Deconstructing Development Discourse
Buzzwords and Fuzzwords

Praise for this book

'This book has emerged from a process that challenged its authors to think "out of the box" of accepted development concepts; to question their continued validity, to speak truth to power. A sparkling addition to the student's tool-kit, and a sobering call for renewed thinking to long-time development thinkers and practitioners.'

Gita Sen, Professor, Centre for Public Policy, Indian Institute of Management

'An important initiative from two seasoned, reflective development practitioner scholars. The chapters in this book will prove a real help in teaching Masters students, as well as stimulating me personally towards new research themes. Are you tired of looking in Google Scholar for academic journal articles that present serious issues in a way that engages students? Then this text provides what you are looking for.'

Helen Hintjens, Senior Lecturer in Development and Social Justice,
International Institute of Social Studies, The Hague

'Timely and emancipatory and long overdue, this is a dissection of how vocabularies trap us ... These terminologies are the underbelly of the modernisation project which has shackled and burned holes into the aspirations and potential of countries of the South. A must-read for those who are working for justice in the public domain.'

Devaki Jain, Member South commission, founder member DAWN

'With a lightness of touch that belies a deadly seriousness of intent, this book is both a useful guide and a powerful antidote to the dangerous oversimplifications of twenty-first century development policy. It is essential reading for researchers, students and development professionals'

David Lewis, Professor of Social Policy and Development,
London School of Economics & Political Science

'An exciting, fun and deeply challenging book for all engaged in development. This timely and highly readable edited volume pushes us to peel back the language of development and grapple with issues that really do matter for global social justice. Congratulations to the editors for taking up where Wolfgang Sach's *Development Dictionary* left off!'

Wendy Harcourt, Editor of Development,
Society for International Development

'As development practice advances on the ground, development discourse becomes more complex. This collection fills the important gap by demystifying the jargon and concepts for practitioners and students of development.'

Rajesh Tandon, President, PRIA, India

'Since its invention post-Second World War, the development industry has cultivated a vast ideological vocabulary to confuse, conceal and mystify the reconstruction by imperial governments of the former colonies to allow super-exploitation by the international oligopolies. Development intellectuals have readily colluded and contributed to this obscurantism. This book goes a long way towards demonstrating the emptiness of development jargon, unveiling the naked emperor.'

Firoze Manji, Editor in Chief, Pambazuka News

'This critical dictionary of development discourse will be enormously useful for those of us who believe that effective communication is essential for positive social change.'

Ricardo Wilson-Grau, independent evaluator, Brazil

Deconstructing Development Discourse
Buzzwords and Fuzzwords

Edited by
Andrea Cornwall and Deborah Eade

Published by Practical Action Publishing in association with Oxfam GB

Practical Action Publishing Ltd
Schumacher Centre for Technology and Development
Bourton on Dunsmore, Rugby,
Warwickshire, CV23 9QZ, UK
www.practicalactionpublishing.org

ISBN 978 1 85339 706 6

This volume is based on *Development in Practice* Volume 17, Numbers 4 & 5, published
by Routledge, Taylor & Francis Limited. The views expressed in this volume are those
of the individual contributors and not necessarily those of the editors or publisher.
For more information about the journal, visit: www.developmentinpractice.org.

Since 1974, Practical Action Publishing (formerly Intermediate Technology
Publications and ITDG Publishing) has published and disseminated books and
information in support of international development work throughout the world.
Practical Action Publishing Ltd (Company Reg. No. 1159018) is the wholly owned
publishing company of Practical Action. Practical Action Publishing trades only in
support of its parent charity objectives and any profits are covenanted back to
Practical Action (Charity Reg. No. 247257, Group VAT Registration No. 880 9924 76).

Oxfam is a registered charity in England and Wales (no 202918) and Scotland
(SCO 039042). Oxfam GB is a member of Oxfam International.

Oxfam GB,
Oxfam House, John Smith Drive,
Oxford, OX4 2JY, UK
www.oxfam.org.uk

Indexed by Andrea Palmer
Typeset by S.J.I. Services
Printed by Information Press
Printed on FSC 100% post-consumer waste recycled paper.

Contents

Preface

Deborah Eade

'When *I* use a word,' Humpty Dumpty said, in a rather scornful tone, 'it means just what I choose it to mean, neither more nor less.'

'The question is,' said Alice, 'whether you can make words mean so many different things.'

'The question is,' said Humpty Dumpty, 'which is to be master – that's all.' (Lewis Carroll, *Through the Looking Glass and What Alice Found There*, 1871)

Winnie-the-Pooh sat down at the foot of the tree, put his head between his paws, and began to think. First of all he said to himself: 'That buzzing noise means something. You don't get a buzzing noise like that, just buzzing and buzzing, without its meaning something.'
(A. A. Milne, *Winnie-the-Pooh*, 1926)

The genesis of the special issue of *Development in Practice* on which this book is based was the 2004 UNRISD conference 'Social Knowledge and International Policy Making', which addressed the role of ideas in shaping policy (Utting 2006). In writing up the official conference report (UNRISD 2004), I was powerfully reminded how deeply the concepts and language of international development are defined by the cultural mindsets of donor agencies, be they bilateral or multilateral (and hence nominally pluri-cultural). The intellectual contribution and cultures of aid-receiving countries, even those where English is the medium of higher education, are, as Adebayo Olukoshi points out, consigned at best to the textboxes of influential reports published by the World Bank and other UN specialised agencies; on average only two per cent of the citations in such reports even include any reference to African research. In this way, scholars in the South are enlisted to provide case studies to suit the 'theoretical frameworks and analysis [for the formulation of policy proposals by] institutions in the North' (UNRISD 2004:11). Where English is not the prime language of scholarship, let alone the language in which most people communicate, the exclusion is greater still. For instance, Mike Powell reports finding 'bilingual, regionally oriented development practitioners in West Africa struggling to interpret and reconcile the very different development discourses coming out of Anglo-Nordic and Francophone intellectual traditions' (Powell 2006:523).[1]

If Southern researchers and development practitioners break into the international market, it is increasingly as consultants, whose conceptual frameworks and the language they are expected to use are by definition determined by the commissioning body. The whole process neatly illustrates Gramsci's notion of cultural hegemony, whereby the values of the ruling culture – in this case, the captains of the Development Industry – capture the ideology, self-understanding, and organisations of the working class – in this case, those whose lives are most significantly affected by international development policies and by the ministrations of development assistance.

It was in the context of these conference discussions that Andrea Cornwall presented a paper co-authored with Karen Brock, 'Taking on Board New Concepts and Buzzwords', in which she dissected the benign-sounding terms that pepper mainstream development policy and whose use is *de rigueur* for anyone working in this field.[2] It is acceptable, sometimes expected, to show a certain critical and even disdainful distance from established shibboleths such as 'community' or 'empowerment'. But there is no pretending they don't exist; the rhetorical trick is to demonstrate one's awareness that the meaning of such words is woolly and imprecise, and then go ahead and employ them, safely quarantined within inverted commas. Sometimes such terms have been captured or co-opted by powerful agencies and in the process have lost any radical or critical edge that they might once have had – rather as a bee's life is doomed once it has lost its sting. The aim then is to decide whether the term has anything left worth saving, or to leave it to its fate. More often, a buzzword will have a multitude of meanings and nuances, depending on who is using it and in what context – what might be called the Humpty Dumpty Syndrome.[3] Or these words appear to convey one thing, but are in practice used to mean something quite different, or indeed have no real meaning at all. The use of tough-sounding language does not provide any immunity to the effects of a deeper ideology. The process by which 'non-negotiable policies' lose their mandatory power is described by Sarah Hlupekile Longwe in her pithy analysis of the 'evaporation of gender policies' somewhere between SNOWDIDA, the international co-operation agency of 'Snowdia, a very isolated nation in the North', and their application in SNOWDIDA's programme in 'the People's Republic of Sundia, one of the least-developed countries of Southern Africa' (Hlupekile Longwe 1997: 149).

Remarkably, it has taken only 60 years or so for Developmentspeak, a peculiar dialect of English, to become the *lingua franca* of the International Development Industry. Its pundits inhabit all the major institutions of global governance, the World Bank – as befits its role as the world's Knowledge Bank (see the chapter by Robin Broad; also Cohen and Laporte 2004) – taking the lead in shaping the lexicon: burying outmoded jargon, authorising new terminology and permissible slippage, and indeed generating a constant supply of must-use terms and catchphrases. Its speakers are found in all corners of the world, giving local inflections to the core concepts, thus making the adoption of Developmentspeak an essential qualification for entry into the Industry.

The extraordinary thing about Developmentspeak is that it is simultaneously descriptive and normative, concrete and yet aspirational, intuitive and clunkily pedestrian, capable of expressing the most deeply held convictions or of being simply 'full of sound and fury, signifying nothing'. This very elasticity makes it almost the ideal post-modern medium, even as it embodies a modernising agenda.

This is certainly not to say that anything goes. Indeed, this collection deliberately brings together a range of scholars, activists, and aid workers – many of whom have at some time played all three roles, and most of them reasonably fluent in Developmentspeak – who nevertheless care about language. Language can confer the power to name, to set out the boundaries of what is thinkable; it can also be used to expose and therefore challenge such power. This is not, therefore, an attempt to establish some kind of Royal Academy of Developmentspeak in order to pronounce on how words may or may not be used; nor to embark on a heroic attempt to restore important terms to their pre-lapsarian state of linguistic innocence. Rather, it reflects a shared concern about the way in which buzzwords serve to numb the critical faculties of those who end up using them, wrapping up all manner of barbed policies and practices in linguistic cotton wool. If this volume convinces readers not to take any item of Developmentspeak at face value, gives them the confidence to identify cant, and emboldens them to be vigilant about (and to expose) its pernicious role in restricting the boundaries of thought, and in shaping policy and practice, then our purpose will have been achieved.

Notes

1. Mike Powell's introductory overview to his guest issue of *Development in Practice* in November 2006 (Volume 16, Number 6) spells out the myriad ways in which the increasing domination of the development sector by the English language both excludes those who are not fully fluent in English, and just as importantly '[disempowers] itself by ensuring its ignorance of vitally (and in the case of China increasingly) important intellectual traditions. By failing to engage systematically with local languages, the sector limits its understanding of and its ability to communicate with most of its intended beneficiaries. Addressing the issue of language fully would have large financial and organisational implications, but failure to do so carries the high costs of ignorance and inefficient communication. If development is to be about life, it has to be able to connect with the languages in which its beneficiaries live' (Powell 2006:523).
2. This paper forms the basis of Cornwall and Brock (2006).
3. The opening quotations clearly betray my middle-class English upbringing of the early 1960s; I make no apology for this, for it would be sad indeed if our childhood left us without cultural roots and reference points. Of course, the fictional works of Lewis Carroll, an Oxford don who was also an Anglican priest, a logician, and a photographer, and A. A. Milne, an obscure playwright, assistant editor of the satirical magazine *Punch*, and author of

children's books and poems, cannot conceivably be regarded as universal or even 'great' authors. But while not universal, they nevertheless form part of the 'globalised' culture of Walt Disney, Inc., albeit in saccharine animated cartoon versions that bear little relation to the original texts and wonderful illustrations.

References

Cohen, Don and Bruno Laporte (2004) 'The evolution of the Knowledge Bank', available at http://siteresources.worldbank.org/KFDLP/Resources/461197-114859 4717965/EvolutionoftheKnowledgeBank.pdf (retrieved 20 March 2007).

Cornwall, Andrea and Karen Brock (2006) 'The new buzzwords', in Peter Utting (ed.), pp. 43–72.

Hlupekile Longwe, Sarah (1997) 'The evaporation of gender policies in the patriarchal cooking pot', *Development in Practice* 7(2): 148–56.

Powell, Mike (2006) 'Which knowledge? Whose reality? An overview of knowledge used in the development sector', *Development in Practice* 16(6): 518–32.

UNRISD (2004) 'Social Knowledge and International Policy Making: Exploring the Linkages', Report of the UNRISD Conference, Geneva, 21–22 April.

Utting, Peter (ed.) (2006) *Reclaiming Development Agendas: Knowledge, Power and International Policy Making*, Basingstoke: Palgrave Macmillan and UNRISD.

CHAPTER 1

Introductory overview – buzzwords and fuzzwords: deconstructing development discourse

Andrea Cornwall

> All things are subject to interpretation; whichever interpretation prevails at a given time is a function of power and not truth.
> (Friedrich Nietzche)

Words make worlds. The language of development defines worlds-in-the-making, animating and justifying intervention in currently existing worlds with fulsome promises of the possible. Wolfgang Sachs contends, 'development is much more than just a socio-economic endeavour; it is a perception which models reality, a myth which comforts societies, and a fantasy which unleashes passions' (1992:1). These models, myths, and passions are sustained by development's 'buzzwords'. Writing from diverse locations, contributors to this volume critically examine a selection of the words that constitute today's development lexicon. Whereas those who contributed to Sachs' 1992 landmark publication *The Development Dictionary* shared a project of dismantling the edifice of development, this collection is deliberately eclectic in its range of voices, positions, and perspectives. Some tell tales of the trajectories that these words have travelled, as they have moved from one domain of discourse to another; others describe scenes in which the ironies – absurdities, at times – of their usage beg closer critical attention; others still peel off the multiple guises that their words have assumed, and analyse the dissonant agendas that they embrace. Our intention in bringing them together is to leave you, the reader, feeling less than equivocal about taking for granted the words that frame the world-making projects of the development enterprise.

The lexicon of development

For those involved in development practice, reflection on words and their meanings may seem irrelevant to the real business of getting things done. Why, after all, should language matter to those who are *doing* development? As long as those involved in development practice are familiar with the catchwords that need to be sprinkled liberally in funding proposals and emblazoned on websites and promotional material, then surely there are more important things to be done than sit around mulling over questions of semantics?

But language *does* matter for development. Development's buzzwords are not only passwords to funding and influence; and they are more than the mere specialist jargon that is characteristic of any profession. The word *development* itself, Gilbert Rist observes, has become a 'modern shibboleth, an unavoidable password', which comes to be used 'to convey the idea that tomorrow things will be better, or that more is necessarily better'. But, as he goes on to note, the very taken-for-granted quality of 'development' – and the same might be said of many of the words that are used in development discourse – leaves much of what is actually *done* in its name unquestioned.

Many of the words that have gained the status of buzzwords in development are (or once were) what the philosopher W.B. Gallie (1956) termed 'essentially contested concepts': terms that combine general agreement on the abstract notion that they represent with endless disagreement about what they might mean in practice. Yet the very contestability of many of the words in the lexicon of development has been 'flattened', as Neera Chandhoke suggests for *civil society*; terms about which there was once vibrant disagreement have become 'consensual hurrah-words' (Chapter 16). They gain their purchase and power through their vague and euphemistic qualities, their capacity to embrace a multitude of possible meanings, and their normative resonance. The work that these words do for development is to place the sanctity of its goals beyond reproach.

Poverty is, of all the buzzwords analysed in this collection, perhaps the most compelling in its normative appeal; as John Toye notes, 'the idea of *poverty reduction* itself has a luminous obviousness to it, defying mere mortals to challenge its status as a moral imperative'. The moral unassailability of the development enterprise is secured by copious references to that nebulous, but emotive, category 'the poor and marginalised' (Cornwall and Brock 2005). Similarly, Elizabeth Harrison draws attention to the 'righteous virtue' of anti-corruption talk, which she argues makes it virtually immoral to question what is being labelled 'corrupt', and by whom. Many of the words that describe the worlds-in-the-making that development would create have all the 'warmly persuasive' qualities that Raymond Williams described for *community* in his memorable 1976 book *Keywords*. Among them can be found words that admit no negatives, words that evoke Good Things that no-one could possibly disagree with. Some evoke futures possible, like *rights-based* and *poverty eradication* (Uvin, Toye). Others carry with them traces of worlds past: *participation* and *good governance* (Leal, Mkwandawire), with their echoes of colonial reformers like Lord Lugard, the architect of indirect rule; *poverty*, whose power to stir the do-gooding Western middle-classes is at least in part due to its distinctly nineteenth-century feel; and *development* itself, for all that it has become a word that Gilbert Rist suggests might be as readily abandoned as recast to do the work that it was never able to do to make a better world.

Alongside words that encode seemingly universal values, the lexicon of development also contains a number of code-words that are barely intelligible to those beyond its borders. They are part of an exclusive and fast-changing vocabulary. These words capture one of the qualities of buzzwords: to sound 'intellectual and scientific, beyond the understanding of the lay person, best left to "experts"' (Chapter 5). Some have their origin in the academy, their meanings transformed as they are put to the service of development. Among them *social capital* and *gender* are two such examples, with applications far distant from the theoretical debates with which they were originally associated (Chapters 11 and 13). Others circulate between domains as different in kind as the worlds that they make: business, advertising, religion, management. Take *empowerment*, a term that has perhaps the most expansive semantic range of all those considered here. Advertisements beckoning consumers to 'empower' themselves by buying the latest designer spectacles mimic the individualism of the use of this term by development banks, just as the brand of 'spiritual empowerment' offered on the websites of the new Christianities lends radically different meaning to its uses by feminist activists to talk about collective action in pursuit of social justice (Chapter 10).

Buzzwords get their 'buzz' from being in-words, words that define what is in vogue. In the lexicon of development, there are buzzwords that dip in and out of fashion, some continuing to ride the wave for decades, others appearing briefly only to become submerged for years until they are salvaged and put to new uses. What we see, in some cases, is less the rise and rise of a term than its periodic resurfacing – evident, for example, in Alfini and Chambers' account of changes and continuities in the language of British aid policies. Tracing the reinvention of ideas, as well as words, over time brings into view some of the paradoxes of development. *Community* and *citizenship* featured, for example, in the vocabularies of the 1950s colonists in Kenya who sought to 'rehabilitate' errant anti-colonial activists through community development programmes that would teach them to become responsible 'citizens' (Presley 1988). *Community participation* came into vogue in the 1970s, taking on an altogether different connotation in the 1980s as 'do it for yourself' became 'do it by yourself' as neo-liberalism flourished (Chapter 8; Cornwall 2000). Toye's Angels are timeless, but their ministrations have their own historicity. Anti-poverty policies have genealogies that can be traced back over centuries: to take one example, Elizabethan provision of 'outdoor relief' to those judged to be the 'deserving' poor, along with 'setting the poor on work', is not far distant from some of today's *social protection* policies described here by Guy Standing.

Among words with familiar referents, there are others in this collection that have an entirely contemporary feel, keywords of the times we live in. *Globalisation* still captures the *Zeitgeist*, however much the term has come to be qualified in recent years (Guttal). *Security* (Luckham) has become emblematic of the new realities of development, and the increasingly polarised worlds that we have come to inhabit. *Faith-based* (Balchin) is a term whose apparent novelty disguises continuities between the three Cs of the age of colonialism (Civilisation, Christianity, and Commerce) and today's mainstream development – continuities that are increasingly visible. As part of the new world that has been constructed with the conjunction of *development* and *security*, talk of 'faith' has come to displace any debate about *secularism,*as Cassandra Balchin contends: 'today in international development policy, religion is simultaneously seen as the biggest developmental obstacle, the only developmental issue, and the only developmental solution' (Chapter 7). And there are words, like *peacebuilding*, which Tobias Denskus compares to the 'non-places' such as airports and supermarkets described by Marc Augé (1995), that arrive in the ether and linger to enchant the consumers of development's latest must-have terms.

The *Development Dictionary* brought together critical genealogies of the key concepts of the age to write the obituary of development. It is a sign of how far, and how fast, things have changed that there is so little overlap between the words that feature there and here. But many of the entries in *The Development Dictionary* appear in today's development discourse in new guises: *state* as *fragile states* (Osague) and *good governance* (Mkandawire); *environment* as *sustainability* (Scoones); *planning* (development institutions' preoccupation of that age) as *harmonisation* (Eyben) (their preoccupation in this one). *Equality* is as much of a concern as ever, but has come to be used in development more often with *gender* (Smyth) in front of it. *Capacity building* (Eade) transforms *helping* into a technical fix, generating its own entourage of 'experts'. International NGOs have made much of a shift from *needs* to *rights* (Uvin). And *progress* continues to be regularly invoked, even as the hopes once associated with it quietly slip away.

The apparent universality of the buzzwords that have come to frame 'global' development discourses masks the locality of their origins. Significantly, few of the words used in Anglo-dominated development discourse admit of translation into other languages: many come to be used in other languages as loan-words, their meanings ever more closely associated with the external agencies that make their use in proposals, policies, strategies, and reports compulsory. Even the word 'buzzword' itself is peculiarly Anglophone. Gilbert Rist notes:

> I eventually decided to write this chapter in English, for the simple reason that 'buzzword' is just impossible to translate into French. It comes under what we call *'la langue de bois'*, whose translation into English does not exactly convey the same meaning.

La langue de bois, the language of evasion, well captures one of the functions of development's buzzwords. But, as Rist rightly observes, buzzwords do not just cloud meanings: they combine performative qualities with 'an absence of real definition and a strong belief in what the notion is supposed to bring about'.[2]

Buzzwords as fuzzwords

> When ideas fail, words come in very handy. (Johann Wolfgang von Goethe)

The language of development is, as Fiona Wilson suggests, a hybrid, not quite the language of social science nor of 'living' English; its 'vocabulary is restricted, banal and depersonalised'. Its 'underlying purpose', she notes, 'is not to lay bare or be unequivocal but to mediate in the interests of political consensus while at the same time allowing for the existence of several internal agendas' (1992: 10). Policies depend on a measure of ambiguity to secure the endorsement of diverse potential actors and audiences. Buzzwords aid this process, by providing concepts that can float free of concrete referents, to be filled with meaning by their users. In the struggles for interpretive power that characterise the negotiation of the language of policy, buzzwords shelter multiple agendas, providing room for manoeuvre and space for contestation.

Scoones' tale of the rise and reinvention of the buzzword *sustainability* draws attention to the 'boundary work' (Gieryn 1999) performed by this concept in bridging discursive worlds and the actors who animate them. Scoones notes that 'to be effective in this boundary work, remaining contested, ambiguous, and vague is often essential'. Yet, as Pablo Leal, Evelina Dagnino, and Srilatha Batliwala make clear in this volume, it is the very ambiguity of *participation*, *citizenship*, and *empowerment* that have made them vulnerable to appropriation for political agendas that are far from those that the social movements that popularised their use had in mind. Their accounts provide powerful examples of the politics of meaning, as differently positioned users put very different versions of these concepts to use.

Leal explores the trajectories of *participation*, showing how amenable the term was to pursuit of a neo-liberal policy agenda, and how divorced its mainstream appropriations are from its more radical roots. Dagnino highlights the 'perverse confluence' that marks the flowing together of neo-liberal and radical democratic meanings of *citizenship*. Batliwala traces the depoliticisation of *empowerment* as it has been converted from an approach that sought to fundamentally alter power relations to a status that constitutes development's latest 'magic bullet'. She asks (p. 112):

> Should we be troubled by what many may consider the inevitable subversion of an attractive term that can successfully traverse such diverse and even ideologically opposed terrain? I believe we should, because it represents not some innocent linguistic fad, but a more serious and subterranean process of challenging and subverting the politics that the term was created to symbolise.

Ines Smyth explores the morass of competing meanings that have come to surround the use of another word that has traversed different domains and ended up depoliticised in the process: *gender*. Noting the 'resounding silence around words such as "feminism" and "feminist"', her analysis gives a compelling sense of the lack of fit between organisational imperatives and the original goals with which *gender* was associated by feminist scholars and activists. She writes (p. 144):

> Real women and men, power and conflict all disappear behind bland talk of 'gender', while the language of 'mainstreaming' creates the possibility of orderly tools... and systems through which profoundly internalised beliefs and solidly entrenched structures are miraculously supposed to dissolve and be transformed.

There are parallels here with Scoones' account of how *sustainability* became subject to 'the default bureaucratic mode of managerialism [...] and its focus on action plans, indicators, and the rest' (Chapter 14). For all the loss of momentum and fragmentation that was a casualty of its institutionalisation, however, Scoones argues that 'sustainability' has retained a 'more overarching, symbolic role – of aspiration, vision, and normative commitment'. It is that combination of aspiration, vision, and commitment that, for Smyth, makes abandoning the term *gender* altogether less attractive than reanimating it by harnessing it to terms that might restore some of its original focus on power relations: *rights-based* and *empowerment*.

Rights-based gains much of its allure from the legitimacy that it promises, grounding development in a more powerful set of normative instruments than Enlightenment ideals. But, as Peter Uvin contends, what exactly development actors mean when they invoke the language of 'rights' needs to be closely examined. As he shows, rights-talk may amount to a thin veneer over development business as usual. Until, as Uvin argues, donors begin to apply some of their high-moral-ground talk about rights to themselves, rights-talk risks remaining fluffy and meaningless: akin to what Mick Moore, in his analysis of the World Bank's new-found enthusiasm for *empowerment*, calls 'cheap talk': 'something that one can happily say in the knowledge that it will have no significant consequences' (2001:323).

Reforming relationships

Many of the words that have enjoyed a meteoric rise in popularity over the past decade are those which speak to an agenda for transforming development's relationships. Today, *civil society, social capital,* and *partnership* are as ubiquitous as *community*, evoking much the same warm mutuality. As Guy Standing puts it, these kinds of word are 'intended to invite automatic approval' (Chapter 5); and their rising fortunes have been as much to do with their feel-good factor as with what they promised to deliver.

Neera Chandhoke's account of the rise and rise of *civil society* shows us what is lost when buzzwords are domesticated by development agencies. From the intense differences in perspective that the term once provoked, it has become – like many of the other expressions analysed in this collection – emblematic

of something that no-one could reasonably argue against: close, convivial relations of solidarity and self-help, and an essential bulwark against the excess-
es of the state and the isolation of the individual. The problem, Chandhoke
argues (Chapter 16), is not that these are not part of what can happen in 'civil
society'. It is that projecting normative desires on to actually existing societies
simply serves to obscure the empirical and analytical question of 'what civil
society actually does and does not do for people'. After all, as Chandhoke reminds us, 'civil society' is only as civil as the society that gives rise to it.

Another facet of buzzwords emerges in Ben Fine's account of *social capital*:
their use as substitutes for terms that are far less easily assimilated into a consensual narrative. Of the buzzwords examined in this collection, *social capital*
is one of the most accommodating: its uses span just about any and every kind
of human relationship, lending it considerable discursive power as a feel-good
catch-all Good Thing. Charting its rise within mainstream development, Fine
shows how it came to be linked to a broader set of personal, institutional,
and professional projects, including that of what he terms 'economics imperialism'. Like *civil society*, the normative appeal of social capital sits uneasily
with its 'darker' sides; the 'wrong kind' of social capital is, after all, *corruption*
(Chapter 25).

Miguel Pickard's account of *partnership* captures some of the ambivalence
that accompanies Northern development agencies' projection of their own desired self-image onto complex power relations in 'the South'. Pickard also highlights the contradictions of donors' demands for an ever-increasing volume of
reporting and planning, with the emphasis on measurable outcomes, and the
realities of working to bring about social change. As Islah Jad contends in her
account of the 'NGOisation' of Palestinian women's movements, the professionalisation and projectisation that have come about in response to these
demands may not only weaken the transformative potential of aid-receiving
organisations, but can also have more far-reaching political consequences. Jad
reminds us that to attribute to NGOs the almost magical democratising properties ascribed to *civil society* is to overlook the extent to which donor intervention has sapped the energies of once-vibrant movements, as they come to
conform to the strictures of NGOisation (Alvarez 1988).

Riding the wave as the self-proclaimed champions of 'global civil society',
international non-government agencies have increasingly turned to *advocacy*
as their new metier. John Samuel shows quite what a mire of meanings now
surrounds the term *public advocacy* as it has become the latest fad in the NGO
world. Drawing on experiences from India that affirm that 'advocacy without
mobilisation is likely to be in vain', he argues passionately for a return to a
more 'people-centred' approach (p. 192):

> We need to become equal participants in social communication, rather
> than playing the role of highly paid experts travelling around with our
> ready-made toolkits and frameworks for prescribing the best communi-
> cation medicine.

Samuel argues that such an approach is grounded in close links with social movements. Yet, echoing themes emerging in the contributions by Leal, Eade, Jad, and Batliwala, these links are being lost as advocacy becomes professionalised and the voices of marginalised people are appropriated by urban and international elites.

Deborah Eade's account of *capacity building*, another buzzword that has come to be closely associated with international NGOs, poses pithy questions about exactly what and whose capacities are seen as worth building. Like Leal, she highlights the left-leaning traditions that originally informed the notion; and, equally, she notes its usage today in the service of neo-liberalism. By troubling an idea that seems at first glance so evidently morally commendable, she identifies the paradoxes and hypocrisies that lie at the heart of the development enterprise. In doing so, she pricks the bubble that surrounds representations of NGOs in development.

Development's remedies

The disconnects described by Leal, Batliwala, Eade, and Samuel are evident on a grander scale in the world of official development agencies – bilateral and multilateral donors and development banks. Among the remedies prescribed by the institutions that populate this world for addressing its manifest failure to achieve its bold and ambitious promises are measures for tackling the structure of the development industry itself. Some have a direct origin in New Public Management, such as donors' current preoccupation with 'results'. Others have echoes of projects of governance of earlier times, whether 1960's budget support or, further back still, the carving up of colonial dominions between the world powers of the age.

Rosalind Eyben's account of *harmonisation* exposes the quixotic nature of the aid world. As she points out, there is a certain attractiveness in the logic of donor co-ordination. Yet in practice, the harmony in *'harmonisation'* is an illusion: instead, she suggests, donors gang up on recipients to drive through their agendas, becoming 'cartels' with whom it may be imprudent to argue. Premised on achieving a noiseless consensus on poverty policy that would be scarcely imaginable in the signatories' home countries, the Paris Agenda contributes to neutralising those who might contest it by draining funding from 'civil society' to channel through direct budget support. Eyben observes some of the contractions. One is the fate of another prevalent piece of donor rhetoric, *country ownership* (see Chapter 21); evident in the perverse contradictions of 'country-owned' but identikit Poverty Reduction Strategies (see Rowden and Irama 2004). Another is the 'strange irony that the economists-turned-managers who govern Aidland advocate *co-operation* among themselves on efficiency grounds, while on exactly the same grounds impose polices based on principles of *competition* on their recipients (Severino and Charnoz 2003)' (Chapter 20).

As *results-based management* has hit mainstream development agencies, a veritable industry has sprung up to measure 'results' and provide the necessary evidence – as ever, sorely difficult to find – that development is working. The days when *process* showed a glimmer of becoming fashionable came and went very quickly; today's development is all about the quantifiable and measurable. *Best practice* – with its implicit assumptions that practices can be found that are 'best' for all – is part of this ever more homogenising world of development prescriptions, indicators, and 'results'. As Warren Feek's contribution makes amply clear, what may make a practice 'best' may come to depend as much on context as anything inherent in what is being done. He argues (p. 234):

> The 'best practice' highlighted after an exhaustive international search may work in the poor barrio on the outskirts of Cali, Colombia, but may be completely inappropriate – perhaps even 'bad practice' – if replicated in Blantyre, Malawi; Puna, India; Kuala Trenggannu, Malaysia; and even the town in which I was raised: New Plymouth, New Zealand. Probably even Barranquilla, Colombia would not do what they do in Cali, Colombia, because it just would not work in Barranquilla. Things are different in Barranquilla!

'And', he continues, 'if the point of labelling something the "best" is not that others replicate it, then why label it the "best"?' Why indeed?

Things may well be different for the people of Barranquilla. But for the aid-agency staff who populate the expatriate enclaves that can be found in the capital cities of any Southern country, the new architecture of aid keeps them insulated from anything that might be happening locally. Denskus' account of *peacebuilding* paints a vivid picture of just how distant aid staff may now find themselves from the realities of the countries that they move between. He cites an aid official's account of the impact of hostilities on the supermarket baskets of expatriate 'peacebuilders'; and talks of hyper-real donor-created bubbles in which aid officials spend their time talking among themselves and come to gain greater knowledge of each other's programmes than what is actually happening out there in the field.

As Guy Standing observes, 'throughout history, institutions have arisen to institutionalise specific discourses and divert knowledge from outside critique' (Chapter 5). Robin Broad's account of the 'art of paradigm maintenance' within the World Bank reveals the work to which *knowledge management* has been put in an era where the Bank needed to reinvent itself to secure its own place in the global order. Her analysis of the politics of 'knowledge management' in the institution that would have us regard it as the Knowledge Bank highlights the sleights of hand and mind that accompany the production of 'knowledge' for development. The philosopher Nelson Goodman argued that 'a statement is true and a description or representation right for a world it fits' (1978:132). Robin Broad's account shows how 'truth' is made to fit the world that the Bank wishes to make; and the tactics that she describes underscore the partiality – in the sense of being partial to, as well as consisting of a partial picture – of the representations of the problems of (and, implicitly, the solutions for) development that emerge from this mighty information machine.

The end of ideology?

Many of the buzzwords analysed in this collection gained popularity precisely through what Fox terms their 'trans-ideological' properties. Yet just as they appear to rise 'above' ideology, they are densely populated with ideological projects and positions. The 'family resemblances' (Wittgenstein 1953) of many of the terms considered here are so diffuse that their ideological implications become clear only in the context of their use by particular, positioned, social and political actors. Unpicking these layers of meaning brings identifiably ideological differences into clearer view.

Good governance appears at first glance to be less ambiguous than many of the terms considered here. Its chief prescriptions are encoded in a universal toolkit for the construction of liberal democratic institutions that closely enough resemble those that facilitated the growth of capitalism in the West that they will do the same wherever they are implanted. Yet, as Thandika Mkandawire's chapter shows, the genesis of 'good governance' in debates with African intellectuals had quite a different project in mind: the transformation of state–society relations to create a more inclusive and accountable state. These meanings continue to circulate within use of the term *governance* in development, which has acquired – as Sierra Leonean commentator Freida M'Cormack (pers. comm.) puts it – the status of 'the mother of all buzzwords'. But, as Mkandawire makes clear, the mantra-like quality that 'good governance' has attained in international policy circles has led to a diminution of concern with democratic citizenship and the privileging of traditional neoliberal remedies. That these remedies continue to fail the people of Africa then becomes ascribable to 'bad governance'.

Security acquires its discursive power through the very opposite of the orderly and predictable world that *good governance* would seek to create: its capacity to evoke the fear of things falling apart. Robin Luckham juxtaposes the framing of security and development discourses (p. 273):

> In contrast to development, whose language is firmly rooted in the grand narrative of the Enlightenment, the discourse of security arises from the double-edged and ambivalent nature of development, including its roots in a destructive capitalism which demolishes livelihoods, communities, and even states – indirectly through the structural violence of poverty, and directly through war and political violence.

Both *security* and *development* come together in talk of *fragile states*, a label whose origins are widely ascribed to the World Bank. Eghosa Osague's exploration of the rise of the idea of the 'fragile state' and the use of this term in the African context makes a convincing case for the need to take a less simplistic view of state capacity and fragility. Highlighting the extent to which the term connotes 'deviance and aberration from the dominant and supposedly universal (but Western) paradigm of the state, which played a key role in the development of capitalism', he argues (p. 291):

> ultimately, the responsibility for determining when states are no longer fragile is that of citizens of the countries concerned and not that of 'benevolent' donors and the international development community whose motivation for supposed state-strengthening interventions is to ensure that fragile states take their 'rightful' places in the hegemonic global order.

It is all the more ironic, then, to observe the extent to which another term that the World Bank launched into circulation – *country ownership* – has become a decorative epithet that promises something quite different from that delivered by the monoculture of 'reform'. 'Country ownership' would, after all, seem to posit quite the converse to the institutional recipes of *good governance*, resonating with the ideals of self-determination that spurred anti-colonial struggles and shaped post-independence nationalist governments. Such are its evident contradictions, Willem Buiter argues, that it needs to be seen as 'a term whose time has gone'. As he points out, to conflate the deployment of the term 'country ownership' by today's development powers with any meaningful opportunity by developing countries to shape their own development would be a grave mistake. Rather, he comments, 'country ownership' boils down to decisions made by the few who own the country – and, by extension, the compacts that they make with the international financial institutions.

Among the panaceas that found their way into mainstream development in the late 1990s, propelled by the 'good governance' agenda, *transparency* and *accountability* are two that achieved instant popularity across the spectrum. In Fox's analysis of these terms, and the none-too-straightforward relationship between them, he illuminates another quality of development buzzwords: their 'trans-ideological character', which allows them to be appropriated by a variety of political and policy actors. As such, he observes, these terms become as amenable to the proponents of New Public Management as to human-rights activists. Fox draws attention to another property of buzzwords that their apparent universality conceals (p. 245):

> One person's transparency is another's surveillance. One person's accountability is another's persecution. Where one stands on these issues depends on where on sits.

Much the same could be said for *corruption*; quite what and who is judged to be 'corrupt' is, as Harrison points out, just as much a matter of positionality. Commenting on the growth of a veritable anti-corruption industry geared at cleaning up the state, she notes the extent to which this has come to deflect attention from the probity of other actors, including development agencies themselves. The ironies of the confluence of anti-corruption efforts with neo-liberal policy prescriptions raises further questions. Harrison asks: 'does the focus on anti-corruption, with its attendant increase in privatisation, concessions, and contracting-out, in turn open the door for greater corruption among multi-national corporations?' (p. 261).

The ambivalent nature of development, in Luckham's terms, is more than evident in the effects of the kind of *globalisation* that mainstream development's lenders and donors have sought to foster. Shalmali Guttal's analysis draws attention to the discursive moves that equate 'globalisation' with 'development', 'democracy', 'rights', and 'choice'. This, she argues, provides a convenient cover for the sanction and support for corporate expansion that forms part of the agenda of neo-liberal states and multilateral institutions. But, Guttal argues, 'globalisation' has, equally, fostered the flowering of resistance: 'the same technology that has exacerbated the financial insecurity of countries has also been used by people's movements and activists to jam the gears of globalisation' (Chapter 6).

Language matters

If terms that were once calls to mobilisation in pursuit of social justice, or concepts that were good to think and debate with, have been reduced to vague and euphemistic buzzwords by their incorporation by the development establishment, what is to be done? As Scoones puts it, 'can an old buzzword be reinvigorated and reinvented for new challenges, or does it need discarding with something else put its place?' Some contributors to this volume would argue that there are words that are beyond redemption; others would contend that it is necessary to reclaim some of the associations once conveyed by terms that are too precious to lose and use them to give 'mainstreamed' buzzwords new vigour and purpose. Their analyses suggest a variety of strategies and tactics.

Out with the old, in with the new

One way of dealing with a denatured buzzword is to dump it altogether, and hope that others will follow suit. Replacing tired old buzzwords with captivating new alternatives, or rehabilitating the 'lost' words that spoke for hopes and dreams that never went away, is to play the development-buzzword game on its own terms. It is worth considering some of the words that might be put in the place of today's fuzzwords. *Justice, solidarity,* and *redistribution* are attractive candidates, resonant with the demands of countless movements in their struggles to make a fairer, better world. They are resounding calls to action. And they are words that mainstream development agencies might sooner choke on than assimilate. But there is no guaranteeing that they would not become smoothed out, stripped of any disruptive meanings, and incorporated. Think, for instance, of how *power* and *political agency*, words that might seem at first sight to be anathema, have come to enter the discourse of the World Bank in recent years (see, for example, Alsop 2005).[3]

Another approach is to propel into popularity words whose very dissonance with mainstream development lends them their potential as alternative frames for thought and action. A number of the missing words identified by Alfini and Chambers – like *love, peace, respect* – would seem to fit the bill. But they share the warm, persuasive qualities of other buzzwords; and they are no less vague in what they might come to mean. Better, perhaps, to seek out words that are less ambiguous and which might provoke development actors out of the complacency of othering 'the poor'. What would it take, for example, to make *pleasure* the buzzword of today? As a former bilateral donor commented, 'the very idea of talking about pleasure in the context of development makes me very uncomfortable'. This is precisely what is needed, it might be argued: words that provoke discomfort, that shake people up. Talk of 'pleasure' takes us beyond monochromatic representations of abjection, reminding us of the humanity of those whose lives development agencies would wish to improve.

Pleasure-based approaches suggest more prospect of enhancing well-being and saving lives than current development models (Jolly 2006). But there is equally no guarantee that as a result of its incorporation, *pleasure* would not become tomorrow's *freedom*.

Leveraging incorporated buzzwords

Gita Sen proposes that rather than abandoning terms that are felt to have become corrupted, a more productive approach might be to 'recognise that the fact that new terms and frameworks are being taken up by the opposition is an important sign not of failure, but of success in the first level of the struggle for change' (2004: 13). Citing Sun Tzu's *Art of War*, she argues, 'if knowledge is power, then changing the terrain of discourse is the first but very important step. It makes it possible to fight the opposition on the ground of one's choosing' (*ibid.*). As Hilary Standing (2004) points out, it is naive to expect bureaucrats to be either willing or able to carry out the transformative work that those who advocate the adoption of radical concepts expect of them. But this does not mean that the inclusion of these words in development policies is not useful to others, including those within development bureaucracies who are able to use them as levers for change.

For all the association of Foucault's work with the totalising power effects of discourse, his work on 'governmentality' reminds us that even the most powerful masters of meanings can never completely secure the capture of language for their own projects. It is in the 'strategic reversibility' (1991:5) of discourse, he argues, that the potential for resistance and transgression lies. As we have seen with the reclaiming by social movements of words used to denigrate and exclude, such as 'queer' and 'mad', the words that make the worlds of the powerful can be used as tools for mobilisation and resistance. It is, after all, in the very ambiguity of development buzzwords that scope exists for enlarging their application to encompass more transformative agendas.

Incorporated buzzwords may, indeed, serve as bridges from one domain into another: allowing activists and progressive bureaucrats to enlist each other in efforts to refashion development policy and practice, and providing a discursive meeting ground on which actor-networks come together around a shared 'story-line' (Hajer 1993). While rejection may be a necessary precursor to reinvention, then, ditching terms whose symbolic potency is not yet spent in favour of novel but unfamiliar terms may leave practitioners at the periphery of the worlds of discourse-making, bemused and adrift. For all the emptying of meaning that occurs as words come to be institutionalised by development agencies, spaces for contestation and resignification of meaning are never completely closed. Even the most unpromising of buzzwords can provide entry points for the mobilisation of alternatives: take, for example, the reworking of meanings for *security* described by Luckham, in efforts to claim normative and discursive ground within the ambit of development policy.

Constructive deconstruction

Tackling what Guy Standing (2001) calls development's 'linguistic crisis', some might argue, calls for more than tactical resistance and for making the most of the room for manoeuvre offered by the appropriation of the language of social movements by the development establishment. What would it take to rehabilitate words that have been reduced to feel-good fuzzwords, to turn the uneasy silence of consensus into vigorous debate, and to revive denatured and depoliticised buzzwords?

Constructive deconstruction – the taking apart of the different meanings that these words have acquired as they have come to be used in development discourse – provides an opportunity for reflection, which is a vital first step towards their rehabilitation. By making evident the variant meanings that popular development buzzwords carry, this process can bring into view dissonance between these meanings. If the use of buzzwords as fuzzwords conceals ideological differences, the process of constructive deconstruction reveals them: and, with this, opens up the possibility of reviving the debates that once accompanied the use of bland catch-all terms like *civil society* and *social capital*. And if this is accompanied, as in the genealogical accounts in this and Sachs' collections, with tracing their more radical meanings, it can also help to wrest back more radical usages of even some of the most corrupted of terms in the current development lexicon, such as *empowerment*.

What this requires is not only close attention to meaning. It also calls for a disentanglement of the normative and the empirical, a focus on 'actual social practices rather than wishful thinking' (Chapter 2). This can clear the ground for the more politicised and indeed explicitly normative discussion that Leal proposes in this volume for *participation* when he asks (p. 97):

> What exactly do we wish to participate in? Can we continue to accept a form of participation that is simply added on to any social project, i.e.

neo-liberal modernisation and development, creating an alibi for development by transferring ownership to the poor in the name of empowerment? Or should participation be re-located in the radical politics of social transformation by reaffirming its counter-hegemonic roots?

Such a process, as Rist argues for *development*, would enable us to 'be aware of its inclusion in a corpus of beliefs that are difficult to shatter, expose its mischievous uses, and denounce its consequences'. Dislocating naturalised meanings, dislodging embedded associations, and de-familiarising the language that surrounds us becomes, then, a means of defusing the hegemonic grip – in Gramsci's (1971) sense of the word 'hegemony', as unquestioned acceptance – that certain ideas have come to exert in development policy and practice.

Reclaiming meaning through reconfiguration

For all that might be done to seek more specificity in definition, words gain their meanings in the contexts of their use; and these meanings are relative to the other words that surround them. Raymond Williams points out that particular combinations of words 'establish one set of connections while often suppressing another' (1976: 25). The very mobility of meanings of many of the words that make up the development lexicon makes them difficult to resignify without the help of other words that can moor them to specific projects. Ernesto Laclau's (1997) notion of 'chains of equivalence' offers further insights, as well as a strategy for reanimating denatured buzzwords. As terms are added to others, Laclau argues, 'chains of equivalence' are formed: the more words in the chain, the more the meaning of any of those words comes to depend on the other words in the chain.

Used in a chain of equivalence with *good governance, accountability, results-based management, reform*, and *security*, for example, words like *democracy* and *empowerment* come to mean something altogether different from their use in conjunction with *citizenship, participation, solidarity, rights*, and *social justice*. In either chain, other words that might be added – such as *freedom* – would come to mean quite different things. Thinking of words in constellations rather than in the singular opens up further strategies for reclaiming 'lost' words, as well as salvaging some of the meanings that were never completely submerged. Embedding words in chains of equivalence that secure meanings that would otherwise be pared away, and employing a politics of hyphenation that lends particular meanings to words with multiple potential referents, can serve as means of resisting decoupling and recombination – and give tired buzzwords a new lease of life.

Conclusion

Different words, different contexts, different actors, and different struggles call for different strategies: some combination of any or all of those outlined here may be required at some times and for some purposes. As the contributions to this volume make clear, engagement with development's language is far more than a matter of playing games with words. These reflections on the language of development evoke bigger questions about the world-making projects that they define and describe. Pablo Leal contends: 'our primary task is, as it should always have been, not to reform institutional development practice but to transform society'. Whether *development* has a place in that process of transformation may come to depend on our willingness to resignify it.

Acknowledgements

I would like to thank Deborah Eade, Ian Scoones, Fiona Wilson, and Karen Brock for their contributions to the arguments developed here, and Robert Chambers for all the conversations we have had about our shared interest in development language over the years.

Notes

1. For further information about England, see www.victorianweb.org anti-poverty policies in Elizabethan /history/poorlaw/elizpl.html.
2. Although Internet searches failed to track down a site dedicated to development's buzzwords, there are numerous others devoted to the management-speak that is becoming pervasive in development institutions. See, for example, the Official Bullshit Generator at www. erikandanna.com/Humor/bullshit_generator.htm and the Systematic Buzz Phrase Projector at www.acronymfinder.com/buzzgen. asp?Num=111&DoIt=Again. My personal favourite is the Elizabethan Buzzword Generator at www.red-bean.com/kfogel/hypespeare.html And you can send your most reviled buzzword to www.buzzwordhell.com. *La langue du bois*, the language of evasion, has its own generator: www. presidentielle-2007.net/generateur-de-langue-de-bois.php.
3. To take an example, in a major 2003 report on inequality in Latin America and the Caribbean, senior bank staff – including the Vice-President and Chief Economist for the region – conclude that 'breaking with the long history of inequality in Latin America' depends on 'strong leadership and broad coalitions' ... to mobilise 'the political agency of progressive governments and the poor'. See http://wbln0018.worldbank.org/LAC/LAC. nsf/PrintView/4112F1114F594B4B85256DB3005DB262?Open document.

References

Alsop, Ruth (2005) *Power, Rights and Poverty: Concepts and Connections*, Washington, DC: The World Bank.

Alvarez, Sonia (1998) 'The 'NGOization of Latin American feminisms' in S. Alvarez, E. Dagnino and A. Escobar (eds.) *Cultures of Politics, Politics of Cultures: Re-visioning Latin American Social Movements*, Boulder, CO: Westview.

Augé, Marc (1995) *Non-Places: Introduction to an Anthropology of Supermodernity*, London: Verso.

Cornwall, A. (2000) *Beneficiary, Consumer, Citizen: Perspectives on Participation for Poverty Reduction*, Stockholm: Sida Studies 2.

Cornwall, A. and K. Brock (2005) 'What do buzzwords do for development policy? A critical look at "participation", "empowerment" and "poverty reduction", *Third World Quarterly*, 26 (7): 1043–60.

Foucault, M. (1991) 'Governmentality', in G. Burchell, C. Gordon and P. Miller (eds.) *The Foucault Effect: Studies in Governmentality*, Chicago, IL: University of Chicago Press.

Gallie, W.B. (1956) 'Essentially contested concepts', *Proceedings of the Aristotelian Society* 56: 167–9.

Gieryn, T. (1999) *Cultural Boundaries of Science: Credibility on the Line*, Chicago, IL: Chicago University Press.

Goodman, Nelson (1978) *Ways of Worldmaking*, Indianapolis, IN: Hackett.

Gramsci, Antonio (1971) *Selections from the Prison Notebooks*, London: Lawrence & Wishart.

Hajer, Maarten (1993) 'Discourse coalitions and the institutionalisation of practice', in F. Fischer and J. Forester (eds.) *The Argumentative Turn in Policy Analysis and Planning*, Durham, NC: Duke University Press.

Jolly, Susie (2006) *Sexuality and Development*, IDS Policy Briefing, Issue 29.

Laclau, Ernesto (1997) 'The death and resurrection of the theory of ideology', *MLN* 112.3: 297–321.

Moore, Mick (2001) 'Empowerment at last?', *Journal of International Development* 13 (3): 321–9.

Presley, Cora Ann (1988) 'The Mau Mau rebellion, Kikuyu women, and social change', *Canadian Journal of African Studies / Revue Canadienne des Études Africaines* 22(3:) 502-27.

Rowden, R. and J. Irama (2004) 'Rethinking Participation: Questions for Civil Society about the Limits of Participation in PRSPs', Washington, DC: ActionAid International.

Sen, Gita (2004) 'The Relationship of Research to Activism in the Making of Policy: Lessons from Gender and Development', paper prepared for the UNRISD conference on Social Knowledge and International Development Policy: Exploring the Linkages, Geneva, 21–22 April.

Severino, J.-M. and O. Charnoz (2003) 'A paradox of development', *Revue d'Économie du Développement* 17(4): 77–97.

Sachs, Wolfgang (1992) *The Development Dictionary: A Guide to Knowledge as Power*, London: Zed Books.

Standing, Guy (2001) *Globalization: The Eight Crises of Social Protection*, Geneva: ILO.

Standing, Hilary (2004) 'Gender, myth and fable: the perils of mainstreaming in sector bureaucracies', *IDS Bulletin*, 35(4): 82–8.

Williams, Raymond (1976) *Keywords*, London: Picador.

Wilson, Fiona (1992) *Faust: The Developer*, CDR Working Paper 92.5.

Wittgenstein, Ludwig von ([1953] 2001) *Philosophical Investigations*, Oxford: Blackwell.

About the author

Andrea Cornwall is a Professorial Fellow of the Institute of Development Studies at the University of Sussex, where she specialises in the anthropology of participation and democracy, masculinities, women's empowerment and women's rights, and sexualities. Recent co-edited works include *Feminisms in Development: Contradictions, Contestations, and Challenges* (2007), *The Politics of Rights: Dilemmas for Feminist Practice* (2007), and *Development with a Body: Sexualities, Development and Human Rights* (2008).

CHAPTER 2
Development as a buzzword

Gilbert Rist

Despite its widespread usage, the meaning of the term 'development' remains vague, tending to refer to a set of beliefs and assumptions about the nature of social progress rather than to anything more precise. After presenting a brief history of the term, the author argues that not only will development fail to address poverty or to narrow the gap between rich and poor, but in fact it both widens and deepens this division and ultimately creates poverty, as natural resources and human beings alike are increasingly harnessed to the pursuit of consumption and profit. The survival of the planet will depend upon abandoning the deep-rooted belief that economic growth can deliver social justice, the rational use of environment, or human well-being, and embracing the notion that there would be a better life for all if we moved beyond 'development'.

The meaning(s) of 'development'

To regard 'development' as a buzzword strikes me as highly apposite, for although it has been in vogue for almost 60 years (a record indeed!) its actual meaning is still elusive, since it depends on where and by whom it is used.[1] It is also part of the ordinary buzz or hubbub to be heard in countless meetings devoted to issues ranging from agriculture, urban planning, and international trade to poverty reduction, personal well-being, and industrial production. Everyone may use it as she or he likes, to convey the idea that tomorrow things will be better, or that more is necessarily better. But there is more to it than that. To 'get a buzz from something' also means 'to get a boost' or 'to be perked up'. In this respect, 'development' has beyond doubt been widely used as a hard drug, addiction to which, legally tolerated or encouraged, may stimulate the blissful feelings that typify artificial paradises. So it may also be legitimate to regard the word 'development' as toxic.

Strangely enough, the international career of the term 'development', coupled with the notion of 'underdevelopment', started as a 'public relations gimmick thrown in by a professional speech-writer',[2] since President Truman merely wanted to include in his 1949 Inaugural Address a fourth point that would sound 'a bit original'. So from the very beginning, when the idea was first aired in international circles, no one – not even the US President – really knew what 'development' was all about. This did not, however, prevent the word from gaining wide acceptance.[3] Nevertheless, this unintentional stroke of genius turned the two antagonists – colonisers vs. colonised – into seemingly equal members of the same family, henceforth considered either more or less 'developed'. The dominant view was that time – but also money and political will – would suffice to fill the gap between the two sides.

This global promise of generalised happiness had immediate appeal, not only for those who expected an improvement of their living conditions, but also for those who were committed to international social justice. In other words, 'development' – with all the hopes and expectations that it conveyed – was at first taken very seriously, even by those who were later to count among its critics. As Teresa Hayter recalls, in the 1960s 'there was little attempt [...] to define development. Instead, there was an unquestioned assumption [...] that "development", whatever it was, could lead to improvement in the situation of poor people' (Hayter 2005: 89). This comment gives a clue to the reasons why the word 'development' started buzzing in dominant parlance: it rested on a mere – albeit unquestioned – assumption, and no one cared to define it properly. Both elements characterise a buzzword: an absence of real definition, and a strong belief in what the notion is supposed to bring about.[4] 'Development' therefore became a sort of performative word: saying by doing. Any measure (foreign investment, lowering – or raising – of trade barriers, well-digging, literacy campaigns, and the like) was from now on justified 'in the name of development', making even the most contradictory policies look as if they were geared to 'improving the lives of poor people'. This extensive use of the term 'development' to delineate policies that were assumed to be necessarily good also helped to build up new schemas for perceptions of reality. In other words, 'development' was no longer considered a social construct or the result of political will, but rather the consequence of a 'natural' world order[5] that was deemed just and desirable. This trick – which is at the root of what Bourdieu calls 'symbolic violence'[6] – has been highly instrumental in preventing any possible critique of 'development', since it was equated almost with life itself.

'Development' also did sterling service during the Cold War period. At that time, the Great Powers disagreed on almost all issues except one: 'development', the magic word that reconciled opposite sides. Its necessity and desirability were not debatable, and the two ideological adversaries vied with each other in promoting it across what was then known as the Third World. To be sure, there was some shared and genuine intention to improve the lot of the poor, viewed as potentially interesting future customers of the industrialised countries, but beyond the routine discourse on 'the challenge of our times', 'development' was mainly used as an excuse for enticing 'developing countries' to side with one camp or the other. No wonder, therefore, that this political game turned to the advantage of the ruling 'elites' who were influential in international arenas, rather than grassroots populations. But this lasted only for a time, since it was easy to see through. Progressively, 'white elephants' and gargantuan projects came under criticism and, after two 'development decades' – promulgated under the auspices of the United Nations – had failed to deliver the goods, a generalised 'development fatigue' overcame both developed and developing countries.

The buzz seemed to fade away, but the catchword had proved so helpful in sanctifying so many different ventures and in giving them an aura of legitimacy that every effort had to be made to restore its former lustre. This was indeed no easy task, but the solution was found by adding to the word 'development' a series of adjectives that were supposed to dignify it. Thanks to the experts' imagination, 'development' was successively qualified as 'endogenous', 'human', 'social', and, eventually, 'sustainable' – as if, when standing alone, 'development' had become a dirty word. Why was it suddenly necessary to specify that 'development' had to be 'human'? Was it a form of tacit avowal that, left to its plain meaning, it could also be inhuman? This might have been the case, but no one seriously raised the question.

The height of absurdity was reached when the Brundtland Commission (WCED 1987) tried to reconcile the contradictory requirements to be met in order to protect the environment from pollution, deforestation, the greenhouse effect, and climatic change and, at the same time, to ensure the pursuit of economic growth that was still considered a condition for general happiness. This impossible task resulted in the coining of the catchy phrase 'sustainable development', which immediately achieved star status.[7] Unfortunately it only meant exchanging one buzzword for another. 'Sustainable development became a global slogan that all could readily endorse, and one that was sufficiently vague to allow different, often incompatible interpretations' (South Centre 2002:15). Again, it is impossible to bring together a real concern for environment and the promotion of 'development'. 'Sustainable development' is nothing but an oxymoron, a rhetorical figure that joins together two opposites such as 'capitalism with a human face' or 'humanitarian intervention'.[8] The defenders of the environment and of economic growth respectively were both eager to claim that they drew their inspiration from the same notion, which could be used for different purposes. Hence the battle to define what 'sustainable development' is really about. But Brundtland's plea for a 'new era of economic growth' was certainly not in favour of those who considered environmental sustainability a top priority. It is true that concern for protecting the environment has grown recently, but this can hardly be attributed to the popularity enjoyed by the idea of 'sustainable development'. If an increasing number of people – everywhere and at all levels of society – feel that something has to be done to lessen the impact of human activity on the biosphere, this is rather due to the mounting environmental crises that we are witnessing, from recurrent hurricanes to the melting icecap, or from progressive desertification of large inhabited areas to urban pollution. And yet, 'development' – be it sustainable or not – remains high on the agenda, and no one seems about to forsake it.

So far, I have concentrated on the reasons why 'development' has survived despite (or because of) its ambiguities. But its persistence as a vogue word in economic and political discourse also rests on an even more important

foundation, namely that 'development' corresponds to a generalised and firmly rooted modern belief. Without entering into too much theoretical detail,
it should be remembered that, according to Durkheim, no society can exist
without religion, since religion is an 'eminently social thing' and religious representations 'express collective realities' (Durkheim 1995:9). Religion, in this
sense, has therefore nothing to do with the commonsense view that associates it with the idea of the supernatural or with intimate personal convictions
regarding the existence of God and with attendance at church or mosque. It
relates to the belief of a given social group in certain indisputable truths, a
belief that determines compulsory behaviour in such a way as to strengthen
social cohesion (Rist 1997: 20). In any (democratic) society, various ideologies, whether or not they are related to political parties, are tolerated; but, in
Durkheim's sense, religious beliefs are, as it were, above ideologies; they are
shared by all, as everyone believes that any person belonging to the social
group also shares these beliefs (despite possible private disagreement). They
are beyond dispute and entail various practices on the part of believers who
cannot evade them without endangering the cohesion of the group or risking
being considered social outcasts.

This summary account of the concept of religion should help to explain
why 'development' can be considered one of the indisputable truths that
pervade our modern world.[9] Whatever their ideological creed, no politician
would dare to run on an election platform that ignores economic growth or
'development', which is supposed to reduce unemployment and create new
jobs and well-being for all. Small investors and ordinary people expect an
increase in profits or wages that is supposed to follow a 'secular trend'. 'Development' has become a modern shibboleth, an essential password for anyone
who wishes to improve their standard of living.

A down-to-earth definition

The undeniable success of 'development', linked to its undeniable failures in
improving the condition of the poor, therefore needs to be called into question.[10] The time has come to get rid of this buzzword and demystify the beliefs
associated with it. To neutralise the damaging power of a buzzword amounts
to producing a down-to-earth definition that plainly states what it is all about
and what it actually promotes. In this particular case, the difficulty lies in
the *a priori* positive meaning of the word 'development', which derives both
from its supposedly 'natural' existence and from its inclusion in a cluster of
unquestionable shared beliefs. This is why those who are ready to recognise
that 'development' has not really kept its promises are also loath to discard the
notion altogether. Failures, they would say, do not result from 'development'
itself, but rather from erroneous interpretation or ill-considered implementation. Even in the most dramatic situations it is always possible to appeal to the
presumed existence of a 'good development'. After all, God himself may not

answer all our prayers or grant all our requests, but his righteousness remains beyond doubt...

So, to formulate a proper, sociological, definition of 'development', one has to put aside its emotional and normative connotations and also to incorporate all the external characteristics – which anyone can observe – that are related to the subject matter. In other words, the definition of 'development' should not be based on what one thinks it is or what one wishes it to be, but on actual social practices and their consequences, i.e. things that anyone can identify. What needs to be highlighted is an historical process that concerns not only the countries of the 'South', or only operations conducted under the umbrella of 'development co-operation', which started some two centuries ago and continuously transforms our world.[11]

On this basis and to put it in a nutshell, my definition reads as follows: *the essence of 'development' is the general transformation and destruction of the natural environment and of social relations in order to increase the production of commodities (goods and services) geared, by means of market exchange, to effective demand.* This formulation may appear scandalous compared with the wishful thinking that usually characterises definitions of 'development'. But I contend that it truly reflects the actual process observable when a country or a region is 'developing'. (For a more detailed formulation, see Rist 1997: 12–18.)

First, as far as the natural environment is concerned, it is well documented that the industrialisation process in England took place alongside the enclosure movement. In other words, open fields or commons that anyone could use became private property, to be bought or sold. 'Development' starts when land is transformed into what Polyani (1957) calls a 'fictitious commodity', and when the natural environment is turned into a 'resource'. The progress of the Industrial Revolution, along with increased demand for energy, led to the exploitation of new mineral and non-renewable resources. Ore was transformed into steel to be used in the production of new objects, and oil was transformed into exhaust gas: in both cases, destruction is the reverse side of production – a fact that goes unnoticed by the economist – since recycling is either problematic (requiring new energy costs) or impossible. And, of course, the whole process ends up in increased pollution. But the exploitation of the natural environment does not stop there. Anything can be converted into a commodity and, therefore, into an opportunity for profit. Hence the tremendous efforts made by transnational corporations in favour of licensing procedures to appropriate all kinds of living organisms and biodiversity generally. The best-known example is that of farmers who are no longer able to use part of the previous harvest to sow their crops and are forced to buy new seed every year. A country is the more 'developed' the more limited the number of free things that are available: to spend an afternoon on the beach, to go fishing, or enjoy cross-country skiing is nowadays impossible unless one is prepared to pay for it.

With regard to social relations, the picture is no different, since these are also subject to the rule of commodity and exploitation. The major change took place with the gradual generalisation of wage-labour in modern societies, i.e. when labour also became another 'fictitious commodity', to use Polanyi's phrase. What used to be freely exchanged within the family circle or among neighbours has been progressively converted into paid employment. Since everyone has to earn a living, expensive day nurseries have replaced grand-parents in looking after small children, marriage bureaux have replaced vil-lage dances as opportunities for those in quest of marriage partners, and the tedious chore of walking the dog twice a day can be contracted out to a jobless person keen to make a little money. Such is life in a fully 'developed' country... These anecdotal examples may be laughable, but they are also indicative of a sweeping trend that is jeopardising social bonds. What used to be intimate and personal, supposedly outside the realm of the market, can today be the object of a contract for paid services, such as the practices of womb-leasing, drawing on sperm banks, or buying 'human spare parts' (eyes, kidneys, livers, etc.) from the destitute or condemned in 'Southern' countries. Finally, in a 'developed' country, human beings are also turned into 'resources' and are expected to know how to sell themselves to potential employers. Prostitution may be officially condemned, but it has become the common lot: everyone is for sale.

To complete this already rather grim description of what 'development' is really about, one should add an inventory of its devastating side effects, not only on the environment and the precarious equilibrium of the biosphere, or on the conservation of natural resources (forests, arable land, fish stocks) which are overexploited, but above all on the continuous impoverishment of millions of people. As Jeremy Seabrook (1998) has it, poverty is not a form of 'illness' that demonstrates the malfunctioning of capitalism and can be 'cured'. On the contrary, poverty is proof of the 'good health' of the capitalist system: it is the spur that stimulates new efforts and new forms of accumula-tion. To put it differently, economic growth – widely hailed as a prerequisite to prosperity – takes place only at the expense of either the environment or human beings. World segregation is such that those who enjoy a so-called 'high standard of living' hardly come into contact with the poor and may thus cherish the illusion that their privileged circumstances may sooner or later spread to humankind as a whole. But climatic change, the greenhouse effect, and nuclear clouds cannot be contained and may affect everyone, rich and poor alike, perhaps in the not-too-distant future. This is the real meaning and the real danger of globalisation. It first and foremost concerns the globe, or our 'blue planet', and its fragile balance, which is being progressively destabi-lised by human activities, and not – as we are given to believe – international trade, new information and communication technologies, or round-the-clock stock-market trading.

It should be clear by now why 'development' must be considered a toxic word, as I half-jokingly suggested at the beginning of this chapter. As a buzz-word, it has been used time and again to promote a system that is neither viable, nor sustainable, nor fit to live in. The (substantial) benefits that it still confers on a tiny minority are not enough to justify its continuing acceptance, in view of the lethal dangers that it entails. This is being progressively, if reluctantly, admitted. The question therefore remains: given the amount of information that scientists have gathered on the manifold natural (actually human-made) hazards that may impinge on our daily lives, why is it that we do not believe in what we know to be certain? The answer, probably, lies in the fact that our belief in 'development' is still too strong to be undermined by scientific certainty. Our collective behaviour is strangely determined by what Levy-Bruhl, almost a century ago, described as the 'pre-logical mentality' held to be characteristic of 'primitive peoples'! A radical change of mind is therefore required in order to anticipate possible – or likely – catastrophes. The idea is not to revive the figure of the prophet of doom, nor to wring one's hands, but to take the impending catastrophe so seriously that it will eventually not happen (Dupuy 2002): just as the Japanese anticipate earthquakes or tsunamis, take catastrophes for granted, adapt their behaviour to this conviction and enforce anti-seismic construction standards so that, when earthquakes actually occur, casualties are minimal in comparison with what would happen in other countries. From then on, we must resort to the heuristic of fear, to anticipate what we might experience when the worst happens, in order to prevent it from happening, instead of deluding ourselves with the unverified idea, implicit in the notion of 'development', that tomorrow things will be better.

A change could be conceivable if we recall the Amerindian wisdom that teaches us that 'we hold the Earth in trust for our children'. But it also entails changes in our daily life, particularly in the Northern hemisphere. These are often presented, in a moralistic tone, as a way of vindicating austerity or as a rationing process. But these measures should be considered not as entailing a loss, but rather a gain: there is a positive side to restoring a sense of limits. Instead of viewing 'development' as the history of progress, we could also look upon it as *eine Verlustsgeschichte*, a history of successive losses – which, again, mainly concerns not only the natural environment, but also social bonds and conviviality.[12]

The time has come – and it is indeed high time – to debunk the 'development' buzzword. To do so means that we must define it properly – relying on actual social practices, rather than wishful thinking. We must be aware of its inclusion in a corpus of beliefs that are difficult to shatter, expose its mischievous uses, and denounce its consequences. The most important thing, however, is to make it plain that there is life after 'development' – certainly a different one from what we in the privileged regions are used to, but there is no evidence to suggest that we would lose on such a deal.

Notes

1. To my knowledge, there is no French word that could properly translate 'buzzword'. Hence I opted for the challenge of writing this chapter in

English, even if playing on and with words in another language is always risky. I am therefore grateful to Roy Turnill for revising an earlier version of this essay.

2. The appalling history of the drafting of Point IV of President Truman's Inaugural Address of 20 January 1949, in which the idea of 'development' vs. 'underdevelopment' was launched, is related by Louis J. Halle, who served at the time in the State Department. See his article: 'On teaching International Relations', *The Virginia Quarterly Review* 40(1), Winter 1964 (reprint, no pagination). The phrase 'public relations gimmick' is Halle's.

3. For a more detailed presentation of this episode, see Rist 1997, pp. 70 *et seq.*

4. The process leading to the creation of buzzwords or 'plastic words' is highlighted by Pörksen 1995. See also Rist 2002.

5. The linkage of 'development' (or growth) with nature can be traced back to Aristotle: in Greek, the noun 'nature' (*phusis*) derives from the verb *phuo* (to grow, to develop). For plants, animals, human beings, or institutions, to behave 'according to its nature' simply means 'to develop'.

6. The expression 'symbolic violence' has been coined to explain how those who wield power exert their domination with the tacit consent of the dominated party, by imposing a particular world view, usually considered to be 'natural'. From then on, there is no choice but to match one's behaviour to it and thus to reinforce it. See Bourdieu 1980: 215 *et seq.* and Rist 2006.

7. In fact, the term was already used at a United Nations Seminar in 1979 and in a study jointly sponsored in 1980 by the International Union for the Conservation of Nature and Natural Resources (IUCN): *World Conservation Strategy: Living Resources Conservation for Sustainable Development.*

8. In poetic or mystical writings, expressions such as 'dark brightness' or 'presence of the absent God' are not out of place, as they produce an excess of meaning without establishing a hierarchy between the signifiers. But the Brundtland Report was neither a poem nor a mystical utterance.

9. Since religious beliefs come in clusters, one could identify some other 'truths' that pertain to the same corpus, such as 'democracy', 'human rights', 'market', etc., but that would go beyond the ambit of this chapter. To question one means questioning all of them. See also Perrot *et al.* 1992.

10. According to UNDP statistics, the gap between the 20 per cent poorest and the 20 per cent richest of the world has more than doubled over the last 40 years of so-called development aid.

11. As a symbolic date to mark the beginning of the process, 1776 is probably the most appropriate. It corresponds to the publication by Adam Smith of the *Inquiry into the Nature and Causes of the Wealth of Nations* (the beginning of economics); the Declaration of Independence of the United States (first occurrence of the concept of human rights); and the perfecting by James Watt of the steam engine (production of energy based on fossil ore – coal – rather than wind- or water-mills).

12. I hasten to say that I am not against electricity, antibiotics, or the Internet. I do not suggest 'going back' (which would be nonsense) to caves. I do not think that people are happy just because they are poor. But I am

convinced that economic growth, as such, is unable to solve (and is rather likely to increase) the survival problems of those who are faced with water pollution, depletion of fish resources, desertification etc., not to mention the millions of displaced persons in the wake of international or civil wars who are the first victims of the 'growth' in the arms industry.

References

Bourdieu, Pierre (1980) *Le sens pratique*, Paris: Editions de Minuit.
Dupuy, Jean-Pierre (2002) *Pour un catastrophisme éclairé. Quand l'impossible est certain*, Paris: Le Seuil.
Durkheim, Emile (1995) [1912] *The Elementary Forms of Religious Life*, New York, NY: The Free Press.
Hayter, Teresa (2005) 'Secret diplomacy uncovered: research on the World Bank in the 1960s and 1980s', in Uma Kothari (ed.) *Radical History of Development Studies: Individuals, Institutions and Ideologies*, London: Zed Books.
Perrot, Marie-Dominique, Fabrizio Sabelli, and Gilbert Rist (1992) La mythologie programmée. *L'économie des croyances dans la société moderne*, Paris: PUF.
Polanyi, Karl (1957) [1944] *The Great Transformation, The Political and Economic Origins of Our Time*, Boston, MA: Beacon Press.
Pörksen, Uwe (1995) *Plastic Words: The Tyranny of Modular Language*, Philadelphia, PA: Pennsylvania University Press [trans. *Die Plastikwörter. Die Diktatur einer internationalen Sprache*, Stuttgart: Klett-Cotta, 1989].
Rist, Gilbert (1997) *The History of Development, From Western Origins to Global Faith*, London: Zed Books.
Rist, Gilbert (ed.) (2002) *Les mots du pouvoir, Sens et non-sens de la rhétorique internationale*, Nouveaux Cahiers de l'IUED, n° 13, Paris and Geneva: PUF/IUED.
Rist, Gilbert (2006) 'Before thinking about *What Next*: prerequisites for alternatives', *Development Dialogue* (special issue 'What Next') 1(47): 65–96.
Seabrook, Jeremy (1988) *The Race for Riches: The Human Cost of Wealth*, Basingstoke: Marshall Pickering.
South Centre (2002) *The South and Sustainable Development Conundrum*, Geneva: South Centre.
World Commission on Environment and Development (1987) Our *Common Future*, Report of the World Commission on Environment and Development, with an introduction by Gro Harlem Brundtland, Oxford: Oxford University Press.

About the author

Gilbert Rist is a Professor of Political Science and teaches social and cultural anthropology, inter-cultural relations, and the history of development theories at the Institut universitaire d'études du développement (Graduate Institute of Development Studies) in Geneva.

CHAPTER 3

Words count: taking a count of the changing language of British aid

Naomi Alfini and Robert Chambers

A word analysis of six UK Government White Paper policy statements on aid (selected between 1960 and 2006) compares the top 20 words and key word pairs used in each document. Characteristic sentences are composed of the top 20s to represent the spirit of each paper. Results illuminate changes in the context of White Papers on aid, and point to trends in the history of the UK's approach to international development. A characteristic sentence to illustrate the 2005 Paris Declaration on Aid Effectiveness is contrasted with a series of words that did not appear in that document. Readers are invited and challenged to identify words they would like to be used and acted on more commonly in development.

Introduction

> In language we coordinate our behaviour, and together in language we bring forth our world. (Fritjof Capra 1996: 282)

The prevailing words and expressions in development discourse keep changing. Some become perennials, long-term survivors year after year, like *poverty, gender, sustainable*, and *livelihood*. Others have their day and then fade, like *scheme* and *integrated rural development*. Yet others mark major shifts in ideology, policy, and reality, as have *liberalisation, privatisation*, and *globalisation*.

There is, too, a vocabulary to mock these fashions in the lexicon of development; we talk of the *alphabet soup* of acronyms and the *PC* (politically correct) *buzzwords* that are *flavours of the month* in *development-speak*. During lectures, development students play Development Bingo,[1] ticking off combinations of the latest *vogue words* and *weasel words* as a speaker uses them: *capacity building, harmonisation, good governance, transparency, accountability* and the like, startling speakers and waking up colleagues with cries of 'Development!' when a column is complete.

An Internet search provides several definitions of *buzzword*: 'a word or phrase that takes on added significance through repetition or special usage'; 'a word or phrase connected with a specialised field or group that usually sounds important and is used primarily to impress lay persons'; and 'a stylish or trendy word or phrase'. In recent decades, the English forms of buzzwords have tended to be adopted in Washington, DC and then disseminated around the world as instruments of power.

The words we use (especially buzzwords) frame our perceptions and thoughts, and affect our mind-sets, ways of ordering our world, and actions. Embedded through use and repetition, our language influences both policies and practice in development. Thus, studying how the language of development policy has changed can give us a sense of the historical shifts in development thinking and priorities, and help us to reflect on where we are going (or could go) in the future.

With this in mind, we have made word counts of relatively comparable statements of policy to see what their language reveals or suggests. We confined our research to White Papers (official government statements) published on British aid policy between 1960 and 2006.[2] Two dimensions of historical context can aid our understanding and interpretation of the content of these papers. First, there were the well-known changes in the world and in the priorities of aid generally. Among the more relevant have been decolonisation and post-colonial relationships; the shift from industrialisation and import substitution to agriculture and cash-crop exports as development strategies; the oil shock of 1973 and the concurrent shortage of world food stocks; and the U-shaped curve of Northern and donor intervention (high in the colonial period, low in the 1970s, and then rising to levels in the 1990s and 2000s that would have been unthinkable two decades earlier). Second, British domestic politics were significant. After 1963, White Papers were published only in the periods when Labour governments were in power (1964–1970 and 1974–1979, and from 1997 onwards). Under Conservative governments, the responsible Overseas Development Administration (ODA) produced only brief technical reports, while under the current Labour government, the Department for International Development (DFID) has produced White Papers that are fuller and more detailed, and presented to educate and persuade as well as to articulate policies.

The following White Papers were selected for this study:[3]

- **1960** *Assistance from the United Kingdom for Overseas Development*, Cmnd. 974, H M Treasury, London: HMSO, March.
  This paper conceptualises aid as investment (both private and government), similar to the way British 'investment' was made in the Americas throughout the seventeenth, eighteenth, and nineteenth centuries. Being written by Her Majesty's Treasury, it reads somewhat like an accounts update for shareholders.

- **1967** *Overseas Development: The Work in Hand*, Cmnd. 3180, Ministry of Overseas Development, London: HMSO, January.
  This paper recognises more complexities and challenges entailed in overseas development than does the 1960 paper. It seeks to assure the UK's approach to overseas aid (which includes greater emphasis on technical assistance and research) will eventually achieve a successful

endpoint and does not undercut Britain's competitive standing in the world market.

- **1975** *Overseas Development: The Changing Emphasis in British Aid Policies. More Help for the Poorest*, Cmnd. 6270, Ministry of Overseas Development, London: HMSO, October.
  This paper was written during the world food shortage, following the oil crisis of 1973. It shifts the focus of overseas aid to the *poorest* countries and their poorest communities, largely through strategies of rural development and short-term food aid.

- **1997** *Eliminating World Poverty: A Challenge for the 21st Century, White Paper on International Development*, Cmnd. 3789, Department for International Development, London: HMSO, November.
  This paper re-orients overseas aid towards the target for aid contributions of 0.7 per cent of GNP. It links development to human rights and stresses the need for public understanding about global mutual dependence and the benefits that *poverty elimination* would bring to the world.

- **2000** *Eliminating World Poverty: Making Globalisation Work for the Poor, White Paper on International Development*, Cmnd. 5006, Department for International Development, London: HMSO, December.
  This paper 'stands alongside' the 1997 White Paper by setting out an agenda for managing the processes of globalisation to achieve *poverty reduction*. It raises many issues related to globalisation, portrayed as having the potential to make or break development. It advocates *good globalisation* policies, building efficient governments and effective markets, and raising the UK's rate of aid contributions to 0.7 per cent of GNP.

- **2006** *Eliminating World Poverty: Making Governance Work for the Poor, White Paper on International Development*, Cm 6876, Department for International Development, London: HMSO, July.
  This paper presents a four-pronged approach to poverty reduction: strengthening good governance in poor countries; increasing aid funds (doubling aid to Africa); mitigating and preventing impacts of climate change; and reforming international development systems, such as the United Nations. Along with reducing poverty, it stresses development's role in building security and reducing violent conflict, including terrorism.[4]

Method and limitations

Our word analysis consists of two examinations. First, we conducted counts to ascertain the top 20 words used in each paper.[5] We eliminated common words like *the, then*, and *should* and others like *million* which seemed unlikely to tell us much, and retained words with a clearer development significance. Noting the relative frequency and manner in which these top 20s are used, we constructed a characteristic sentence for each document, trying to express some of its spirit and content. Second, we tracked the frequency with which pairs of key contrasting words (*economic: social; rural: urban; women: gender;* and *agricultural: industrial*) are used throughout the documents.[6]

Our method and presentation have limitations. Comparability is limited, because White Papers were not all conceived for the same purpose or written in the same fashion. Their different emphases were in part intended to complement rather than fully supplant their immediate predecessors. Their formats vary. Some aim to give an account of the UK's general activities in development, while others more explicitly focus on themes (such as Globalisation in 2000 and Governance in 2006). Also, intervals between publications are inconsistent. Labour governments published White Papers related to overseas development every two to eight years, but we could find nothing comparable produced during the Conservative governments of the Thatcher and Major years between 1979 and 1997.[7] Finally, our characteristic sentences cannot pretend to be summaries of the White Papers, but rather intend to give an impression of the framework of the language used.

Word counts: the top 20s

Lists rank the top 20 development-related words used in each paper. The number shows how many times a word appears in the paper. Numbers are divided by the total word count (given above each list) to find the percentage (%) that top words constitute of a paper's full word content. 'Rank' refers to a word's standing relative to the others in the top 20. Some words share a rank, because they occur the same number of times within a paper. These have been organised alphabetically. A few words which were also much used but did not quite make it to the top 20 are included in the characteristic sentences.

Findings

We were struck by the fact that the top 20s include nouns like *country, world, aid,* and *poverty* and general adjectives like *public* and *international,* but very few of what would typically be considered buzzwords. Exceptions could be *community* in 1975, *sustainable* and *partnership* in 1997, and *global* in 2000. There are notable shifts in these top 20s over time. First, descriptions of the political and international context changed. Countries receiving assistance, mainly *Colonial, Commonwealth,* and *newly independent* in 1960, became *overseas* (1967), and then *developing* (1975–2006). In 2006 *developing* lost some ground, but *Africa* appeared for the first time, in twelfth place. *People* first entered the top 20 in 1975 and then continued to score, ranking fifth in 2006. Astonishingly, the *poor* were entirely absent from the 1960 text and barely mentioned in 1967. The *United Kingdom* (1960) became *Britain* (1967), disappeared in 1975 and 1997, and resurfaced in 2000 and 2006 as the *UK. World*

Table 1. Assistance from the United Kingdom for Overseas Development (1960) (Total words in document = 4973)

	Rank	Word	Number	%
1	1	United Kingdom	78	1.57
2	2	assist/s/ance	72	1.45
3	3	country/ies	66	1.33
4	4	Kingdom	63	1.27
5	5	loan/s	37	0.74
6	6	Colonial	36	0.72
7	7	Commonwealth	33	0.66
8	8	development	28	0.56
9	9	overseas	26	0.52
10	9	technical	26	0.52
11	10	Government/s	25	0.50
12	11	international	24	0.48
13	12	provide/s/ed/ing	23	0.46
14	13	fund/s	21	0.42
15	14	invest/ed/ment	20	0.40
16	15	bank/s	19	0.38
17	16	territory/ies	18	0.36
18	17	private	16	0.32
19	18*	economic	15	0.30
20	18*	independent	15	0.30

* *subscription/s* and *training/ed* also occur 15 times, and so are jointly ranked 18 with the last two words in the list.

Characteristic sentence:

The *assistance provided* by the *United Kingdom* for *overseas development* is mainly to *Colonial territories* and newly *independent countries* of the *Commonwealth*, and while primarily *economic* – as *loans* to *governments*, *funds subscribed* to *international banks*, and *private investment* – also includes *technical assistance* and *training*.

became a regular member of the top 20 from 1975, and *international* scored among the top four from 1997 onwards, reflecting perhaps an expanded consciousness of international co-operation and the increased importance of multilateral organisations like the World Bank.

Second, there are shifts in the terminology of aid. The highest-scoring word and its cognates began as *assistance* (1960) and then became *aid* (1967 and 1975), *support* (1997 and 2000), and finally *help* (2006). The most mentioned means of aid also changed. In 1960, discussion began in terms of *loans* and *investment plans*. Thereafter, these terms all but disappeared from the top 20s

Table 2. Overseas Development: The Work in Hand (1967) (Total words in document = 46, 237)

	Rank	Word	Number	%
1	1	country/ies	422	0.91
2	2	British	343	0.71
3	3	overseas	289	0.64
4	4	aid/s/ed/ing	280	0.61
5	5	development	279	0.60
6	6	ministry/'s	263	0.57
7	7	government/s	236	0.51
8	8	assist/s/ed/ing/ance	204	0.44
9	9	technical	177	0.38
10	10	provid/es/ed/ing	166	0.36
11	11	developing	164	0.35
12	12	programme/s	156	0.33
13	12	train/s/ed/ing	156	0.33
14	13	university/ies	151	0.33
15	14	service/s	146	0.32
16	15	economic/s/ally/ist/ists/; economy/ies	144	0.31
17	16	Britain/'s	142	0.31
18	17	help/s/ed/ing	123	0.27
19	18	staff	120	0.27
20	19	research	117	0.25

Characteristic sentence:

Britain's overseas aid to *developing countries provides help* through *programmes* and *schemes* for *economic development, technical assistance, training services* for *staff* of *government ministries,* courses in *British universities,* and *research.*

(*investment* resurfaced once, in 2000). The 1975 emphasis on *schemes* and *programmes* indicates support for activities that were geographically or sectorally bounded. *Policy* appeared first in 1975, rose in 1997 and 2000, but dropped out in 2006, perhaps in part replaced by *public services*. In addition to economic inputs, aid provided *technical assistance* and *training* (including *education*) in 1960 and 1967, indicating a focus of the decolonisation process early on. In 1975 the principal term used was *education*. *Training* and *education* did not score later, perhaps subsumed in the 2000s under the term 'capacity building'. *Rural, poorest,* and *food* are all one-hit wonders in the 1975 top 20s, reflecting the short-term nature of the response to the food crisis of the time.

Table 3. Overseas Development: The Changing Emphasis in British Aid Policies. More Help for the Poorest (1975) (Total words in document = 24, 104)

	Rank	Word	Number	%
1	1	country/ies	392	1.63
2	2	aid	230	0.95
3	3	development	190	0.79
4	4	developing	178	0.74
5	5	poorest	134	0.56
6	6	rural	117	0.49
7	7	food	96	0.40
8	8	programme/s	94	0.39
9	9	need/s	74	0.31
10	10	community	69	0.29
11	11	government/s	66	0.27
12	12	world/s	65	0.27
13	13	scheme/s	63	0.26
14	14	income/s	60	0.25
15	14	provide/d	60	0.25
16	15	assistance	58	0.24
17	16	help	56	0.23
18	17	fund/s	55	0.23
19	17	policy/ies	55	0.23
20	17	produc/tive/tivity/tion/ing	55	0.23

Characteristic sentence:

Government assistance will provide *funds* and *other resources* to *help* meet short and long *term needs* of the *poorest developing countries* and *low income communities*, with support to *rural development schemes, education projects* and international aid including the *World Food Programme.*

Counts also shed light on the changes that aid was intended to achieve. In 1975 *poorest* burst into the top 20 at fifth place, despite the fact that even *poor* had been scarcely mentioned earlier. From 1997 onwards, concern focused on *poor people* and *poverty. Poverty elimination* was the overarching goal in 1997, which in the text, though not the title, shifted to poverty *reduction* in 2000. (*Elimination* is used 10 times, whereas *reduction* is used 99 times in 2000. In 2006 *elimination* is used only once, in the title, and *reduction* is used 23 times.) *Need* first appeared in 1975 and reappeared in 1997 and 2006. *Right(s)* featured only in 1997. Until 1997 the *environment* did not score (it barely enters into previous White Papers at all). It remained in 2000 and then was supplanted by *climate* in 2006.

Table 4. Eliminating World Poverty: A Challenge for the 21st Century (DFID) (1997) (Total words in document = 26, 375)

	Rank	Word	Number	%
1	1	development	334	1.27
2	2	country/ies	330	1.25
3	3	international	146	0.55
4	4	developing	139	0.53
5	5	support/s/ed/ing	131	0.50
6	6	poor	123	0.47
7	7	government/s	118	0.45
8	8	people/s	117	0.44
9	9	poverty	112	0.42
10	10	world/s	100	0.38
11	10	policy/ies	100	0.38
12	11	environment/s/al/ally	95	0.36
13	12	sustainable/ability	91	0.35
14	13	economic	80	0.30
15	14	right/s	78	0.30
16	15	resource/s	77	0.29
17	15	partner/s/ship/ships	77	0.29
18	16	need/s	72	0.27
19	17	help/s/ed/ing	70	0.27
20	18	assistance	69	0.26

Characteristic sentence:

Sustainable development to eliminate *poverty* requires *support* for human *rights*, and *international help* with more *resources* of *development assistance* in *partnership* with *developing countries*, ensuring that government and *world economic policies* address the *needs* of *poor people* and the *environment*.

Tracking key words and significant shifts

Throughout the White Papers we tracked the frequency with which the following pairs of significant development-related words were used.

woman/en/'s	gender
social	economic
industry/ial	agriculture/al
rural	urban

The changes in each word's frequency, and possible relationships between paired words, are illustrated in Table 7 and Figure 1.

Table 5. Eliminating World Poverty: Making Globalisation Work for the Poor (2000) (Total words in document = 39, 222)

	Rank	Word	Number	%
1	1	country/s/ies	631	1.61
2	2	development	363	0.93
3	3	developing	264	0.67
4	4	international	237	0.60
5	5	government/s	219	0.56
6	6	poor	197	0.50
7	7	UK/s	190	0.48
8	8	poverty	171	0.44
9	9	world/s	169	0.43
10	10	policy/ies	160	0.41
11	11	people/s	158	0.40
12	12	trade	149	0.38
13	13	invest/ed/ing/ment/ments	141	0.36
14	14	environment/s/al/ally	131	0.33
15	15	DFID	129	0.33
16	16	global	124	0.32
17	17	support/s/ed/ing	108	0.28
18	17	finance/ial/ed/ially/ing	108	0.28
19	18	effective/ly/ness	106	0.27
20	19	globalization	99	0.25

* reduction also occurs 99 times and is jointly ranked with globalisation

Characteristic sentence:

Since *globalisation* leads to *international development* with potential for *poverty reduction*, the *UK Government* will *support global policies* that *assist developing countries* to benefit from *world trade, investment* and *finance* and build *effective governments* which *support poor people* and the *environment*.

Discussion

The words *women* and *gender* follow similar patterns. Until 1997 *women* was low and *gender* non-existent. Both peaked in 1997, and then dropped by more than half in 2000 (when the focus was *globalisation*). Interestingly, *women* has been used consistently almost three times as often as *gender*, despite concerns by some that the Gender and Development (GAD) agenda had shifted attention away from women in development (Cornwall *et al.* 2004).

Industry showed the expected decline over the whole period, as industrialisation became a less favoured strategy, while *agriculture* rose to a plateau in 1967 and 1975, dropped in 1997, and declined to another plateau in 2000

Table 6. Eliminating World Poverty: Making Governance Work for the Poor (2006) (Total words in document = 39, 822)

	Rank	Word	Number	%
1	1	country/ies/s	452	1.14
2	2	help/ing/ed/s	307	0.77
3	3	international	293	0.74
4	4	development	273	0.69
5	5	people/s	248	0.62
6	6	world/s	218	0.55
7	7	UK	204	0.51
8	8	developing	195	0.49
9	9	government/s	184	0.46
10	10	support/s/ed/ing	183	0.46
11	11	aid	158	0.40
12	12	Africa/n	154	0.39
13	13	work	151	0.38
14	13	poverty	151	0.38
15	14	poor	133	0.33
16	15	service/s	131	0.33
17	16	public	124	0.31
18	17	need/s	124	0.31
19	18	bank/s	123	0.31
20	19	climate	120	0.30

Characteristic sentence:

Poverty reduction requires *international development* efforts to *help* strengthen *governments* in *developing countries (supporting poor people's* access to *public services*), increase *international aid* (doubling G8 *countries' aid* to *Africa*), tackle *climate* change, and reform *international development* systems such as the *World Bank* to better fit the *needs* of today's *world*.

Table 7. Paired words as percentage of word-counts in White Papers on aid (1960–2006)

	1960	1967	1975	1997	2000	2006
woman/en/s	0.02	0.03	0.02	0.17	0.07	0.08
gender	0.00	0.00	0.00	0.06	0.02	0.01
social	0.14	0.06	0.08	0.15	0.14	0.14
economic	0.30	0.22	0.15	0.30	0.21	0.21
agricultur/al	0.10	0.21	0.19	0.09	0.05	0.07
industry/ial	0.20	0.11	0.07	0.05	0.03	0.02
urban	0.00	0.00	0.12	0.04	0.01	0.01
rural	0.00	0.01	0.49	0.04	0.02	0.03

and 2006. *Rural* was low in 1960 and 1967, but then rose to a dramatic peak in 1975, immediately after the oil-price shock and concurrent drop in world food stocks. It was then on a much lower plateau through 1997, 2000, and 2006. Apart from a notable rise in 1997, *urban* features little throughout the White Papers.

Economic was about twice as commonly used as *social* until 2000, when it dropped by a third. It is still more used than *social*, which rose in 1997 and subsequently maintained its position (similar to where it started in 1960).

Analysis

This simple analysis cannot pretend to give detailed insights into British aid policy. But it does confirm and illuminate changes over time. The increasing length of White Papers can be interpreted as in part reflecting the growth in knowledge and specialisation as development has evolved into its own industry over the years. Word frequency indicates and illustrates the trend of British aid towards the international, with a steady shift away from the narrow 1960 emphasis on the Britain–Commonwealth relationship to the attention given in 2006 to reorganising international development systems like the UN. Or again, 1997 was a time of prominence for social issues in development, as indicated by the new words that appeared or rose in its top 20, for example *rights, partnership, poor, people, sustainability, environment*, and *gender*. The paired words *women/gender* and *social/economic* all also peaked in 1997. This was the first White Paper to use all words on the word-pair list, and it used them all proportionately more than the 2000 and 2006 papers. In part this is explained by the 2000 and 2006 focus on themes – globalisation and governance respectively – and in part by the social orientation of the new Labour government in 1997 and the radical influence of then Secretary of State for International Development, Clare Short. Then, after the socially oriented rhetoric of 1997, the 2000 White Paper assumes a more practical-sounding tone, using words like *reduction* and *effectiveness*.

This word analysis raises other intriguing questions and conjectures. Why, for example, do some words disappear or not appear at all? What is not noted or said may be as significant as what is. Why is Iraq never mentioned in the 2006 White Paper? A strength of the word-search technology is being able to confirm guesses about what is *not* there.

There remains the issue of the use of buzzwords. Although the top-20 analysis does not adequately pick this up, a reading of the White Papers gives the impression that their use has increased over this period (1960–2006). One can speculate whether word-counts of policy documents can reveal more now, in the early twenty-first century, than in the past. If, as findings of this study suggest, the international dimension is becoming more central to development policy, then there could perhaps be more value attributed to the use of the same standard lexicon. There have been many calls, such as the Rome Declaration (Rome–HLF 2003), for harmonisation of lender and donor policies. As

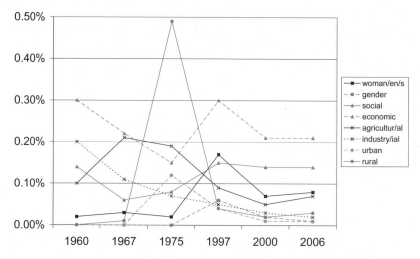

Figure 1. Frequency of paired words throughout White Papers on aid (1960–2006)

donors engage in this, do they also harmonise their vocabulary and syntax so that they are not only 'singing from the same hymn sheet', but also singing the same tune? The question is whether harmonisation drives standardisation and a narrowing of vocabulary, with more use of the same fewer words. If so, this is likely to reduce diversity, choice, and subtlety of expression. Too much standardisation may also lead to new hegemonies.

An example is provided by the OECD Paris Declaration on Aid Effectiveness (DAC 2005). In this, the density of keywords is striking.[8] An appropriate characteristic sentence to describe it reads as follows:

> To *monitor indicators* of *effective performance* from *aid, donors* and *partners* need the *capacity* to *manage* the *mutual harmonisation* of *programmes* and to *assess, measure* and *report* on *results*.

Paradigmatically, this presents a mechanistic world without people, where aid effectiveness is achieved through top–down, standardised bureaucratic norms, with measurements and upwards reporting. A shadow sentence of words never used in the Declaration might read:

> To *negotiate* and *evolve agreements* that *optimise outcomes* for *poor, vulnerable*, and *marginalised people* requires *compromises* and *trade-offs* based on *personal conviction, interactions*, and *relationships* that *nurture trust*, together with *reflective appreciation* of *power* and *conflicts*.[9]

Paradigmatically, this is for a world that names and recognises the realities and significance of power, trust, negotiation, and relationships in aid (see, for example, Eyben 2006).

Words for the future

The words left out of White Papers may be as significant as those that appear and those that make the top 20s. Throughout the years, White Papers have not used words such as *critical, reflection, self-awareness, empathy, solidarity, compensation, personal development, love, happiness, pleasure, hope, spiritual,* or *holistic*. Only in recent years have terms like *marginalisation, exclusion*, and *professionalism* begun to appear. Negative dimensions such as *conflict* and *corruption* are beginning to be addressed, although statements still dwell upon the roles and responsibilities of poorer countries. Similarly, papers since 1997 have included *needs, rights, accountability*, and *justice,* but there continues to be a lack of language articulating the *responsibilities* and *obligations* of the powerful countries and international organisations towards those who are marginalised and excluded. Attention remains focused on the poor and relatively powerless, not on the wealthy and powerful.

When invited to name positive words expressing concepts, values, and actions that they would like to be given greater emphasis in future development, participants in workshops have often proposed and given high scores to *critical, empathy, ethics, honesty, humility, justice, listen, love, peace, reflect, respect,* and *redistribution*.

If Fritjof Capra is right, that together in language we bring forth our world, let us end with an invitation and a challenge. We have reviewed some of the words most common in past and current British aid-policy documents that have both reflected and redirected much thinking and action. If you have read this far, may we invite you to join us in reflecting critically on the words and concepts that you habitually use and how they frame, influence, and reinforce your own thinking and action. And may we then challenge you, and ourselves, to name words that we wish to be used or used more, together to bring forth our future world; and then to use and act on them and spread their use.

Acknowledgements

We thank Andrea Cornwall for many helpful corrections and suggestions at the draft stage, and also David Wendt, who spent many hours on the technical side of data analysis. We are grateful to Henry Rowsell of the British Library of Development Studies for help and advice in tracing these and other documents. The usual disclaimers apply.

Notes

1. Reportedly invented and originally played as 'Buzzword Bingo' by students at the Massachusetts Institute of Technology during a commencement speech by Vice President Al Gore in 2001, (http://everything2. com/index.pl?n ode_id=431890).

2. Although the organisation responsible for aid has been known variously as Ministry of Overseas Development (1964–1979), Overseas Development Administration (ODA) (1979–1997), Department for International Development (DFID) (1997–present), there was much continuity of staff and location during this period (from correspondence with staff from DFID's Stationery Office www.dfid.gov.uk/pubs/ in August 2006, and from http://en.wikipedia.org/wiki/Department_for_International_Development, on 12 February 2007).

3. The search for comparable policy statements on British overseas aid was challenged by the fact that DFID's Stationery Office does not have a list of their titles, nor are copies of them available on-line. This is in part due to the fact that overseas aid was handled by various bodies until 1997, when DFID was formed (see Note 2). Thus, our initial search consisted of finding out which bodies these were (through contacting communications staff at DFID, on-line searches, and paper searches through the archives at the British Library for Development Studies, at the Institute of Development Studies in Brighton, England). Of the eight papers that we were able to locate, we used six. The papers in 1963 (*Aid to Developing Countries*) and 1965 (*Overseas Development: The Work of the New Ministry*) have not been included, since they were published so close to 1960 and 1967 that we deemed them unlikely to contribute much more insight. Unable to trace any White Paper or comparable policy statement between 1975 and 1997, we analysed *Common Crisis*, the British Government's response to the Brandt Commission, but found it too specific for useful comparability.

4. Before 1997, *conflict*, *violence*, and *violent* were not mentioned in the selected White Papers. In 2006 these words were used proportionately more than in the previous papers (for example, although the 2000 and 2006 have similar total word counts, *conflict* is used 95 times in 2006 and 53 times in 2000). Further, a full chapter of the 2006 paper is devoted to 'Promoting Peace and Security', which makes frequent reference to conflict.

5. Word-counts were conducted using software called Automap, which provides a total count of every word in a simple text (.txt) document (www.casos.cs.cmu.edu/projects/au tomap/software.html). Thus, we converted the electronic versions of White Papers produced from 1997 onwards (available on-line at www.dfid.gov.uk/pubs) from pdf to .txt format, using MS Word. Since White Papers that pre-date 1997 are not available electronically, we scanned paper versions into MS Word documents and then converted these to .txt format. All papers were imported into Automap for analysis. Resulting word-counts were 'cleaned'. This involved removing any software commands that were picked up (which are unrelated to the text), as well as a list of commonly occurring but irrelevant words, such as *the*, *of* and *and* – although these were included in the total word-count used to calculate percentages. We then read through lists and removed other words that we thought had no significance to the study (such as *million* and *work*). Next, we searched out the different forms of high-scoring words by stem searches (for example, 'econ' for *economy*, *economic*, *economically*), and by tense searches (*help*, *helps*, *helping*, *helped*). Words were added together with the others in their stem and tense groups, and then lists were re-ordered according to the new figures.

6. For the word-pair analysis, we drew up a list of words that we thought fitted into pairs that indicated contrasts in development. These words were: *economic, social, rural, urban, women, gender, agricultural,* and *industrial.* The words that we selected undoubtedly also reflect our own interests and priorities in development. Therefore, we encourage other people to create and investigate their own lists.

7. We tried to fill the 22-year gap between 1975 and 1997 with *The Common Crisis* (1983), the government's official response to the Brandt Commission report, but found it was too different and specific to be included.

8. A simple manual method of counting for chosen words was used for the Paris Declaration. This was repetitive use of CTRL + H in MS Word.

9. *Conflict* does, however, show up once in *'potentially conflicting targets'. Poor* and *trust* appear once each, but in the titles of organisations: The Consultative Group to Assist the Poorest and the Tanzania Social and Economic Trust. None of the other words in italics is to be found in the document.

References

Capra, Fritjof (1996) *The Web of Being: A New Synthesis of Mind and Matter,* London: HarperCollins.

Cornwall, Andrea, Elizabeth Harrison, and Ann Whitehead (eds.) (2004) 'Repositioning feminisms in development', special issue of *IDS Bulletin* 35(4): October.

Development Advisory Committee (DAC) (2005) 'Paris Declaration on Aid Effectiveness: ownership, harmonisation, alignment, results and mutual accountability', endorsed 2 March, Paris: DAC/OECD, available at www.aidharmonization.org/ahoverview/secondary-pages/editable?key=205.

Eyben, Rosalind (ed.) (2006) *Relationships for Aid,* London and Sterling, VA: Earthscan.

Eyben, R., A. Hughes and J. Wheeler (2005) 'Rights and power: the challenge for international development agencies', *IDS Bulletin* 36(1): 63–72.

Rome High-Level Forum on Harmonisation (2003) 'Rome Declaration on Aid Harmonisation', endorsed 25 February, Rome:
High-Level Forum on Harmonization, available at www.aidharmonization. org/ahoverview/secondary-pages/why-RomeDeclaration.

About the authors

Naomi Alfini is an independent researcher on power dynamics in development contexts, particularly in relation to children and young people's participation.

Robert Chambers is a Research Associate in the Institute of Development Studies at the University of Sussex. His main research and operational experience has been in East Africa and South Asia. His books include *Rural Development: Putting the Last First* (1983), *Whose Reality Counts? Putting the First Last* (1997), and *Ideas for Development* (2005).

CHAPTER 4
Poverty reduction

John Toye

The idea of poverty reduction naturally attracts all kinds of angels – in NGOs, government departments and international financial institutions – but their ministrations are frustrated by many obstacles. These include the narrow and static way in which economists define the poor; the remoteness of the poor, their social invisibility and elusiveness to most forms of targeting; and the absence of political will to engage in poverty-reduction policies. The angelic response to these obstacles has been to trumpet a global campaign of poverty reduction with millennial goals, international aid targets, and poverty-reduction strategy papers. It would be better to re-discover the language of risk, vulnerability, and social insurance. The message of the association between risk and reward, and the collective need for social mechanisms that will allow individuals to bear increased risk without exposure to irreversible damage, is the one that really needs to be delivered.

Mediaeval theologians debated how many angels could dance on the head of a pin. Sometimes one wonders if the equivalent modern question should not be: *'How many angels can dance on the head of the poor?'* The answer to both questions may be the same: *an infinite number.* Once those angels get into their high-tech tap shoes, there is no stopping them.

The idea of *poverty reduction* itself has a luminous obviousness to it, defying mere mortals to challenge its status as a moral imperative. Poverty reduction thus has a natural attraction for angels of all kinds: the angels of non-governmental mercy, the great and good angels of the government aid bureaucracies and international financial institutions – not forgetting the cohorts of angelic academics. To be a moral imperative, however, an action must be capable of being performed. The determined angel will therefore need to be armed with a definition of poverty, a method of reducing poverty, and the political will to implement the method.

What poverty is to be reduced?

Poverty is now thought of as a kind of generalised lacking, or a state of being without some essential goods and services. Poor people are people deprived of things that they need to live a normal life. Identifying poor people then becomes a matter of tallying up how much people consume, often using a household survey, and discovering what percentage of them fall below some pre-set threshold that is meant to represent the minimum standard of a normal life. This percentage is called the 'headcount ratio' of the poor.

There are various ways to define the cut-off point between the poor and the non-poor. The scientifically minded go straight to the science of nutrition and call on the calorie as the bedrock of need: allegedly 2300 calories a day per person is required. Then they price the minimum survival calorie intake and allow a percentage above that for non-food expenditure. The fact that there is no uniform standard of this kind, and that in general calorie requirements vary with climate and the amount of physical work performed is often quietly ignored.

Attention is usually paid, however, to one special case of this variation: the difference in food needs between adults and children. Much ingenuity is devoted to deciding the adult-equivalence scale in order to convert children's minimum consumption needs into that of an adult. Is a child's basic need one half or one third of an adult's? Does the proportion vary with the age of the child? Does it vary with the number of children in the household, for example, because of economies of scale in the production of household services?

The household itself, which is taken as the unit for accounting for consumption, is also a somewhat dubious concept, when stretched over heterogeneous continents and cultures. Different patterns of family formation, of migrant employment, of the adoption and fostering of children sometimes make it difficult to decide on which groups of people are 'eating out of a common pot' and thus forming a household for statistical enumeration purposes.

The use of a pre-set threshold implies that need is absolute. Once basic needs are met, poverty is no more. Others, however, have argued that poverty is relative, and that when economic growth raises living standards altogether beyond some minimum threshold, the poor do not vanish, but are still there, trapped in the bottom deciles of the income distribution. Others again have argued that poverty is both absolute and relative at the same time. It is absolute in that, in any given society, minimum essential goods can be listed and priced. It is relative because in different societies – or indeed the same society at different points in time – the lists of basic needs and their costs might be different.

This definition of poverty is manifestly far too narrow. Its focus is on consumption (or income), and it ignores both the productive assets of the poor and a range of communal and social resources that the poor use to supplement their consumption. Such resources are vital to well-being. Lack of access to public health and education services and public utilities, such as clean water and public security, may be as damaging to a person's life chances as inadequate nutrition and the absence of some household effects. Yet these aspects of welfare are usually missing when the poor are being counted.

What to do to achieve poverty reduction?

Having counted the poor, however partially, the determined angel now faces three options for what to do about it. They are *poverty alleviation, poverty reduction,* and *poverty elimination.* Poverty alleviation sounds rather namby-pamby, as if one were temporising with poverty rather than really confronting it. Poverty elimination has the right degree of gritty determination and radicalism, but it has a utopian feel about it, and it seems to fly in the face of the Gospel of Saint Matthew, which tells us 'the poor are with you always'. Poverty reduction, which sounds both resolute and realistic, is the golden mean between these two, and is therefore the angelic policy of choice.

The absolute and the absolute-cum-relative definitions of consumption poverty preserve the idea that poverty could conceivably be reduced to zero, while consumption inequality remains. This keeps the poverty-elimination option open in principle. However, if poverty is relative, it would have to continue until all households are consuming an equal amount – a state of affairs that definitely has a utopian feel to it.

How should poverty reducers go about their task? It might seem that their aim should be to redistribute consumption such that the number of people lifted out of poverty, i.e. hoisted over the minimum consumption threshold, is maximised, subject to a government budget constraint. Yet to do so would be a very ineffective way of reducing poverty. Maximising the numbers who cross the poverty line is best achieved by concentrating budget transfers on those poor people who are already closest to the minimum standard. More poor people can be moved across the poverty line, the closer to it they are already. A policy that reduces poverty by reducing the headcount ratio helps only the richest of the poor and leaves the rest untouched.

If reducing the poverty of the poorest of the poor is the priority, the aim should be to reduce the intensity of poverty, the size of the wedge between the incomes of the poor and the poverty threshold. This can be done, at least in the first instance, without any effect on the headcount ratio. Just as a very poor person can get poorer without changing the headcount ratio, so that same person can get richer without changing it.

If poverty is to be reduced by making income transfers, these can be universal or can be targeted on the poor. Universal transfers command wider political support, but they are more expensive and they benefit rich and poor indiscriminately. Targeted transfers are less wasteful, but can suffer from targeting errors: failure to reach all of the poor, failure to disqualify some of the rich, or both at once. The best targeting is self-targeting, a transfer that only the genuinely poor would apply for. Self-targeting may, however, awaken the collective memory of the Victorian workhouse and its principle of 'less eligibility', i.e. the notion that conditions there should be such that nobody would choose to enter it if they had any better option. Self-targeting and the principle of less eligibility are but two terms for the same thing.

Helping the poorest of the poor raises other kinds of problem. The poorest of the poor tend to be the most remote of people, most subject to the vagaries of geography, weather, and disease, and the most subject to the sorts of social discrimination that renders them all but invisible. They are the least connected to each other and the rest of society, the least organised for self-help or social action, and the least prepared for political engagement. In short, they are the most recalcitrant to all forms of angelic ministration.

Summoning Political Will

If the poorest of the poor do not organise themselves to demand their right to poverty reduction, poverty reduction can be achieved only by summoning up a huge effort of Political Will. Yet Will is elusive, more Will o' the Wisp than Will to Power. Like the Scarlet Pimpernel, they seek him here, they seek him there. Among the national elites of the developing world he is usually absent without leave for long periods. If only these elites were more haunted by the spectres of crime, disease, and insurrection emanating from the hovels of the poorest of the poor, Political Will might return. If only the elites were more moved by the piteous sights in their streets and shantytowns and could feel a sense of common humanity with their inhabitants, Will might be summoned. But, no! Many national elites seem pretty comfortable with things exactly as they are – with *zero poverty reduction*, or even *negative poverty reduction* – and the absence of Political Will.

Global poverty reduction

In these circumstances, the obvious Angelic Alternative is to go global. For this, what is needed is a global definition of poverty, a global-transfer technology, and a global summoning of Political Will for poverty reduction. No problem. Or is there?

Globally speaking, the poverty to be reduced is *dollar-a-day poverty*. What is that? It is the number of people in the world who live on less than one dollar a day. One might want to be a little curious about this concept, since poor people in developing countries rarely have any dollars at all. If they have any paper money, it will be their local currency, not the mighty greenback. So we are talking about the local-currency equivalent in cash or kind of one US dollar per day, calculated through the foreign-exchange rate adjusted for purchasing power parity. How much consumption can that amount of local currency buy? That will depend on the types of goods that the poor eat, and on their prices. In some countries, the staple of the poor is rice, in others manioc, in others potato. There is no single basket of consumption goods that the poor of all countries consume. There are also plenty of obstacles to perfect price arbitrage, so in some countries the price of the staple of the poor is relatively high, while in others it is relatively low. Thus the local-currency equivalent of one dollar a day in country A will purchase a different type and amount of basic consumption for its poor person than will the local-currency equivalent of one dollar in country B. Although neither poor consumer in A or in B can in any sense be called rich, the degree and urgency of their poverty may be quite different. Nevertheless, they are lumped together as the dollar-a-day poor for the purpose of achieving *global poverty reduction.*

The global-transfer technology for poverty reduction is foreign aid, a.k.a. international development co-operation assistance, a.k.a. international partnership agreements. In recent years, bilateral aid agencies and international financial institutions have proclaimed that their paramount mission is nothing but poverty reduction. This came after a decade (the 1980s) during which conservative governments in the West had instructed them to focus their efforts exclusively on increasing economic growth by adopting a range of neo-liberal policies. The disappointing results from these policies created the public mood to resume the drive for poverty reduction. Increasingly, aid transfers have become conditional on the aid-recipient country adopting a *Poverty Reduction Strategy Paper*, a plan outlining national poverty-reduction policies.

International poverty-reduction targets are disembodied poverty targets, in that they are not integrated into particular transfer schemes of bilateral and multilateral foreign aid. Such targets (for example, those included within the Millennium Development Goals for 2015) do not represent the degree of poverty reduction that such aid schemes can be expected to achieve. They are chosen primarily for their political impact, and hence they have an element of arbitrariness about them. If they seem bold and dramatic (but not absurdly so), they will help to summon Political Will in the developed countries to foot the bill for the aid transfers.

The problem of linkage between targets and transfers re-surfaces in another form, however: the question of *poverty-efficient aid allocation*. If the target is to reduce dollar-a-day poverty by half by 2015, the question is how shall aid be allocated across countries between now and 2015 to get as close to the target as possible? The resolution of this question requires one not only to establish the number of poor in each country today (which is supposedly given by the dollar-a-day calculation), but also to estimate the rate at which aid will be able to reduce poverty in each country in the future. Suffice it to say that the margins of error in doing so are extremely wide.

The Advocate of the One We Don't Speak Of has long argued that the only reliable way to reduce poverty is by means of economic development, and that aid will not reduce poverty in a sustainable way unless it first stimulates economic development. The empirical evidence is not wholly inconsistent with his claim. It does show that poverty tends to fall when economic growth takes place. Yet it also shows that the rate of poverty reduction during periods of economic growth varies widely between countries. Growth evidently brings more benefits to the poor in some places than in others. Perhaps not surprisingly, where the initial income distribution is more unequal, there is less poverty reduction per unit of growth than in countries with a more equal distribution. One of the secrets of achieving *pro-poor growth* (now re-labelled *shared growth*) is thus to embark on measures of *re-distribution with growth* – a venerable angel chorus that has survived long enough to be re-discovered and become fashionably popular again.

Poverty and vulnerability

Something else that is being re-discovered is the original motivation for embarking on poverty measurement and analysis. The original concern was not the modern one of bringing about poverty reduction by reducing the numbers of those deemed to be in poverty. Rather it was to prevent the working poor from falling into destitution, and into the moral turpitude that was believed to be inseparable from destitution. The problem that the Victorian angels addressed was that the respectable poor seemed to be at risk of tipping over irreversibly into a condition of life that was immeasurably worse than mere poverty, which continued to be seen as normal for much of the population. The Victorian angels' ambition, paradoxically to modern eyes, was to stop the numbers of the poor from decreasing – by stopping the numbers of the destitute from rising. This is what motivated Charles Booth's study of poverty in London and Seebohm Rowntree's study of poverty in York.

The foundational concern was thus not with a current state of lacking or scarcity of consumption of those who had some regular income. It was about their exposure to future risks that could plunge families into dependence and depravity – and do so irreversibly. In short, the focus of concern was not their poverty, but their *vulnerability*. The social reforms that followed from these poverty studies were addressed to the causes of the vulnerability of the poor. For the risk of loss of employment, the state would provide labour exchanges and unemployment insurance. When work was no longer possible, the state would pay an old-age pension to those who had contributed during their working lives. The solution was for the government to provide social safety nets for those among the working poor affected by stochastic risk. It was not for the government to try to raise their general standard of living.

Amid all the angelic rhetoric, reports, and resolutions on global poverty reduction, it is encouraging that the words *risk*, *vulnerability*, and *social insurance* are beginning to buzz around once more. Why so? It is surely because we are beginning to re-discover that risk and reward go hand-in-hand. Individuals' willingness and ability to accept greater risk can result in increased incomes for themselves, and often for the whole community. Willingness to accept risk is a matter of individual attitudes, but a community's ability to accept risk (assuming that some individuals are willing risk takers) is a matter of having access to mechanisms of insurance, in case the risk goes badly for the individual risk taker. Any community that wants to get beyond the standard of living afforded by a simple subsistence economy has to be willing and able to engage in a greater division of labour, and a wider array of markets – over the workings of which it will, almost by definition, have little control. Expanding the division of labour is a high-risk process, in the course of which the daring and the innovators in the community may come terminally unstuck.

Yet this vulnerability need not claim many victims, if it provokes the search for effective ways of limiting individual liability. Some social-insurance mechanisms already exist in subsistence societies, and care must be taken not to destroy them gratuitously in the search for something better. However, they are rarely robust enough to take the full strain of insuring against the greater risks that will arise as the division of labour deepens and reliance on distant markets becomes more pervasive. In a time of increasing globalisation, something new will be required. In building more robust institutions of insurance, the demons of moral hazard and adverse selection must be confronted. Economists will give more practical help to the poor by designing the incentives of insurance schemes correctly, than by further refining the buzz-buzz of poverty reduction.

About the author

John Toye is Professor of International Development at the University of Oxford, and was previously Director of the Institute of Development Studies at the University of Sussex. From 1998 to 2000 he was Director of the Globalisation Division of the UN Conference on Trade and Development (UNCTAD). His most recent book, *The UN and Global Political Economy* (Indiana University Press 2004), was co-authored with his son, the historian Richard Toye.

CHAPTER 5
Social protection

Guy Standing

The term 'social protection' has been widely used around the world and is often treated as synonymous with 'social security', which is misleading. This chapter considers the numerous terms that have become part of the language of social protection, indicating that the image conveyed by the term is rather different from what is meant by it.

Introduction

In their first year at university, all students should have a mandatory course in linguistic manipulation. There is nothing new about the use and misuse of words, images, similes, and metaphors in shaping the way we think, act, formulate hypotheses, and assess evidence. But the intensity with which modern communications bombard our senses has reached such a pitch that we need to develop skills of resistance.

The notion of 'social protection' is peculiarly susceptible to the seductiveness of buzzwords and euphemisms. Elsewhere, I have argued that the linguistic distortion of debates on the direction of certain policies constitutes one of the eight 'crises' of social protection (Standing 2002a, 2002b). This chapter now reviews the main terms that have been used by analysts, politicians, their well-paid advisers, 'think tanks', and commentators. The underlying theme is that the mainstream terminology has evolved as part of a strategy to adapt systems of social protection to the perceived pressures of globalisation and the process of labour re-commodification. One could make a case for arguing that those using the key buzzwords have been contributing to a particular orientation, which *inter alia* envisages a shrinking role for the state, moving away from provision of a comprehensive relatively universalistic system of social support and from a wide range of enterprise benefits unrelated to the performance of labour.

Before we start: an incidental observation. We should be serious. This means we should be prepared to treat the perpetrators of buzzwords with more wit. We should require social scientists to define those colourful phrases and to justify their use. More mockery would not go amiss.

Several other contextual points are worth bearing in mind. It is surely true that ordinary language is idealised, giving the impression that words and phrases mean the same thing to all of us. In an age dominated by *techne* and information technology, it is easy to overestimate the extent of consistency and comprehensibility of ordinary communication. This was a point made by Jürgen Habermas in his classic theory of communicative action. It is easy for those who dominate public discourse to assume that there is more potential for communication than is the case, to presume that there is a consensus, and to insist or imply that a convenient consensus does exist. Language is a social force. Throughout history, institutions have arisen to institutionalise specific discourses and divert knowledge from external critique.

Social protection: the key terms

The following will do no more than list and comment on what seem to be the key terms in the modern lexicon of social protection. Others would compile a different list. But one hopes that what follows captures the essence of the matter. Words in inverted commas are those that are considered separately or that are susceptible to several interpretations.

1. 'Social protection', 'social security', and 'welfare'

Let us start with the basics. These three terms are often used as if they were synonyms. They are not. *Social protection* is the broadest, signifying the full range of protective transfers, services, and institutional safeguards supposed to protect the population 'at risk' of being 'in need'. *Social security* is the term that covers the state-based system of entitlements linked to what are often called *contingency 'risks'*.[1]

The word *welfare* is peculiar, in that it has been used very differently in the USA and western Europe, although as with so many terms the hegemonic culture seems to be reshaping the perception of welfare in Europe. In the USA, the word has a derogative connotation, and one is advised to say it with a slight sneer. In Europe, for several decades one could reasonably demand that policies should enhance our welfare. In the USA, polite talk refers to 'bums on welfare' and 'welfare dependency'. The defining moment was when Bill Clinton gave the warming pledge in 1996 to 'end welfare as we know it'.

'The welfare state' as a term has been subject to a bewildering battering since Richard Titmuss first coined the term. One reason was Gösta Esping-Andersen's (1990) typology of three worlds of welfare state, which has given a generation of sociologists enriching opportunities to stay off the streets through boosting their CVs with outpourings on typologies, often with the word 'regime' added. It is a matter of personal judgment whether one finds the vast literature illuminating or confusing, or both.[2]

What is the primary objective of the welfare state? Some believe it should promote 'happiness', others that it should promote social justice, or income equality or equal life chances. Jürgen Habermas, among others, has depicted welfare legislation as having a *normalising* effect, and supporting established stereotypes. While a lack of consensus on the objective has helped to erode the legitimacy of the welfare state, there should be little doubt that it has promoted social norms of behaviour, and little doubt that social scientists have assisted in making it more efficient in doing so.

For many years in the twentieth century, welfare policies to protect individuals in need were seen as valuable for society as a whole. But the welfare state's collective insurance functions, based on principles of social solidarity, have been gradually reduced by the rhetoric of individual rights-and-responsibilities and the rhetoric of user services, taxpayers' money, and efficiency. Some now see the welfare state as primarily safeguarding the market economy while protecting market-oriented individuals against contingency losses, stabilising labour-based earnings. Many others make a name for themselves by proposing that 'welfare states' must become 'enabling states' (oppose that!) or 'social investment states'.[3] No doubt they will have a lot of 'social capital' (a clever term that came into popularity when the supply-siders began to wish to see a role for the state, having spent a decade denigrating anything to do with it – see Ben Fine's contribution to this volume).

With the thousands of publications devoted to the welfare state and its 'regimes', one is left with the impression that it has been an instrument for preserving societies based on the performance of labour, in which it has reinforced social stratification rather than the reverse. That may be contestable, but there is a fuzziness about the term that is used by the vast majority of social scientists and policy makers as if it had a single, uncontested meaning.

2. 'Need' and 'poverty'

One should not consider social protection without mentioning that the two most fundamental words of all are ambiguous and contested. Rarely are the words 'poverty' and 'need' defined in any detail when discussing social protection.

Contrary to liberal tradition, which sees pursuit of individual interests as legitimate, *discursive theory* maintains that needs must be determined and adjudicated rationally and socially. Wants and needs become negotiable by public standards, transforming 'economic man' into social citizen. This involves deliberative justice, which can only be developed in conditions of basic security.

As various analysts have recognised, we require a politics of need interpretation, which could be constructed in three stages, according to Nancy Fraser (1989):

- a struggle to validate a need as a politically legitimate one, or to have it defined as a non-political matter;
- a discourse on what is needed to satisfy the need;
- a struggle to have the need alleviated: a resource struggle.

Neither rights nor needs exist as objective facts that are determined scientifically, outside society. They are social constructs, determined by a process of consciousness. They are always relative and subject to refinements of definition. In practice, social-protection systems evolve, and in doing so modify what is covered by the notion of need.

3. 'Social insurance'

This term has been used to justify social security and social protection for more than a century. Often one hears Eurocrats (a buzzword in itself) extol 'the European social model', and state with disarming candour that it will be 'defended'. The image that those who use the term are trying to project is social insurance, implying a model by which 'contributions' are matched by 'entitlements', and by which the more fortunate not only cover their risks in case of need but also express 'social solidarity' by contributing to the transfers to less fortunate neighbours, who have also contributed in their time. It is a comforting model, easily understood.

Unfortunately, it is a model of privilege, one at best suited to an economy in which almost everybody is in full-time, well-paid, stable jobs and in which contributions can be levied equitably and efficiently. It apparently thrived in a 'golden age' that never existed, even though that age is located in the minds of some social scientists in the late 1960s.

In the twenty-first century, this is even more a fiction than when the proselytisers of social insurance succeeded in selling the labourist model in the middle decades of the twentieth century. Now, if a person has casual labour, or is unemployed, he or she is unlikely to have contributions paid or be able to make them. If a person is working hard in caring for his or her children or elderly frail relatives, ditto. Enormous numbers of European workers – and even more of the migrants in their midst – do not qualify for the range of social-insurance benefits that define the European social model that is being defended so stoutly. And the number is growing.

Recognising such realities, astute policy makers keen to increase 'coverage' (see [6] below) introduced 'fictitious contribution periods' to bolster the edifice of social insurance. For example, during a period designated as legitimate unemployment, or maternity leave, or sick leave, a person may be classified as having made social-insurance contributions, even though they have not done so, or the fictitious contribution may be deducted from the amount of transfer, as it were. This opens up a pseudo-world of unreality: fictitious contributions from fictitious work, and contributions without contributing. Policy makers could preach the virtues of social insurance, when in fact a rising proportion of beneficiaries were fictitious contributors, leaving governments having to top up social-insurance funds from general taxation. This has led to pressure to cut benefits and to make them harder to obtain or to retain, so as to balance the funds.

4. 'Social safety net'

This is a candidate for the title of Most Obfuscating Euphemism of the 1990s. With the ascendancy of supply-side economics, it was noticed that the roll-back of public social spending meant that a lot more people were becoming economically insecure, 'vulnerable', and 'impoverished'. Supply-side economic orthodoxy had argued that cutting social spending and removing 'rigidities' that were forms of protection would boost economic growth. Adding to the colourful imagery, it was said with fervour that 'a rising tide would lift all ships'. Imagine! When this metaphor ran into the sand (sic), due to the evidence of rising inequalities and insecurities, a new metaphor had to be added to the lexicon. So, economists, particularly in the World Bank, IMF, and OECD, urged governments to develop a 'social safety net' for the 'really poor'.

It has such a nice image – catching all those unfortunate enough to fall from the mainstream of society into 'need' or 'poverty', a net under the high-wire risk society, enabling them to avoid pain and to bounce back. Unfortunately, in reality the term has been a euphemism for 'selective', 'targeted' measures, usually 'means-tested', supposedly intended for those deemed to be the 'most needy'. One could argue that it has been a ruse to cut public social spending, and one is inclined to tell those who use the term that a feature of the net is that the holes are so large that many of the victims fall through it.

Because they feel that a safety net suggests lack of active intervention, some sages have resorted to the image of a *'trampoline net'*, implying that what governments should do is help those falling into need to bounce back up by one means or another. It is easy to stretch this image to one of condemnation. Those not bouncing back must be unfit or lazy or shirking, and as such should be 'retrained' or compelled to take up an available 'work opportunity'.

All this amounts to a model of statistical discrimination, sifting out the 'undeserving' (see [9] below). Even if there were an empirically supported tendency for certain types of people to fail to take available jobs, or an adequate income, that would not mean that *all* people of that type would have those tendencies. The term 'safety net' should be avoided.

5. 'Targeting', 'selectivity', and 'means-testing'

Targeting is another word intended to invite automatic approval. It came into vogue with supply-side economics and structural adjustment programmes in developing countries. The image is that policy should focus on the groups most in need, rather than being universal or untargeted. It goes with the notion of 'selectivity', and with the special case of 'self-targeting', prompting a rather painful image for the uninitiated. Thus, Amartya Sen, among many others, lauds public-works schemes as an ideal form of social protection because they involve self-targeting (Sen 1999). Only if you are really desperate will you queue up in the heat and dust to beg for a place in the road-digging gang. That is the idea. But why one should favour such a scheme is unclear.

The implied reasoning is surely fallacious. Those most in need of income support are likely to lack the energy to reach the queue, let alone be able to work well in the mid-day sun and dust.

Targeting and selectivity have been the rationale behind the global trend towards 'means testing'. Here the image is that people should receive support from the state only if they have insufficient 'means' to support themselves. The means usually means income. But what counts as income? Some policies have counted only earned income, others have included savings, rent, dividends, etc. Some have included the imputed value of property. Some have included the income of others on whom the person might (or might not!) depend for support.

Whatever the design, means testing produces poverty traps (see [10] below), and may induce 'relationship traps' as well, in that it might pay a couple to separate, at least during the day time. A modern variant is what might be called the *old-age care trap*, whereby frail elderly people have to sell their last-remaining assets in order to qualify for means-tested care. This growing practice is unedifying, demeaning, and stigmatising. But it goes with the drift to means testing.[4]

Above all, means testing and other schemes based on selectivity criteria fail to satisfy any principle of social justice worthy of the name, because they tend not to reach those most in need of income support, a fact which research around the world has consistently demonstrated. This is most dramatically the case in developing countries. It recalls the aphorism (attributed to Richard Titmuss) that benefits that are only for the poor are invariably poor benefits.

6. 'Coverage'

A common assertion is that a primary objective should be to increase the 'coverage' of social protection, the implicit suggestion being that more people should be 'covered' by schemes protecting them from contingency risks. The ILO has launched what it calls a 'campaign' to increase social-security coverage. It is spending a lot of money on the campaign, holding lots of costly meetings in exotic places. But it is unclear what 'extending coverage' means. For example, suppose a country is operating a social-insurance system to which only 10 per cent of the population are making contributions. If the government abolished it and replaced it with a wholly means-tested social-assistance scheme, by definition the whole population would be 'covered'. Would that be a great achievement?

Coverage conveys another comforting image, that of a blanket. But it should be attached to a specific type of scheme. There are many forms of social-protection scheme that one might wish to cut, thereby reducing 'coverage'. For example, it is far from clear that one would wish to see a growth of coverage in the form of 'workfare' schemes.

7. 'Social inclusion'

Over the past three decades, social protection has gradually become a euphemism for altering the behaviour and attitudes and 'capabilities' of those perceived to be 'marginalised' and 'socially excluded'. None of the words in inverted commas in the previous sentence was part of the lexicon of mainstream social-security discourse in the 1960s and 1970s.

The imagery has mirrored the reorientation of policy. Increasingly, those in need are characterised as socially and emotionally defective, in need not of financial resources but of moral fibre, confidence, and 'emotional intelligence' (sic). The perception that society's 'losers' are in need of help because of their attitudinal and behavioural failings has led to more emphasis on protection by 'case work', by 'processing clients', if necessary by compulsion, which is 'good for them', even if they do not appreciate it. Overall, social protection has been shifting from the domain of economics and sociology to one of psychology. The paternalistic triumph is a frightening spectre of increasingly sophisticated social engineering, in the guise of protection. The tragedy is not that some people do need help, but that there are few safeguards against therapising people into being 'helpless' victims (Furedi 2004). A new occupation has emerged in the lexicon of social protection: 'people changers'. *What do you want to be when you grow up? A human case worker.*

8. 'Active' versus 'passive' policy

Not so long ago, the language of social protection was enriched by the enthusiastic adoption of the view that most social and labour-market policies were 'passive' and that they should become, or be replaced by policies that were, 'active'. As buzzwords go, the related term 'Active Labour Market Policy' should be a candidate for a BBA (Best Buzzword Award), although there are other worthy candidates.

The distinction between passive and active social policy has been based on the image that whereas the former gives money or services with few or no conditions, active policy provides jobseekers with services that enable them to hold jobs with pride. Policies should 'activate' and be 'pro-active'. The macho imagery is blatant. Who could be in favour of being 'passive'? Being passive implies being inactive, lazy, feeble, and lacking in sexual energy. 'Active' implies being energetic, strong, aroused. *'Yes, Minister, of course we are in favour of active policies'.*

The active–passive distinction was derived from a rather different image and policy. In the Rehn-Meidner model that guided Swedish macro-economic policy in the post-1945 era, the term 'active labour-market policy' meant counter-cyclical, implying that, as unemployment rose, state spending should rise to absorb the unemployed in training or public works. When the recession receded, it was expected that such policies should be cut back. By contrast, 'active' now means 'corrective', enabling the poor and unemployed to be more 'competitive' and 'employable'.

In the new idiom, active policy means inducing those at the margin of the labour market to be 'socially integrated'. Advocates go further. If the marginals do not take up the 'opportunity', they must be compelled to do so, because in the longer term they will be happier, even if they do not appreciate that now.[5]

The imagery of the dichotomy leads the observer down a familiar path. What if someone does not believe that she needs to be made more 'employable' and 'socially integrated'? Clearly, she is 'undeserving' of public support. Are we sure?

9. 'Deserving' versus 'undeserving' poor

The undeserving poor have been around for a very long time. All social-protection systems make moralistic judgments. Who deserves support? And who deserves it more or less than others? The distinction between deserving and undeserving poor crystallised in the nineteenth century. But by early in the twentieth century research had shown that the distinction was arbitrary and unfair, and pernicious. It was resurrected in the 1980s and 1990s, as a generation of technocrat advisers to keen young politicians realised that identifying the undeserving was a good way of justifying cuts in public social spending, at a time when more attempts were being made to explain unemployment as essentially 'voluntary', the fault of the individual rather than the state of aggregate demand.

The word 'undeserving' implies that the person is to blame for his plight. The notion has been enriched in recent years through the addition of what should be called 'the transgressing poor', i.e. those who are not only undeserving but break the law, once denied benefits, simply in order to survive. They fall foul of 'immoral hazards' (see [10] below). Once caught, they may be incarcerated, which conveniently removes them from the poverty and unemployment statistics. In some states in the USA, that may be sufficient to result in their losing the right to vote. Pollsters monitor the way the undeserving poor are prone to vote. The politicians monitor the pollsters.

10. 'Moral hazards' and 'immoral hazards'

The widely used notion of 'moral hazard' is a term of sublime sophistry. It is another candidate for Best Buzzword Award, in that it sounds intellectual and scientific, beyond the understanding of the lay person, best left to 'experts', sorting out the men from the boys.

A moral hazard arises from a tendency for someone to be in a situation where it pays to stay in it rather than move out of it into something that is socially better. In social-protection discourse, it is associated with two appealing terms: 'the poverty trap' and 'the unemployment trap'. An irony of the dominant welfare reforms since the 1980s and 1990s was that they have spread such traps, because there was a strong shift to means-tested social assistance around the world. If you can receive a state benefit only if you are 'poor', why try to move out of poverty if you would lose more in withdrawn benefits than you would gain from doing a low-paid job? The international drift to means testing led to many more people facing effective marginal tax rates in excess of 100 per cent, and many others facing rates not much below 100 per cent.

Once policy makers realised this, they tried to combine incentives with coercion to push people through the poverty-trap zone, making it harder to continue to receive out-of-job benefits, and often providing so-called 'in-work benefits', i.e. earned-income tax credits or marginal employment subsidies designed to top up the incomes of those entering low-wage jobs.

These words suffer from awkward drawbacks. But they convey a picture of millions of people trapped in moral hazards, manipulating the system while lying in bed and becoming obese, living a life of idleness and debauchery.

Remarkably, moral hazards breed 'immoral hazards'. Some people actually cheat. Instead of taking low-paid jobs legally or staying idle, they take jobs without declaring them. It should not be surprising if systems that are intentionally manipulative lead to manipulative responses. But of course it takes only a few newspaper stories to fan middle-class indignation to the point of demands for benefit cuts and acceptance of more policing of recipients of such benefits, intensifying the stigma, leading to lower take-up of benefits by those desperate for help, and encouraging identification of 'welfare cheats', who are criminalised. The final irony here is that this leads not only to a further erosion of public support for universal social protection but also to a process whereby a growing number of people are 'disqualified' from receiving any state benefits. *Dear reader, you will murmur that I exaggerate. Really?*

11. 'The reciprocity principle'

This high-sounding notion is how modernist policy advisers describe the claim that 'there are no rights without responsibilities'. This is linked to the rhetorical question, 'Why should taxpayers be expected to pay for beneficiaries of state transfers if the latter give nothing back to society?' Implicit is the double claim that their plight is their fault and that they must take a job, and be grateful.

This is disingenuous. A right is a right, and should not be made conditional on some type of behaviour that some bureaucrat determines is appropriate.[6] If there are forms of behaviour that policy makers believe are socially inappropriate, they should be ruled out for all citizens equally. Should the idle rich be entitled to the right to eat extravagantly, when they give so little to society? Forcing the victims of economic mishap to behave in certain ways when others more fortunate are not forced to do so is to treat them as second-class citizens. Such questions soon expose the 'reciprocity principle' for what it is: a bogus argument for inequality.

12. 'Dependency'

This word came to exert a powerful hold on the minds of policy makers in the 1990s. The claim was that vast numbers of people receiving income transfers were guilty of relying on them, becoming demotivated and indolent. Dependency goes with 'addiction'. The pejorative word was used to justify cuts in benefits and make them more conditional (as in 'active'), tightening eligibility, restricting the length of time that a person could receive them, and so on.

Dependency may be juxtaposed with 'independence'. Again, who could possibly favour the former, a supine condition? Well, this simplistic imagery could be challenged by the claim that most of us are dependent on others in many ways. Biologically, the human species has survived through mutual dependency and collaboration. Recognition of our dependencies is a healthy response to our humanity. The assurance of some state transfer may provide just the degree of economic security to enable us to gain the confidence to make rational, 'socially responsible' decisions. Taking it away in the guise of reducing 'dependency' may be just what is required to lead to anomic, irresponsible, and ultimately self-destructive behaviour.

13. 'Workfare'

Social protection was supposed to be about 'welfare'. But as means-testing and social-assistance schemes were failing, a new word came into fashion: 'workfare'. What politicians and supporters have tried to convey when using the word is simply that they are in favour of easing the unemployed into jobs instead of 'passive' unemployment benefits. But in reality workfare means making the taking of a job or training place the formal condition for obtaining a state transfer. It goes with the 'reciprocity principle' and 'active' labour-market policy.

As argued elsewhere, workfare schemes have many disadvantages (Standing 2002b: 173-95). Unfortunately, many Ministers of Labour or Social Affairs, in developing countries as well as in industrialised countries, have been drawn into using the language of workfare, without appreciating all the failings of what is actually involved. Among the latest to be converted is the government of India, where elderly women who were entitled to a widow's pension have been told that they cannot have it any more, and must take a job as a child-carer, thereby enabling younger women to take a job in a public-works scheme launched as part of the so-called Rural Employment Guarantee Scheme. The disruptive consequences and the distributive effects of this set of workfare rules will eventually be the subject of a host of PhD dissertations.

14. 'Social protection as a productive factor'

Social democrats met market liberals in the late 1990s in the report-strewn terrain of European Union meetings, by linking social protection to production in this clever phrase.[7] Those wishing to 'defend' social protection realised that public social spending was being depicted as a 'drag' on economic growth, productivity, and 'development', by 'crowding out' private investment, lowering savings, and threatening national 'competitiveness'. Clearly, this was 'unsustainable'.

It would be churlish to suggest that none of this was proven. The trick was to disarm the supply-side critics. So, the adopted ruse was to shift the imagery, by presenting social protection as 'a productive factor', like 'capital' and 'labour'.

Of course, the ruse was also an attempt to shift the composition of public social spending from universal, relatively unconditional transfers and services, deemed to be deplorably 'unproductive', to certain selective measures deemed to be 'productive'. This is another route to 'activation' policies, and to 'targeting' and 'selectivity'. It is a term that can justify a reorientation and a re-prioritising of social spending. It means that 'workfare' is better than 'welfare'. Who could be against making social protection a productive factor? Imagine the shame: he wants to make it unproductive!

A minor drawback of the dichotomy is that it could lead to a focus on what is easy to measure in conventional economic terms. There are other drawbacks as well. For instance, if you justify social spending as conducive to efficiency and labour productivity, then you risk being unable to justify spending that is not 'productive'. An alternative view, with a long pedigree of respectability, is that social protection should be about giving human beings a sense of social, cultural, and economic security, as a human right. That was what inspired the United Nations Declaration of Human Rights in 1948, the Covenant of Social, Economic and Cultural Rights of 1966, and the Charter of Emerging Human Rights of 2004.

15. 'Privatisation' and 'public–private partnerships'

The words 'privatisation' and 'social protection' have come together with increasing ease. In the early 1990s, in developing countries and in the newly defined 'transition countries', the main reform promoted by the international financial institutions was the privatisation of pensions, with dreams of privatising health care and other aspects of social protection soon afterwards. Millions of dollars were devoted to the promotion of pension privatisation.

The 'Chilean model' became a symbol, and numerous special trips, often financed by the World Bank and other financial agencies, were arranged so that budding politicians in other parts of the world could go on pilgrimage there. The zeal was dimmed by subsequent evidence showing the failings of the scheme, particularly its lack of equity as the privatised 'individual accounts' came into effect.

With privatisation came 'liberalisation' and 'commercialisation'. And quietly there emerged 'private–public partnerships', or as, inevitably they became known, 'PPPs'. This is related to the new preference for 'welfare pluralism', and is a euphemism for a trend towards private financing and provision.[8] Of course, the word 'partnership' is not exactly neutral. Is it a partnership of equals, with each gaining as much, and paying as much? Who is really in control? Consider the claim, *'We must have more PPPs, partnerships!'* Unless it is defined, the term is dangerously vague. But the tendency is to favour 'partnership'. It has a nice cuddly sound to it. The provision of subsidies to those dubious private 'providers' is downplayed.

The acronym PPP is not a short form of a descriptive compound noun but an ideological concept. One may like it or not, but the objectives and motives are concealed. Probably, it is a mechanism for enabling multinationals to penetrate a particular social service. When a politician or policy adviser says there should be incentives for PPPs, what he or she probably means is that there should be subsidies for foreign capital, to 'encourage' foreign firms to invest in the country. It is unlikely that the politician will join the board or take a consultancy with the firm shortly afterwards. Perish the thought. That is possibly covered by the hyphen in the full term. But such cynicism is surely misplaced.

16. 'Social dumping' and 'the race to the bottom'

'Social dumping' is a myth, claims Professor Lord Anthony Giddens, commonly called the 'high priest' of the Third Way and long-time adviser to Tony Blair (Giddens 2006). This term is a source of anguish among social-protection specialists. It originated as analogous to the dumping of goods, sold in a foreign market at less than the cost of production in order to capture market share. But social dumping is really about the argument that we in country X cut social benefits in order to make our production more 'competitive' than those in country Y, and to retain jobs that would otherwise go to country Y. The image goes further with *a race to the bottom*, suggesting that all countries are cutting back on social benefits in order to become more competitive than others, lowering their 'non-wage labour costs'.

It is not very nice, this race. It is good to know that Lord Giddens regards social dumping as a myth. He believes that moving jobs to countries with lower social protection will result in pressure there to raise benefits. This is really a delightful example of wishful thinking. Total labour costs in western Europe in, say, car production are about 50 times what they are in China. It will take rather a long time for those benefits to rise to narrow the difference.

The reality is that governments and companies are using international competitiveness and the desire to preserve jobs as justification for benefit cuts. Those are not myths. But we can be carried away by the euphemisms. To some extent, benefits are dwindling. But quietly, governments are responding by raising subsidies to capital, to lower the costs borne by corporations. One day that will come on to the agenda of the WTO, as a form of unfair competition and trade distortion. Meanwhile, the pace and extent of social dumping may have been lessened, but not stopped. Rather than a race to the bottom, it is likely that there is a trend towards convergence, to below what was the dream of social democrats in the mid-twentieth century.

Concluding reflections

Social protection has been misused. Poverty and economic insecurity are reflections of inequality, of income, wealth, power, and status. A society in which everybody had a right to basic security would address inequality directly. But in the globalisation era, so far, there has been a drift to a *charity* perspective, not a rights-based one. We are all urged to contribute, altruistically, to charities, to adopt a goat, fund an African child's schooling, and so on. Pity, as Bernard Shaw so memorably put it, is akin to contempt.

Alongside charity, there is a slide into coercion and a slide into *discretion* as a principle of social benefits. Local bureaucrats are given the quiet nod to decide on who should receive benefits, who should not, and what conditions on which those chosen should be given the benefit. It is all very paternalistic, leaving the inequalities unchallenged.

Linguistically, we must never forget that language can be used as a means of resistance, even though we have focused on how policy makers and ideological proponents of particular changes manipulate language. Claimants of public assistance in the UK and elsewhere use the language of the elites to turn against them, as when they refer to using 'enterprise' and 'responsibility' by doing undeclared work for cash. We have not assessed the buzzwords of resistance in this chapter. They merit a separate treatment.

One extraordinary feature of the topic of social protection – and it is by no means unique in this respect – is the proliferation of acronyms. These are rarely innocent. But what they tend to do is to give insiders an advantage, a capacity to blind outsiders with science. The PRSP must help to deliver the MDGs, and the IFAs will support that.

More generally, social protection is not a fixed concept; it is an elastic notion that every user of the term can define differently. A statement such as 'we must devote more resources to social protection' might elicit consensus support and nods of agreement. But few might agree if what the speaker meant was that more resources should be devoted to workfare schemes, or conversely to give every citizen a basic income without obligations. Now, that *is* a good idea.

Notes

1. Social protection is supposed to compensate for risks, but it is not clear what types of risk should be included. Analysts have differentiated

between idiosyncratic and systemic risk, and between risks, shocks, and hazards. It all becomes a little confusing. But the key point is that different systems of social protection cover different types of situation needing some form of social protection.
2. This writer's views about the vagueness of the original effort were given in a review of the book at the time in the *Journal of European Social Policy* (Standing 1991).
3. On the former, see Gilbert 2002; on the latter, see Giddens 2000.
4. As this chapter was being finished, the Bush Administration in the USA was announcing that it was extending means testing to its old-age Medicaid programme, ostensibly to prevent the non-poor receiving subsidised health care. A predictable result will be that many more of the near-poor will slip into impoverishment.
5. This is the explicitly stated view of Blair-adviser Richard Layard (2005), ennobled by New Labour for his policy contributions.
6. For a defence of this view, drawing on the idea of republican, or claim, rights, see Standing 2005.
7. Not surprisingly, the ILO took up the subject several years later, by when the proposition had descended into confusion.
9. For useful reviews, see Mehrotra and Delamonica 2005; Webster and Sansom 1999.

References

Esping-Andersen, Gösta (1990) *Social Foundations of Postindustrial Economies*, Oxford: Oxford University Press.
Fraser, Nancy (1989) 'Talking about needs: interpretive contests as political conflicts in welfare-state societies', *Ethics* 99(X): 291–313.
Furedi, Frank (2004) *Therapy Culture: Cultivating Vulnerability in an Uncertain Age*, London: Routledge.
Giddens, Anthony (2000) *The Third Way and Its Critics*, Cambridge: Polity Press.
Giddens, Anthony (2006) *Europe in the Global Age*, Bristol: Polity.
Gilbert, N. (2002) *Transformation of the Welfare State: The Silent Surrender of Public Responsibility*, Oxford: Oxford University Press.
Layard, Richard (2005) *Happiness: Lessons from a New Science*, London: Penguin.
Mehrotra, S. and E. Delamonica (2005) 'The private sector and privatisation in social services: is the Washington Consensus "dead"?', *Global Social Policy* 5(2):141–74.
Sen, Amartya K. (1999) *Development as Freedom*, Oxford: Oxford University Press.
Standing, Guy (1991) 'The three worlds of welfare capitalism', *Journal of European Social Policy* 1(1): 71–5.
Standing, Guy (2002a) *Beyond the New Paternalism: Basic Security as Equality*, London: Verso.
Standing, Guy (2002b) 'Globalisation: the eight crises of social protection', *The Indian Journal of Labour Economics* 45(1): 17–46.

Standing, Guy (ed.) (2005) *Promoting Income Security as a Right*, London: Anthem.

Webster, Mike and Kevin Sansom (1999) 'Public–Private Partnerships and the Poor: An Initial Review', Task No. 164, WELL: Loughborough University, available at www.lboro.ac.uk/well/ resources/well-studies/full-reports-pdf/ task0164.pdf (retrieved 26 January 2007).

About the author

Guy Standing is Professor of Economic Security at the University of Bath in the UK and Professor of Labour Economics at Monash University in Australia. He is also economic adviser to the United Nations Department of Economic and Social Affairs, and was formerly Director of Socio-Economic Security in the International Labour Organisation. His publication of greatest pertinence to this volume is *Beyond the New Paternalism: Basic Security as Equality* (2002).

CHAPTER 6
Globalisation

Shalmali Guttal

The term 'globalisation' is widely used to describe a variety of economic, cultural, social, and political changes that have shaped the world over the past 50-odd years. Because it is a complex and multifaceted phenomenon, globalisation has been credited with a wide range of powers and effects. Its proponents claim that it is both 'natural' and an inevitable outcome of technological progress, and creates positive economic and political convergences. Critics argue that globalisation is hegemonic and antagonistic to local and national economies. This chapter argues that globalisation is a form of capitalist expansion that entails the integration of local and national economies into a global, unregulated market economy. Although economic in its structure, globalisation is equally a political phenomenon, shaped by negotiations and interactions between institutions of transnational capital, nation states, and international institutions. Its main driving forces are institutions of global capitalism – especially transnational corporations – but it also needs the firm hand of states to create enabling environments for it to take root. Globalisation is always accompanied by liberal democracy, which facilitates the establishment of a neo-liberal state and policies that permit globalisation to flourish. The chapter discusses the relationship between globalisation and development and points out that some of the most common assumptions promoted by its proponents are contradictory to the reality of globalisation; and that globalisation is resisted by more than half of the globe's population because it is not capable of delivering on its promises of economic well being and progress for all.

Definitions and debates

The term 'globalisation' is widely used to describe a variety of economic, cultural, social, and political changes that have shaped the world over the past 50-odd years, from the much-celebrated revolution in information technology to the diminishing of national and geo-political boundaries in an ever-expanding, transnational movement of goods, services, and capital. The increasing homogenisation of consumer tastes, the consolidation and expansion of corporate power, sharp increases in wealth and poverty, the 'McDonaldisation' of food and culture, and the growing ubiquity of liberal democratic ideas are all, in one way or another, attributed to globalisation. It is certainly one of the most contested topics in the social sciences, and – possibly because it is a complex and multifaceted phenomenon – it has been accorded multiple definitions, and a wide range of powers and effects have been ascribed to it.

Debates about globalisation abound, not only about how to define it but also about its origins, central actors, driving forces, and transformative powers. Supporters and detractors alike agree that advancements in applied sciences, technology, and communications have played central roles in making globalisation possible. US and British banks deal with their customers through call centres in Asia; popular brands of clothing and sportswear design their products in the USA or Europe, manufacture them in developing countries, and sell them all over the world at comparable prices; the Internet allows commodities, futures, and currencies to be traded across the globe, taking advantage of time differences in different bourses and exchange markets; legal and medical establishments in the affluent North outsource much of their processing to selected developing countries such as India, to take advantage of a skilled and educated labour force that costs a fraction of what these establishments would pay in their home countries.

There is, however, far less agreement on the nature, powers, and origins of globalisation. Is globalisation civilising or destructive? Powerful or feeble? Politically neutral or ideology-driven? And when did it start? With Columbus as he set out to conquer new worlds for the Spanish Crown? Or when the East India Company laid the foundation of the British Empire in India? Or when the USA took over the reconstruction of war-ravaged Europe through the Marshall Plan? Many argue that globalisation is a 'natural' outcome of technological, scientific, and economic progress and is irreversible. Others claim that globalisation is driven by greed and the desire for accumulation and control of material wealth, for which capitalism provides a rational ideology and operational framework. Among those on the left, globalisation is viewed as an undeniably capitalist process that has its roots at least as far back as the industrial revolution in Europe and the rise of the British Empire, and has rapidly gained ground since the collapse of the Soviet Union and of socialism as a viable form of economic organisation.

Globalisation is both a result and a force of modernisation and capitalist expansion, entailing the integration of all economic activity (local, national, and regional) into a 'global' market place: that is, a market place that transcends geo-political borders and is not subject to regulation by nation states. The practical manifestations of this integration are the dismantling of national barriers to external trade and finance, deregulation of the economy, export-driven economic growth, removal of controls on the transnational mobility of finance capital, expansion of portfolio capital, privatisation, and the restructuring of local and national economies to facilitate free-market capitalism. This is not to say that the cultural and social dimensions of globalisation are unimportant, but that contemporary culture and society are increasingly shaped by neo-liberal economic measures that supposedly enhance 'economic freedom' and 'consumer choice'. Most significant among these measures are the liberalisation of trade and finance, deregulation, and privatisation, which have been nailed down over the past three decades by the Washington Consensus, the unprecedented rise of corporate power, the formation of the World Trade Organisation (WTO), and burgeoning bilateral and regional free-trade and investment agreements.

The proponents of globalisation claim that it will create convergences of income, access to knowledge and technology, consumption power, living standards, and political ideals. By integrating local and national economies into a global economy that is unfettered by protectionism, economic growth will increase, wealth will be created, and more people in the world will be able to enjoy the advantages and fruits of modernisation, technological progress, and civilisation. Its critics, on the other hand, argue that globalisation is hegemonic, antagonistic to the poor and vulnerable, and is debilitating local and national economies, communities, and the environment.

Globalisation is also a deeply political phenomenon. It is shaped by complex negotiations and interactions between institutions of transnational capital (such as corporations), nation states, and international institutions charged with bringing coherence and order in an increasingly interdependent world. The economy does not exist outside the actions and choices of individual and collective actors, be they private corporations, sovereign governments, United Nations (UN) agencies, the WTO, or international financial institutions (IFIs) such as the World Bank and the International Monetary Fund (IMF). Globalisation is enabled through the facility of neo-liberal policies. An integral companion to globalisation is liberal democracy, which cloaks neo-liberal policy prescriptions in the language of individualised rights, liberties, and choice. Neo-liberal, so-called 'democratic' states are both convenient and necessary for capitalism to expand its frontiers and reach.

Origins and actors

The roots of globalisation can certainly be traced back to the colonisation of Asia, Africa, and the Americas by the dominant economic powers of Europe. However, the expansion of capitalism as a globalising force has not been uniform in successive eras since then. Impelled by the search for new markets and new sources of wealth, and fanned by the industrial revolution, colonialism resulted in the establishment of international commodity markets and mercantilist trade. Although economic protectionism deepened following the First World War and the Great Depression in the early twentieth century, the end of the Second World War provided an impetus for a new bout of capitalist expansion, which, however, was tempered by the establishment of the Soviet bloc and socialism as an alternative form of capital accumulation and distribution.

Since the Second World War, much of the world has indeed become more inter-linked through innovations and advances in applied sciences, travel and transportation, communications, and information technology. But globalisation as we know and experience it today is not simply an inevitable outcome of scientific advancement and technological progress, and there is little that is 'natural' or even autonomous about it. Rather, it is the result of specifically conceived, planned, and targeted neo-liberal policy and structural measures that sought to bring all aspects of social, economic, and political life under the rubric of market capitalism. This era of globalisation took hold in the early 1980s with the coming to power of the Reagan administration in the USA and the Thatcher government in the UK, the eruption of the global debt crisis, the fleshing out of neo-liberalism as an economic framework (which eventually came to be known as the Washington Consensus), and the IFIs' imposition of structural adjustment programmes (SAPs) on developing countries. The fall of the Berlin Wall, the collapse of the Soviet Union, and the end of the Cold War hastened the acceptance by nations of capitalism as the only viable economic order that could create wealth. New nation states that emerged from territories previously under the Soviet umbrella were quick to embrace the economic, institutional, and political support extended by the well-established capitalist powers of North America and Western Europe, especially the USA.

An extremely important development during the later part of the twentieth century was the unprecedented increase in the economic capacities, power, and reach of private corporations, many of which were already operating transnationally. Not only were corporations economically equipped to take advantage of advances in science and technology, but many of these same advances were financed, promoted, and marketed by corporations. The Thatcher and Reagan era signalled an end to state-enforced regulations to curb corporate power. The widespread adoption of neo-liberalism in many of the world's nations led to sharp increases in state support for the private sector and allowed companies to concentrate resources through mergers and acquisitions. Soon, corporations were often bigger sources of capital than the state and its financial institutions. By the mid 1990s, 51 of the world's top 100 economic entities were transnational companies (TNCs), including General Motors, Wal-Mart, Exxon Mobil, Toyota Motor, Royal Dutch Shell, and IBM (for current information, see www.corporations.org).

Today, national and transnational corporations are the main drivers of neo-liberal, economic globalisation. They are the principal beneficiaries of international trade, finance, and investment agreements, and the most powerful advocates of liberalisation, deregulation, and privatisation in every area of commerce and production. While maintaining control over manufacturing, distribution, and service-supply chains, they have lowered their operational costs by outsourcing selected production and services processes to firms in countries where they can get maximum returns. Not only does this result in appreciable increases in their profit margins, but it also allows corporations to shift their sites of production and services processing to wherever they can operate at the lowest costs and with the fewest hindrances from national regulations. Corporations are not in fact advocates of genuine free markets with multiple market actors; rather, their interests lie in securing monopolistic control of markets. On the one hand, TNCs are nationally based corporations that mobilise their country's economic and political power, authority, and diplomacy to operate transnationally and expand their profits. At the same time, TNCs give global endeavours national roots. For example, Nestlé, Proctor & Gamble, Walls, Monsanto, HSBC, and Citibank have bought up local companies, tied local/national employment to the success of their products and services, and completely dominated local/national consumer markets in a large number of countries.

But corporations do not drive globalisation entirely by themselves. Governments are crucial actors in securing domestic and external markets for their pet corporations through subsidies, preferential bidding and contract awards, export credits, development aid, trade and investment agreements, and military aggression. The World Bank and the IMF, the WTO and specialised UN agencies provide the economic and financial architecture for globalisation, while international groupings such as the Organisation of Economic Co-operation and Development (OECD) and the World Economic Forum serve as forums to determine the rules of capitalist global governance. Most of the world's largest TNCs have their home bases in France, Germany, the UK, and Japan, with the largest concentration in the USA. This, coupled with the widespread use of the US dollar as an international currency, has allowed the USA to maintain its dominance over the global economy as well as over the institutions of global governance. The globalisation arena, however, is hardly static: capitalist expansion creates conditions for new actors to enter the fray, challenge existing actors, and compete for economic and strategic dominance.

Possibly the greatest current challenge to US domination of the global economy is from China, which two decades ago decided to use capitalism as an engine of growth. China is using globalisation to establish itself as a modern economic superpower as possibly no other country has done before. It has several attributes upon which globalisation thrives: a rapidly growing economy with the capacity to absorb raw materials, and capital- and technology-intensive goods; an inexhaustible supply of cheap labour for industrial production; and a growing internal market of newly prosperous consumers. China has built up an impressive manufacturing, production, and services base for labour-intensive, skilled, and hi-tech industries by forcing TNCs investing in the country to locate their entire production processes there, rather than outsourcing selected processes. Since 2003, China has become the main destination of Asian exports and served as the principal stimulus of growth in the world economy over the past decade. And finally, China has started to build strategic partnerships with countries rich in natural resources in Asia and Africa, through the provision of foreign aid, preferential loans, and cancellation of interest-free loans owed to China.

Development and globalisation

The development industry has arguably been the most effective portal for globalisation, and some of the most powerful actors in the globalisation arena are members of the mainstream development establishment. These include the IFIs, UN specialised agencies, academics, research institutions, think tanks, civil-society organisations (CSOs), and private consultants and consulting firms, all of whom devise the applications by which economic globalisation is operationalised. Central here are the World Bank, IMF, and regional development banks, who control much of the financing for development, and are instrumental in entrenching globalisation as the only development model available to developing countries.

From its inception, development was conceptualised as a modernising endeavour through which people in the South could consume, think, and act like their counterparts in the North (see Gilbert Rist's contribution to this volume). The euphoria of new technology, knowledge, and science created the myth that the 'economic backwardness' and 'underdevelopment' of newly decolonised nations could somehow be resolved through techno-fixes, regardless of the deep structural inequalities that colonialism had created both among and within nations. Cold War struggles to establish spheres of influence provided incentives for massive aid transfers from wealthy Northern countries to poor Southern nations, and all aid sought greater market openings in aid-recipient countries for Northern products, capital, and services. The explosion of the debt crisis in the 1980s provided opportunities for the North to seal its claims to Southern markets through the SAPs designed by the IFIs.

SAPs were packages of 'economic reforms' aimed at establishing market economies and hastening economic growth in indebted countries, regardless of costs and consequences. They entailed drastically reducing government social spending in areas such as health and education; liberalising imports; removing national restrictions and controls on foreign investment and capital mobility; devaluing the national currency to make exports more competitive and thus generate revenues to service the external debt; privatising state enterprises, utilities, and functions; and removing protections for workers and local producers that were viewed as restrictive to private investment and capital mobility. SAPs sought to 'remove the government from the economy', thus creating spaces for the expansion of private, transnational capital through corporate activity. The ideology underpinning SAPs was the same as that which impelled globalisation: that markets unfettered by national regulation are the most efficient allocators of resources; and, by tying themselves to borderless world markets, poor countries can achieve rapid economic growth, which in turn will generate the revenues needed for national development.

Diverse economic, social, legal, and administrative systems are hindrances to the free play of markets and economic integration that characterise globalisation. SAPs killed this diversity. By the early 1990s, state roles had been transformed in almost all developing countries that operated under IFI loan regimes. Subsidies, welfare, and economic redistribution policies were all but dismantled in a bid to 'streamline' government spending; government enterprises and public assets were privatised in order to achieve greater efficiency; and protectionist measures (such as tariffs, quotas, custom duties, and wage regulations) were drastically reduced in order to make local producers, industries, and workers more 'efficient' by exposing them to foreign competition. The economies of developing countries become ever more closely tied to international markets controlled by corporate powers from the traditional North. And, as states shed their functions of upholding social and economic justice and equity, the provision of physical, social, and financial infrastructure and services started to be farmed out to a variety of civil society and market actors. SAPs laid the foundations of neo-liberal economies ruled by neo-liberal states in developing countries.

SAPs did not, however, deliver the promised economic growth, export revenues, and freedom from debt and poverty. Instead, they led to economic stagnation and increased unemployment, income poverty, economic vulnerability, and environmental destruction. They increased the economic vulnerability of national economies by exposing them to externally triggered economic and financial shocks, and making them dependent on export markets over which they had no control. Borrowing countries became more indebted than before and fell into debt traps whereby they used new loans to repay existing debts. Numerous studies of SAPs reveal that they both created policy-induced poverty and entrenched pre-existing structures of social, economic, and political inequality. (For a sample of critiques, see Bello 2006a, 2006b; Brooks 2006; Roberts 2005; Singh 2005.)

The dangers of neo-liberal economics and globalisation were resurrected in July 1997, when a financial crisis exploded in Indonesia, South Korea, and Thailand and rapidly spread across the region, forcing the collapse of many of the economies of East Asia. The crisis was triggered by currency speculation and sudden massive capital flight, but its foundations had been laid several years earlier, when countries bowed to pressures from the IMF to free speculative capital from the constraints of national regulation. Thanks to the IMF's policy 'advice', the economies of Indonesia, South Korea, and Thailand had become virtual casinos; capital flowed in and out with few restrictions, but also with little substance in the real economy to back it up. The financial collapse was soon transformed into a full-blown economic and structural crisis of enormous magnitude by IFI 'rescue' packages, which were essentially SAPs with a few social programmes thrown in. In less than a year, tens of millions of people were plunged into sudden, abject poverty.

Although IMF, World Bank, and Washington Consensus pundits tried to blame the crisis on Asian 'crony capitalism', the eruption of similar crises in Turkey, Russia, and Argentina clearly showed that not only were Bank–Fund economic reform packages to blame, but also that their so-called rescue packages were intended to save foreign banks, investors, and corporations, and not the crisis-hit countries. By contrast, strict capital controls in Malaysia and China during the crisis protected their economies from unravelling.

In the face of growing international criticism following the Asian crisis, and increasing evidence of the destructive impacts of SAPs, the Bank and Fund changed their tack somewhat. SAPs started to be called 'poverty-reduction strategies', included some social programmes, and put greater emphasis on establishing globalisation-friendly national institutions through a new set of policy reforms called 'good governance' (see Mkandawire's Chapter 2). The core of the IFI development model, however, has remained unchanged, and the assumed inevitability of globalisation appears to have prevented even progressive members of the development establishment from imagining alternative forms of and paths towards development. And, despite mounting evidence to the contrary, developing-country governments continue to maintain what appears to be an almost religious faith in the eventual power of markets to correct imbalances, inequities, and imperfections.

An interesting example here is the micro-credit industry. Possibly because the dominant development model is centred on capital accumulation, the poverty that it creates is also generally attributed to lack of capital, which must then be addressed by creating access to it. For income-poor families, this access is created through loans from micro-credit projects and institutions. Most micro-credit schemes are aimed at women organised in self-help groups (SHGs), run by CSOs and private consultants, and heavily promoted by aid agencies and the IFIs. While some micro-credit schemes may well have helped borrowers to invest in effective income-generating activities, many have created debt traps whereby SHG members borrow from other sources to repay their loans, unfortunately mirroring at the micro level the macro-level financial condition afflicting many indebted governments. Today, micro-credit has become a global debt-creating industry worth billions of dollars. It is favoured by aid agencies and aid-recipient governments alike and relieves the latter of the far less favoured responsibility of controlling markets and redistributing wealth, assets, rights to land, and access to resources which could generate longer-term solutions to poverty.

The experience of the past few decades shows that countries that maintained financial controls and regulated the market to build up infrastructure and agricultural capacity and protect employment (such as China, India, Malaysia, Taiwan, Thailand, and South Korea) did better economically than those that followed the World Bank–IMF development model. However, most countries, rich or poor, have embraced globalisation as the preferred model of development. An important reason for this is political: the top leadership in most countries today consists of people from elite classes (with some exceptions in Latin America) and technocrats who are not committed to seeking credible alternatives to globalisation.

Contradictions and paradoxes

Globalisation is not an inclusive or progressive form of internationalism. Rather, it is the successful expansion on a world scale of particular localisms of social, economic, and political organisation, which are neo-liberal and capitalist in character. The mix of material and ideological elements that make this expansion possible makes globalisation a hegemonic process. Nor does globalisation create or encourage economic freedom, opportunities, and choice at all levels; rather it is more akin to a monoculture of ideas, politics, and economic models.

Globalisation is also contradictory in its effects. Its assumed 'integrative nature' is belied by severe and growing inequalities both within and among nations. While capital and goods may be free to move across boundaries, labour is not. Much of the economic growth attributed to globalisation has been jobless, and has benefited those who are already socially and economically equipped to take advantage of the opportunities offered by economic and financial liberalisation. Recurrent fluctuations in currency and commodity markets and the ability of TNCs to move production sites at whim have wiped out small producers and workers in developing countries. But large national and transnational businesses have benefited from such volatility by acquiring new assets at rock-bottom prices in developing countries. Corporations want protectionism for themselves and *laissez-faire* for their competitors.

Globalisation has integrated rich, affluent, and educated classes, but has fractured working classes and marginalised the poor, who do not have the skills and economic clout to profit from open markets. While trade and financial liberalisation and privatisation have devastated the livelihoods of farmers, fishers, workers, and indigenous peoples in the South, the North too is facing globalisation-induced troubles. The subcontracting and outsourcing of industrial production and services processing to developing countries has created unemployment in the home countries of some of the world's largest TNCs such as the USA, the UK, and France. Contrary to the rosy predictions of its proponents, globalisation has not created a flat, harmonious world with economic prosperity for all. Instead, it has bred imbalances and contradictions that capitalists themselves are hard put to explain.

Paradoxically, the same forces that promote global capitalism also promote democracy, human rights, and government intervention. This is paradoxical, because global capitalism cannot survive in an ethical climate that promotes genuine democracy and fundamental human rights, nor does it favour independent-minded states. Corporations are geared towards profit making and expanding the bottom line for their shareholders, who generally do not include workers, family farmers and fishers, indigenous communities, the urban poor, or even lower-middle-class families. But in order to keep expanding their profits, corporations need the sanction and structural support of nationally and internationally accepted legal, judicial, and political entities that have the moral authority to exercise force through policy and other means. In other words, corporations need a neo-liberal state and multilateral forums and institutions in order to advance their interests. They need the state to act for them: to clear the ground for their entry into domestic arenas; to establish economic, financial, legal, and judicial frameworks that facilitate their operations; and, most important, to provide rational and ethical cover for their operations. This cover is easily conjured by equating globalisation with development, democratic decision making, consumer choice, and the individualised rights of a consuming public.

The role of the governments and state power in the current era of globalisation is a much-debated issue. Many on both the left and the right argue that the state is relatively meaningless in the face of global capital. But state power needs to be examined both within and outside the confines of national arenas. Political structures within nation states are expressions of the economic arrangements and power alignments of interest groups within nations. States that are closely allied to global capital are indeed powerful and they secure for their corporations the most advantageous terms in international and bilateral trade and investment treaties. The withdrawal of the state from economic interventions in most developing countries has been achieved through economic and military aggression by capital-rich countries. At the same time, many developing-country governments have tended to be extremely authoritarian in national arenas and used military force against their own citizens in order to comply with the demands of global capital. State power in relation to globalisation is both contradictory and responsive to the emergence of new forces and trends. India, Brazil, South Africa, and China (the so-called BICS, or BRICS, including Russia) are now forces to reckon with in the WTO. Under the patronage of China, Cambodia – which has been in the grip of post-war reconstruction and SAPs for almost two decades – is now able to thumb its nose at IFIs and wealthy donor countries.

Resistance

As corporate-led globalisation sweeps the world, it transforms those that it touches and, in so doing, it creates spaces and avenues for its dismantling and the possibility of its imminent arrest. Globalisation has not delivered (and cannot deliver) on its promises. Private corporations, national elites, and those able to access higher education have reaped benefits, to be sure. But for hundreds of millions across the world, the actual effects of neo-liberal policies have been inequality, poverty, hunger, increased susceptibility to disease and sickness, and economic and political marginalisation. Peasants, small-scale farmers and fishers, small and medium entrepreneurs, workers, pastoralists, and indigenous communities have faced deep and shattering livelihood crises as a result of free trade and investment, and the depredations of speculative capital. Public goods and services that once were and should still be within equal reach of all those living within a common territory are now being offered as private goods and services accessible only to solvent consumers. Non-state and supra-state actors (such as private corporations and multilateral organisations) often perform the political functions of states, but without being under effective, sovereign control.

For every system of domination, there is a hacker. And progressive civil-society actors are devising increasingly creative and powerful ways of hacking into the neo-liberal regime, exposing its flaws and weakening its institutions.

The hegemony of corporate-led globalisation is being challenged and resisted by a growing, worldwide movement whose base is made up of a wide diversity of people, ideas, cultures, languages, ages, professions, and competencies. These include progressive people's movements, networks, CSOs, independent academics and intellectuals, writers, artists, film makers, small businesses, and even governments, all of whom are using modern information technology to mount well organised, well informed, and sustained challenges to economic globalisation, corporate power, and the key institutions of neo-liberal ideology. The same technology that has exacerbated the financial insecurity of nations has also been used by people's movements and activists to jam the gears of globalisation.

In Latin America, Bolivia has nationalised its energy resources, Argentina has unilaterally restructured the debt owed to Northern bond-holders, and Venezuela has launched the Bolivarian Alternative for the Americas (its Spanish acronym, ALBA, meaning 'dawn') as an alternative plan for regional integration. Larger developing countries are refusing to borrow from the IMF, and those that are under IMF regimes are keen to clear their payments ahead of schedule. The crisis of the trade talks in the WTO, the growing crises of competency and legitimacy of the IMF and World Bank, the intensifying resistance to US occupation in Iraq and elsewhere, and the moves at multiple levels – local, national, and regional – to design, test, and share alternative paths to social, economic, and ecological well-being, are all examples of successes of the counter-hegemonic challenge to globalisation.

References

Bello, Walden (2006a) 'Globalization in retreat', *Foreign Policy in Focus*, 27 December, www.fpif.org/fpiftxt/3826 (retrieved 23 April 2007).

Bello, Walden (2006b) 'Chain-Gang Economics: China, the US, and the Global Economy', 1 November, www.focusweb.org/chain-gang-economics-china-the-us-and-the-global-economy.html?Itemid=94 (retrieved 23 April 2007).

Brooks, Mick (2006) 'Globalisation and imperialism', *In Defence of Marxism*, 11 April, www.marxist.com/globalisation-imperialism-economy110406.htm (retrieved 23 April 2007).

Roberts, Michael (2005) 'Globalisation and empire', *In Defence of Marxism*, 7 December, www.marxist.com/globalisation-empire-barbarism071205.htm (retrieved 23 April 2007).

Singh, Kavaljit (2005) *Questioning Globalization*, New Delhi: Madhyam Books.

About the author

Shalmali Guttal is a Senior Associate with Focus on the Global South (Focus), an activist think tank that monitors development policy and practice. Over the past 20 years, she has worked in India, the USA, and mainland Southeast Asia on issues of social, economic, and political justice.

CHAPTER 7

The F-word and the S-word – too much of one and not enough of the other

Cassandra Balchin

This chapter questions the growing use of the term 'faith-based' in development policy and practice. It is argued that it homogenises people in minority migrant and developing-country contexts and excludes many who are working for human rights and social justice from secular perspectives, thus providing an unsound analytical base for policy. Against the background of the 'war on terror', the author also examines the differences in US and British development policy arising out of the term 'faith-based'.

If you want to get ahead in international development policy today, you've got to use the F-word: *faith-based*. On the other hand, if you want to be dismissed, de-legitimised, silenced in development policy and practice, then you've only got to use the S-word: *secularism*. It has become such an anti-buzzword and has fallen so far out of favour that even secularists have forgotten to carry on developing the concept.

First, some problems of definition. We seem to have slid from identifying certain collections of humans as 'religious groups' to calling them 'faith-based organisations'. Surely, if a bunch of people come together because of their shared religion, then they are a 'religious group'? In old-fashioned political science, 'groups' tended to be linked with the phrase 'interest groups'. But we wouldn't want people to start thinking that any of this had anything to do with politics and power, would we?

There is also a sloppy slippage between *communities, groups, organisations,* and *institutions* – all prefaced by 'faith' and often invoked in the same breath.[1] Sorry, but while I may see myself as part of 'the Muslim community', I most certainly do not see myself as represented by or part of any particular 'faith group, organisation, or institution'. In a report by the Muslim Women's Network, launched on 7 December 2006 to share the voices of women in Britain's Muslim communities, some of the angriest comments were reserved for the way the government seems to talk only to (conservative) male 'community leaders' (Ward 2006). Having been linked with the international network Women Living Under Muslim Laws for some 15 years, I know that women across different geographical and religious contexts make the same criticism of international development policy. Part of the problem here seems to be a conflation of social location, identity, and values,[2] as pointed out by Nira Yuval-Davis (2006).

Studies in developing countries have indeed acknowledged the importance of religion in people's daily lives (Shaheed 1998). In the 1980s and early 1990s, this often came as a rude shock to many international development organisations, especially those based in Western Europe which for decades seemed to operate on the principle that if one shut one's eyes and pretended it wasn't there, the whole 'question of religion' would magically go away. This habit now seems to have been replaced with a tendency to ignore the many in developing countries who do *not* identify as having any specific religion, coupled with a presumption that everyone approaches 'faith' in the same, homogeneous way.[3] One British government website stumbles when it tries to do some defining. It says:

> Faith community [...] can refer to any religiously affiliated group and there is no officially agreed definition. There are core themes, which form the basis for all productive inter-faith activity and for co-operation by all the faith communities in addressing issues of neighbourhood renewal... These centre around: community, personal integrity, a sense of responsibility for future generations – not just the here and now – learning, wisdom, care and compassion, justice and peace, respect for one another and for the earth and its creatures. (Neighbourhood Renewal Unit, available at www.neighbourhood.gov.uk/page.asp?id=1003, retrieved 27 February 2007)

Does this definition mean that people who are not included in the policy-sexy 'faith communities', lack all these 'core themes'? That's a bit unfair on atheists, surely, especially when we all know self-proclaimed devout people who beat their servants and drive 4 x 4s. How is this definitional list of a 'faith community' any different from a list of what it takes to be a decent human being? The website of the World Faiths Development Dialogue (set up in 1998 as an initiative of James D. Wolfensohn, then President of the World Bank, and Lord Carey, then Archbishop of Canterbury) carries an article that proclaims: 'A mark of the great world faiths is the assumption of a moral reality and a critique of the basic human condition' (Abrams 2003:2). I can't quite decide whether that means that Marxism is also a 'great world faith', or that nobody except the Christians, Muslims, Hindus, and Jews (sometimes the Buddhists are also thrown in) has any morals.

Official US development policy is no better. For example, a grandly entitled 'Faith-Based & Community Organizations Pandemic Influenza Preparedness Checklist' (available at www.pandemicflu.gov/plan/faithcomchecklist.html) raises a number of questions. If the presumption is that a 'faith-based organisation' is operating at the community level and can therefore help to deliver health advice during a crisis, then why not call it a 'community organisation'? Or why highlight only religious organisations which can help out? Why not local lesbian support groups or a wheelchair-users' group? And if access to local 'communities' isn't the issue, and the government needs to reach all organisations that can reach people, then why not include trade unions? Very odd.

And also very funny. The World Faiths Development Dialogue website carries an article, albeit with a disclaimer covering all similar documents, which earnestly compares 'Differences between Secular NGOs and Religious based NGOs'. It asserts that while in secular organisations 'The management concept is based on management position and responsibility. The relationship with management is of employer and employee,' in religion-based NGOs 'After God, all are equal, assigned with specific responsibilities based on skills and capacity. The relationship is like members of a family or community. Beneficiaries are members of an extended community' (Sabur 2004). You're kidding, right?

At the level of international development policy, donors and aid agencies have been increasingly obsessed with religion since the mid-1980s, when there was an increase in the strength of extreme right-wing politico-religious groups ('fundamentalists'), combined with a mushrooming of women's and human-rights groups in developing countries, and greater donor commitment to advocacy initiatives (which meant that one had to start talking politics and ideology). For example, international seminars on 'Women, Islam and Development' started appearing (but hardly, if ever, 'Women, Christianity and Development'). All of this long preceded the attacks of 11 September 2001 and the subsequent 'War on Terror', although clearly the latter has led to an increasing desperation in terms of international development policy.

But fundamentalism is on the rise not only in the Global South, where even Sri Lanka's Buddhists now have their very own fundamentalists. Christian fundamentalists are hugely influential in both US and British policy. The US National Security Council's top Middle East aide consults with apocalyptic Christians eager to ensure that US policy on Israel conforms with their sectarian doomsday scenarios (Perlstein 2004), and in recent US elections all candidates seemed to find it obligatory to preface their speeches with a statement of faith. Tony Blair publicly emphasises his Christian beliefs, and no one should be surprised that the former British Secretary of State for Communities and Local Government is a member of Opus Dei, the right-wing Catholic group.

In current international development policy, religion is simultaneously seen as the biggest developmental obstacle, the only developmental issue, and the only developmental solution. The co-existence of these three – seemingly contrary – approaches, which can often be found within a single bilateral or international development agency or NGO, is possible because they all stem from the same Orientalist presumption about the 'underdeveloped Other' (Said 1979). It basically boils down to racism.

Let me simplify an argument that I have made elsewhere (Balchin 2003). In the first approach (seeing religion as the biggest developmental obstacle), 'irrational' people are blamed for their own underdevelopment (as opposed to, for example, gross global trade inequalities perpetuated by the North), and frequently custom is inaccurately conflated with religion. In the second approach, factors influencing poverty such as class, gender, and racial dis-crimination are ignored or downplayed. In the third approach, it is pre-sumed that all 'proper' Indonesians, Ugandans, Moroccans, Chileans, etc. are 'religious'; secular initiatives are de-legitimised, and the work of many local service-delivery and human-rights groups ignored.

Whatever happened to inter-sectionality: the recognition that we are all subject to multiple identities that construct and are constructed by each oth-er? Are my friends in Sisters in Islam a 'faith-based' group or a feminist group or a Malaysian group? I think they see themselves as all of the above – and why can't they be all of these without having to exclusively prioritise one or other aspect of their work?

Added to the problem of prioritising one aspect of our identities to the exclusion of others is the tendency inherent in this 'faith-based' business to conflate ethnicity, culture, race, and religion. International development policy makers do it, the fundamentalists encourage it because it suits their self-importance, and we all slip into the habit. In 2005 I was working with a group of Muslim women in Britain, eliciting the problems that they face as 'women in the community'. A long, angry list of deprivations and discrimi-nations emerged. Do English Muslim converts face these problems, I asked, hoping to help them to identify more clearly the sources of the problems that they faced and thereby to identify what policies should be changed. Stunned silence. Most of the problems were going to drop off the list.

Have we stopped to really think what this whole 'faith groups' business means in terms of international development resources and policies? Under President Bush's Emergency Plan for AIDS Relief (PEPFAR) and related legal measures (which had to be introduced through executive orders and not through democratic congressional process owing to strong opposition), one third of AIDS-prevention money overseas (about US$ 1 billion) had to be spent on programmes that encouraged 'abstinence until marriage'. A report issued in 2006 by the Government Accountability Office, the investigative arm of the US Congress, found that the effort to steer money to abstinence programmes has taken funds away from other anti-AIDS programmes (Kranish 2006). That's an awful lot of money that could have usefully been spent on promoting safe sex or addressing the power imbalances (especially gender-related imbalances) that mean some cannot negotiate safe sex for themselves. That's an awful lot of lives. And if you are a lesbian or a gay man, a child, or a prostitute (or maybe all three), forget any hopes of getting sex education or support if you don't want to become HIV-infected.

Perhaps less dramatic, but no less frustrating, for local rights activists is the recent announcement that the British government will double its aid to Pakistan – and all of the extra money will go to making sure that *madrassahs* don't become terrorist hotbeds (BBC 2006). Perhaps the obsession with reli-gion is also then linked with the neo-conservative economic agenda of winding down state infrastructure and services (and hoping that community services offered by religious groups will plug the gap): investing that much money in the state education sector in Pakistan might ensure that no one *needs* to go to a *madrassah* in the first place.

In the context of the 'War on Terror' especially, 'faith-based' is implicitly counterposed to 'extremism', but this may lead to quite different development policies. To take just one example, in US policy 'faith-based' is short-hand for 'Christians we can do business with', and 'extremism' translates into 'Muslims'. An investigative report by *The Boston Globe* found that USAID spent US$ 57 million from 2001 to 2005 (out of a total of US$ 390 million allocated to NGOs) to fund almost a dozen projects run by faith-based organisations in Pakistan, Indonesia, and Afghanistan. Of the nearly 160 faith-based organisations that have received prime contracts from USAID in the past five years, only two are Muslim. Christian groups' share of USAID funding has roughly doubled under George Bush Jr and accounts for 98.3 per cent of all money given to faith-based groups (Milligan 2006).

By contrast, in British development policy, working with 'faith-based' initiatives has been code for funding 'moderate Muslims'. Progressive Muslim groups rarely get funding, because they don't match the stereotype of what a Muslim should or should not be – a stereotype that suits both the Orientalist and fundamentalist worldviews. Indeed, the word 'moderate' appears in virtually every DFID programme relating to Muslim contexts without definition at any point. The only definition I could find was an indirect one, in an internal document:

> By extremism, we mean advocating or supporting views such as support for terrorist attacks against British or western targets, including the 9/11 attacks, or for British Muslims fighting against British or allied forces abroad, arguing that it is not possible to be British and Muslim, calling on Muslims to reject engagement with British society and politics, and advocating the creation of an Islamic state in Britain. (FCO/HO 2004)

Thus any organisation which holds misogynist, homophobic, or anti-semitic views could, under this categorisation, pass for 'moderate'.

Because many Western governments – and indeed major international development and human-rights NGOs – have been so ignorant about the role of religion in people's lives, particularly about this role in non-Christian contexts, for decades they failed to develop the tools to analyse 'religious groups' and thereby understand which of the groups within this potentially vast ideological array actually work for human rights and equitable development (assuming that these governments and NGOs actually support such rights and development). In their recent rush to 'do religion' or to support 'faith-based initiatives', governments have on occasion made friends with some unsavoury characters (Bright 2006). Meanwhile, gender specialists working in international development and human-rights NGOs still find it hard to get acceptance for the simple message that fundamentalism is bad for women's health.

In the name of 'tradition', the 'faith communities' approach accords some religious figures a place that they have traditionally never had. Women activists in Muslim communities in the Philippines believe that USAID's efforts in

2003 to secure a joint *fatwa* from local religious figures in support of reproductive health was a major factor in enabling the Ulema to overcome previous internal differences and work together to form a united political force that subsequently dominated local councils – until discredited as having no concrete policies to deal with the area's poverty (personal communication).

'Faith-based' always comes with its sidekick, 'inter-faith' dialogue or activities. In contexts where the walls have gone up and war has been declared, dialogue across boundaries is a Good Thing. But sometimes inter-faith dialogue can work to oppress dissenting voices within each religious community, because it easily translates into 'I recognise your hegemonic definition of your identity and you recognise mine, and we'll get along fine'. Remember the 'Holy Alliance' between the Roman Catholic Church and right-wing Muslim governments at the 1994 International Conference on Population and Development, and their concerted attacks on women's bodily autonomy?

In November 2006, the Commonwealth Foundation organised a discussion on 'Faith and Development' which concluded that 'Faith institutions and civil society movements have a key role in providing education and achieving local and global justice, gender equality, and action for non-violent resolutions to conflict'.[4] Its recommendation was the establishment of 'a Multi-Faith Advisory Group that can advise the Foundation on the role of culture and faith in development'. The report stated that this 'will require a balanced membership'. I wonder whether this will include groups like Catholics For a Free Choice, who highlight the current damage being done to gender equality by 'faith institutions'?

This brings us to the thorny question of who gets to define who is a member of a particular 'faith community', or if they qualify for membership at all. What about groups such as the Ahmedis, declared non-Muslims in some countries and visibly not represented in membership, for example, of that supposedly 'umbrella organisation', the Muslim Council of Britain? The whole 'faith communities' policy leaves international development policy makers very close to the highly contested ground of defining who is and is not a 'Muslim', or a 'Christian', or a 'Jew', and so on and so forth.

What is wrong with the focus on 'faith-based groups' is that it misses the crucial point about who is actually exercising power in a community, and for what purposes. At a 2005 Oxfam GB workshop that considered questions of gender and religion, we shared stories of experiences where religion had appeared as the obstacle to a particular development initiative – at the very local, grass-roots level. But when we analysed who was using religion and for what purpose (mostly men, mostly to preserve the *status quo*), it transpired that a religious principle actually lay at the heart of only one of the dozen stories shared.[5]

So where does this leave us? What is the alternative? Secularism? It has become such a dirty word that international development policy makers have not even discussed publicly whether it means non-religious or anti-religious, and how either of these is to be realised in social policy. Ironically, people in developing countries are indeed discussing the issue: for example, Abdullahi an-Na'im on the future of Shari'a (for details, see www.law.emory.edu/cms/site/index.php?id=2383), Juan Marco Vaggione (2002), Asghar Ali Engineer, and Penda Mbow (2006).[6] For many of them, 'having faith' and 'being secular' are not mutually exclusive.

Meanwhile, it is clear that international development policy to date has not been effective in addressing deprivation and discrimination. What is not so clear is what we should do about it. But I would suggest that the 'faith-based' approach is not the best solution, with its treatment of 'faith' as synonymous with organised religion as defined by the powerful within those religions; its dismissal of people who do not wish to assert a religious public identity; its hypocritical support of 'diversity' across religions while ignoring the possibility of contestation within religions; and above all its implicit claim that hungry stomachs can be filled by morality and ideology, rather than by global trade equality, an end to militarisation, and the realisation by all people of their human rights.

Notes

1. An example is the website of the British government's Department for Communities and Local Government (DCLG), notably its sections on Race, Equality, Faith and Cohesion, and the Neighbourhood Renewal Unit.
2. For example, the fact of being born into a Muslim family does not necessarily mean that one identifies as Muslim, and nor does a Muslim identity necessarily mean adherence to a conservative political ideology.
3. For example, see Centre for Islamic Legal Studies (2005), which seems to ignore Nigerian women's secular struggles, as well as progressive interpretations of Islam, and has been heavily criticised by Nigerian women activists.
4. Available at www.commonwealthfoundation.com/uploads/documents/faith_development_recommendations1.pdf (retrieved 27 February 2007).
5. Islam's prohibition against interest or profit on loans affecting micro-credit schemes in Yemen – and even that is contested among Muslim jurists.
6. Dossier No. 28, published in December 2006 by Women Living Under Muslim Laws, reproduces all these articles and many others.

References

Abrams, Len (2003) 'Faith, Development and Poverty – Some Reflections', www.wfdd.org.uk/articles_talks/abrams.pdf (retrieved 27 February 2007).

Balchin, Cassandra (2003) 'With her feet on the ground: women, religion and development in Muslim communities', *Development* 46(4): 39–49.

BBC (2006) 'UK and Pakistan forge terror pact', BBC News, 20 November, http://news.bbc.co.uk/1/hi/world/south_asia/6161500.stm (retrieved 27 February 2007).

Bright, Martin (2006) 'When Progressives Treat With Reactionaries: The British State's flirtation with radical Islamism', Policy Exchange, www.policyexchange.org.uk/Publications.aspx?id=192 (retrieved 27 February 2007).

Centre for Islamic Legal Studies (2005) *Promoting Women's Rights Through Sharia in Northern Nigeria*, Zaria: Centre for Islamic Legal Studies, Ahmadu Bello University, with support from DFID and the British Council.

Engineer, Asghar Ali (2006) 'Secularism in India', parts I and II, *Secular Perspectives*, 16 June – 15 July, www.csss-isla.com/archive.php (retrieved 27 February 2007).

Foreign & Commonwealth Office/Home Office (2004) 'Young Muslims and Extremism', draft report, www.stoppoliticalterror.com/media/youngmuslims070805.pdf (retrieved 27 February 2007).

Kranish, Michael (2006) 'Democrats inspect faith-based initiative', *The Boston Globe*, 4 December, www.boston.com/news/nation/washington/articles/2006/12/04/democrats_inspect_faith_based_initiative/ (retrieved 27 February 2007).

Mbow, Penda (2006) 'The secular state and citizenship in Muslim countries: bringing Africa into the debate', www.ned.org/events/past/events06.html#Jan2606 (retrieved 27 February 2007).

Milligan, Susan (2006) 'Together, but worlds apart: Christian aid groups raise suspicion in strongholds of Islam', *The Boston Globe*, 10 October.

Perlstein, Rick (2004) 'The Jesus landing pad: Bush White House checked with rapture Christians before latest Israel move', *The Village Voice*, 18 May, www.villagevoice.com/news/0420,perlstein,53582,1.html (retrieved 27 February 2007).

Sabur, M. Abdus (2004) 'Case Study of the Asian Muslim Action Network (AMAN)', www.wfdd.org.uk/programmes/case_studies/aman.doc (retrieved 2 March 2007).

Said, Edward (1979) *Orientalism: Western Conceptions of the Orient*, New York, NY: Vintage Books.

Shaheed, Farida (1998) 'The other side of the discourse: women's experiences of identity, religion and activism in Pakistan', in Farida Shaheed, Sohail Akbar Warraich, Cassandra Balchin and Aisha Gazdar (eds.) *Shaping Women's Lives: Laws, Practices and Strategies in Pakistan*, Lahore: Shirkat Gah Women's Resource Centre.

Vaggione, Juan Marco (2002) 'Paradoxing the secular: religion, gender and sexuality at the crossroads', *Transregional Center for Democratic Studies Journal* 3(8): 1–19.

Ward, Lucy (2006) 'Muslim women angry at views being ignored, study shows', *Guardian Unlimited*, 7 December, www.guardian.co.uk/religion/Story/0,,1965867,00.html (retrieved 27 February 2007).

Yuval-Davis, Nira (2006) 'Belonging and the politics of belonging', *Patterns of Prejudice* 40(3):196–293.

About the author

Cassandra Balchin, formerly a journalist based in Pakistan, has been linked with the network Women Living Under Muslim Laws since the early 1990s and is Director of Legal Awareness, Women & Society (LAWS), focusing on Muslim communities in Britain.

CHAPTER 8

Participation: the ascendancy of a buzzword in the neo-liberal era

Pablo Alejandro Leal

Participation was originally conceived as part of a counter-hegemonic approach to radical social transformation and, as such, represented a challenge to the status quo. Paradoxically, throughout the 1980s and 1990s, 'participation' gained legitimacy within the institutional development world to the extent of achieving buzzword status. The precise manipulations required to convert a radical proposal into something that could serve the neo-liberal world order led to participation's political decapitation. Reduced to a series of methodological packages and techniques, participation would slowly lose its philosophical and ideological meaning. In order to make the approach and methodology serve counter-hegemonic processes of grassroots resistance and transformation, these meanings desperately need to be recovered. This calls for participation to be re-articulated within broader processes of social and political struggle in order to facilitate the recovery of social transformation in the world of twenty-first century capitalism.

Somewhere in the mid-1980s, *participation* ascended to the pantheon of development buzzwords, catchphrases, and euphemisms. From that moment on, and throughout the greater part of the 1990s, the new buzzword would stand side by side with such giants as 'sustainable development', 'basic needs', 'capacity building', and 'results based'. *Participation* entered the exclusive world of dominant development discourse; it had gained currency and trade value in the competitive market struggle for development project contracts, an indispensable ingredient of the replies to requests for proposals that issued from multilateral aid agencies everywhere. Development professionals and consultants rushed to attend workshops on how to employ a multiplicity of methodological packages such as Participatory Rural Appraisal (PRA), Participatory Learning and Action (PLA), Appreciative Inquiry (AI), Community Based Needs Assessment (CBNA), and Stakeholder Analysis. Other professionals rushed to lead these workshops, given the growing market for them. There was no doubt: participation was hot, it was in, and it was here to stay – or at least, until it was displaced by another, newer buzzword.

That this happened should be of no surprise to anyone, since the development industry has made an art of reinventing itself in the face of its failure to reduce or alleviate poverty, social and economic inequity, and environmental degradation after more than five glorious development decades. What is striking is the time and manner in which it came upon the institutional development scene, and this chapter seeks to explore this particular issue.

The historic and systemic failure of the development industry to 'fix' chronic underdevelopment puts it in the challenging position of having both to renew and reinvent its discourse and practice enough to make people believe that a change has, in fact, taken place and to make these adjustments while maintaining intact the basic structure of the *status quo* on which the development industry depends. This explains why we have seen, over the past 50 years, a rich parade of successive development trends: 'community development' in the post-colonial period, 'modernisation' in the Cold War period, and 'basic human needs' and 'integrated rural development' throughout the 1970s. The neo-liberal period (1980s to the present day) witnessed a pageant of such trends as 'sustainable development' and 'participatory development' from the late 1980s and all through the 1990s; 'capacity building', 'human rights', and 'good governance' throughout most of the 1990s; and, we must not forget, 'poverty reduction/alleviation' in the dawn of the twenty-first century.

Michel Chossudovsky (2002:37) explains the phenomenon in simple and lucid terms:

> The 'official' neoliberal dogma also creates its own 'counter-paradigm' embodying a highly moral and ethical discourse. The latter focuses on 'sustainable development' while distorting and stylizing the policy issues pertaining to poverty, the protection of the environment and the social rights of women. This 'counter-ideology' rarely challenges neoliberal policy prescriptions. It develops alongside and in harmony rather than in opposition to the official neoliberal dogma.

It is clearly more than coincidence that participation appeared as a new battle horse for official development precisely at the time of the shock treatment of Structural Adjustment Programmes (SAPs) inflicted on the underdeveloped world by the World Bank and the IMF. SAPs were the operational methodology that, in practice, implemented neo-liberalism in poor nations. By using the re-negotiation of Third World debt as leverage, the international financial institutions were able to force poor countries to do things that were clearly against their best interest. Thus the wave of privatisation, denationalisation, elimination of subsidies of all sorts, budgetary austerity, devaluation, and trade liberalisation initiated a deep social desperation throughout the Third World. The anti-SAP riots in Caracas in 1989, which left more than 200 people dead; the bread riots of Tunis in January 1984; the anti-SAP riots led by students in Nigeria in 1989; the general strike and popular uprising against the IMF reforms in Morocco in 1990; and the Zapatista uprising of 1994 against the signing of the North American Free Trade Agreement (NAFTA) are but some of the most emblematic examples of the social and political backlash that the SAPs produced.

In participation, official development found what Majid Rahnema has called 'a redeeming saint' (Rahnema 1990:20). Development's failures were now to be explained by its top-down, blueprint mechanics, which were to be replaced by more people-friendly, bottom-up approaches that would 'put the last first', as Robert Chambers (1983) coined in his well-known book *Rural Development: Putting the Last First.*

What perhaps sets the ascendancy of participation apart from other co-opted development concepts are its radical roots. Arising from the emancipatory pedagogy of Paulo Freire, the Marxist-oriented school of Participatory Action Research (PAR), the principal objective of the participatory paradigm was not development – or 'poverty alleviation' – but the transformation of the cultural, political, and economic structures which reproduce poverty and marginalisation. 'The basic ideology of PAR', according to Mohammed Anisur Rahman (1993:13), 'is that a self-conscious people, those who are currently poor and oppressed, will progressively transform their environment by their own praxis'. Or, in more Freirean terms, development can only be achieved when humans are 'beings for themselves', when they possess their own decision-making powers, free of oppressive and dehumanising circumstances; it is the 'struggle to be more fully human' (Freire 1970:29).

Development *per se* is not excluded from the equation but is seen as something that stems from and is functional to the advancement of social transformation. According to Fals-Borda *et al.* (1991), in the context of the global state of victimisation and oppression of the poor by power-wielding elites, development comes only as a result of individual self-awareness and subsequent collective action. In other words, social transformation can and should produce development, while institutional development historically has not led to social transformation. The reason for this is very clear: institutional development was simply never intended to do so.

Radical neo-liberalism

The World Bank praises the privatization of Zambia's public health system: 'It is a model for Africa. Now there are no more long line-ups in the hospitals'. The Zambian Post completes the idea: 'There are no more long line-ups at the hospitals because people now die at home'. (Galeano 2002)

When taking into consideration the radical nature of the participatory proposal for social transformation and the neo-liberal structural-adjustment context in which it has been co-opted, the incompatibility between the two might seem far too deep-seated to permit such a co-optation to take place. But if we factor in the growing social discontent, popular mobilisations, and anti-SAP riots that were taking place across the Third World, we begin to understand how the development industry could not simply ignore the increasing critiques and challenges to its reigning paradigm. In Rahnema's words (1990:

200), the challenge that participation posed to development orthodoxy was 'too serious to be brushed away or frontally imposed'.

Yet, what exactly does Rahnema mean when he identifies participation as 'a threat too serious to be brushed away'? In what way did participation represent a challenge to the reigning orthodoxy? To understand this issue, we must locate ourselves in the context of the Cold War, whose most significant disputes (which were anything but 'cold') took place not in the First but in the Third World. National liberation struggles were on course in Africa in countries like Namibia, Angola, and Guinea Bissau. Tanzania had undertaken its historic project of *Ujamaa* socialism under the leadership of Julius Nyerere. In Central America, the Sandinista rebels had triumphed in Nicaragua, and revolutionary insurgencies in El Salvador and Guatemala were underway. In South America, the brutal dictatorships of the Southern Cone were confronting an increasingly belligerent popular opposition. In all of these cases, popular education and participatory grassroots action were playing an active role.

In 1971, Freire would travel to Tanzania and, along with Budd Hall, a renowned PAR activist and thinker, would assist the socialist government in the design of its educational programme. In the mid-1970s, Freire would serve as an adviser to the revolutionary government of Guinea Bissau. He would later provide similar services for the Sandinista government of Nicaragua. Popular education would play a significant role in the construction of grassroots guerrilla support in El Salvador and Guatemala throughout the 1980s, while it would help to consolidate popular resistance to the fascist dictatorships in South America[1] throughout the 1970s and 1980s. In 1977, radical Colombian sociologist and participatory research pioneer, Orlando Fals-Borda, would be instrumental in organising a world conference on PAR which, according to Budd Hall, reflected the decision of researchers and activists to 'use their intellectual skills and connections to strengthen the political movements associated with revolution and democracy of the time' (Hall 1997). From this conference, the participatory action-research movement received a global push and expansion.

It was clear that in the Cold War dispute, participation and popular education had taken sides with the Left and not the Right, and, in the world run by the ultra-reactionary Reagan–Thatcher politics of the 1980s, the very decade in which participation began its ascendancy, this would not go unnoticed. The threat was real and palpable and needed to be reckoned with.

If we add to the above the fact that the SAP politics of 1980s and 1990s would only serve to heighten popular resistance throughout the Third World, it would become imperative for the global power elites to seek some kind of palliative solution, to put a 'human face' on inhumane policies; at the very least, to create the illusion that they were not indifferent to the suffering inflicted upon the poorest of the poor by the new neo-liberal shock treatment (Leal and Opp 1999). Consequently, a 1989 World Bank Report entitled *Sub-Saharan Africa: From Crisis to Sustainable Growth* advocated creating new institutions and strengthening civil-society organisations (CSOs), inclusive of groups such as NGOs and voluntary organisations such that these might create channels of participation, by establishing 'links both upward and downward in society and [voicing] local concerns more effectively than grassroots institutions' (World Bank 1989:61, cited in Leal and Opp 1999). According to the Bank, with the creation of a proper 'enabling environment', poor nations can 'channel the energies of the population at large', and 'ordinary people should participate more in designing and implementing development programs' (*ibid.*).

But the mutations of the official discourse did not stop there, and the irony that they produced was indeed something to behold. By employing the language of 'empowerment', 'self-reliance', and 'participation', the Bank assumed a populist appearance reminiscent of PAR. The new rhetoric assumed a pseudo-political stance in its suggestion that the 'crisis of governance' in many countries is due to the 'appropriation of the machinery of government by the elite to serve their own interests', and went so far as to state that a 'deep political malaise stymies action in most countries' (*ibid.*). At a first glance, one might naively infer that the logical implication is to call for people to be empowered to overturn the current and oppressive state of affairs through increased political participation. However, the actual intent is somewhat different. By having identified the nasty state as the culprit, the World Bank was not advocating a popular government, but rather creating a populist justification for the removal of the state from the economy and its substitution by the market. As Moore (1995:17) asserts:

> ...the World Bank is not about to give the state to these people even though it contends that the state has taken the resources from them. Rather than have the state controlled by the common people, the World Bank would control the local state's withdrawal from the economy. Resources must be taken away from the state and placed in the 'market,' where all citizens will supposedly have equal access to them.

Thus liberation or empowerment of poor people in this rationale is not linked with political or state power. Rather, the implication is that empowerment is derived from liberation from an interventionist state, and that participation in free-market economics and their further enlistment into development projects will enable them to 'take fuller charge of their lives', and it is this which is cast as inherently empowering (Leal and Opp 1999).

The World Bank would go on to manufacture products such as the *Participation Source Book* in 1996, a methodological guide to 'doing' participatory development. And later it would produce the stirring report *Voices of the Poor* (Narayan *et al.* 2000), making heart-felt calls for all development institutions to pay closer attention to the needs, aspirations, and subjectivities of the planet's marginalised classes and to consider how these might influence development policy. Linked to *Voices of the Poor* were the Poverty Reduction Strategy Papers (PRSPs), an initiative also led by the World Bank, that sought to articulate poverty reduction with participation, 'with empowerment as an implicit adjunct' (Cornwall and Brock 2005: 1045). And finally, the cherry on the cake, were the Millennium Development Goals (MDGs), ratified by the United Nations General Assembly in 2000, in which the world's governments committed themselves to the goal of halving global poverty by 2015. The declaration is peppered with buzzwords such as 'sustainability', 'participation', 'empowerment', 'equality', and 'democracy', but it makes no reference to what might be the forces that produce and perpetuate poverty. Maintaining a politically and conceptually ambiguous stance, the MDG declaration affirms that 'the central challenge' faced by the planet's governments and respective institutions is 'to ensure that [*neo-liberal*] globalization becomes a positive force for all the world's poor' (United Nations General Assembly 2000: 2).

People's participation and empowerment filter into all of the above equations, sometimes implicitly, but more often than not explicitly identified as foundational pillars of the global poverty-reduction crusade. According to Cornwall and Brock (2005: 1046), by remaining 'politically ambiguous and definitionally vague, participation has historically been used both to enable ordinary people to gain agency and as a means of maintaining relations of rule'. However, in the hands of the development industry, the political ambiguity has been functional to the preservation of the *status quo*.

Preserving the hegemony of the *status quo*, in the Gramscian sense, entails the reproduction of discourse through various channels in order to create and maintain a social consensus around the interests of the dominant power structures, which in the twenty-first century are encased in and are functional to the neo-liberal world order. Thus, the manipulations required to neutralise challenges and threats to its dominant rationale and practice cannot afford to lack sophistication. Whatever the method used to co-opt, the dominant order has assimilated an historic lesson, as White (1996) affirms with simple clarity: 'incorporation, rather than exclusion is the best form of control'. Since frontal negation or attacks to those challenges to the dominant order often serve only to strengthen and legitimate the dissent in the eyes of society, co-option becomes the more attractive option for asserting control. Counter-ideology is thus incorporated as part of the dominant ideology, as Chossudovsky (2002: 37) argues:

> Within this counter-ideology (which is generously funded by the research establishment) development scholars find a comfortable niche. Their role is to generate within this counter-discourse a semblance of critical debate without addressing the social foundations of the global market system. The World Bank plays in this regard a key role by promoting research on poverty and the so-called 'social dimensions of adjustment'. This ethical focus on the underlying categories (e.g. poverty alleviation, gender issues, equity, etc.) provides a 'human face' to the World Bank and a semblance of commitment to social change. However, inasmuch as this analysis is functionally divorced from an

understanding of the main macro-economic reforms, it rarely constitutes a threat to the dominant neoliberal economic paradigm.

For participation to become part of dominant development practice, it first had to be modified, sanitised, and depoliticised. Once purged of all the threatening elements, participation could be re-engineered as an instrument that could play a role *within* the *status quo*, rather than one that defied it. Co-optation of the concept depended, in large measure, on the omission of class and larger social contradictions. As such, participation became another ingredient in the prevailing modernisation paradigm. This conceptualisation holds that poverty, inequity, and marginalisation are results of a lack of application of technology, capital, and knowledge combined successfully through appropriate policy and planning mechanisms, leading to pertinent reforms of institutional structures (i.e. SAPs) (Escobar 1995; Tandon 1996). The dominant discourses of mainstream development hold as fundamental the assertion that the pattern for these types of intervention are found in the Western rationalist tradition which focuses on behavioural models of rational choice rather than structural inequity or the human response to oppression (Cowen and Shenton 1995; Porter 1995; Pieterse 1991).

As such, institutional development opts for the route of *technocracy* or the technification of social and political problems. By placing emphasis on the *techniques* of participation, rather than on its meaning, empowerment is thus presented as a *de facto* conclusion to the initiation of a participatory process – part and parcel of technical packages like PRA, PLA, and stakeholder analysis. Power – or political – issues are thus translated into technical problems which the dominant development paradigm can easily accommodate (White 1996).

Freed from its originally intended politics and ideology, participation was also liberated from any meaningful form of social confrontation, aside from the very superficial dichotomy between 'outsiders' and 'insiders', or 'uppers' and 'lowers'. Power, in the current global context, and especially so in the context of Third World societies, implies significant degrees of social confrontation and contradiction which are inherent and imminent in processes of social change and transformation. However, for reasons that should by now be self-evident, social confrontation is an issue that the development industry has never been able or willing to address.

This process of depoliticisation has been well documented in a series of critiques, culminating with Cooke and Kothari's (2001) *Participation: The New Tyranny?* Nevertheless, to say that institutional development effectively 'depoliticised' participation is not entirely true. Either tacitly or overtly, participation is either functional to the dominant social order or it defies it. The 'depoliticised' versions of participatory action (participatory development, PRA, etc.), 'liberated' from their transformative elements, are still, in fact, political, since they inevitably serve to justify, legitimise, and perpetuate current neo-liberal hegemony. As such, by having been detached from its radical nature, participatory action was consequently *re*-politicised in the service of the conservative neo-liberal agenda. As Williams (2004:1) states:

'If development is indeed an 'anti-politics machine', [...] participation provides a remarkably efficient means of greasing its wheels.'

Returning to politics and power

It should come as no surprise then, that a very relevant and legitimate call has been made to politically relocate participation and rescue its transformative potential. One good example is the edited volume *From Tyranny to Transformation? Exploring New Approaches to Participation* (Hickey and Mohan 2004). This book is based on the idea that while the critical backlash has been legitimate and necessary, one must be careful not to throw the baby out with the bathwater and discard participation in its entirety. The merits of participation as a political and methodological approach that makes social transformation possible remain, but participation must be re-articulated to serve broader struggles, as Hickey and Mohan (2004:1) point out:

> [...] participatory approaches are most likely to succeed where they are pursued as part of a wider (radical) political project and where they are aimed specifically at securing citizenship rights and participation for marginal and subordinate groups.

Since it is abundantly clear that 'wider radical political projects' are unlikely ever to be on the agenda of development industry, the re-politicisation of participation must take place outside the institutional development agenda and within the social, political, and cultural context of grassroots struggle.

Power is, as it has always been, at the centre of the participation paradigm. But, as we have discussed, the institutionalised understandings of empowerment seek to contain the concept within the bounds of the existing order, and empowerment becomes the management of power when in the hands of the powerful. Institutionalised development, unable to accept or assume the original connotations of power and empowerment that participation carried with it, manoeuvred to create new interpretations of the concept. Principal among them is the idea of power as something which could be 'given' by the powerful to the powerless. Of course, as Tandon (1996:33) points out, this is highly problematic:

> Those who 'give' power condition it; it has to be taken. It is through the active struggle for rights that you secure those rights. It is through the active struggle for resources that you secure those resources. That is the lesson of history.

Empowerment, disassociated from the broader societal issues that generate poverty and disenfranchisement, is reduced to sharing in the cycle of development projects; but, as White (1996) notes, 'sharing through participation does not necessarily mean sharing in power'. If empowerment, as Guijt (1998) states, is about the transformative capacity of people or groups, and there is no collective analysis of the causes of oppression or marginalisation and what actions can be taken to confront and affect those causes, then any efforts are unlikely to be empowering. Genuine empowerment is about poor people seizing and constructing *popular power* through their own praxis. It is not handed down from the powerful to the powerless, as institutional development has conveniently chosen to interpret the concept. Those who give power condition it, for, as Paulo Freire (1970) best put it himself: 'Freedom is acquired by conquest, not by gift'.

Towards other, better possible worlds

> I am not a subject but rather I create myself as one, as a subject. I continually become; I continually place myself as a subject. There is no subject without becoming one as such. To become is a verb and not a noun. If others place me as a subject, I am not a subject but an object, because I have been placed as one. All domination is based on positioning the other as an object. (Drí 1998: 1)

Today's globalised world is characterised by a vast concentration of wealth that implies a parallel concentration of political power. This has led to the exclusion of the global majorities, denying them any meaningful economic or political participation. The inability of these expanding majorities to attain a dignified life, not in consumer-led opulence espoused by the modernisation paradigm, but at least free from misery, renders political democracy meaningless. Rather than being subjects of their own political power, the global poor are objects of neo-liberal capital, overwhelmed by global forces that they do not see or comprehend. After all, political power is nothing if it does not serve as a vehicle to assert control over – or *govern* – one's present and future life. One cannot speak of participation when a few global power brokers decide the fates of more than two thirds of the world's population.

Most Third World societies are experiencing crisis in governance, brought on by militarisation, transnational corporate control, and corrupt governments created in the service of neo-liberal globalisation. These phenomena have undermined all democratic capacity at the formal institutional level and created a sort of political vacuum. This political vacuum could be interpreted as *a strategically favourable situation for building upon local people's decision-making capacity and grassroots action,* for building popular power and self-governance. However, this first political vacuum is related to a second, which can be called *the absence of spaces and a culture for meaningful participation.* In societies with historically paternalistic or authoritarian structures or current de-democratised neo-liberal regimes, the spaces for meaningful social and popular participation are constantly reduced. As a consequence, the necessary *culture of participation* is displaced by the Freirean 'culture of silence'.

The above begs the question: *What exactly do we wish to participate in?* Can we continue to accept a form of participation that is simply added on to any social project, i.e. neo-liberal modernisation and development, creating an alibi for development by transferring ownership to the poor in the name of empowerment? Or should participation be re-located in the radical politics of social transformation by reaffirming its counter-hegemonic roots?

We must not lose sight of the fact that the underlying principle of those approaches to participation was the struggle for deep social transformation. This is something quite different from institutional reform, or development. The context of the global political economy of power and powerlessness places new responsibility on participatory activists and practitioners to reconstitute participation as an instrument for promoting social transformation. The recovery of the emancipatory meaning of participation implies re-grounding in the radical roots of liberatory/popular education and participatory action research, to re-situate the transformative proposal in the twenty-first century neo-liberal world order and reconstruct the spaces and culture for participation and the exercise of popular power. In this logic, Orlando Fals-Borda (2000), the renowned PAR pioneer, creates the concept of *people's SpaceTimes* as the 'place' where we, as grassroots practitioners and activists, can initiate our political–pedagogic work:

> [...] people's SpaceTimes are concrete social configurations where diversity is part of normality, and 'where people weave the present into their particular thread of history' (Sachs 1992:112). Local affirmation, collective memory, and traditional practices are fundamental in such SpaceTimes. Here life and cultural identities, mutual aid and cooperative institutions are formed, personality is shaped, and collective rights have priority over individual rights. Hence it is not surprising that many of the mechanisms used in SpaceTimes by the common people to defend themselves are those to which they have had recourse throughout the centuries, mechanisms and practices which they know best for survival in basic struggles such as those for land, power, and culture. (Fals-Borda 2000: 628)

The struggle to fill people's SpaceTimes is the struggle to counteract the hegemony of global capitalist power. It is thus the struggle for political power; it is the struggle for cultural recognition or affirmation of alternative constructs of 'the good life'; it is the struggle for control over territories, communities, and their resources or the defence of the space of material and cultural reproduction (Fals-Borda 2000). For local people to construct this type of popular power, they must engage in their own political and economic analysis of the local, national, and global realities, which will in turn determine their capacity to influence and affect power relations at higher social levels.

As such, there lies before us the historic task, as participatory practitioners and activists, to be active protagonists in the reconstruction and re-dimensioning of the social subject which will frontally engage the world of twenty-first century capitalist society by creating new political and cultural imaginaries and make the push towards transformation. This juncture drives us all to make value-based, philosophical, and ideological stands with respect to our own praxis, beginning with the recognition that our primary task is, as it should always have been, not to reform institutional development practice but to transform society.

Note

1. For some examples, see John Hammond (1998), Bud Hall (1997), and Paulo Freire (1978).

References

Chambers, Robert (1983) *Rural Development? Putting the Last First*, Harlow: Longman.

Chossudovsky, Michel (2002) *The Globalization of Poverty: The Impacts of IMF and World Bank Reforms*, Mexico: Siglo XXI Editores. (Spanish version)

Cooke, Bill and Uma Kothari (eds.) (2001) *Participation: The New Tyranny?*, London/New York: Zed Books.

Cornwall, A. and K. Brock (2005) 'What do buzzwords do for development policy? A critical look at "participation", "empowerment" and "poverty re-duction"', *Third World Quarterly* 26 (7): 1043–60.

Cowen, Michael and Robert Shenton (1995) 'The invention of development', in Jonathon Crush (ed.) *Power of Development*, London: Routledge.

Drí, Rubén (1998) 'Crisis y reconstruccio´n del sujeto polí´tico popular', paper presented at Primeras Jornadas de Teoría y Filosofía Política, Buenos Aires, 21–22 August, Facultad de Ciencias Sociales, Universidad de Buenos Aires. Available at: www.clacso.org/ www.clacso/espanol/html/biblioteca/sala/sala2.html.

Escobar, Arturo (1995) 'Imagining a post-development era', in J. Crush (ed.) *Power of Development*, London: Routledge.

Fals-Borda, Orlando (2000) 'People's SpaceTimes in global processes: the response of the local', *Journal of World-Systems Research* 3 (Fall/Winter): 624–34.

Fals-Borda, Orlando, and Muhammad Anisur Rahman (eds.) (1991) *Action and Knowledge: Breaking the Monopoly with Participatory Action-Research*, New York, NY: Apex Press.

Freire, Paulo (1970) *The Pedagogy of the Oppressed*, New York, NY: Continuum.

Freire, Paulo (1978) *Pedagogy in Process: Letters to Guinea Bissau*, New York, NY: Continuum.

Galeano, Eduardo (2002) 'Paradojas', *La Jornada*, México City, 19 October.

Guijt, Irene (1998) 'Waking up to power, conflict and process', in I. Guijt and K. Shah (eds.) *The Myth of Community*, London: IT Publications.

Hall, Budd L. (1997) 'Reflections on the Origins of the International Participa-tory Research Network and the Participatory Research Group in Toronto, Canada', paper presented to the Midwest Research to Practice Conference in Adult, Continuing and Community Education, Michigan State Univer-sity East Lansing, Michigan, 15–17 October.

Hammond, John (1988) *Fighting to Learn: Popular Education and Guerrilla War in El Salvador*, Piscataway, NJ: Rutger's University Press.

Hickey, S. and G. Mohan (eds.) (2004) *From Tyranny to Transformation? Exploring New Approaches to Participation*, London: Zed Books.

Leal, Pablo and Robert Opp (1999) 'Participation and Development in the Age of Globalization: Institutional Contradictions and Grassroots Solutions', available at www.pdforum.org. Abridged version published in *Development Dialogue*, published by CIDA.

Moore, David (1995) 'Development discourse as hegemony: towards an ideological history – 1945–1995', in David Moore and Gerald Schmitz (eds.) *Debating Development Discourse: Institutional and Popular Perspectives*, London: Macmillan.

Narayan, Deepa, Raj Patel, Kai Schafft, Anne Rademacher and Sarah Koch-Schulte (2000) *Voices of the Poor: Can Anyone Hear Us?*, New York, NY: Oxford University Press/World Bank.

Pieterse, Jan Nederveen (1991) 'Dilemmas of development discourse: the crisis of developmentalism and the comparative method', *Development and Change* 22(1): 5–29.

Porter, Doug J. (1995) 'Scenes from childhood: the homesickness of development discourses', in Jonathan Crush (ed.), *Power of Development*, London and New York: Routledge.

Rahman, Muhammad Anisur (1993) *People's Self-Development: Perspectives on Participatory Action Research*, London/Dhaka: Zed Books and Dhaka University Press.

Rahnema, Majid (1990) 'Participatory action research: the "Last Temptation of Saint Development"', *Alternatives* 15:199–226.

Tandon, Yash (1996) 'Poverty, process of impoverishment and empowerment', in Vangile Titi and Narech Singh (eds.) *Empowerment for Sustainable Development: Toward Operational Strategies*, London: Zed Books.

United Nations General Assembly (2000) United Nations Millennium Declaration: Resolution adopted by the General Assembly, www.un.org/millennium/declaration/ares552e.pdf.

White, Sarah C. (1996) 'Depoliticising development: the uses and abuses of participation', *Development in Practice* 6(1): 6–15.

Williams, Glyn (2004) 'Towards a re-politicisation of participatory development: political capabilities and spaces of empowerment', in S. Hickey and G. Mohan (eds.) *From Tyranny to Transformation? Exploring new approaches to participation*, London: Zed Books.

World Bank (1989) *Sub-Saharan Africa: From Crisis to Sustainable Growth*, Washington, DC: World Bank.

About the author

Pablo Alejandro Leal is Professor of Political Economy at the Benito Juárez University of Oaxaca State and a professor of development theory, popular education, and participatory action-research at the Oaxaca campus of the National Pedagogic University. He is also an active member of the Zapatista Collective of Oaxaca.

CHAPTER 9
Citizenship: a perverse confluence

Evelina Dagnino

This chapter discusses the different meanings that citizenship has assumed in Latin America in the past few decades. Its main argument is that, in the perverse confluence between neo-liberal and democratic participatory projects, the common reference to citizenship, used by different political actors, projects an apparent homogeneity, obscuring differences and diluting the conflict between those projects.

Citizenship has become an increasingly recurrent term in the political vocabularies of social movements, and more recently NGOs, governments, and international development agencies. In Latin America, its emergence is linked with the experiences of social movements during the late 1970s and 1980s, reinforced by democratisation efforts, especially in those countries still under authoritarian or military regimes. It swiftly became a common reference point among a range of social movements such as those of women, black people and ethnic minorities, gays, older people, consumers, environmentalists, urban and rural workers, and those organised around urban issues such as decent housing, health, education, unemployment, and violence (Foweraker 1995; Alvarez *et al.* 1998).

For Latin American social movements, the reference to citizenship was not only a useful tool in their own specific struggles but also a powerful link among them. The general claim for equal rights already embedded in the conventional concept of citizenship was both expanded and given particular meanings in relation to specific claims. The process of redefinition placed a strong emphasis on the cultural dimension of citizenship, incorporating contemporary concerns with subjectivities, identities, and the right to difference. This new citizenship was seen as reaching far beyond the acquisition of legal rights: it depended on citizens being active social subjects, defining their rights, and struggling for these rights to be recognised. At the same time, the emphasis on culture asserted the need for a radical transformation of cultural practices that reproduce social inequality and exclusion.

As a result of its growing influence, citizenship soon became a contested concept in Latin America (Dagnino 2004). From the 1990s onwards, it has been appropriated by the elites and by the state to encompass a variety of meanings. In the neo-liberal perspective, citizenship is understood primarily as the integration of individuals into the market, while at the same time previously acquired rights, in particular labour rights, are being progressively eroded. Meanwhile, in response to increasing poverty and social exclusion, there has been a resurgence of philanthropic endeavours from the so-called Third Sector, which convey their own version of citizenship.

The contested definitions of citizenship are the principal axis of political struggles in Latin America today, a reflection of the confrontation between a democratising, participatory project to extend the meaning of citizenship and the neo-liberal offensive to curtail any such possibility. In this chapter, I draw on the experience of Brazil in relation to these issues in order to highlight the challenges and contradictions to be addressed in using the term *citizenship* in international development discourse.

A perverse confluence

Today's democratisation processes are locked in a perverse confluence of two distinct political projects. On the one hand, many countries have seen the increasing involvement of civil society in discussion and decision making about public policy. In Brazil, in particular, efforts to enlarge democracy through participation have been recognised and incorporated in the 1988 Constitution. As a result, the confrontational relations between the state and civil society have been largely replaced by an investment by social movements in the possibility of joint initiatives and in institutional participation in the newly created participatory spaces (see, for example, Abers 1998; Dagnino *et al.* 1998; Fedozzi 1997; Santos 1998). At the same time, neo-liberal governments throughout Latin America are bent on achieving a reduced, minimal state[1] that progressively abandons its role in guaranteeing universal rights by rolling back its social responsibilities and transferring them to civil society, now envisaged as a mere implementer of social policies.

The perverse nature of the confluence between the participatory and the neo-liberal projects lies in the fact that both not only require a vibrant and proactive civil society, but also share several core notions, such as *citizenship*, *participation*, and *civil society*, albeit used with very different meanings. The common vocabulary and shared institutional mechanisms obscure fundamental distinctions and divergences. The apparent homogeneity conceals conflict and contradictions by displacing dissonant meanings.

The neo-liberal project has also re-defined meanings in the cultural sphere. The notion of citizenship offers perhaps the most dramatic case of how such meanings are displaced. First, because it was precisely through the notion of citizenship that the participatory project managed to achieve its most important political and cultural gains, to the extent of generating an innovative definition that has penetrated deep into Brazil's political and cultural fabric (Dagnino 1994a; 1998). And second because such a displacement determines how the most critical challenge facing Latin America – inequality and poverty – is addressed.

Participatory citizenship

Citizenship came to prominence as a crucial weapon in the struggle against social and economic exclusion and inequality, and in broadening the prevailing conception of politics. Thus, the struggles for a deepening of democracy that were undertaken by social movements in Latin America sought to redefine citizenship by challenging the existing definition of what constituted the political arena – its participants, its institutions, its processes, its agenda, and its scope (Alvarez *et al.* 1998).

Adopting as its point of departure the notion of *a right to have rights*, this new definition of citizenship enabled new social subjects to identify what they considered to be their rights and to struggle for their recognition. In contrast to a view of citizenship as a strategy by the elites and by the state for the gradual and limited political incorporation of excluded sectors of society, or as a legal and political condition necessary for the establishment of capitalism, this is a definition of non-citizens, of the excluded: a citizenship 'from below'.

Much of the attraction of citizenship and its core category of rights lies in the dual role that it has played in the debates on democracy that characterise contemporary politics in Latin America. The struggle for the recognition and extension of rights helped to make the argument for the expansion and deepening of democracy much more concrete. And the reference to citizenship provided common ground and shared principles for a huge diversity of social movements that adopted the language of rights as a way to express their demands. This in turn helped these movements to avoid fragmentation and isolation. Thus the building of citizenship was always conceived as a struggle for the expansion of democracy that could incorporate both a broad range of demands and particular concrete struggles for rights, such as the rights to housing, education, and health care, whose achievement would further deepen democracy.

The focus of social movements on the need to assert the right to have rights is clearly related to extreme levels of poverty and exclusion, but also to the pervasive authoritarianism and hierarchical organisation of Brazilian society. Class, race, and gender differences have historically underpinned the social classification that pervades our cultures by establishing each person's 'place' in the social hierarchy. Thus, for marginalised sectors, the political relevance of cultural meanings that are embedded in social practices is part of their daily life. As in most Latin American societies, to be poor means not only to experience economic or material deprivation, but also to submit to cultural rules that convey a complete lack of recognition of poor people as subjects, bearers of rights. In what Telles (1994) called the incivility embedded in that tradition, poverty is a sign of inferiority, a form of existence that makes it impossible for individuals to exercise their rights. The cultural deprivation imposed by the absolute absence of rights – which is essentially the denial of human dignity – finds its expression in material deprivation and political exclusion.

The perception of cultural social authoritarianism as a dimension of exclusion, in addition to economic inequality and political subordination, constituted a significant element in the struggle to redefine citizenship. First, it made clear that the struggle for rights, for the right to have rights, had to be a political struggle, thus enabling the urban popular movements to establish the link between culture and politics which became embedded in their collective action. The experience of the *Assembléia do Povo* (People's Assembly) from 1979 to the early 1980s, a movement of *favelados* (shanty-town dwellers) in Campinas in the state of São Paulo, illustrates this. Right from the start of their struggle for the 'right to the use of the land', *favelados* knew that they would have to struggle first for their very right to have rights. Thus, their first public initiative was to ask the media to publicise the results of their own survey of the *favelas*, in order to show the city that they were not idlers, misfits, or prostitutes, as they were assumed to be, but decent working citizens who therefore should be seen as bearers of rights (Dagnino 1994b).

Making this connection made it possible to establish alliances with other social movements – such as ethnic, feminist, gay, ecological, and human-rights movements – in seeking more egalitarian social relations and helping to articulate a distinctive, enlarged view of democracy. Rights and citizenship (Santos 1979) became the core of a common ethical–political field in which many of these movements and other sectors could share and reinforce each other's struggles. For instance, the emergence of the *Sindicato Cidadão* (Citizen Trade Unions) in the early 1990s shows that this vision penetrated even the Brazilian labour movement (Rodrigues 1997), traditionally associated with a more strictly class-based stance.

Secondly, the broader scope of citizenship went far beyond the formal legal acquisition of a set of rights within the political–judicial system. Rather, it represented a *project for a new sociability*: a more egalitarian way of organising all social relations, new rules for living together in society (new ways to deal with conflicts, and a new sense of a public order, of public responsibility, a renewed social contract) and not only the incorporation into the political system in the strict sense. More egalitarian social relations imply recognising the other as having valid interests and rights, and the constitution of a public domain in which rights determine the parameters for discussion, debate, and the negotiation of conflicts, thus bringing in an ethical dimension to social relations. Such a vision is profoundly unsettling for both the social authoritarianism that characterises Brazilian society and for more recent neo-liberal discourses that elevate the importance of private interests at the expense of an ethical dimension to social life (Telles 1994).

Thirdly, once rights are no longer limited to legal provisions, access to existing rights, or the implementation of formal rights, it is possible to include new rights that emerge from specific struggles or campaigns. In this sense, the definition of rights and the assertion of something as a right become themselves the objects of political struggle. The rights to autonomy over one's own body, to environmental protection, or to housing, for instance, illustrate something of the diversity of these new rights. The inclusion not only of the right to equality, but also the right to difference, specifies, deepens, and broadens the right to equality (Dagnino 1994a).

Fourthly, an additional element in this redefinition transcends a central reference in the liberal concept of citizenship: the claim to access, inclusion, membership, and belonging to an already given political system. What is really at stake in struggles for citizenship in Brazil is more than the right to be included as a full member of society; it is the right to participate in the very definition of that society and its political system, to define *what we want to be members of*. The direct participation of civil society and social movements in state decisions constitutes one of the most crucial aspects in the redefinition of citizenship, because it conveys a potential for radical transformations in the structure of power relations that characterise Latin American societies.

A further consequence of such a broadening in scope is that citizenship is no longer confined to the relationship between the individual and the state, but becomes a parameter for all social relations. This may be more evident for social movements of women, blacks, or gays, for example, since such a significant part of their struggles is concerned with fighting the discrimination and prejudice that they face in every aspect of daily life. The process of building citizenship as the affirmation and recognition of rights was seen as a way to transform deeply embedded social practices. Such a political strategy implies moral and intellectual reform: a process of social learning, of building new kinds of social relations in which citizens become active social subjects. It also means that all members of society have to learn to live on different terms with citizens who refuse to accept the social and cultural places previously ascribed to them.

Social movements, whether organised around basic claims such as housing, water, sewage, education, and health care, or broader interests such as those of women, blacks, or ecological movements, emphasised that citizenship meant the constitution of active social subjects who can thus become political actors. Some even defined citizenship as consisting of this very process. Thus consciousness, agency, and the capacity to struggle are evidence of one's citizenship, even if other rights are absent. Among 51 activists interviewed in Campinas, São Paulo, in 1993, most members of popular movements and of workers' unions expressed this view. By contrast, answering the same question – *'Why do you consider yourself a citizen?'* – members of business organisations stressed the fact that they *'fulfil their duties'* and *'have rights'*, whereas the middle-class activists highlighted their *'position in society'*, derived from their professional activities, as indicators of citizenship. Interestingly, while a large majority of these two sectors considered that they were treated as citizens, a similar majority of those belonging to social movements and workers' unions expressed the opposite view (Dagnino 1998: 40–41).

The role of the social movements of the 1970s and 1980s in shaping this redefinition of citizenship is obviously rooted in their own struggles and practices. Although they drew on a history of rights that had given rise to *regulated citizenship* (Santos 1979), they reacted against the conception of the state and of power embedded in that history. They also reacted against the control and tutelage of the political organisation of popular sectors by the state, political parties, and politicians. Their conception of rights and citizenship embodied a reaction against previous notions of rights as favours and/or objects of bargain with the powerful (as in the case of citizenship by concession, *cidadania concedida*) (Sales 1994). In this sense, the struggle for rights, also influenced by the 1970s human-rights movements against the military regime, encapsulated not only claims for equality but the negation of a dominant political culture deeply rooted in Brazilian society.

This notion of citizenship and the participation of civil society as a mechanism for its extension were formally recognised in the 1988 Constitution. The Collor government, brought to power in 1989, began the move to neo-liberalism, which reached its peak under Cardoso from 1994 to 2002, and created what we have referred to as the perverse confluence between the two political projects. Citizenship was once again redefined in neo-liberal terms, in order to neutralise the meanings that the term had acquired in its use by social movements while trying to retain its symbolic power.

Neo-liberal versions of citizenship

Some neo-liberal definitions of citizenship retrieve the traditional liberal conception, while others address new elements in the contemporary political and social configurations in Latin America. First, the collective meaning given by the social movements is reduced to a strictly individualistic understanding. Second, neo-liberal discourses establish an alluring connection between citizenship and the market. To be a citizen is equated with individual integration in the market, as a consumer and as a producer. This seems to be the basic principle underlying the vast number of projects to enable people to 'acquire citizenship': that is to say, to learn how to start up micro-enterprises, or how to become qualified for the few jobs still available. As the state retreats from its role as guarantor of rights, the market is offered as a surrogate for citizenship. Hence, social rights enshrined in the Brazilian Constitution since the 1940s and reaffirmed in 1988 are now being eliminated, on the grounds that they impede the freedom of the market and therefore restrict economic development and modernisation. This rationale effectively casts bearers of rights/ citizens as unpatriotic, privileged enemies of political reforms intended to shrink state responsibilities. Previously guaranteed rights to social services are increasingly viewed as commodities to be purchased by those who can afford them. This effectively turns the market into a surrogate for citizenship, the incarnation of modernising virtues and the sole route for the Latin American dream: inclusion in the First World.

A further aspect of neo-liberal versions of citizenship is in the formulation of social policies on poverty and inequality. Many of the struggles organised around the demand for equal rights and the extension of citizenship focused on how such policies should be defined. The participation of social movements and other sectors of civil society was a fundamental claim in the struggles for citizenship, in the belief that this would contribute to social policies that would ensure that all citizens enjoyed universal rights. With the rolling back of the state, these social policies are increasingly formulated as emergency responses for those whose very survival is at risk. The targets of these policies are not seen as citizens who are entitled to rights but as 'needy' (*carentes*) human beings requiring public or private charity. In the face of the gravity and urgency of the situation, reinforced by cuts in social spending, many sectors of civil society called upon to participate in the name of 'building citizenship' choose to subordinate their belief in the universality of rights and surrender to the immediate practical possibility of helping a handful of the destitute.

The notion of a 'Third Sector' (the others being the State and the Market) as a surrogate for civil society is particularly expressive of this attempt to implement a 'minimalist' politics and to collapse the public spaces for political deliberation that had been opened up by the democratising struggles of previous decades (Avritzer 2002). The relationship between the state and NGOs exemplifies this perverse confluence. Endowed with technical competence and social insertion as 'reliable' interlocutors in civil society, NGOs are frequently seen as the ideal partners to assume the responsibilities handed over by the state to civil society or to the private sector (see also Alvarez 1999 for the impact of this process in depoliticising feminist organisations in Brazil). Parallel to this is the government's tendency to 'criminalise' social movements that remain combative and well organised, such as the Landless Movement (MST) and some trade unions. Reinforced by the mass media and international aid agencies, there is a growing sense that 'civil society' is synonymous with NGOs, if not equated with the 'Third Sector'. In this scheme of things, 'civil society' is thus reduced to those sectors whose behaviour is 'acceptable' to the government, or to what one analyst referred to as 'the five-star civil society' (Silva 2001).

Conclusion

This analysis has important consequences for the contested conceptions of citizenship, such as the displacement of issues such as poverty and inequality: in being addressed solely as technical or philanthropic issues, poverty and inequality are effectively withdrawn from the public (political) arena and so from the proper domain of justice, equality, and citizenship, and reduced to a problem of ensuring minimum conditions for survival.

Moreover, the solution to the problem of poverty and inequality is presented as an individual moral duty. The idea of a collective solidarity that underlies the classical reference to rights and citizenship is being replaced by an understanding of solidarity as a strictly private moral responsibility. This is why civil society is being urged to engage in voluntary and philanthropic work. It is no coincidence that voluntary work is becoming the favourite hobby of the Brazilian middle class. This understanding of citizenship also accords with that held by corporate foundations. Seeking to maximise profits while also nurturing a public image of 'social responsibility', these foundations also view solidarity as a question of individual ethics, with no reference to universal rights or to the political debate on the causes of poverty and inequality.

This 're-signification' of the notions of citizenship and solidarity block off their political dimension and erode the sense of public responsibility and public interest that had been so hard-won in the democratising struggles of Brazil's recent past. As the targeted distribution of social services and benefits comes to occupy the place formerly held by rights and citizenship, so the institutional channels through which to claim rights are closed down; instead, distribution depends only on the good will and competence of those involved. It becomes increasingly difficult, therefore, even to formulate the notion of rights within the public sphere (Telles 2001). The symbolic importance of rights as the cornerstone of an egalitarian society is thus being dismissed in favour of social relations based on individualism.

A second set of consequences relates to the participation of civil society, another central plank of the democratising project that has been re-signified. While the neo-liberal project requires the participation of civil society, this increasingly means that organisations of civil society take over the role of the state in providing services. The effective sharing of decision-making power, i.e. the full exercise of citizenship as conceived by democratising forces, takes place in most cases within the limits of a neo-liberal framework, with decision-making power remaining the preserve of the 'strategic nucleus' of the state (Bresser-Pereira 1999). The political meaning of participation has thus been reduced to management, and related concerns with efficiency and 'client satisfaction' have come to replace the political debate on inequality and social justice.

The perverse confluence described here constitutes a minefield in which sectors of civil society, including NGOs, that do not support the project of the minimal state feel deceived when, motivated by the shared vocabulary of citizenship, they get involved in initiatives with government sectors that are committed to rolling back the state. Many of the social movements who participate in public spaces to formulate public policies share the same reaction. Some of them define this situation as a dilemma, and several contemplate rejecting altogether any further joint initiatives, or being extremely cautious with respect to the correlation of forces within these initiatives and the concrete possibilities opened by them (Dagnino 2002).

Under an apparent homogeneity of discourse, what is at stake in these spaces is the advancement or retreat of very different political projects and conceptions of citizenship. Although the election in 2002 of Luís Inácio Lula da Silva of the Workers' Party (PT) renewed hopes that the democratic participatory project would advance, his broad coalition government has not been immune to the effects of the perverse confluence described in this chapter. Ironically, since the PT itself emerged in the 1980s as a result of civil society's struggles around the building of citizenship, the government's social policies – an increase in their number and scope notwithstanding – are still largely following the same neo-liberal directions. Resolving the perverse confluence and reaffirming a radical conception of citizenship is the difficult and urgent task now facing social movements and democratic sectors of civil society.

Acknowledgement

This chapter draws on the author's earlier work '"We all have rights but…": contesting conceptions of citizenship in Brazil', in Naila Kabeer (ed.) *Inclusive Citizenship: Meanings and Expressions of Citizenship*, London: Zed Books, 2005, pp. 147–63.

Notes

1. Clearly, this state is only selectively minimal: it is minimal regarding social policies towards the poor, but not with respect to the protection of capitalist interests, as in the case of government efforts to save banks from financial failure.

References

Abers, Rebecca (1998) 'From clientelism to cooperation: local government, participatory policy, and civic organizing in Porto Alegre, Brazil', *Politics & Society* 26(4): 511–37.

Alvarez, Sonia E. (1999) 'Advocating feminism: the Latin American feminist NGO "boom"', *International Feminist Journal of Politics* 1(2): 181–209.

Alvarez, Sonia E., Evelina Dagnino, and Arturo Escobar (eds.) (1998) *Cultures of Politics/Politics of Cultures: Revisioning Latin American Social Movements*, Boulder, CO: Westview Press.

Avritzer, Leonardo (2002) *Democracy and Public Spaces in Latin America*, Princeton, NJ: Princeton University Press.

Bresser-Pereira, Luiz Carlos (1999) 'From bureaucratic to managerial: public administration in Brazil' in *Reforming the State: Managerial Public Administration in Latin America*, Luis Carlos Bresser Pereira and Peter Spink (eds.) Boulder, CO: Lynne Rienner, pp. 115–46.

Dagnino, Evelina (1994a) 'Os movimentos sociais e a emergência de uma nova noção de cidadania', in E. Dagnino (ed.) *Os Anos 90: Política e Sociedade no Brasil*, São Paulo: Brasiliense

Dagnino, Evelina (1994b) 'On becoming a citizen: the story of D. Marlene', in Rina Benmayor and Andor Skotnes (eds.) *International Yearbook of Oral History and Life Stories*, Oxford: Oxford University Press.

Dagnino, Evelina (1998) 'Culture, citizenship, and eemocracy: changing discourses and practices of the Latin American left', in S. Alvarez, E. Dagnino, and A. Escobar (eds.).

Dagnino, Evelina (2002) *Sociedade Civil e Espaços Públicos no Brasil*, São Paulo: Paz e Terra.

Dagnino, Evelina (2004) 'Sociedade civil, participação e cidadania: de que estamos falando?', in Daniel Mato and Illia Garcı́a (eds.) *Políticas de Ciudadania y Sociedad Civil en Tiempos de Globalización*, Caracas: Universidad Central de Venezuela.

Dagnino, Evelina, Ana Cláudia Chaves Teixeira, Daniela Romanelli da Silva, e Uliana Ferlim (1998) 'Cultura democrática e cidadania', *Opinião Pública*, V(1), November, 11–43.

Fedozzi, Luciano (1997) *Orçamento Participativo – Reflexões sobre a experiência de Porto Alegre*, Porto Alegre: Tomo Editorial/FASE.

Foweraker, Joe (1995) *Theorizing Social Movements*, London: Pluto Press.

Rodrigues, Iram Jácome (1997) *Sindicalismo e Política: A Trajetória da CUT*, São Paulo: Scritta/ FAPESP.

Sales, Teresa (1994) 'Raízes da desigualdade social na cultura Brasileira', *Revista Brasileira de Ciências Sociais* (ANPOCS) 9(25): 26–37.

Santos, Boaventura de Souza (1998) 'Participatory budgeting in Porto Alegre: toward a redistributive democracy', *Politics and Society* 26(4): 461–510.

Santos, Wanderley Guilherme dos (1979) *Cidadania e Justiça*, Rio de Janeiro: Campus.

Silva, Cátia Aida (2001) Comment during a debate transcribed in *Os Movimentos Sociais, a Sociedade Civil e o 'Terceiro Setor na América Latina: Reflexões Teóricas e Novas Perspectivas*, (co-organização com Sonia E. Alvarez) *Primeira Versão 98*, Outubro, Campinas: IFCH, UNICAMP, pp. 1–77.

Telles, Vera da Silva (1994) 'A sociedade civil e a construção de um espaço público', in E. Dagnino (ed.), *Os Anos 90: Política e Sociedade no Brasil*, São Paulo: Brasiliense.

Telles, Vera da Silva (2001) *Pobreza e Cidadania*, São Paulo: Editora 34.

About the author

Evelina Dagnino is a Professor of Political Science at the State University of Campinas (Unicamp) in São Paulo and has been a Visiting Professor at the Universities of Yale and Göteborg. She has published extensively on the relations between culture and politics, social movements, civil society and participation, and democracy and citizenship.

CHAPTER 10

Taking the power out of empowerment – an experiential account

Srilatha Batliwala

This chapter traces the centuries-long evolution of the concept and practice of empowerment, its adoption by radical social movements, especially women's movements from the 1970s onwards, and its conversion, by the late 1990s, into a buzzword. Situating the analysis in the context of women's empowerment interventions in India, the chapter describes the dynamic of the depoliticisation and subversion of a process that challenged the deepest structures of social power. The 'downsizing' and constriction of the concept within state policy, the de-funding of genuine empowerment strategies on the ground, and the substitution of microfinance and political quotas for empowerment are examined and analysed.

Of all the buzzwords that have entered the development lexicon in the past 30 years, *empowerment* is probably the most widely used and abused. Like many other important terms that were coined to represent a clearly *political* concept, it has been 'mainstreamed' in a manner that has virtually robbed it of its original meaning and strategic value. It is one of the best examples of what I have elsewhere described as the

> ...distortion of good ideas and innovative practices as they are lifted out of the political and historical context in which they evolved and rendered into formulas that are 'mainstreamed'. This usually involves divesting the idea of its cultural specificity, its political content, and generalizing it into a series of rituals and steps that simulate its original elements, but lacking the transformative power of the real thing. Thus good ideas – evolved to address specific development challenges – are altered into universally applicable panaceas. Transferring the correct rhetoric – buzzwords and catch phrases emptied of their original meaning – is a vital part of this legerdemain. (Batliwala 2007:89)

A brief history

Both the word itself and the concept of empowerment have a fascinating history.[1] According to some recent research into the term's origins and meanings (Gaventa 2002), it can be traced back as early as the Protestant Reformation in

Europe and it reverberates through the centuries in Europe and North America through Quakerism, Jeffersonian democracy, early capitalism, and the black power movement. The concept of empowerment, although expressed in other linguistic equivalents, was embedded in many other historic struggles for social justice: in my own state of Karnataka in southern India, for instance, the twelfth-and thirteenth-century Veerashaiva movement against caste and gender oppression called for the redistribution of power and access to spiritual knowledge through the destruction of these forms of social stratification. But the term became revitalised and acquired a strongly political meaning in the latter half of the twentieth century, when it was adopted by the liberation theology, popular education, black power, feminist and other movements engaged in struggles for more equitable, participatory, and democratic forms of social change and development.

From these historically, politically, and geographically diverse locations, empowerment was hijacked, in the 1990s, into increasingly bizarre locations, converted from a collective to an individualistic process, and skilfully co-opted by conservative and even reactionary political ideologies in pursuit of their agenda of divesting 'big government' (for which read: the welfare state) of its purported power and control by 'empowering' communities to look after their own affairs. Management gurus discovered 'empowerment' and infused it into the human-resource development and motivational practices of the corporate world, turning it to the service of profit making and competitiveness in the market place. Thus the 1990s witnessed a widespread co-option of the term by corporate management, neo-con political movements, and consumer-rights advocates.

What's in a word?

Should we be troubled by what many may consider the inevitable subversion of an attractive term that can successfully traverse such diverse and even ideologically opposed terrain? I believe we should, because it represents not some innocent linguistic fad but a more serious and subterranean process of challenging and subverting the politics that the term was created to symbolise. This political project is most clearly evident in the domain of women's empowerment, and I shall use the subversion and de-politicisation of the term within this context, particularly in my country – India – to demonstrate why it is a matter of concern.

The concept of women's empowerment emerged from several important critiques and debates generated by the women's movement throughout the world during the 1980s, when feminists, particularly in the Third World, were increasingly discontent with the largely apolitical and economistic 'WID', 'WAD', and 'GAD' models in prevailing development interventions. There was growing interaction between feminism and the concept and practice of popular education, based on the 'conscientisation' approach developed by Paulo Freire in Latin America in the 1970s as part of his 'liberation theology'. The latter, though representing a powerful new framework that contested the more top–down, paternalistic 'community development' approach that had remained prevalent until then, nevertheless ignored gender and the subordination of women as a critical element of liberation. The re-discovery of Gramsci's 'subalterns' and the hegemonic role of dominant ideologies, and the emergence of social construction theory and post-colonial theory were also important influences on activists and nascent social movements at this time.

The interplay of these powerful new discourses led, by the mid-1980s, to the spread of 'women's empowerment' as a more political and transformatory idea for struggles that challenged not only patriarchy, but also the mediating structures of class, race, ethnicity – and, in India, caste and religion – which determined the nature of women's position and condition in developing societies. By introducing a hitherto absent gender dimension to theories of conscientisation and popular education, by recognising women as part of Gramsci's subaltern classes, feminists incorporated gender subordination and the social construction of gender as a fundamental category of analysis in the practice of social change and development. Feminist movements in the Third World, but particularly in Latin America and South Asia, evolved their own distinctive approach, pushing consciousness-raising into the realm of radical organising and movement building for gender equality. The influence of these discourses had led to the widespread adoption of the empowerment concept in many other development and social-justice arenas, such as education, health care, rural development, and workers' rights. By the beginning of the 1990s, empowerment held pride of place in development jargon. And though it was applied in a broad range of social-change processes, there is little doubt that the term was most widely used with reference to women and gender equality.

It is not surprising, therefore, that 'empowerment' – if not the concepts that informed it – soon became a trendy and widely used buzzword. The sharp political perspective from which it arose became diffused and diluted. Development-assistance agencies (multilateral, bilateral, and private), eternally in search of sexier catchphrases and magic bullets that could somehow fast-track the process of social transformation, took hold of the term and began to use it to replace their earlier terminology of 'people's participation' and 'women's development'. The 1995 Fourth World Conference on Women in Beijing played a critical role in introducing the 'e' word to state actors, and governments anxious to demonstrate a progressive approach to gender quickly adopted the catchphrase of women's empowerment. For instance, signatories to the Beijing Declaration stated that they would dedicate themselves to 'enhancing further the advancement and empowerment of women all over the world ...' (United Nations 1995: 7).

The most important point, however, is that all efforts to conceptualise the term more clearly stressed that empowerment was a *socio-political* process, that the critical operating concept within empowerment was *power*, and that empowerment was about shifts in political, social, and economic power between and across *both* individuals *and* social groups.

How power left empowerment: the Indian experience

Let us now use the Indian case to demonstrate how the once powerful idea and practice of women's empowerment degenerated into a set of largely apolitical, technocratic, and narrow interventions that create nothing like the radical transformation envisaged by early women's movement leaders – and how it was brought to serve neo-liberal economic ends.

Borrowing from the usage of the term by feminist popular educators in other parts of the world, 'empowerment' entered the women's movement lexicon in India by the mid-1980s. Almost at the same time, it replaced the earlier terminology of 'women's welfare', 'women's development', and 'women's up-liftment' in use by the government and major donor agencies supporting work with marginalised women. In 1986, for instance, I co-designed a critical new programme template for the Department of Education, Ministry of Human Resource Development, entitled 'Education for Women's Equality' in which the *empowerment* approach (roughly similar to feminist popular education methods) was strongly advocated. Thus, empowerment as a term entered the gender-equality arena in India through distinctly different political routes: those of feminists challenging patriarchal gender relations, of progressive government policy, and of aid agencies anxious to do something new. By the beginning of the 1990s, therefore, everybody concerned with women's issues and gender equality – state actors, aid agencies, development professionals, and feminist activists and advocates – was using the term 'empowerment'. But in this latter-day development Babel, there was no clarity about what exactly it meant to its various proponents, since the meanings that they attached to it were seldom articulated in any clear or specific way. It was common, in those days, to find the annual reports of NGOs or donor agencies talking about how their objective was empowerment, but it was impossible to find a comprehensive definition of what it signified to them.

In an attempt to clear the conceptual and strategic cloud, I was invited, in 1992, to undertake an exercise of examining how empowerment was understood and operationalised across South Asia by grassroots women's and development organisations with a stated objective of women's empowerment. Through a process of wide consultation and discussion with more than 25 organisations across South Asia and a number of leading feminist activists, a (then) new conceptual and strategic framework was collectively and painstakingly developed over the course of a year, and presented under the title 'Women's Empowerment in South Asia: Concepts and Practices' (Batliwala 1993). At the time, this document provided one of the first detailed conceptualisations of empowerment, constructed from the perception and practice of those consciously engaged in the empowerment of women and in advancing gender equality. This coincided with Naila Kabeer's own research and her influential book *Reversed Realities*, which reflected and greatly enhanced the framework in the South Asia document (Kabeer 1994).

The South Asia document defined empowerment as a process, and the re-sults of a process, of transforming the relations of power between individuals and social groups. Since feminist activists were among the first to use this word widely, it also had a specific gendered meaning: the transformation of the relations of power between men and women, within and across social categories of various kinds. The document defined empowerment as a process that shifts social power in three critical ways: by challenging the ideologies that justify social inequality (such as gender or caste), by changing prevailing patterns of access to and control over economic, natural, and intellectual re-sources, and by transforming the institutions and structures that reinforce and sustain existing power structures (such as the family, state, market, education, and media). The document emphasised that transformatory empowerment could *not* be achieved by tackling any one of these elements of social power – even at that early stage, its architects were clear that there was no 'one-shot' magic-bullet route to women's empowerment, such as providing women with access to credit, enhanced incomes, or land titles. The framework stressed that the ideological and institutional change dimensions were critical to sustaining empowerment and real social transformation.

Through the 1980s and early 1990s, initiatives around the subcontinent, and particularly in India, were engaged in a diverse range of experiments that attempted to enact the process of empowerment on the ground with various marginalised communities, but most often focused on poor rural and urban women. These approaches tried to depart from past interventions that treated women either as beneficiaries of services or as producers or workers. Instead they adopted feminist popular-education strategies that created new spaces for women to collectivise around shared experiences of poverty, exclusion, and discrimination, critically analyse the structures and ideologies that sustained and reinforced their oppression, and raise consciousness of their own sense of subordination. These spaces and the activists working within them facilitated women to recognise their own agency and power for change – their power to organise themselves to confront and transform the social and economic arrangements and cultural systems that subjugated them. The main inputs in these processes were new ideas and information, not hand-outs or services; an opportunity for women to locate and articulate the changes that they wanted to make, and evolve strategies to do so. Grassroots women in different corners of the country, in cities, towns, and villages, were mobilised into *sanghs* or *samoohs*[2] through which they developed a political and personal agenda for change, and the collective strength and creative power to move their agendas forward.

These basic strategies found expression in a range of activities across the country. Women's groups and grassroots women's collectives began to address their unequal access to economic and natural resources, to education, health services, to reproductive health and rights, aiming to change the gender division of labour and access to training, technical skills, and employment. Micro-credit programmes successfully shifted productive resources into poor women's hands and they, in turn, were demonstrating how women's enhanced incomes were applied to raise household nutrition levels and improve the health and education status of their children. There were struggles to make visible and redress the pervasive and diverse forms of violence against women – dowry-related violence and murders, rape, female infanticide and foeticide, domestic violence, caste-based and communal violence that targeted women, and state-sanctioned violence. Major public campaigns were launched for legislative reform and enforcement – for special cells for women in police stations, for greater representation of women in *Panchayat Raj*[3] institutions, for changes in the rape law that would shift the burden of proof from the victim to the perpetrator, for banning or regulating sex-determination and sex-selection technologies, and for more stringent punishment for dowry harassment and domestic violence (see Kumar 1993).

Interestingly, during this entire phase, women's movements saw the state as a critical enabler of the empowerment process, even if their stance was adversarial. In turn, several arms of the Indian state – and especially some committed senior bureaucrats – took the lead in supporting and launching programmes that were built upon a transformative notion of empowerment, providing space for the mobilisation and organisation of some of the country's poorest and most oppressed women to challenge and change their social, political, and economic conditions, even when this meant confronting other sections of the state and its policies and programmes.[4] This support was not entirely altruistic, of course, but often sprang from an astute understanding that these women's empowerment processes might better enable the administration to deliver its schemes and services, outperform other states and provinces in development indicators, and lower the poverty line.

Donor agencies quickly followed suit and abandoned their earlier 'WID', 'WAD', and 'GAD' approaches to adopt the empowerment framework as both an objective and a methodology. While donors did not play a critical role in India in defining or advancing the empowerment approach, they quickly promoted it among their development partners, and many NGOs and women's development organisations were compelled to switch their language, if not their strategies, to fit the new empowerment mantra. This was a huge factor, along with government adoption of the term, in spreading the use of the empowerment terminology and eventually rendering it into a meaningless buzzword.

In retrospect, it is the early successes of the empowerment approach – despite contemporary angst about how difficult it was to measure, or how it took too long to demonstrate impact, and other anxieties – that contributed inadvertently to its subsequent instrumentalisation, and its conversion into not only a buzzword but a magic bullet for poverty alleviation and rapid economic development, rather than a multi-faceted process of social transformation, especially in the arena of gender equality. By the mid-1990s, India had enthusiastically embraced neoliberal economic policies, but it was also an electoral democracy where the poor – particularly the rural poor – were the largest vote banks, who routinely threw out regimes that failed their interests and needs. Opening up rural markets and raising incomes of the poor was thus critical to political survival. In India's populist politics, empowerment was a natural target for co-option by varying political players, most of whom were anxious to limit its transformatory potential.

Consequently, ruling regimes and political parties of various hues rapidly adopted and simultaneously constricted the concept and practice of women's empowerment into two relatively narrow and politically manageable arenas: (1) the so-called 'self-help' women's groups (SHGs) which were meant to simulate the empowering nature of the *sanghs* and *samoohs* mentioned above, but in reality engage in little else but savings and lending; and (2) reservations for women within local self-government bodies which are deemed to lead to political empowerment. Both of these are described as 'women's empowerment' approaches, although there is little evidence that either result in sustained changes in women's position or condition within their families, communities, or society at large. Indeed, there is a growing body of analysis that argues that the empowering effects of these interventions are complex, and that they can consolidate existing power hierarchies as well as create new problems, including manipulation and co-option by dominant political interests, growing indebtedness, doubling and tripling of women's workloads, and new forms of gendered violence (Cornwall and Goetz 2005: 783-800; Burra et al. 2005; Fernando 2006). On the other hand, policies such as rural development, which have the widest sway, have determined that the goals of poverty alleviation and empowerment will be achieved through self-help groups and *panchayats*.[5]

Although virtually every government policy claims to support women's empowerment, a deeper scrutiny of both policy and implementation strategies (available on the websites of every ministry concerned with poverty eradication, marginalised social groups, women and girls) reveals that the broad-based, multi-faceted, and radical consciousness-raising approaches fostered in programmes like Mahila Samakhya in the 1980s and early 1990s have more or less disappeared. Every department's narrow-bandwidth intervention, in the era of increasing divestment and privatisation, is packaged in the language of empowerment. India's rural development policy describes its objectives as poverty alleviation and empowerment, claiming that these will be achieved through the strategies of self-help groups and strengthening local governments, the twin sites of 'women's empowerment'. The Education Department's Women's Empowerment Project offers an even better example of this 'downsized' empowerment strategy:

> Since the overall empowerment of women is crucially dependent on economic empowerment, ... the main purpose of the Women Empowerment Project (WEP) is to organize women into effective Self Help Groups.[6]

In the larger political arena, there has been an equally disturbing trend whereby the idea of women's empowerment has been distorted and co-opted into the ideological frameworks of the religious fundamentalism that has become deeply entrenched in Indian politics: the status of women in certain minority groups, and their need for 'empowerment' (in its vernacular equivalents), was a key component of the Hindu nationalists' ideological and political project, as was the construction of the Hindu woman as the educated, equal, empowered opposite – despite the fact that they remain deeply hostile to the questioning of the disempowerment and subjugation of millions of women with the spread of particular regional and upper-caste Hindu practices such as dowry or female foeticide through sex-selective abortions (Hassan 1998; and Sarkar 1998).

A requiem

In the new millennium, the once-ubiquitous term 'empowerment' has virtually disappeared from the Indian development discourse, including in the context of gender equality, except in a few niches of government policy.[7] I attribute this to several tendencies that began emerging in the late 1990s: the overwhelming sway of the micro-credit model and SHGs as substitutes for the more comprehensive empowerment processes of early feminist activism; the displacement of empowerment by the emergence of the 'rights-based approach' within critiques and counters to neo-liberal reductionist and instrumentalist strategies for economic development and social justice; and the management-influenced 'results-based' approach that has been adopted by a large number of development-assistance programmes and donors, including those that had remained steadfastly opposed to fast-track strategies.

With donors increasingly abandoning empowerment as a no-longer-fashionable – indeed *practical* – methodology, and enthusiastically championing (with a few exceptions) large-scale micro-finance programmes as the quickest route to women's empowerment (*and* overall economic development!), the old feminist concept and practice of empowerment have been interred without ceremony. Grassroots practitioners and movements find that they can no longer raise funds with the language and strategies of empowerment, or that they must disguise these within *au courant* frameworks or rhetoric (such as rights, micro-finance, transparency, accountability, and so forth). Some donors have moved resources out of broader-based empowerment approaches, because they don't show 'countable' results and/or because empowerment doesn't work fast enough.

Because the process – and its effects and impacts – was so shaped by the interests and contexts of those engaged in it, and hence less predictable in its outcomes, the empowerment approach is not sufficiently 'results-oriented', an important priority in current development funding. In such agencies, the 'rights-based' approach (as though empowerment is about anything but rights!) finds greater favour, because rights-based interventions – greater access to redress, achievements of the Millennium Development Goals, new legislation

– are more readily quantified. But these approaches often shift agency into the hands of professional intermediaries (lawyers, NGO activists, policy specialists) and away from marginalised women and communities. They also focus on formal structures and equality, rather than on the informal institutions and cultural systems that older empowerment processes attempted to transform (though not always successfully).

Meanwhile, in keeping with the insidious dominance of the neo-liberal ideology and its consumerist core, we see the transition of empowerment out of the realm of societal and systemic change and into the individual domain – from a noun signifying shifts in social power to a verb signalling individual power, achievement, status. *'Empower yourself'* screamed a billboard advertisement for jobs in yet another IT company in Bangalore, my home town, last year. Ironically, the permeation of the concept into corporate management practices reflected some of the principles that infused it in the world of social change: reducing hierarchy, decentralisation, greater decision-making power and autonomy for managers on the ground – all essential to efficiency and competitiveness in the era of global corporations (Morris and Willocks 1995; Cook and Macaulay 1996). But this journey out of social struggles and into management practice is deeply disturbing: can the empowerment of the local manager of a multinational corporation achieve the same social good as the struggles of impoverished Dalit women with whom I have worked to claim the right to burn their dead in the upper-caste cremation ground or have their children seated in the classroom with caste-Hindu classmates, or the efforts of indigenous women to regain their traditional rights to forest produce, or the campaigns of pavement dwellers to secure housing in India's burgeoning metros? Would these women equate their experience to that of the manager who is advised to hold an exercise on Friday afternoon, with the advice to 'Present a daft award for the best bit of empowerment, the most empowered person of the day' (Morris and Willcocks 1995:77, quoted in Gaventa 2002)?

Postscript

I called this chapter an experiential account, because I did not want to pretend to be presenting an exhaustive, thoroughly researched analysis of the buzzword 'empowerment' – and also because I was an unapologetic champion of the powerful and transformatory concepts and practices that it represented at the height of feminist grassroots organising in another India. But today, I ask myself a simple question: if this word, and the idea that it represented, has been seized and re-defined by populist politics, fundamentalist and neo-con ideologies, and corporate management, if it has been downsized by microfinance and quota evangelists, and otherwise generally divested of all vestiges of power and politics, is it worth reclaiming? These very processes signal the vagueness and lack of political accuracy that its critics always highlighted. They also warn us that the subversion of powerful political techniques that organise the marginalised will always first occur through the co-option and distortion of its language.

Clearly, we need to build a new language in which to frame our vision and strategies for social transformation at the local, national, or global level. I for one intend to do so not by re-reading Foucault or Gramsci or other great political philosophers, but by listening to poor women and their movements, listening to their values, principles, articulations, and actions, and by trying to hear how they frame their search for justice. From this, I suspect, will emerge not only a new discourse, but also new concepts and strategies that have not yet entered our political or philosophical imaginations.

Notes

1. I am deeply indebted to John Gaventa (2002) for his masterly overview of the origins, meanings, and usages of empowerment.
2. Several sections of this chapter also borrow heavily from my chapter 'Women's empowerment in 21st century India – changing meanings, contexts and strategies', in Shiva Kumar and Rajani Ved (eds.), *The Wellbeing of India's Population*, forthcoming.
3. *Sanghs* and *Samoohs* are local terms for collectives or informal organisations.
4. The structures of local self-government at the village and provincial level based on a pre-colonial Indian units of local government that existed in some parts of the country.
5. See section on 'Rural Development' in http://india.gov.in/sectors/ruraldev1.php, retrieved 6 February 2006.
6. See http://india.gov.in/outerwin.htm?id=http://education.nic.in/ (retrieved 6 February 2006).
7. The Women's Development Programme in Rajasthan, the Mahila Samakhya Programme in several states of the country, are the earliest examples of this.

References

ASPBAE/FAO (1993) *Women's Empowerment in South Asia: Concepts and Practices*, New Delhi: ASPBAE (Asia South Pacific Bureau of Adult Education).

Batliwala, Srilatha (2007) 'When rights go wrong', *Seminar* 569: 89–94.

Burra, Neera, Joy Deshmukh-Ranadive, and K. Murthy, Ranjani (eds.) (2005) *Micro-Credit, Poverty and Empowerment: Linking the Triad*, New Delhi: Sage.

Cook, Sarah and Steve Macaulay (1996) *Perfect Empowerment: All you need to get it right first time*, Arrow: London, quoted in Gaventa 2002.

Cornwall, Andrea, and Anne Marie Goetz (2005) 'Democratizing democracy: feminist perspectives', *Democratization* 12(5): 783–800.

Fernando, Jude L. (2006) *Microfinance: Perils and Prospects*, London: Routledge.

Gaventa, John (2002) 'Empowerment: A Briefing Note', unpublished monograph, Brighton: Institute of Development Studies.

Government of India, Ministry of Human Resource Development, Dept of Education, 2006, http://india.gov.in/outerwin.htm?id=http://education.nic.in/, retrieved February 2006.

Hassan, Zoya (1998) 'Gender politics, legal reform, and the Muslim community in India', in Patricia Jeffery and Amrita Basu (eds.), *Appropriating Gender: Women's Agency, the State, and Politicized Religion in South Asia*, London: Routledge.

Kabeer, Naila (1994) *Reversed Realities – Gender Hierarchies in Development Thought*, London: Verso.

Kumar, Radha (1993) *The History of Doing – An Illustrated Account of Movements for Women's Rights and Feminism in India, 1800–1990*, New Delhi: Kali for Women.

Morris, Steve and Graham Willcocks (1995) *Successful Empowerment in a Week*, London: Hodder & Stoughton for the Institute of Management.

Sarkar, Tanika (1998) 'Woman, community and nation – a historical trajectory for Hindu identity politics', in Patricia Jeffery and Amrita Basu (eds.), *Appropriating Gender: Women's Agency, the State, and Politicized Religion in South Asia*, London: Routledge.

United Nations (1995) 'Beijing Platform for Action', Annexe 1, para 7, www.un.org/esa/gopher-data/conf/fwcw/off/a–20.en/, retrieved 12 February 2006.

About the author

Srilatha Batliwala is a Civil Society Research Fellow at the Hauser Center for Nonprofit Organizations at Harvard University, but is based in her home city of Bangalore. She is widely known for her work on gender equality and women's empowerment.

CHAPTER 11
Social capital

Ben Fine

In parallel with, and as a complement to, globalisation, 'social capital' has enjoyed a meteoric rise across the social sciences over the last two decades. Not surprisingly, it has been particularly prominent across development studies, not least through heavy promotion by the World Bank. As a concept, though, as has been argued persistently by a minority critical literature, social capital is fundamentally flawed. Although capable of addressing almost anything designated as social, it has tended to neglect the state, class, power, and conflict. As a buzzword, it has heavily constrained the currently progressive departure from the extremes of neo-liberalism and post-modernism at a time of extremely aggressive assault by economics imperialism. Social capital should not be ignored but contested – and rejected.

Introduction

Social capital as a concept rose to prominence during the 1990s, towards the latter half as far as development is concerned. Although before then it had scarcely warranted a mention[1], its leading proponent, Robert Putnam, was acknowledged in the 1990s to be the single most cited author across the social sciences. As a word, or two, *social capital* had certainly raised a buzz. What, how, and why is the subject of this contribution.

This chapter is written from a highly personal point of view: I was heavily involved, if critically, with social capital from an early stage, and have disseminated my views in a number of publications. I draw on my own writings extensively in this piece, along with an anecdote or two that might shed some light on the source and nature of buzzwording. Throughout, I assume at least a passing knowledge of what social capital is or is about – although, as will become clear, it has far exceeded its initial popularisation as *'It's not what you know, it's who you know that counts'*.[2]

In the next section, I offer a short account of the key features of social capital as it has come to be deployed across the social sciences. This is followed by a discussion of its role within development studies, and how it came to acquire it. The final section offers some more general commentary on social capital as buzzword.

Social capital is as social capital does

My own interest in social capital arose accidentally, although it was possibly an accident waiting to happen. In the mid-1990s, I had begun to study the relationship between economics and the other social sciences. I had become convinced, initially on casual but soon to be cumulative evidence, that economics imperialism (or colonisation of the subject matter of other social sciences) had entered a new, aggressive, wide-ranging, and yet more palatable and successful phase. Consequently, I was understandably intrigued to find that two individuals at the opposite extremes of social science, Pierre Bourdieu and Gary Becker, were both using the term 'social capital': not least because Becker was and remains the leading practitioner of an economics imperialism of an older, longer-standing kind. Becker's form of economics treats all economic *and* social phenomena as if they could be reduced to optimising individuals interacting as far as possible as if a market were present. His so-called 'economic approach' to social science has obvious affinities to rational choice, differing only in subject matter (and knowledge of non-economic literature).[3]

From the simple question of how the two Bs could be deploying the same concept, I became embroiled in the meteoric rise of social capital across the social sciences. My investigation bordered on the obsessive as I meticulously sought out literature on social capital, ultimately culminating in the writing of a book (Fine 2001). Since then I have limited myself to a watching brief, complemented by the occasional assault, with the intention of renewing my obsession at a later date to assess once more where social capital has got and where it is going.[4] My conclusions, and continuing perspective, on social capital have moved far beyond the 'two Bs' conundrum. In retrospect, it is obvious that social capital has become a buzzword. As such, it has reflected individual and collective degradation of scholarship. And it is this that needed to be addressed.

This is a powerful indictment. It can be justified by laying out the key features of social capital. First, collectively, users of the concept have developed a gargantuan appetite in terms of what it is, what it does, and how it is understood. Almost any form of social interaction has the potential to be understood as social capital. As a positive resource, it is presumed to have the capacity to facilitate almost any outcome in any walk of life, and to be liquid or fluid across them to a greater or lesser extent. And it is equally adaptable across subject matter, disciplines, methods, and techniques, at least within the social sciences. In short, in principle, and to a large (if selective) degree in practice, social capital can be anything you like.

Second, this imparts to users of the concept of social capital the property of being able to reinterpret all previous social science through its prism. Hence, social capital has been presumed to be a more general approach than that individually attached to notions such as networks, trust, linkages, and so on. Through its prism, however, these concepts and their lineage lose their force.

Social capital is equally at home as a residual or complementary category, explaining what was previously inexplicable in its absence. Thus, for example, *social inclusion* might be a form of social capital, it might be explained by social capital, or it might reinforce the effects of social capital (with social exclusion as the corresponding dark side). Inevitably, though, the social-capital prism filters out more light than it lets through, in drawing simplistically upon basic categories of social analysis, stripped of their rich traditions and contested meanings.

Third, 'social capital' is an oxymoron. It presumes that there can be a capital that is not social. It is rarely made explicit what this asocial capital is, where the boundary lies between it and social capital, and what role is played by that other capital in itself and as complement to, or constraint upon, its *alter ego*. Social capital might be the counterpart to economic capital (asocial?), the state, or even personal capital. In what respect it is *social* and/or *capital*, and hence distinctive as such, is under-explored.

Fourth, as a result, the economy, and economic theory, tend to remain unexamined in the context of social capital. There is some loosely formulated presumption that markets cannot work at all or cannot work perfectly in the absence of social capital. This opens the potential for (more) social capital to enhance the working of the market, just as it enriches non-economic behaviour and outcomes through collectivity.

Fifth, social capital offers a highly attractive analytical fix for economics, as a *residual* theoretical and empirical factor. Differences in economic performance had traditionally been seen as the consequence of different quantities of capital and labour. The former had been refined to various types, such as physical, financial, environmental, and human capital. Social capital, for economists in their own limited departure from neo-liberalism, could be added to capture anything else that might contribute to performance, with the non-market such as social capital understood as the path-dependent response to market imperfections.

Sixth, despite its wide scope of definition in principle, social capital in practice has exhibited a number of taboo aspects, despite these being at the core of social interaction. Generalising over such an extensive literature is dangerous, but omissions (apart from the economy other than as something given but to be enhanced), despite being significant elements in social interaction, include class, the state, trade unions, and political parties and organisations.[5] And, by the same token, co-operation and collectivity have been emphasised at the almost absolute expense of power and conflict.

Seventh, the policy perspective induced by uses of the concept of social capital, although never put in these terms, is self-help raised to the level of the collective. However good or bad things might be, they could be better if people interacted more, trusted one another, and co-operated. Social capital offers the golden opportunity of improving the *status quo* without challenging it. *Everything* from educational outcomes through crime prevention to better psychological health can be improved if neighbours and communities would only pull together and trust one another.

Eighth, Bourdieu is acknowledged to have been an early purveyor of social capital, and he placed considerable emphasis on both its class dimensions and its contextual content. He offered a much deeper understanding of social capital than what has followed, but also a narrower definition, as he distinguished it from cultural and symbolic (and economic) capital. These differences have been lost in subsequent literature by subsuming the symbolic and the cultural into the social, while equally dropping the class and contextual content for universal notions of any collectivity across time, place, and application. In place of Bourdieu, the rational choice or individualistic foundations of other renditions of the concept of social capital, drawing on the influence of the rational-choice sociologist James Coleman, have come to the fore.[6] The most recent literature has begun to bring Bourdieu and context back in and to stand aloof from rational choice. Yet this renders the concept different in every application, so that transposability between case studies and analytical categories relies upon a leap of faith. In this respect, social capital is treated as if it were capital in money form, along with presumptions of fluidity between its various components and effects (something of which Bourdieu himself was guilty).

Ninth, precisely because of its amorphous, all-encompassing nature, social capital is an ideal category, for want of a more tempered term, for the hack academic (hackademic?). Apart from a focus for conferences and research-grant applications, it has given rise to a typical article – *X and Social Capital*. So, whatever has been done before can be done again, with social capital serving as anything from organising theme to tangential by-line. In this respect, at least, there are parallels with the ubiquity of studies of *X and Globalisation*.

Tenth, purveyors of social capital have exhibited a capacity to absorb criticism by continuing to move forward. Opposition is readily perceived as seeking the addition of an otherwise missing variable or method, so that the remedy is to incorporate what is otherwise absent. Where criticism is offensive to the core values of social capital, it is usually simply ignored, especially in relation to the points already elaborated. This is so much so that those contributions that do acknowledge criticism do so selectively for the purpose of supporting their own particular contributions.

Personally, I have found this so frustrating that I began to preface the frequent seminars that I have given on social capital with the explicit challenge to the audience that they indicate where I am wrong or where there is disagreement. This has rarely solicited a public response. But in private, individuals say they agree with me but were going to use social capital anyway as a means to further their own contributions (which would, nonetheless, make correctives in the light of my criticisms). And, it would be claimed, at least economists are being civilised by bringing non-economic factors into their considerations. For the latter, however, the problem is less a matter of persuading economists to be civilised by continuing their colonisation of the other social sciences and more one of constituting an alternative economics. In short, social capital has created a *cordon sanitaire* around itself, through which criticism is ignored, incorporated, or even serves as a sort of repressive tolerance, legitimising the idea through acknowledging opposition. In place of the global, the economic, class, the state, conflict, gender, power and so on, social capital offers a bland alternative, highly conciliatory in principle and practice, with more humanely presented forms of neo-liberalism, with token incorporation on narrower terms of other buzzwords such as *empowerment* and *participation*.

Eleventh, as should be apparent, irrespective of other criticisms, social capital has become definitionally chaotic, as it is imbued with so many different variables, approaches, and applications. Again, this has frequently been acknowledged in the literature, only for another definition or approach to be adopted, compounding rather than resolving the collective conceptual chaos (the social capital of social capital!).There is a significant, if heavily outweighed, literature that is critical of social capital and, almost certainly, a body of social scientists who will have nothing to do with it because of its conceptual chaos and incoherence. Yet this aversion to social capital inhabits a parallel universe with limited dialogue with, or response from, the purveyors of social capital.

Last, social capital thrived in the particular intellectual context peculiar to the 1990s, in which there was a reaction against the extremes both of neo-liberalism and post-modernism. Like its counterpart, globalisation, but as its complement and opposite in many respects, purveyors of social capital have rejected the belief that markets work perfectly and have embraced the idea of 'getting real' about how people go about their (daily) lives. The global, though, is notable for its absence from the world of social capital; it is more about communities accepting the world as it is and bettering themselves on this basis as a form of 'participation' and 'empowerment'.[7] Thus, and further, the 'dark side' of social capital, as in corruption and community or racist violence for example, is often acknowledged – only to be ignored. Even so, the World Bank's use of social capital has tended not even to acknowledge criticism, but see below.

Social capital and development

In view of the above, it is hardly surprising that development and social capital should be brought together. But the prominence of social capital within development has been considerably strengthened by its heavy promotion from an early stage by the World Bank. Why should this have been so?

In many respects, social capital offered, alongside other complementary buzzwords like 'participation' and 'empowerment', the dream concept for the challenges faced by the World Bank in the 1990s. The decade had brought a crisis of its (and the IMF's) legitimacy, with mounting criticism of the neo-liberal policies attached to loans. The Comprehensive Development Framework (CDF) and post-Washington Consensus (PWC) were designed to restore that legitimacy (Fine *et al.* 2001). The rejection of the Washington Consensus at the rhetorical level was evident. This was even carried through in scholarship to some extent, even if not immediately, for example in the case of privatisation. Yet it is arguable whether these shifts had any impact on policy itself, as an even wider range of market-supporting interventions than under the Washington Consensus became legitimised through a rationale of correcting market and non-market interventions.

These shifts also reflected changes underway within the discipline of economics in general and development economics in particular (Jomo and Fine 2006). The old 'informal', 'classical' development economics had long given way to the 'new', with its emphasis on mathematical techniques, econometrics, the virtues of the market, and the corresponding need not to distort it through rent-seeking, corruption, and the like. But, in its reaction against neoliberalism, mainstream economics had begun to emphasise the importance of market imperfections and the need to correct them through non-market mechanisms. This has fed through into what I have termed the 'newer' development economics, with the PWC to the fore.

In one major respect, the CDF and PWC exhibit a marked difference from earlier ideologies emanating from the World Bank. Although completely different, the Keynesian/welfarism/modernisation stance of the McNamara period and the neo-liberalism of the Washington Consensus had their own relatively simple message on how to achieve development. In contrast, the PWC emphasises that the incidence of market and non-market imperfections is uneven and contingent in form, extent, and consequences, so that not one model fits all, and so on, and everything is micro. Social capital is at its core the negative mirror-image of rent-seeking, etc., with the same analytical framework but diametrically opposed conclusions – that non-market influences can be beneficial (rather than detrimental) to the market. As such, it incorporates the non-economic in a way that is consistent with the (non-) market imperfections approach and is sensitive in principle to difference from one application to another. I hasten to add that this does not necessarily make a policy difference; rather, it simply offers richer scope in justifying policy. After all, there are limits to using neo-liberalism as the rationale for substantial intervention.

In short, social capital offered considerable leverage in the World Bank's dealings with the external world. In addition, it allowed for certain internal institutional interests to be promoted. The World Bank is dominated by economists, numerically and intellectually, and of the worst type from the perspective of the social scientists under the shadow of the Washington Consensus. The CDF and PWC offered some opportunity for non-economists to be taken seriously. Social capital was strategically chosen as a judicious concept for that purpose. In a paper that is unusual for its information and honesty over the internal workings of the World Bank (Bebbington *et al.* 2004), all this is revealed: from Putnam's initial invitation to be involved, through the attempts to engage (successful), but not to be dominated by (unsuccessful) the economists. Not surprisingly, this is not entirely the take of the paper's authors.

Rather, they see themselves as the heroes, unrecognised, strategically compromising and so reviled, of a hidden internal battle to civilise the World Bank's economists, and so bring the progressively social to the intellectual and policy practices of the World Bank (Fine 2007b) for response.

In this respect, for them, criticism of social capital has missed the point of its inner significance in shifting the Bank's thinking and hence policy. Of course, this leaves aside both the other influences on the thinking and practice of the World Bank and the broader impact of the promotion of social capital in development thinking and practice elsewhere. Essentially, at least in retrospective self-justification, these authors are asking us to devolve our intellectual responsibilities to them, in order that they can promote their own positions within the World Bank around a concept that they themselves admit to be flawed. The parallels with the 'never mind the arguments, just do it' stance on privatisation are striking. And they are ironic. For whatever the impact of social capital on the design and implementation of particular World Bank *projects*, the strategy of the organisation in practice has been to shift as much of its finance as possible from the public to the private sector. This is so despite a World Bank rethink on privatisation, adjudging it to have been previously too premature a gamble (Bayliss and Fine 2007).

Polemics aside, the account of Bebbington *et al.* (2004) is a striking illustration of how strategic thinking within the World Bank is forced, individually and institutionally, to conform to its shifting needs and practices, and how limited is the scope to buck its requirements. Such is the case on a grander scale for the resignations of Joseph Stiglitz, Ravi Kanbur, and others. But where professional recruitment and careerism prove insufficient to serve the World Bank's scholarship, rhetoric, and policy, the delusion of internal influence and reform incorporates those who offer a little more by way of free thinking and altruistic motivation. This is not to say that the scholarship, rhetoric, and policy of the World Bank are pre-determined in and of themselves and in relation to one another. But they are embedded, to coin a phrase, in an institution and its practices that are heavily constrained and can be perverse in attaching intentions to outcomes. The reduction of the impact of social capital to the activities of a few scholars within the World Bank is at best partial and at worst misleading.

Given my own interest in social capital for other reasons, I was alert to its importance for the World Bank from an early stage. I dredged through the Bank's dedicated website, http://worldbank.org/poverty/scapital, and initially exaggerated its importance as a way of circumventing the idea of the developmental state as an alternative to the Washington Consensus (Fine 1999b), although that the PWC would circumvent the developmental state proved correct. But my efforts did prompt a mole within the World Bank to contact me with three gems of wisdom in terms of the reaction that I was likely to receive to my criticisms. First, I would be asked to back off, as the World Bank was changing for the good. Second, none of my criticisms would be addressed.

And, third, I would be offered a job of sorts, to internalise and incorporate criticism.

I am sorry to say, even moles can get it wrong, and the last of these responses never materialised. Only on one occasion, the exception that proves the rule, has there been any serious attempt to engage in discussion with me. This was a seminar organised jointly by the London School of Economics and the Overseas Development Institute, specifically to provoke debate, and with Michael Woolcock as opponent.[8] To my astonishment, he insisted as precondition for participation that I provide him with three questions to answer, and he would reciprocate. I offered the following:

1. Discuss critically the relationship between social capital and globalisation.
2. Assess critically what is the social capital of the World Bank and other IFIs.
3. Discuss critically what social capital understands as, and adds to the understanding of, development; with what economic analyses it is consistent; and how it understands 'non-social', especially economic, capital, and capitalism.

These questions were indicative of a wish to explore the relationship between social capital and globalisation, economic development, and the practices of the World Bank itself. I do not have a record of Woolcock's questions, but one was to ask what I would say to a South African nurse asking me how I would deal with HIV/AIDS,[9] and another was why I did not publish in respectable journals. The latter is ironic in view of the knowledge Bank's total exclusion of my work from its social-capital website (including its extensive annotated bibliography) and from its overall website altogether (other than once for a legitimising exercise[10]). In the event, while I did answer his questions, he totally ignored mine, preferring to offer a tangential discourse on some obscure management framework before departing to survey the implementation of the World Bank's social-capital toolkit household survey for Albania. With social-capital surveys having been widely adopted across developed and developing countries, whatever the intentions of the World Bank's social capitalists in moving internal dialogue and practice, the external impact has been considerable in this respect at least.[11]

Deconstructing the buzz

In discussing consumer culture, I have argued that it can be characterised by six Cs (Fine 2002b; 2005). While I hesitate to extrapolate from consumer culture to buzzwords, doing so does offer some insight. The first C is **constructed**. Social capital has been constructed through a combination of academic and, to a much lesser extent, developmental practices that have mutually reinforced one another – but to the exclusion of others, especially where critical (myself) or inconvenient (Bourdieu, power, class, state, etc.).

Second, social capital is *contextual*, like all concepts, in the more general sense of itself being a specific product of the material and intellectual circumstances that mark the turn of the millennium. This aspect of social capital is brought out by Putnam's foisting it, as an afterthought, upon his study of regional disparities in Italy from the twelfth century onwards. He then exports it to the twentieth-century USA as the way to understand the decline of bowling clubs and the rise of television prior to finding an entrée into the World Bank. Today's context allows this to happen, and for social capital to be accepted and promoted as a legitimate and legitimised concept. It is the contemporary phlogiston of social theory.

Third, social capital is *chaotic*, not least in its multifarious uses and meanings. Far from this resulting in its dismissal from the intellectual arena, this appears to have promoted its use. It has been subject to hundreds of measures, or elements that make up a measure, so much so that it has been felt necessary to re-aggregate into intermediate categories such as linking, bonding, and bridging. These all mutually contradict one another across traditional social variables (such as class, gender, ethnicity), quite apart from the conundrum of its perverse, dark, or negative side (mafia and the like).

Fourth, social capital is *construed*, that is it is not simply passively received as a well-defined and given concept but is reinterpreted and worked upon by those who engage with it. One aspect of that reworking, for example, has been to disassociate social capital both from Bourdieu (too radical) and from Coleman (too reactionary), unless one or other of these is the intent.

Fifth, social capital is the product of *contradictory* pressures, as it seeks to accommodate both material and intellectual developments. How can the World Bank legitimise itself while pretty much continuing business as usual? How can the economy be ignored when we are deploying social *capital*? And how can we set aside power and conflict when we are addressing social capital?

Last, then, social capital is *contested*, or subject to conflict over its meaning. Among social capitalists themselves, this is resolved through chaotic compromise. Otherwise, contestation takes the form of exposing and rejecting social capital for its sore conceptual inadequacies and corresponding consequences for practice. Social capital has in part risen to prominence because it has been allowed to do so by those who have not engaged critically with it. One index of this is that my polemic in *Antipode*, according to its editors, has been one of its most accessed pieces (Fine 2002c). I suspect that this reflects its racy title, the prominence of social capital, and silent but unengaged opposition to it. By contrast, while globalisation has been shown to be equally flawed as a conceptual panacea, it has been universally addressed by its critics and won away, not only from neo-liberalism but also from the intellectual Third Wayism characteristic of social capital.

The current intellectual scene is marked by the demise within academia of the extremes of (attention to) neo-liberalism and post-modernism, and by the coincidental rise of economics imperialism in the form of market and non-market imperfections as universal explananda. The consequence is that the content and dynamic within and between disciplines is extremely open, and to be determined by the integrity and values that scholars bring to their scholarship. Much the same applies to the more general influence of scholarship on development thinking and practice. In this light, the point is not so much to deplore the six Cs and how they characterise social capital, as they must bear on any concept, whether buzzword or not. Rather, social capital has a content and dynamic that severely constrain progressive developmental thinking. It must be more heavily contested, but through argued rejection, in terms of its own inner weaknesses as well as its strategic consequences – irrespective of the odd individual or case-study advantage that might appear to accrue.

Acknowledgement

Thanks to the editors for comments on an earlier draft.

Notes

1. For debate about the (absence of) history of social capital, see Fine (2007a) and Farr (2004, 2007). The latter's response, to the effect that there is a history, reports six million items for social capital on an Internet search. Yet his own history is more or less forcibly confined to a single source, John Dewey, with a few other bit players.
2. Key texts include Harriss (2001), Smith and Kulynych (2002), and Bebbington *et al.* (2004). See also Fabio Sabatini's website www.socialcapitalgateway. org/. For my own works, and more general context of economics imperialism, see www.soas.ac.uk/departments/departmentinfo.cfm?navid¼490
3. On Becker and Bourdieu, see Fine (1999a). For a fuller account of economics imperialism, see Fine and Milonakis (2007).
4. See especially Fine (2002a, 2003).
5. Although there is a healthy literature on social capital and political activity as such.
6. Note that Coleman as individual tends to be acknowledged more than his 'rational choice' approach, explicit reference to which would deter many punters.
7. See Moore (2001) for a more general critique of incorporation of such notions in anaesthetised forms.
8. Given the excellent Woolcock (1998), it seems that the mole's condition three is operative on occasion.
9. I cannot resist pointing to the answer that might have been given by a World Bank 'lead economist', Bonnel (2000: 849), who, in discussing social capital, argues that 'Reversing the spread of the HIV/ AIDS epidemics and mitigating its impact' require three sets of measures: (1) sound macroeconomic policies; (2) structural policy reform; and (3) modifying further the systems of incentives faced by individuals.
10. See Foreword to Fine (2004).

11. Note, though, that Bebbington *et al.* do at least reference (and essentially accept) my criticisms of social capital (other than strategically), but in the context of its having served its purpose within the Bank, which can now, with its civilised economists, move on to issues of empowerment and the like. The mind boggles.

References

Arestis, P. and M. Sawyer (eds.) (2004) *The Rise of the Market*, Camberley: Edward Elgar.

Bayliss, K. and B. Fine (eds.) (2007) *Privatization and Alternative Public Sector Reform in Sub-Saharan Africa: Delivering on Electricity and Water*, Basingstoke: Palgrave Macmillan.

Bebbington, A., S. Guggenheim, E. Olson and M. Woolcock (2004) 'Grounding discourse in practice: exploring social capital debates at the World Bank', *Journal of Development Studies* 40(5): 33–64.

Bonnel, R. (2000) 'HIV/AIDS and economic growth: a global perspective', *South African Journal of Economics* 68(5): 820–55.

Farr, J. (2004) 'Social capital: a conceptual history', *Political Theory* 32: 6–33.

Farr, J. (2007) 'In search of social capital', *Political Theory*.

Fine, B. (1999a) 'From Becker to Bourdieu: economics confronts the social sciences', *International Papers in Political Economy* 5(3): 1–43, reproduced with afterword in Arestis and Sawyer (eds.) (2004).

Fine, B. (1999b) 'The developmental state is dead – long live social capital?', *Development and Change* 30(1): 1–19.

Fine, B. (2001) *Social Capital versus Social Theory: Political Economy and Social Science at the Turn of the Millennium*, London: Routledge.

Fine, B. (2002a) 'It ain't social, it ain't capital and it ain't Africa', *Studia Africana* No. 3: 18–33.

Fine, B. (2002b) *The World of Consumption: The Material and Cultural Revisited*, London: Routledge.

Fine, B. (2002c) 'They f**k you up those social capitalists', *Antipode* 34(4): 796–99.

Fine, B. (2003) 'Social capital: the World Bank's fungible friend', *Journal of Agrarian Change* 3(4): 586–603.

Fine, B. (2004) 'Economics and ethics: Amartya Sen as point of departure', *ABCDE Conference*, Oslo, 24–26 June, 2002, published in The New School Economic Review 1(1):151–62, available at www.newschool.edu/gf/nser/articles/0101_fineb_econandethicssen_fall04_final.pdf

Fine, B. (2005) 'Addressing the consumer', in Trentmann (ed.) (2005).

Fine, B. (2007a) 'Eleven hypotheses on the conceptual history of social capital', *Political Theory* 35(1): 7–53.

Fine, B. (2007b) 'Social Capital in Wonderland: the World Bank Behind the Looking Glass', mimeo available from author.

Fine, B. and D. Milonakis (2007) *From Political Economy to Freakonomics: Method, the Social and the Historical in the Evolution of Economic Theory*, London: Routledge.

Fine, B., C. Lapavitsas and J. Pincus (eds.) (2001) *Development Policy in the Twenty-First Century: Beyond the Post-Washington Consensus*, London and New York: Routledge.

Harriss, J. (2001) *Depoliticizing Development: The World Bank and Social Capital*, New Delhi: Leftword Books, revised edition, London: Anthem Press, 2002.

Jomo, K. and B. Fine (eds.) *The New Development Economics: After the Washington Consensus*, Delhi and London: Tulika and Zed Press.

Moore, M. (2001) 'Empowerment at last', *Journal of International Development* 13(3): 321–29.

O'Connor, J. (1973) *The Fiscal Crisis of the State*, New York, NY: St Martin's Press.

Oishi, T. (2001) *The Unknown Marx: Reconstructing a Unified Perspective*, London: Pluto Press.

Smith, S. and J. Kulynych (2002) 'It may be social, but why is it capital? The social construction of social capital and the politics of language', *Politics and Society* 30(1): 149–86.

Trentmann, F. (ed.) (2005) *The Making of the Consumer: Knowledge, Power and Identity in the Modern World*, Oxford: Berg.

Woolcock, M. (1998) 'Social capital and economic development: toward a theoretical synthesis and policy framework', *Theory and Society* 27(2): 151–208.

About the author

Ben Fine is Professor of Economics at the School of Oriental and African Studies at the University of London. Recent and forthcoming publications include *The New Development Economics: A Critical Introduction* (2006), *From Political Economy to Freakonomics: Method, the Social and the Historical in the Evolution of Economic Theory* (2007), and *Reinventing the Economic Past: Method and Theory in the Evolution of Economic History* (2008).

CHAPTER 12

Reflections on relationships: the nature of partnership according to five NGOs in southern Mexico

Miguel Pickard

This chapter is based on interviews with several staff members of NGOs located in San Cristóbal de Las Casas, Chiapas, Mexico, regarding partnerships between them and their funding sources, such as foundations or agencies of the North that do or support development work in the South. The motive behind the interviews was an interest in the word 'partnerships', in particular strategic ones. Do partnerships exist now and, if they do, what does it mean for the NGOs to have a partnership with a funding source? The general conclusion was that strategic partnerships have indeed existed in the past, and may again emerge in the future, but that currently they exist only sporadically, given the distinct ways of viewing and carrying out development work within NGOs on the one hand, and foundations or agencies on the other.

Introduction

Funding organisations have a plethora of terms for the intended targets of their largesse: *recipients, beneficiaries, counterparts, clients, grantees, partners,* etc. But what do these terms mean? Are they equivalents, interchangeable synonyms? And, specifically, under what circumstances is a *partnership* said to exist between development-oriented funding organisations in the global North and their, well, whatever, in the global South?

What follows is a general reflection on the term *partnership*, undertaken by activists working in NGOs in Mexico. We suggest here that *partnership* denotes a special relationship between equal participants or, yes, *partners*, who enjoy a distinctive bond of trust, a shared analysis of existing conditions in society, and thus in general a common orientation of what needs to be done to construct a more just, equitable, and democratic world.

This chapter surveys how partnerships are regarded in the eyes of five informants, all of whom are currently working at NGOs in southern Mexico. The work of these non-profit NGOs centres on specific themes: for example, economies of solidarity, conflict resolution, human rights, citizens' participation in formal electoral politics, and alternative information and analysis for grassroots organisations. It is worth stating at the outset that these themes are not the NGOs' *raisons d'être*. Rather, they are *means* to a greater end, which might be summarised as a long-term commitment to the empowerment of social and civil organisations. These NGOs believe in general that such organisations will be the agents of change, or perhaps will combine, mutate, and permutate into new *social actors* or *agents* who will undertake the task of societal transformation.

For the purposes of this chapter we use two (what we hope are) generic terms for donor and donee within the 'development' field: *agencies* in the North and *recipients* in the South. The term *agency* annoys some Northern aid workers, yet it is our generic term in Mexico for external, non-government, non-corporate sources of funding, and it is used here and in general with no derogatory intention.

The NGOs surveyed share one important trait. We are dependent on funding from Northern agencies for our existence and survival. There is no tradition in our area of the global South, or an extremely weak one at best, of individual donations to 'good and noble causes'. Self-financing schemes cover at best only a small percentage of the budget. The only in-country sources of funding in our field are government coffers or corporate profits. To accept funds from the first would, in the minds of many, convert NGOs to Government Organisations, and corporate funding is seen to be too tainted, especially in a moral or ethical sense, to accept. None of the NGOs interviewed for this discussion accepts corporate funding. One does accept government funds within a trilateral (government/NGO/agency) scheme described below.

A word about the word

There is no universal standard definition of partnership within the development world. For our purposes here, we have imbued it with a particular meaning, as noted above. For this reason, there is no exact translation of 'partnership' into Spanish. It is a word that must be given meaning within a specific context, although one informant reports that the Spanish equivalent of *strategic relationship* is one 'real-life' term for what one agency and one NGO established at the start of this century. In any event, the word is generally construed to mean equal standing among participants, with perhaps differentiated responsibilities. And once this was explained, informants readily accepted that a partnership can, in fact, exist between aid agencies and recipients in certain situations, as we shall see.

The fact that funding flows from North to South may, however, have important implications for the theoretical equality of standing within a partnership. One informant rejects the proposition that a proper partnership can ever exist where, at some point in the relationship among agencies and recipients, financial assets are transferred in a non-commercial transaction from the former to the latter. Only agencies have final judgement in the matter of grants, while recipients can do little more than wait for the decision on their funding request. The power to grant or withhold funding is unequally shared, and so, for our informant, a true partnership can never be said to exist, since an unequal power relationship inevitably prevails, at least on the question of funding.

A historic setting

For two of our informants, chequered relationships between Northern agencies and Southern recipients have been the rule for the past several decades. After World War II, the relationship was essentially paternalistic, even neo-colonial. One part of the world was 'developed', the other 'underdeveloped'. One part of the world had 'solutions' to underdevelopment, the other lacked them, and the received wisdom of the time posited simply transferring knowledge, technology, and resources from the North to jumpstart development in the South. In this rather linear way of thinking, development was a matter of inputs.

During the late 1950s and into the 1960s, as the global South gained greater political independence, the prevailing development paradigm increasingly met with criticism and rejection. After decades, transfers of millions of dollars had had no appreciable effect on poverty or underdevelopment. With time, development practitioners and academics agreed: poverty in the developing world was less a cause, and more an effect, of overarching structural problems. It was these structures, then, that had to be transformed or eliminated in order for poverty to be reduced. The focus of attention shifted from poverty to the root causes of underdevelopment.

In Latin America during the 1970s and 1980s, wars of national liberation, though often unsuccessful in overthrowing political and economic elites, nonetheless were important in instilling at the grassroots a sense of nationalism and self-determination. This idea percolated to the development sector, where, over time, it altered the existing paternalistic and neo-colonial paradigm.

What emerged was the determination of stakeholders in developing countries to be considered 'social subjects', i.e. actors fully capable of participating in the development debate and proposing innovative and 'home-grown' solutions to structural problems affecting the majority of the population. These local social subjects had to be seen as autonomous, in the sense that they had a particular, perfectly valid understanding of their own reality and could act to transform it. Thus the global South was more than capable of generating its own objectives, perspectives, and strategies. The top-to-bottom, North-to-South chain of command of ideas, methods, and strategies in the development field underwent a radical transformation. Other more horizontal, or democratic, models appeared. And Northern agencies that resisted changes found themselves increasingly estranged from their Southern counterparts.

Increasingly, the proper role of development agencies was thought to be participation with, and strengthening of, 'local social subjects', to collaborate in building alternative social and economic paradigms. From a Southern perspective, it was incumbent upon the Northern agencies to join the South. As participants in an effort to help to eradicate the structural causes of poverty, Northern agencies were always welcome, but now the relationship with the South had to be put on a more equal footing.

Some Northern agencies enthusiastically took up the challenge. In this new context, the idea of a shared commitment between Northern and Southern organisations to help to create socially based alternatives took hold. One informant says that during this period, which covered roughly the 1970s, 1980s and into the 1990s, Northern and Southern entities considered themselves 'allies'. In fact, a wide range of terms came into the development lexicon to describe this new-found relationship. For some Northern agencies, the Southern allies were counterparts, colleagues even; one agency in Germany coined the term 'mutual parts', in an effort to express the commonality of action and commitment, harkening back to our word 'partnership'. A US agency preferred to talk of 'associates'. It is at this time that informants agree that something akin to a partnership existed among the Northern and Southern institutions working to eliminate the root causes, or structural reasons, behind the lack of opportunity that characterised the lives of most of the world's population.

Behind this blossoming spirit of collegiality there was in addition an effort to define what a new society might look like. This was a joint activity among various actors within the development field, such as Northern agencies, Southern social and civil organisations, and the greater civil society. And, as such, a new actor (or, to use the Latin American term, 'social subject') was in the making. This actor undertook actions in favour of social change, thought about social change as a strategic goal, and recognised that, in order to create, change introspection and self-criticism were necessary, as was a willingness to change established modes of thinking, acting, working, and relating to the greater community.

In other words, belonging to a partnership required a shared vision; but, just as important, that vision had to be jointly constructed, never imposed. It also, in the end, required a shared ideology, though not necessarily one that arose from any particular political current. It was rather a matter of opposing the *status quo* where it had proved unjust, undemocratic, discriminatory, and exclusionary. Structural changes could be brought about through greater political awareness and mobilisation on the part of the oppressed majority, not only by resisting and rejecting existing structures and ways of thinking, but also by building alternatives.

Importantly, within this partnership a common dialect evolved which recognised the role that imperialism, colonialism, racism, capitalism, and (later) patriarchy had played in forming the current *status quo*.

Given this search for greater equality and collegiality, most Southern partners sought to ensure that funding from outside sources would not interfere with their own priorities, objectives, and goals. Suggestions from the North were of course welcome, and so were technical, methodological, or knowledge inputs, but funding had to be given without attached strings. It was impermissible to use funding to influence a Southern partner's activity to conform to Northern priorities. A new ethics became a part of this new-found *partnership*: the South gained a greater independence in thought and movement, and funding requests were granted for overall strategic objectives, rather than mere specific activities. But likewise, Southern partners were expected to exercise grants with professionalism, with timely and transparent accountability.

Further, mutual commitments were intended to apply to the long term. Structures were not easily modified, and it was thought quite useless to insist on deadlines. Northern partners either had to commit support for an undefined future in the South or, if they withdrew earlier, had to be satisfied with having contributed to modifying the *status quo*, even if concrete results were difficult to identify. That was the nature of the beast, or so it appeared at the time.

The paradigm shifts

The majority of our informants agree that the 'good times' of shared hopes and visions between Northern and Southern partners began to show signs of strain in the late 1990s, although one claims to have seen the writing on Northern walls years before. Several reasons are behind the disaffection.

One is identified as a general conservative political attitude that accompanied the implementation from the mid-1980s of neo-liberal economic policy virtually throughout the world. Another reason was, surprisingly, the transition to more democratic regimes in many Southern countries, particularly in Latin America. As governments became more democratic through the exercise of formal democracy, particularly at the ballot box, their legitimacy increased, more so in the global North than in the South. People in the South continued to be disenfranchised, disempowered, and mired in a stubbornly resistant poverty that seemed to deepen and spread, notwithstanding the democratic veneer of political representation.

Yet an important shift in emphasis occurred: funds and efforts now poured into the South to support fledgling democracies. The logic was seemingly irrefutable: if impoverished countries were remodelled after European or North American democracies, diverse 'stakeholders' would be able to push their particular agendas forward within the political arena and generate an overall distribution of political power and economic resources. But it did not take long for reality to trump logic. Entrenched elites learned to play the democratic game and gain legitimacy on the world stage, while denying their population real access to power.

One effect of more legitimate Southern governments among Northern agencies was the willingness of the latter to work with the former to find supposed new ways of overcoming poverty. Schemes of 'co-investment' were hatched, whereby local governments equalled or exceeded funds transferred by Northern agencies. Multilateral organisations, such as specialised agencies of the United Nations, were often eager to make their own contributions. In line with the democratic glaze that accompanied this new age, 'trilateral' or 'multilateral' boards of directors were established over these joint investments, giving Northern agencies, local governments, and grant recipients voice and vote to administer funds and decide on specific grant proposals.

These new arrangements pleased some Southern recipients. They took pains to argue that the boards were indeed representative and non-coercive, and, perhaps most importantly, afforded innovative means whereby Southern organisations could legitimately access tax revenues, since 'part of that money is ours to begin with'. The funding, they argued, could be destined to meeting the needs of the poor, the disenfranchised, the disempowered. Other Southern organisations were less than pleased, however, and refused to participate, alleging that involvement in these schemes legitimised governments that still did not represent majority interests.

Further, in the intervening neo-liberal years, efforts to *eliminate* poverty had given way to *alleviating* poverty and *attending* to the poor, or rather, to the 'losers' of the new economic game. And neo-liberal economists were quite willing to admit that there would be losers. A large amount of government funding for social causes was admittedly used to prop up the consumption of the most impoverished. And with token exceptions, governments had little tolerance for rude questions regarding the *status quo* or even ruder talk of changing it.

Yet another reason behind the paradigm shift was the supposed accession of some countries to the status of 'developed' countries. For example, in the case of Mexico, one president's decision to join the Organisation for Economic Co-operation and Development (OECD), and then negotiate a free-trade agreement with the USA, was sufficient reason for some Northern agencies to channel grants elsewhere. A publicity campaign to convince world opinion of the country's arrival in the 'First World' was successful, but unsubstantiated by basic economic data that pointed to persistent and widening poverty and unemployment, greater wealth concentration, and increasing rates of emigration.

Finally, another turning point during the 1990s was the shift of fundraising strategies among Northern agencies. The decades-old practice of appealing to the general public for funds was not entirely forgotten, but certainly downgraded in importance. Agencies of all sizes chose to accept increasingly wider slices of their budget pie from their governments. Southern recipients immediately detected the change. Beholden to government back-funders and anxious to demonstrate 'success' of resources applied, or required to do so by management in order to justify renewed grant applications, Northern agencies now distanced themselves from the previous thinking that associated poverty reduction with long-term processes.

Unfortunately for all, those processes had been especially difficult to document. They involved qualitative changes that were nothing if not subjective. Since such processes involved inherently slow social evolution, many agencies, as mentioned earlier, had to end their commitments without conclusive proof that their participation had indeed wrought greater empowerment of the people.

By accepting government funding and quickly becoming dependent on it to sustain programmes, projects, and bureaucracies, Northern agencies began to turn screws on Southern recipients to show conclusive 'results'. Indicators, especially quantifiable ones, became important. Certain agencies emphasised particular themes (gender, AIDS, environmental issues, agro-ecology, fair trade) in an effort to distinguish their 'brand' of overseas aid, or to hop on to fashionable development bandwagons in order to please governments in the North. At times, concern about particular themes was welcomed in the South; one informant says that, for example, stimulating greater gender awareness was in itself not a problem, although sometimes the way it was done caused friction.

But more importantly, there was a dramatic change in the way in which priorities were determined. Harkening back to the 1950s, once again it was the North that set priorities, often unilaterally. Conceptual gains of previous decades were wiped away, as Northern agencies scrambled to satisfy back-funders' criteria. For example, the idea that partners in the North and South had to jointly design priorities and strategies to have an impact on a long-term process suddenly disappeared. Now, funds were very often conditioned on recipients taking on particular themes, or adjusting on-going programmes and projects to highlight aspects thought to be important in the North.

Part and parcel of this shift towards quantifiable and supposedly more objective criteria was the emphasis on finding indicators of 'success'. This continues to be an on-going debate (or battle) between Northern funders and Southern recipients, given the latters' frequent insistence on working within long-term processes of social transformation that are unsuited to easy, short-term quantification. The main problem, says one informant, is that funders are asking to see quantitative indicators that come from financial-investment circles and have nothing to do with social processes. At best, says another informant, these indicators are an interesting and useful means of looking at activities but they cannot, and should not, be converted into objectives. In other words, she adds, Northern funders have begun requesting 'a logic of methodological construction that does not respond to the construction of social subjects'.

A consequence of the paradigm shift and the newly imposed emphasis on quantifiable indicators was that some Northern agencies concluded that Southern counterparts lacked the basic skills to address basic poverty. This, once again, was a task to be carried out at the behest and direction of Northern agencies, which supposedly did have the required skills set. Southerners could be selected to help with specific inputs, according to demonstrated competencies. What ensued was the contracting-out of these competencies, so that a local NGO could be called in to conduct workshops on specific topics, from bee keeping to human rights. One informant recounted the unsettling prospect of being hired to give human-rights workshops to indigenous communities selected by a Northern agency. Rather than 'accompanying' communities, establishing long-term relations of confidence and trust, the NGO faced the prospect of 'dropping in' for the sole purpose of a workshop that would conceivably be entirely disconnected from the local context. Although the option might be a means of funding this particular human-rights centre, in the end it was rejected since it ran counter to its logic, strategies, methodology, and *raison d'être*. But it pointed to disturbing trends within the development field.

In summary, real development, as understood by a great many Southern organisations, e.g. designed, controlled, and operated by social agents, is being thwarted by a Northern vision too often driven by the need to please back-funders. When these back-funders are governments controlled by parties (of whatever complexion) with neo-liberal economic worldviews, there is often a regression to the logic of decades past, when development was thought to entail a transfer of resources. The current received wisdom emanating from governments adds new requirements for approval of Northern agencies' funding requests: transparency, accountability, input–output methodologies for tabulating indicators. These are useful tools that should be incorporated as auxiliaries in all processes of transformation. But the essence of social-development processes lies elsewhere, in the empowerment of social-change agents, many of which are nascent, or under construction, and by definition resist quantification.

Real epistemological and ideological barriers currently prevent *partnerships* from prospering. In the unanimous opinion of those whose views have contributed to this study, real partnerships within the development world will again be forged and thrive when Northern and Southern organisations meet on an equal footing and support social subjects working to construct a new world order.

About the author

Miguel Pickard is a Mexican economist who has worked with several NGOs, both local and international. He is currently a researcher at CIEPAC (Centre for Economic and Political Investigation for Community Action) in San Cristóbal de las Casas, Chiapas, which he co-founded in 1998.

CHAPTER 13

Talking of gender: words and meanings in development organisations

Ines Smyth

This chapter reflects on the vocabulary commonly used within development organisations to communicate about 'gender and development'. It argues that the relevant terminology, though frequently used, remains problematic. Some terms are almost entirely absent, while others are used loosely and inappropriately – with the subtleties of carefully developed and much-debated concepts often lost. Terms such as 'empowerment', 'gender', and 'gender mainstreaming' which originated in feminist thinking and activism have lost their moorings and become depoliticised. Despite these problems, there are indications that debates and language may be taking a more radical turn with the acknowledgement of the shortcomings of the practices of gender mainstreaming, the deepening of interest in the notion of empowerment, and the explicit adoption of a human-rights language.

Introduction

Why do so many of us use the language of gender as a camouflage that fools no one and does none of us any favours? (Cornwall 2006:1)

Several years ago I wrote an article (Smyth 1999) reflecting on how development organisations appeared to be afraid of using feminist language and concepts, opting instead for safer and less challenging discourses. My reflections focused most directly on Oxfam GB, since as a staff member of that organisation I inhabited, heard, and spoke its language.

Enough time has gone by to warrant revisiting these thoughts and expanding them. Here I am not attempting to 'monitor progress' in Oxfam GB, in the manner often required in development work. Even if this was the intention, changes in knowledge-management systems at different levels of the organisation would not allow for a methodical review of whether the language of feminism is any more in favour now than it was in 1999. What I seek to do here is to consider more broadly the vocabulary that we use in the development world to communicate about what is often referred to, in its most common short-hand, as 'gender and development'. Oxfam GB remains the main subject of this investigation.

This is not an easy piece to write, since it requires using language that has become densely layered with contradictory meanings and interpretations, and which, in the rest of the chapter, I challenge and criticise. In so doing I am chipping away at the very blocks that should be building my argument, or turning them into traps of my own making.

'Gender talk is everywhere'

Reflections on and celebrations of the progress made by women and in gender relations in recent decades are always tempered by the realisation that change is never linear, and that current circumstances and trends are full of intractable problems and new threats (Kerr 2006).

What is undisputed is that in the past 30 years or so concerns about 'gender issues' have shifted from being seen as a minor but irritating diversion from the more urgent questions of poverty and globalisation, to being a *lingua franca* in which so many actors appear to be fluent. As Gita Sen says: 'Across a sweeping range of issues, from macroeconomics to human rights and political participation, feminist researchers and activists from women's movements appear to have succeeded in bringing about significant changes both in discourse and in actual policy' (Sen 2006: 128). Thus the fact that, as Ruth Pearson puts it, 'gender talk is everywhere' (Pearson 2006:157) is a victory in terms of conveying the pervasive presence of certain concerns in the field of development.

If words are important, silences are important too and a reflection of what is excluded from daily exchanges – verbal or written – among development practitioners and policy makers. What is also important is the frequency and clarity with which certain terms are used, the first as a sign of what gets given priority and air space, the latter because on the clarity of key terms depends whether and how policies are developed and then implemented.

I would argue, however, that the terminology associated with 'gender', though encountered everywhere, remains problematic. Some terms are almost entirely absent, while others are used loosely and inappropriately – with the subtleties and rigour of carefully developed and much-debated concepts utterly lost, so that words are left empty of meaning. Other terms are connected in what Cornwall and Brock (2006: 48) call 'chains of equivalence', where new meanings emerge according to the proximity between chosen words. This lack of clarity in language and concepts affects Oxfam GB too. In a review of its use of human-rights instruments, Marsha Freeman concludes: 'Lack of clarity as to "gender", "mainstreaming" and the role of human rights impedes achievement of the goals of equality between women and men, historically referred to as gender equity' (Freeman 2002: 7).

Confusion can thus compromise the entire purpose for which such language is developed. Something more complex is also happening, however: real women and men, power and conflict all disappear behind bland talk of 'gender', while the language of 'mainstreaming' creates the possibility of orderly tools (an interesting term in itself) and systems through which profoundly internalised beliefs and solidly entrenched structures are miraculously supposed to dissolve and be transformed. At the root of all this is the fact that terms that originated in feminist thinking and activism have somehow lost this mooring, although there are indications that the emerging 'rights' language could be heralding a return to such foundations.

Speech impediments

What are the terms that are being used or deleted from daily spoken and written language in the field of international development?

Silence on feminism

The first thing to note is that there is still a resounding silence around words such as *feminism* and *feminist* (as well as *class*). This was the subject of my article of 1999, and nothing seems to have changed much, either in Oxfam GB or in other organisations. Occasionally the connection with feminism is acknowledged. This is the case, for example, with various documents in which ActionAid acknowledges feminism as the inspiration for some of its thinking.

These remain exceptions, however, and it would seem that the 'fear of feminism' to which I had earlier attributed the absence of certain terms is still dominant. While, as I stressed in my earlier article, feminist-inspired work can take place even in the absence of such explicit language, *feminist, feminists*, and *feminism* are certainly not the kind of 'warm and reassuring' (Cornwall and Brock 2006: 45) words of which the discourse of development organisations has become redolent. On the contrary, they either evoke the derogatory and faintly ridiculous notions through which feminists of all eras have been belittled and demonised, or they instil fear by pointing, accurately, to an arena of struggle and contestation. For this reason they are avoided.

This absence is perhaps also a consequence of the fact that individuals (the majority of whom are women) who are engaged in intrinsically feminist work seem to inhabit two separate domains: that of the women's movement on the one hand, and that of development bureaucracies (including NGOs) on the other. This was certainly the consensus expressed at the AWID Forum held in Bangkok in November 2005, where there was a real sense of the existence of these two separate worlds, as echoed in the repeated calls for creating new bridges and connections (see *Development* 49(1), 2006 for all the key speeches at the Forum).

Contrary to what happens within the women's movement, those who, for whatever reasons, choose to inhabit the so-called 'mainstream development sector' (Win 2006:62) struggle to champion gender equality and women's rights, in speech and in practice. This has to do with organisational structures and changes, and with the power relations inherent in hierarchies. The common experience, as House remarks in relation to the water sector, is one where being a 'gender activist' 'often mean[s] receiving the negativity that appears to be integral to the raising of this subject' (2005: 212). It is thus understandable that many such activists, let alone others whose world views differ and whose priorities lie elsewhere, choose not to use the explicit language of feminism, with all its negative associations.

Empowerment

Empowerment perhaps has the richest and most complex history and evolution of all relevant terms: from the seventeenth-century meaning of delegation and granting licence (Pieterse 2003) to its reverse meaning – in a feminist sense – of self-generated positive change. In this long trajectory, the term has attracted contributions from the most extreme traditions: 'feminist scholarship, the Christian right, New Age self-help manuals, and business management' (Cornwall and Brock 2006: 50).

When the term *empowerment* is used, the emphasis is often on the idea of 'processes' leading to broader outcomes. According to the UK government's Department for International Development (DFID), empowerment refers to 'individuals acquiring the power to think and act freely, exercise choice, and to fulfil their potential as full and equal members of society' (DFID 2000:11). Oxfam GB has adopted this definition verbatim, adding: 'This will of course take different forms and move at different paces according to the particular social, cultural, economic and political context. It is a critical part of working toward the attainment of gender equity ...' (Oxfam 2001).

There are, however, two common problems with the way the term is used. one is that it can easily become too broad and generalised, and thus the answer to questions on 'life, the universe and everything'.[1] An example is the DFID definition quoted above, which continues that empowerment is also about 'negotiating new kinds of institutions, incorporating new norms and rules that support egalitarian and just relations between women and men'.

The other, more common, problem occurs especially within development agencies when they attempt to 'operationalise' the term and shift the focus from empowerment as process to empowerment as end product. The Millennium Development Goals (MDGs) are an example of this, quantifying as they do women's empowerment in the specific and rather limited fields of education, waged employment, and participation in formal politics.

This focus on outcomes has been amply criticised by feminist analysts, not least because it predefines what are highly individual experiences and perceptions. As Mosedale (2005a: 244) points out: '[E]mpowerment is an on-going process rather than a product. There is no final goal. One does not arrive at a stage of being empowered in some absolute sense. People are empowered, or disempowered, relative to others or, importantly, relative to themselves at a previous time.'

In some of the NGO literature, the distinct impression is also given that development programmes can 'empower' women, while a feminist perspective would emphasise that only women themselves can be agents of such a process of change. The first approach is typical of many microfinance projects. For example, the US Grameen Foundation states: 'Our programs are designed to empower the world's poorest by providing affordable capital, financial services, appropriate technology, and capacity building resources to those front-line microfinance institutions (MFIs) that serve them' (www.grameenfoundation.org/programs).

Finally, a feminist tradition understands relevant processes of empowerment as being collective endeavours, versus those that promote individualism and even consumerism (Rowlands 1998), again as appears to be the case among popular microfinance interventions.

Despite the problems, current research on how women's empowerment can be achieved in practice through development interventions is allowing different agencies to engage in dialogue on shared concerns, and to link abstract notions of empowerment to concrete attempts to establish how development programmes can genuinely contribute to women's empowerment (Mosedale 2005b).

Gender

Perhaps the most confusing of all terms is that of *gender* itself. We know that often the word is used to mean 'women'. At a more basic level, words such as *engendering* and *gendered* are usually helpful, for example in titles such as *Engendering Development* (World Bank 2001; for Oxfam see Zuckerman 2002). Other expressions, such as *genderising, doing gender,* and even *you are gender* (though admittedly those are mostly verbal rather than written usages), are certainly much less so.

The transition that seems to have occurred in this case is one that gradually has eroded any meaning from the term gender. Emptied of meaning, it pops up in the most inappropriate places and manners. Clearly 'gender ...is a widely used and often misunderstood term' (Momsen 2004:2).

I am not suggesting with these comments that the term *gender* and those associated with it should be entirely dropped. On the contrary: with increased clarity and consistency of use, they can provide important bridges between understandings and practices of feminist activists on the one hand, and those of feminists and others operating within the confines of development organisations, on the other.

Gender mainstreaming

The most common use of the term *gender* is in association with *mainstreaming*. The notion of gender mainstreaming grew out of the realisation that the concerns for women and gender issues should not remain marginal to the ideas and practices of development organisations, but should be central to them, and hence located in their 'mainstream'. How this should happen, whether by being integrated into them or radically *transforming* them, has long been debated.

Most organisations have opted for a language of transformation. For Oxfam GB, for instance, gender mainstreaming is 'a process of ensuring that all of our work, and the way we do it, contributes to gender equality by transforming the balance of power between women and men' (Gell and Motla 2003). This approach has helped to emphasise that gender issues must be addressed in *all* aspects and stages of development work, including the necessity to do the same internally within development organisations (Mukhopadhyay *et al.* 2006). But it is exactly here that organisations appear reluctant to consider fundamental transformations and are content to tinker at the margins of their structures and practices. It is for this reason that much feminist-inspired literature has long concluded that gender mainstreaming has not been successful. As Aruna Rao puts it: 'While the intention of gender mainstreaming is transformation, it has been chewed up and spit out by development bureaucracies in forms that feminists would barely recognise' (Rao 2006:64).

Ironically, at a practical level the dominance of 'gender mainstreaming' has led to a decline in the resources devoted to programmes and projects explicitly addressing women's disadvantage, or supporting women's organisations, on the understanding that there is no need for gender-specific activities because all concerns have been thoroughly 'mainstreamed'.

In terms of language it can be said that the association between the term *gender* on one hand and *mainstreaming* – with its bureaucratic associations – on the other has created a 'chain of equivalence' that hides the element of power relations so essential to the original feminist understanding of the term. This terminology also helps to smooth over the fact that 'doing gender' within development organisations is itself an arena of dissent and struggle (see earlier discussion on the fate of many feminists inhabiting development agencies).

With 'gender mainstreaming' it is also easier to put real women and men, and the messy realities of their lives and relations, at a certain distance, and turn them into the neat categories necessary for log frames, monitoring tools, and management systems. The experience of Oxfam is interesting here too. Oxfam Great Britain was one of the first NGOs to have a Gender Policy, and the very process of developing it – let alone the contents – was unique in terms of using consultations through which people could internalise essential principles. Ten years or more later the Policy still stands, but it is accompanied by what are called 'non-negotiables': a very small set of basic rules for management and for humanitarian practices. While clearly it is essential that systems themselves embody principles of gender equality, these rules suggest that a commitment to gender equality can be 'ordered' by diktat once and for all, rather than growing out of sustained and continuous efforts to encourage an organic transformation of people's views and actions.

As Joanna Kerr is reported to have said: 'All of us were very excited in Beijing, in governments, donor agencies and women's organizations. But something has happened since then: the last few years a terrible gender fatigue has developed within governments and within donor agencies.... Possibly one of the explanations is that the use of the concept of gender mainstreaming led to an overemphasis on instruments and tools, whilst neglecting to look at the political process' (Hivos 2006: 4).

Thus the term *gender mainstreaming* as a 'chain of equivalence' has become highly depoliticised, in the sense that it is 'disconnected from political and structural realities, and alternative or radical ideas are diluted or neutralised' (Utting 2006: 4).

Conclusions: new words, threats, and promises

Despite the problems discussed so far, new expressions have been finding their way into development language in recent years. In most cases they are not entirely new: rather they are terms that have been rediscovered and adapted to new contexts. *Diversity* is certainly one. However, while this opens the possibility of bringing into development organisations discussions and approaches typical of debates on intersectionality (a difficult term in itself), it also carries new threats. One is that of encouraging a belief that gender disparities and inequalities have been overcome, and that our work therefore needs a new focus; the other is that gender becomes 'dissolved' into more generic categories of disadvantages, with the associated risk of losing even more institutional profile and resources (Pearson 2006:159).

A source of innovation and promise is the spread of rights-based language and approaches to development. In ActionAid the move from a core statement focusing on 'Fighting Poverty Together' to that of 'Rights to End Poverty' has been accompanied by supplementing the 2000 Gender Policy with a firm statement to the effect that Women's Rights are to be one of the main priorities of the organisation (although the original Policy had also made clear reference to women's rights and their empowerment).

This revision is certainly welcome, as it bases efforts to promote gender equality on intrinsic rather than instrumental arguments (Kabeer 2003). Furthermore, an emphasis on women's human rights helps to re-politicise debates and also practices, by offering opportunities to use human-rights treaties as tools of advocacy (Freeman 2002).

Oxfam GB has also adopted a Rights-Based Approach, both in its overall analysis of poverty, and as a specific area of intervention (known as the 'Right to be Heard'). In its approach to gender equality, things are not so clear. Recent attempts to transfer the emphasis of the organisation from 'gender mainstreaming' to women's rights have met with the expressed fear that this is 'a step backwards to WID [Women in Development] and away from GAD [Gender and Development]', and a sign that 'we are neglecting men' (various personal communications). These discussions are on-going. It is to be hoped that they will lead to a consensus on the fact that, given that women continue to face specific and substantial barriers to the enjoyment of their rights, the promotion of women's human rights is the logical and necessary aim for a rights-based development organisation.

In summary, there are major problems associated with the absence of certain terms, the 'emptying' of meaning and depoliticisation of others. At the same time there are indications that debates and language may be taking a more radical turn, with the acknowledgement of the shortcomings of gender mainstreaming, the deepening of interest in the notion of empowerment, and the explicit adoption of a human-rights language.

Note

1. The question concerning Life, the Universe, and Everything was posed and answered by Douglas Adams in his series *The Hitchhiker's Guide to the Galaxy*.

References

Cornwall, A. (2006) 'Ten Years After Beijing –Time to Bid Farewell to Gender?', IDS News Archive, www.ids.ac.uk/IDS/news/Archive/BeijingCornwall.html (retrieved 16 November 2006).

Cornwall, A. and K. Brock (2006) 'The new buzzwords', in P. Utting (ed.) *Reclaiming Development Agendas*, Basingstoke: Palgrave Macmillan and UNRISD.

DFID (2000) Poverty Elimination and the Empowerment of Women, DFID Target Strategy Paper, London: Department for International Development.

Freeman, M. (2002) 'Women's Human Rights Evaluation', unpublished paper written as part of the Oxfam GB Gender Review, September 2001–May 2002, Oxford: Oxfam GB.

Gell, F. and M. Motla (2002) 'Gender Mainstreaming Tools, Questions and Checklists, to Use Across the Programme Management Cycle', unpublished paper, Oxford: Oxfam GB.

HIVOS (2006) 'Women's Rights – Unfinished Business. What Should International NGOs Be Doing?' Report of International NGO Conference, Amsterdam, 15–17 November 2006.

House, S. (2005) 'Easier to say, harder to do: gender, equity and water', in A. Coles and T. Wallace (eds.) *Gender, Water and Development*, Oxford: Berg.

Kabeer, N. (2003) *Gender Mainstreaming in Poverty Eradication and the MDGs: A Handbook for Policy-makers and Other Stakeholders*, Ottawa: Commonwealth Secretariat, IDRC, and CIDA.

Kerr, J. (2006) 'Women's rights in development', *Development* 49(1): 6–11.

Momsen, J. (2004) *Gender and Development*, London: Routledge.

Mosedale, S. (2005a) 'Assessing women's empowerment: towards a conceptual framework', *Journal of International Development* 17: 243–57.

Mosedale, S. (2005b) 'Strategic Impact Inquiry On Women's Empowerment, Report of Year 1'.

Mukhopadhyay, M., G. Steerhouwer, and F. Wong (2006) *Politics of the Possible: Gender Mainstreaming and Organisational Change – Experiences from the Field*, Amsterdam: KIT and Novib.

Oxfam, GB (2001) 'Guidelines for Assessing Impact on Gender Equality', unpublished paper available at http://homepage.oxfam.org.uk/sco/gender/resources/airguide.htm.

Pearson, R. (2006) 'The rise and rise of gender and development', in U. Kothari (ed.) *A Radical History of Development Studies: Individuals, Institutions and Ideologies*, London: Zed Books.

Pieterse, J. (2003) 'Empowerment: snakes and ladders', in K. Bhavnami, J. Foran, and P. A. Kurian (eds.) *Feminist Futures: Re-imagining Women, Culture and Development*, London: Zed Books.

Rao, A. (2006) 'Making institutions work for women', *Development* 49(1): 63–7.

Rowlands, J. (1998) 'A word of the times: but what does it mean? Empowerment in the discourse and practice of development' in H. Afshar (ed.) *Women and Empowerment: Illustrations from the Third World*, London: Macmillan.

Sen, G. (2006) 'The quest for gender equality', in P. Utting (ed.) *Reclaiming Development Agendas: Knowledge, Power and International Policy Making*, Basingstoke: Palgrave Macmillan and UNRISD.

Smyth, I. (1999) 'A rose by any other name: feminism in development NGOs' in F. Porter, I. Smyth, and

C. Sweetman (eds.) *Gender Works: Oxfam Experience in Policy and Practice*, Oxford: Oxfam GB.

Utting, P. (2006) 'Introduction: reclaiming development agendas', in P. Utting (ed.) *Reclaiming Development Agendas: Knowledge, Power and International Policy Making*, Basingstoke: Palgrave Macmillan and UNRISD.

Win, E. (2006) 'Building an international feminist space: reflections from Bangkok', *Development* 49(1): 60–62.

World Bank (2001) *Engendering Development: Through Gender Equality in Rights, Resources, and Voice*, Oxford: Oxford University Press.

Zuckerman, E. (2002) 'Evaluation of Gender Mainstreaming in Advocacy Work on Poverty Reduction Strategy Papers (PRSPs) Synthesis Report', unpublished paper written as part of the Oxfam GB Gender Review, September 2001–May 2002, Oxford: Oxfam GB.

About the author

Ines Smyth is Oxfam GB's Global Gender Policy Adviser. She also worked at the Asian Development Bank in Manila and for several years at the Institute of Social Studies in The Hague, the University of Oxford, and the London School of Economics.

CHAPTER 14
Sustainability

Ian Scoones

As a consummately effective 'boundary term', able to link disparate groups on the basis of a broad common agenda, 'sustainability' has moved a long way from its technical association with forest management in Germany in the eighteenth century. In the 1980s and 1990s it defined – for a particular historical moment – a key debate of global importance, bringing with it a coalition of actors – across governments, civic groups, academia and business – in perhaps an unparalleled fashion. That they did not agree with everything (or even often know anything of the technical definitions of the term) was not the point. The boundary work done in the name of sustainability created an important momentum for innovation in ideas, political mobilisation, and policy change, particularly in connection with the UN Conference on Environment and Development (UNCED) held in Rio in 1992. All this of course did not result in everything that the advocates at the centre of such networks had envisaged, and today the debate has moved on, with different priority issues, and new actors and networks. But, the author argues, this shift does not undermine the power of sustainability as a buzzword: as a continuingly powerful and influential meeting point of ideas and politics.

Introduction

Sustainability must be one of the most widely used buzzwords of the past two decades. There is nothing, it seems, that cannot be described as 'sustainable': apparently everything can be either hyphenated or paired with it. We have sustainable cities, economies, resource management, business, livelihoods – and, of course, sustainable development. Sustainability has become, par excellence, what Thomas Gieryn (1999) calls a 'boundary term': one where science meets politics, and politics meets science. The 'boundary work' around sustainability – of building epistemic communities of shared understanding of and common commitment to linking environmental and economic development concerns – has become a major concern across the world. In the past two decades, networks of diverse actors have been formed, alliances have been built, institutions and organisations have been constructed, projects have been formulated, and money – in increasingly large amounts – has been spent in the name of sustainability. It is at this complex intersection between science and politics where boundary work takes place, and where words, with often ambivalent and contested meanings, have an important political role in processes of policy making and development.

A (very) short intellectual history

But like all buzzwords, the term *sustainability* has a history. It has not always had such significant connotations. The term was first coined several hundred years ago by a German forester, Hans Carl von Carlowitz, in his 1712 text *Sylvicultura Oeconomica*, to prescribe how forests should be managed on a long-term basis. It was, however, not until the 1980s that the term attained much wider currency. With the birth of the contemporary environment movement in the late 1960s and 1970s, and debates about the limits to growth, environmentalists were keen to show how environmental issues could be linked to mainstream questions of development. The commission chaired by Gro Brundtland, former Prime Minister of Norway, became the focal point for this debate in the mid-1980s, culminating in the landmark report entitled *Our Common Future* in 1987. This report offered the now classic modern definition of sustainable development:

> Sustainable development is development that meets the needs of the present without compromising the ability of future generations to meet their own needs. (WCED 1987a: 43)

The terms *sustainability*, and more particularly *sustainable development*, drew on longer intellectual debates across disciplines. From the 1980s there was a global explosion of academic debate and policy debate on these issues, particularly in the run-up to the United Nations Conference on Environment and Development (UNCED), held in Rio in 1992.

Ecologists had long been concerned with the ways in which ecosystems responded to shocks and stresses; and mathematical ecology had blossomed through the 1970 and 1980s, with important work from the likes of Buzz Holling and Bob May on the stability and resilience properties of both model and real biological systems (Holling 1973; May 1977). Sustainability could thus be defined in these terms as the ability of a system to bounce back from such shocks and stresses and adopt stable states.

Neo-classical economists drew on theories of substitutable capital to define (weak) sustainability. And within economics, debates raged over whether such a 'weak' definition of sustainability was adequate or whether a stronger definition, highlighting the lack of substitutability of 'critical natural capital' was needed (cf. Pearce and Atkinson 1993). Ecological economics meanwhile traced more tangible links with ecological systems, generating such fields as life-cycle analysis, ecological footprint assessment, and alternative national accounting systems (Common and Stagl 2005). Elements of these debates were picked up by the business community, where notions of the 'triple bottom line' emerged, in which sustainability was seen as one among other more conventional business objectives, resulting in a whole plethora of new accounting and auditing measures which brought sustainability concerns into business planning and accounting practice (Elkington 1997). And at Rio, the World Business Council for Sustainable Development was launched with much fanfare (Schmidheiny and Timberlake 1992), bringing on board some big corporate players. Drawing on wider popular political concerns about the relationships between environment, well-being, and struggles for social justice, political scientists such as Andrew Dobson (1999) delineated political theories that incorporated a 'green' politics perspective, placing sustainability concerns at the centre of a normative understanding of social and political change. Others offered integrative syntheses, linking the economic, environmental, and socio-political dimensions of sustainability into what Bob Kates and colleagues have dubbed a 'sustainability science' (Kates *et al.* 2001).

By the 1990s, then, we had multiple versions of sustainability: broad and narrow, strong and weak, big S and small s sustainability, and more. Different technical meanings were constructed alongside different visions of how the wider project of sustainable development should be conceived. Each competed with the others in a vibrant, if confusing, debate. But how would all this intense debate translate into practical policy? 1992 was the key moment for this.

Coming of age in Rio

The 1992 Rio conference, convened by the United Nations and attended by representatives of 178 governments, numerous heads of state, and a veritable army of more than 1000 NGOs, civil-society, and campaign groups, was perhaps the high point – the coming of age of sustainability and sustainable development. Many people believed that this was the moment when sustainability would find its way to the top of the global political agenda and would become a permanent feature of the way in which development, both North and South, would be done (Holmberg *et al.* 1991).

The Rio conference launched a number of high-level convention processes – on climate change, biodiversity, and desertification – all with the aim of realising sustainable-development ideals on key global environmental issues. Commissions were established, and national action-planning processes set in train for a global reporting system against agreed objectives (Young 1999). At the same time, a more local-level, community-led process was conceived – *Agenda 21* – which envisaged sustainability being built from the bottom up through local initiatives by local governments, community groups, and citizens (Selman 1998).

These were heady days indeed. Environment and development had, it seemed, finally come of age. Groups such as the London-based International Institute for Environment and Development (IIED), the Delhi-based Centre for Science and Environment, the Washington-based World Resources Institute, and the Manitoba-based International Institute for Sustainable Development had access to and influence over policy debates that a few years before they could only dream of. The challenge for such organisations – and many others besides who adopted the creed of sustainable development as central to their mission – was to move from theory to practice, from ideals to real results on the ground. What did implementing sustainable development mean? The result was an exponential growth in planning approaches, analysis frameworks, measurement indicators, audit systems, and evaluation protocols designed to help governments, businesses, communities, and individuals to make sustainability real. This was great business for consultants, trainers, researchers, and others. But did it make a difference?

Sustainable livelihoods as boundary work

In the late 1990s, particularly in the UK but also more broadly, the term 'sustainable livelihoods' became the signifier of 'good' development. For a period this word-pairing became enormously influential in UK international development policy, and a quintessential example of how 'sustainability' – especially when connected to another term – can be a prime mover in boundary work, linking science and policy in novel and potentially positive ways.

Originally coined by a committee working on agriculture and food for the Brundtland Commission during the 1980s (reputedly emerging one evening over discussion in a Geneva hotel), the term 'sustainable livelihoods' first appeared in the 1987 Food 2000 report (WCED 1987b). This particular linking of terms was given definitional flesh by Robert Chambers and Gordon Conway in a discussion paper published by the Institute of Development Studies in 1992 (Chambers and Conway 1992). For a time it languished out of the policy limelight, but with the publication of the UK government's White Paper on international development in 1997 (DFID 1997), it was suddenly centre-stage, and seen as a critical element of development thinking for the new department (the Department for International Development, DFID), now with ministerial status and with a dynamic minister – Clare Short – in the lead role.

William Solesbury (2003) lucidly documents the policy history of 'sustainable livelihoods' over this period, tracing linkages between researchers, White Paper drafting teams, advisory committees established by the new department, and the bureaucratic manoeuvrings of key individuals within government. Before long a large section of the department, with a substantial spending budget and a dedicated cadre of staff, had adopted the name 'sustainable livelihoods'. In a few short, if busy, months the old style 'natural resource' department had been transformed, according to the promotional rhetoric, into something forward-looking, cross-cutting, and dynamic that could meet the 'New Labour' political demands of doing something effective about poverty and development.

Government enlisted external experts, including researchers, NGO workers, and others, to think through the implications. A researchers' checklist developed by a team at the Institute of Development Studies (Scoones 1998) was adapted and embellished and became a 'framework', and, later, a whole suite of 'approaches' (Carney 1998; 2002). And, with this, the acronyms started to flow, a brand was created, and a whole industry of trainers, consultants, web-based information specialists, and others were commissioned to make 'sustainable livelihoods' a central thrust of UK development policy.

This flurry of activity and discussion was not confined to the new DFID: other aid agencies looked with interest at what was happening in London. NGOs such as Oxfam GB were also developing their own approaches (Neefjes 2000), and even large UN agencies such as the FAO became interested in the approach as one that transcended narrow sectoral concerns and took a more integrative approach to development and poverty reduction.[1]

This was classic boundary work. Scientific concerns, drawing from ecology, economics, and politics, merged with specific political and bureaucratic agendas in a process of mutual construction of both science and policy. Alliances were formed, spanning government, NGOs, private consultants, and academia, linking often unlike organisations and individuals, both North and South. It seemed that a word (or in this case two) had created a whole network, loosely affiliated around a set of often rather vague and poorly defined understandings of a complex and rather ambiguous concept. But at the time – and in certain places, notably DFID – it had an important uses, both conceptual and political.

Things fall apart

But all good things must come to an end. While the DFID-centred network disintegrated for parochial, bureaucratic–political reasons, a wider crisis of confidence overwhelmed the confident, positive members of networks centred on ideas of sustainability by the late 1990s. Why was this?

The 1992 Rio agenda was of course extravagantly ambitious, and high hopes depended on the processes that arose from it. But not everyone was playing ball. Commercial interests lobbied hard in the USA, for example, to dilute the conventions, and, in the end, the USA did not sign up. Beyond the geopolitics of sustainability and the particularly recalcitrant role of the USA in its new-found position as sole global superpower, there were other impediments to the realisation of the ambitious aims of Rio. Once the heads of state had left, the often newly created Environment Ministries had the task of seeking budgets and creating a political space back home for environment and development agendas. Given other pressing issues, this was usually an up-hill struggle. For those governments that had signed up to conventions, much energy was spent on complying with the elaborate consultation, planning, and reporting requirements. For cash-strapped new ministries in developing countries, this was not easy. For sure, aid flows helped as agencies re-geared their funding to accommodate the new enthusiasm for environmental issues, but this was often not enough to bring sustainable development beyond the rhetorical gloss and the often half-hearted routinisation of action planning, indicator monitoring, and 'sustainable development' projects.

Buzzwords – and the ambitions with which they are associated – that become mainstream and incorporated into routine, bureaucratic procedures often (perhaps always) suffer this fate. For many commentators writing since 2000, the simplistic managerialism of many initiatives labelled 'sustainable development' left much to be desired (Berkhout *et al.* 2003). Critiques focused on the lack of progress on major targets set in 1992, the endless repackaging of old initiatives as 'sustainable' this or that, and the lack of capacity and commitment within governments and international organisations to make the ideals of sustainability real in day-to-day practice (Vogler and Jordan 2003). With the default bureaucratic mode of managerialism dominating – and its focus on action plans, indicators, and the rest – the wider political economy of sustainable development was being neglected, many felt. *'It's politics, stupid'*, commentators argued. And, with mainstreaming and bureaucratisation, the urgency and political vibrancy is lost, and, with this, comes a dilution and loss of dynamism in a previously energetic and committed debate.

Long live sustainability

But all was not lost. While the coalitions formed before and after the Rio conference may have dispersed, fragmented, and turned in on themselves, since the late 1990s there has been a revival – but in different guises – of sustainability debates. And this time politics is more to the fore.

Rather than emerging from a rather ethereal and abstract idea of sustainability derived from theory, debates in recent years have focused on some big issues that have hit the international headlines. These have resulted in both public and, usually later, political reactions. For example, the controversy about genetically modified (GM) crops, which peaked in Europe in the late 1990s and early 2000s, had many political and policy reverberations internationally. This was a debate about, among other things, the sustainability of farming systems, the future of food, human health, and biodiversity, and corporate control of the agri-food system (GEC Programme 1999). In the same way, the debate on climate change did not really begin to be taken seriously until after the year 2000. No longer was this a discussion on the arcane specifics of global climate models, but a real political and economic issue, to which people and governments had to pay attention. Concerns about the environment-and-development drivers of new global diseases and pandemics were also pitched into the public and political realm, first with SARS and then avian 'flu.

All of these issues – and the list could go on – are centred around classic 'sustainability' questions: they each involve complex and changing environmental dynamics which have an impact on human livelihoods and well-being; they all have intersecting ecological, economic, and socio-political dimensions; and, as with an increasing array of environment–development issues, they have both local and global dimensions.

But what is equally sure is that the existing 'sustainable development' institutional and policy machinery is incapable of dealing with them effectively. The Kyoto Protocol on climate change has all but collapsed, and the options for a post-Kyoto settlement that involves the USA, China, and India have yet to be elaborated. Questions of biosafety surrounding GM crops have not been resolved, and the UN Biosafety Protocol seems far from an effective answer. And recent disease scares have shown that neither global institutions nor local health systems are able to deal with the likelihood of a global pandemic.

So how have new coalitions, networks, and affiliations formed around the concept of 'sustainability'? In contrast to the Brundtland–Rio period of the 1980s and 1990s, today there is nothing that can be constructed as a global consensus. While the post-Rio institutions – such as the UN Commission for Sustainable Development and the secretariats of the different conventions – still exist, they are not necessarily seen as the rallying points for new initiatives. For these we have to look beyond these institutions to new actors and groupings.

The 2002 'Rio-plus-10' conference in Johannesburg was not such a big deal as its predecessor, but it did attract some interesting groups and some strong debate – and, importantly, much dissent. Conflicts were sparked by the still very live GM debate, for example, where anti-GM activists and social movements were pitched against corporations that had re-branded themselves as committed to 'sustainable agriculture' globally. More generally, there was a heated debate about whether the 'sustainable development' mainstream had sold out to the needs of business and global capital, or whether such accommodation and dialogue with big business was the only route to getting corporate responsibility on sustainability issues (Wapner 2003).

Debate also flourished around the pros and cons, successes and failures of the divergent routes of the Rio commitments – between local solutions (around Agenda 21) and international legal processes (around the global conventions). Some groups argued that local solutions had shown more promise, particularly where intransigent governments subject to extreme corporate lobbying pressure (notably the USA, but perhaps increasingly in Asia) were unable to realise any sustainable development goals, yet cities and neighbourhoods could make great strides towards, for example, tackling the effects of climate change, conserving green spaces, or meeting recycling targets. Others, by contrast, argued that the big sustainability agendas remain global, and, in an increasingly globalised economy and inter-connected world, seeking some form of international agreement on such issues – perhaps with new institutions such as a World Environmental Organisation – remained, despite the pitfalls and obstacles, a key objective for achieving sustainability (Newell 2001).

Thus by 2002, the 'sustainable development' movement, so confidently ambitious at Rio a decade before, was more muted, more fractured, and perhaps a bit more realistic. The term 'sustainability' has however persisted, and indeed been given more conceptual depth in explorations of resilience (cf. Folke *et al.* 2002; Clark and Dickson 2003). As a boundary term, linking diverse groups

– even those who violently disagree with each other – it remains a useful unifying link. To be effective in this boundary work, it is often essential to remain contested, ambiguous, and vague. While academics continue to endeavour to refine its meaning, locating it in ever more precise terms within particular disciplinary debates, it is the more over-arching, symbolic role – of aspiration, vision, and normative commitment – that remains so politically potent.

Where next? Reinventing a buzzword

So what of the future? Will sustainability become the unifying concept of the twenty-first century, as many so boldly proclaimed just a few years ago? Certainly the managerialism and routinised bureaucratisation of the 1990s have been shown to have their limits. While sustainability-related commissions, committees, and processes persist in various guises, they have perhaps less political hold than before. But with climate change in particular – and wider risks associated with environmental change, whether epidemic disease or biodiversity change – now being seen as central to economic strategy and planning, there are clear opportunities for the insertion of sustainability agendas in new ways into policy discourse and practice.

But can an old buzzword be reinvigorated and reinvented for new challenges, or does it need discarding, with something else put its place? Certainly terms associated with sustainability – such as resilience, robustness, diversity, and precaution – are all seen more frequently in policy debates these days (Stirling 2007). But they all have direct links to sustainability, both intellectually, institutionally, and politically. So the lineage persists. Future buzzword archaeologies will no doubt trace transmutations, adaptations, and shifts, but, in my view at least, sustainability – and the wider agenda that it inspires – is here to stay.

Note

1. See information on the £5m DFID-supported FAO Livelihoods Support Programme at the IDS-hosted information portal, Livelihoods Connect, at www.livelihoods.org/lessons/project_summaries/ supp4_projsum.html

References

Berkhout, F., M. Leach, and I. Scoones (eds.) (2003) *Negotiating Environmental Change. New Perspective from Social Science*, Cheltenham: Edward Elgar.

Carney, D. (ed.) (1998) *Sustainable Rural Livelihoods: What Contribution Can We Make?* London: Department for International Development

Carney, D. (2002) *Sustainable Livelihoods Approaches: Progress and Possibilities for Change*, London: Department for International Development.

Chambers, R. and G.R. Conway (1992) 'Sustainable Rural Livelihoods: Practical Concepts for the 21st Century', *Discussion Paper 296*, Brighton: Institute of Development Studies.

Clark, W. and N. Dickson (2003) 'Sustainability science: the emerging research program', *Proceedings of the National Academy of Sciences* 100: 8059–61.

Common, M. and S. Stagl (2005) *Ecological Economics – An Introduction*, Cambridge: Cambridge University Press.

DFID (1997) 'Eliminating World Poverty: A Challenge for the 21st Century', *White Paper on International Development*, Cm 3789. London: Stationery Office.

Dobson, A. (1999) *Justice and the Environment: Conceptions of Environmental Sustainability and Dimensions of Social Justice*, Oxford: Oxford University Press.

Elkington, J. (1997) *Cannibals with Forks: The Triple Bottom Line of 21st Century Business*, London: Capstone.

Folke, C., S. Carpenter, T. Elmqvist, L. Gunderson, C. S. Holling, and B. Walker (2002) 'Resilience and sustainable development: building adaptive capacity in a world of transformations', *Ambio: A Journal of the Human Environment*, 31(5): 437–40.

GEC Programme (1999) *The Politics of GM Food: Risk, Science and Public Trust*, University of Sussex: ESRC Global Environmental Change Programme.

Gieryn, T. (1999) *Cultural Boundaries of Science: Credibility on the Line*, Chicago, IL: Chicago University Press.

Holling, C.S. (1973) 'Resilience and stability of ecological systems', *Annual Review of Ecology and Systematics* 4: 1–23.

Holmberg, J., S. Bass, and L. Timberlake (1991) *Defending the Future: A Guide to Sustainable Development*, London: Earthscan.

Kates, R.W., W.C. Clark, R. Corell, J.M. Hall, C. Jaeger, I. Lowe *et al.* (2001) 'Environment and development: sustainability science', *Science* 292: 641–2.

May, R. (1977) 'Thresholds and breakpoints in ecosystems with a multiplicity of stable states', *Nature* 269: 471–7.

Neefjes, K. (2000) *Environments and Livelihoods: Strategies for Sustainability*, Oxford: Oxfam (UK and Ireland).

Newell, P. (2001) 'New environmental architectures and the search for effectiveness', *Global Environmental Politics* 1(1): 35–44.

Pearce, D. and G. Atkinson (1993) 'Capital theory and the measurement of sustainable development: an indicator of "weak" sustainability', *Ecological Economics*, 8: 103–8.

Schmidheiny, S. and L. Timberbake (1992) *Changing Course: A Global Business Perspective on Development and the Environment*, Cambridge, MA: MIT Press.

Scoones, I. (1998) 'Sustainable Rural Livelihoods: A Framework for Analysis', Working Paper 72, Brighton: Institute for Development Studies.

Selman, P. (1998) 'Local Agenda 21: substance or spin?', *Journal of Environmental Planning and Management* 45(5): 553.

Solesbury, W. (2003) 'Sustainable Livelihoods: A Case Study of the Evolution of DFID Policy', ODI Working Paper 217, London: Overseas Development Institute.

Stirling, A. (2007) 'Resilience, Robustness, Diversity: Dynamic Strategies for Sustainability', paper submitted for ESEE Conference, Leipzig, 3–5 June.

Vogler, J. and A. Jordan (2003) 'Governance and the environment', in F. Berkhout, M. Leach, and I. Scoones (eds.) pp. 137–58.

Wapner, P. (2003) 'World Summit on Sustainable Development: toward a post-Jo'burg environmentalism', *Global Environmental Politics* 3: 1–10.

World Commission on Environment and Development (1987a) Our Common Future: Report of the World Commission on Environment and Development, Oxford: Oxford University Press.

World Commission on Environment and Development (1987b) 'Food 2000: Global Policies for Sustainable Agriculture', *Report of the Advisory Panel on Food Security, Agriculture, Forestry and Environment*, London: Zed Books.

Young, O. (ed.) (1999) *The Effectiveness of International Environmental Regimes: Causal Connections and Behavioral Mechanisms*, Cambridge MA: MIT Press.

About the author

Ian Scoones is a Professorial Fellow at the Institute of Development Studies at the University of Sussex, where he is co-director of the Social, Technological and Environmental Pathways to Sustainability (STEPS) Centre.

CHAPTER 15

From the right to development to the rights-based approach: how 'human rights' entered development

Peter Uvin

This chapter offers an intellectual genealogy of how the concept of human rights has entered the development discourse – from the formulation of a 'right to development' to the rhetorical incorporation of rights within prevailing discourse, to the articulation of a 'rights-based approach' to development. It concludes with some propositions about the important role that a focus on rights might play in the practice of international development.

Introduction

'Rights', 'human rights', and 'rights-based' are relatively recent additions to the development lexicon (Tomasevski 1993; Sano 2000). For decades, the development enterprise lived in perfect isolation, if not ignorance, of the human-rights system and its implications for development. During the 1990s this began to change, for three main reasons. The first was the end of the Cold War, which opened the door to greater missionary zeal. The second was the manifest failure of structural adjustment programmes, which came to be seen as caused by a lack of government accountability and prompted a major push for good governance and democracy. And thirdly, development thinkers always seek to redefine development as being about more than economic growth: talking about human rights is one way to construct a more holistic definition.

By the end of the 1990s, both the PowerPoint presenters and the dirty-fingernails folk had converged around some acceptance that human rights ought to play a larger role in development. But quite what role, and what this might mean for the development enterprise itself, has remained both vague and contested. This chapter offers an intellectual genealogy of rights in development – from the formulation of a 'right to development' to the rhetorical incorporation of rights within prevailing development discourse, to the articulation of a 'rights-based approach' to development.[1]

The right to development

Development as a concept first entered the human-rights edifice through the debate on the 'right to development'. The idea was launched by the Senegalese jurist M'Baye in 1972 – a period of radical debate about the New International Economic Order (NIEO). During the first half of the 1970s, Third World countries used their numerical majority in the United Nations to try to negotiate reforms in the global political economy of trade, finance, investment, aid, and information flows. This effort was led by well-known Third World nationalists, emboldened by the success of the OPEC oil embargo, which many believed was the beginning of a fundamental reshuffling of the world's economic power cards.

The notion of a right to development provided legal and ethical authority to the Third World's request for the international redistribution of resources. In addition, it acted as a counter-argument against rich countries' exclusive insistence on political and civil human rights. Acrimonious discussions about the NIEO persisted for years, but led to no concrete results, apart from the signing of a few weak international commodity agreements. By 1985, the intellectual and political pendulum had swung dramatically rightwards, and structural adjustment had replaced international reform as the talk of the day. The notion of a right to development did not die altogether, partly because the developing countries had learned that, in the words of Ian Brownlie, 'it had become evident that the political futures market was in the area of human rights and it was therefore prudent to pursue policy goals under that banner' (1989:3, cited in Slinn 1999: 370). After much legal wrangling, in 1986 a 'right to development' was adopted as a UN General Assembly resolution (i.e., not a treaty, and thus without binding force), stating as follows:

> The right to development is an inalienable human right by virtue of which every human person and all peoples are entitled to participate in, contribute to, and enjoy economic, social, cultural and political development, in which all human rights and fundamental freedoms can be fully realized. (www.unhch.ch/html/menu3/b/74.htm)

This was the kind of rhetorical victory that diplomats cherish: the Third World got its right to development, while the First World ensured that the right could never be interpreted as a greater priority than political and civil rights, that it was totally non-binding, and that it carried no resource-transfer obligations.

Human rights, once set down on paper, never die, even though no one may care much about their survival. Rather, they mutate into working groups, commissions, and expert panels, each of which produces reports that are occasionally the subject of discussions in low-level meetings. Sometimes, however, out of this patient work contested or marginal rights obtain a second lease of life. This is what happened to the right to development. At the 1993 World Conference on Human Rights in Vienna, the right to development was re-adopted, this time unanimously, as part of the broader Vienna Declaration and Programme of Action. Thus it can be claimed that the right to development now reflects a global legal consensus, and as such represents a victory for its advocates, pyrrhic as it may be. Following this, in 1997 the right to development was honoured with its very own 'independent expert', Indian economist Arjun Sengupta, who has produced a series of fine reports.

From a political, real-world, perspective, the track record of the right to development is catastrophic. According to most legal scholars, the declaration was bad law: vague, internally contradictory, duplicating other already codified rights, and devoid of identifiable parties bearing clear obligations (Slinn 1999; Rosas 1995; Obiora 1996). Affirming that all people have the right to development, and that such development consists of, and is realised through, the realisation of every existing category of human rights is surely a beautifully worded statement, but it is also operationally meaningless. This quality is nicely exemplified in the following quote from the UN Working Group on the Right to Development, which describes the right as being

> ...multidimensional, integrated, dynamic and progressive. Its realization observes the full observance of economic, social, cultural, civil, and political rights. It further embraces the different concepts of development of all development sectors, namely sustainable development, human development, and the concept of indivisibility, interdependence, and universality of all human rights. (Approvingly quoted in UNDP 1998: 3)

It is little wonder that the right to development has so rarely been invoked by a social movement or by a major organisation promoting social change.

Rhetorical-formulaic incorporation

During the 1990s, bilateral and multilateral aid agencies published a slew of policy statements, guidelines, and documents on the incorporation of human rights in their mandate. An enormous amount of this work was little more than thinly disguised presentations of old wine in new bottles. A few quotes suffice. '[The World Bank's] lending over the past 50 years for education, health care, nutrition, sanitation, housing, environmental protection and agriculture have helped turn rights into reality for millions' (Lovelace 1999: 27; World Bank 1999: 3, 4). Or UNDP, claiming that it 'already plays an important role in the protection and promotion of human rights. ...Its program is an application of the right to development' (UNDP 1998: 6). What these statements essentially do is colonise the human-rights discourse, arguing, like Molière's character who discovered that he had always been speaking prose, that human rights is what these development agencies were doing all along. Case closed; high moral ground safely established.

A more benign interpretation is that these verbal changes constitute the first steps towards a true change of vision. Indeed, much scholarship argues that discourse changes have real-world impacts: they slowly redefine the margins of acceptable action, create opportunities for redefining reputations and shaming, change incentive structures and the way in which interests and preferences are defined, influence expectations, etc. This is, after all, a key proposition of all international law: that even in the absence of enforcement mechanisms, international law does matter by affecting actors' perceptions, calculations, reputations, and norms. Hence, rhetorical incorporation, while it may change little in the immediate term, may make a real difference in the longer run.

Until now, however, what this approach has produced is not only a simple sleight-of-hand. It has also overlooked the tensions between the different logics of human rights and of development. As Donnelly (1999: 611) convincingly argues, referring to the UNDP's new work on human development,

> Human rights and sustainable human development 'are inextricably linked' only if development is defined to make this relationship tautological. 'Sustainable human development' simply redefines human rights, along with democracy, peace, and justice, as subsets of development. Aside from the fact that neither most ordinary people nor governments use the term in this way, such a definition fails to address the relationship between economic development and human rights. Tensions between these objectives cannot be evaded by stipulative definitions.

To work out the relations between development and human rights requires more than simply stating that one automatically implies, or equals, or subsumes, the other. Michael Windfuhr (2000: 25), founder of FIAN, one of the world's foremost human-rights organisations devoted to an economic right (the right to food), adds:

> Besides the general misconceptions related to ESC [economic, social, and cultural] Rights – that they are costly to implement, that implementation can only be done progressively and that they are therefore not rights at all but rather political objectives – one additional basic misunderstanding often comes up in discussions on how to integrate ESC-Rights into development cooperation, the concept that development cooperation automatically implements ESC-Rights because it is oriented to improve health or food situations of groups of the population. A rights-based approach means foremost to talk about the relationship between a state and its citizens.

There is a real danger, then, in this kind of rhetorical discourse. Far from constituting the first step towards a fundamental re-conceptualisation of the practice of development co-operation, it seems merely to provide a fig-leaf for the continuation of the *status quo*. By postulating that development projects and programmes by definition constitute an implementation of human rights, the important difference between a service-based and a rights-based approach to development is obscured. To have a right to something – say, food – it not just about having enough of that: a slave can be well nourished too. It is about having a 'social guarantee' (Shue 1980), which implies that it is about the way the interactions between citizens, states, and corporations are structured, and how they affect the most marginal and weakest in society. This is obfuscated in a lot of the easy and self-serving rhetoric that agencies produce.

Human rights and good governance

Human rights came, in the 1990s, to be harnessed to the 'good governance' agenda (see Thandika Mkandawire's contribution to this volume). Initially developed by the World Bank as an extension and deepening of the economic-conditionality agenda contained in the classical structural adjustment programmes of the 1980s, the terminology of 'good governance' has been taken over by some bilateral donors and the entire UN system. Governance specialists, indicators, programmes, and conferences have multiplied like mushrooms after a rainy night. In *Development and Human Rights: The Role of the World Bank*, the Bank declares:

> By helping to fight corruption, improve transparency, and accountability in governance, strengthen judicial systems, and modernize financial sectors, the Bank contributes to building environments in which people are better able to pursue a broader range of human rights. (World Bank 1998: 3)

As this quote suggests, and as discussed above, much of the conversion to human rights still amounts to little more than rhetorical repackaging: policies that were once justified by their potential to improve investor confidence are now justified for their human-rights potential, at least in brochures destined for the human-rights community. Nothing else, however, changes. It takes more than a few ideological leaps to see how strengthening financial systems is a human-rights activity. One feels sure that the framers of the Universal Declaration and the two Covenants were not thinking of shoring up banking-reserve requirements, improving accounting standards, or current-account liberalisation when they were building the human-rights edifice.

In statements like these, the many faces of power, and their associated discourses, come together. Human rights, free trade, or the willingness to let rich-country multinational corporations (MNCs) buy national assets become conflated. All amount to re-statements of the 'good world' as the powerful see it. They are decreed from above, morally self-satisfying, and compatible with the *status quo* in the centres of power. A huge range of other rich-country behaviours remains immune to criticism. Northern over-consumption, a history of colonialism, lopsided environmental degradation, protectionism, the dumping of arms in the Third World, the history of shoring up past dictators, the wisdom of structural adjustment, and globalisation– all are off the discussion table. No wonder so many people resent the human-rights agenda.

Freedom as development

A new paradigm emerged in the early 2000s. In it, development and rights become different aspects of the same dynamic, as if different strands of the same fabric. Development comes to be re-defined in terms that include human rights as a constitutive part: all worthwhile processes of social change are simultaneously rights-based and economically grounded, and should be conceived of in such terms. Without doubt the most referred-to reflections on this new paradigm are found in Amartya Sen's *Development as Freedom*, in which he defines development as the expansion of capabilities or substantive human freedoms, 'the capacity to lead the kind of life he or she has reason to value' (Sen 1999: 87). He argues for the removal of major factors that limit freedom, defining them as 'poverty as well as tyranny, poor economic opportunities as well as systematic social deprivation, neglect of public facilities as well as intolerance or over-activity of repressive states' (Sen 1999:1).

Sen treats freedom as simultaneously instrumental, constitutive, and constructive for development, setting out the deep mutually constitutive links that exist between these two concepts and domains in ways that make their inseparability clear. With Sen as their champion, these ideas have made great inroads in international development discourse. But they are not in themselves new: democracy and development have long been linked in political and development discourse. Take this statement, for example, from the UN Secretary-General's *Agenda for Development*:

> Democracy and development are linked in fundamental ways. They are linked because democracy provides the only long-term basis for managing competing ethnic, religious, and cultural interests in a way that minimizes the risk of violent internal conflict. They are linked because democracy is inherently attached to the question of governance, which has an impact on all aspects of development efforts. They are linked because democracy is a fundamental human right, the advancement of which is itself an important measure of development. They are linked because people's participation in the decision-making processes which affect their lives is a basic tenet of development. (United Nations 1994, para. 120)

This was written five years *before* Sen's book, by an institution that is not exactly the hotbed of philosophical innovation. We have to acknowledge that these ideas have been around a long time in the development field. Rather than congratulating ourselves on how smart and perceptive we have become since reading and discussing Sen's work, we ought to ask why we have not acted on these ideas before. And this is where we encounter the limits of Amartya Sen's major contribution to development. There is no politically grounded analysis of what stands in the way of his approach. This is hardly cause for discarding his contribution: no man is obliged to do everything. What it does mean, though, is that agencies, by signing up to

Sen's vision, remain committed to little more than improved discourse – in this case in a well-appreciated economic-sounding form.

It is interesting here to consider UNDP, the institution whose discourse has adopted Sen's ideas most enthusiastically. Its milestone *2000 Human Development Report* dealt with human rights and human development, and the relations between the two. The section that describes the practical implications of 'promoting rights in development' (UNDP 2000:112) proposes five concrete things:

- launch independent national assessments of human rights
- align national laws with international human-rights standards and commitments
- promote human-rights norms
- strengthen a network of human-rights organisations
- promote a rights-enabling economic environment.

As we can see, four of the five implications are of the largely meaningless legalistic and technical kind that will not challenge anyone: ensure that governments make references to human rights in their constitutions and remove laws that are contrary to human rights; educate, sensitise, or mobilise people in human rights; create national human-rights commissions, ombudsmen, and the like. These are all potentially useful activities, but they do not reflect any mainstreaming of human rights into development practice; they are simply small, technical add-ons, of doubtful operational relevance. Only the fifth seems to offer the potential of going further. Allow me to quote from it at some more length:

> How to create an enabling environment in which public policy can most effectively provide resources for advancing human rights? First, the public sector must focus on what it can do and leave for others what it should not do. ...Second, with this division of labour, the state can focus on the direct provision of many economic, social, and civil rights. ...Third, the major economic ministries, such as finance and planning, need to integrate rights into the economic policy-making process. ...Fourth, the private sector also has responsibilities in creating an enabling economic environment. Chambers of commerce and other business organizations should contribute to efforts to further improve human rights... (UNDP 2000: 118-19)

This is all that the new approach amounts to: a standard repetition of the end-of-the-1990s liberal dogma of the sanctity of economic growth combined with some human-resource development and a few pious recommendations that ministries and corporations – and the Chamber of Commerce? – ought to think about human rights. Vagueness dominates. Note also that none of the human-rights objectives relates to UNDP, the aid enterprise, or the international community itself. All of them are to be implemented out there, in the Third World, without requiring a critical look at oneself.

The 'rights-based approach'

Others – mainly NGOs – have gone much further, erecting a new vision of their work, the so-called 'rights-based approach'. The rights-based approach to development is useful not so much because it posits rights as fixed properties or legal certainties, nor because it somehow leads us to engage in actions or supply services that we would never have thought of beforehand. Rather, its use lies in two things that are both important for development specialists: one about claims, and one about processes – in other words, one about ends and one about means (Sengupta 2000a: 568).

First, the rights-based approach to development encourages a redefinition of the nature of the problem and the aims of the development enterprise into claims, duties, and mechanisms that can promote respect and adjudicate the violation of rights. Typically, this brings about a 'root cause' approach, focusing primarily on matters of state policy and discrimination. The move from needs to rights, and from charity to duties, also implies an increased focus on accountability. Indeed, at the heart of any rights-based approach to development are concerns with mechanisms of accountability, for this is precisely what distinguishes charity from claims (Frankovits and Earle 2000:7; Mukasa and Butegwa 2001; de Feyter 2001: 285; UNDP 2000; HRCA 2001: 2). If claims exist, methods for holding to account those who violate claims must exist as well. If not, the claims lose meaning. Note that this is not the same as saying that only 'justiciable' legal remedies – suing people before courts of law – are suitable remedies: many forms of social counter-power, administrative mechanisms, open discussion, and shared ideological constraints can act as mechanisms of accountability as well. At the end of the day, although they seem to rest on a clear and fixed legal basis, the nature of the claims and the duties created by human-rights claims is a deeply political and constantly shifting matter; for what is socially and legally feasible today is never fixed, but a matter of political struggle.

Second, a rights-based approach brings to development work the realisation that the processes by which development aims are pursued should themselves respect and fulfil human rights (Sengupta 2000b; UNDP 2000). The human-rights approach to development argues that any process of change that is being promoted through development assistance ought to be 'participatory, accountable, and transparent, with equity in decision-making and sharing of the fruits or outcome of the process' (Sengupta 2000b: 21–22; see also Frankovits and Earle 2000; Mukasa and Butegwa 2001; DFID 2000). In other words, it ought to respect the dignity and individual autonomy of all those whom it claims to help, including the poorest and the most excluded, including minorities and other vulnerable groups, often discriminated against; it ought to create opportunities for their participation – opportunities that are not dependent on the whim of a benevolent outsider, but rooted in institutions and procedures.

Nice as this all sounds, it still poses the 'so what?' question rather acutely. After all, the insight that all development ought to take place in a participatory manner, with priority given to the poorest and the most excluded, is hardly revolutionary for the development community. All these issues have been on the agenda for anywhere between ten and 30 years. Development practitioners did not need to wait for human-rights lawyers to tell them that these things are important; rather, what they need is a sense of the extent to which the human-rights paradigm can constitute the basis for a different practice. And of course that has been much, much harder to achieve, or to implement. The risk always exists that taking up a rights-based approach amounts to little more than making nice statements of intent regarding things that it would be nice to achieve, or duties we would like the world to assume one day, without setting out either the concrete procedures for actually achieving those rights or methods of avoiding the slow and dirty enterprise of politics. A number of more progressive NGOs are trying to think through what it concretely means to apply a rights-based approach, but the jury is still out on whether this makes any difference in either programming or impact on the people for whom and with whom they work.

Conclusion

As might be expected, there is a lot less in the emerging human-rights-in-development regime than meets the eye. Much of it is about the quest for the moral high ground: draping oneself in the mantle of human rights to cover the fat belly of the development community, avoiding challenging the *status quo* too much, or questioning oneself or the international system. As a result, one can see power at work here. This is to be expected: most of this rethinking constitutes a voluntary act by people in New York, Washington, London, or Geneva – smart and well-intended, most of them, but not exactly those in great need of overthrowing the established order. This stuff has not been fought for by the masses in whose name it is adopted. It is not part of a fundamental reshuffling of the cards of power, or a redistribution of resources worldwide: no such dynamic has occurred. As a result, one could expect little more, maybe, than fluff, self-congratulation, and more or less hidden transcripts of power.

At the same time, there is no reason to be exclusively cynical. Major change always starts small, and even rhetorical gains sometimes turn out to be the snowballs that set in motion fresh avalanches. In addition, there are organisations and people, in both rich and poor countries, who are courageously rethinking their long-held ideologies and practices in terms of human rights. And there are many more development practitioners, everywhere, who debate questions in a new manner and try to add layers of accountability, transparency, and organisation to their own work. Much more can be done with human rights.

If a rights-based approach to development means empowering marginalised groups, challenging oppression and exclusion, and changing power relations, much of this task lies outside the legal arena, falling squarely in the political realm. Support for the development of international coalitions mobilising shame; the creation of ideational and normative pressure through the spread of convergent shared expectations and discourses; the mobilisation of grassroots and citizen power in favour of certain rights; the certainty that international aid actors will speak out loudly against violations and will extend support to local actors opposing these violations; the creation of ombudsmen, whistle-blowers, and other complaint mechanisms: all these are means – not purely legalistic – of promoting human rights.

If the development community is serious about human rights, then the rights focus cannot be limited to projects. This is an issue of coherence: why use the approach for one part of life and not for another? If donors, be they governments, NGOs, or international organisations, profess attachment to human rights in their development aims, they must be willing to apply the rights agenda to all of their own actions (the inward focus), and to the global political economy of inequality within which they occupy such privileged places (the outward focus). In the absence of such moves, the human-rights focus is little more than a projection of power, and the world has had enough of that already (Duffield 2000; Windfuhr 2000). In other words, the promotion of human rights begins with oneself.

As with most ethically desirable aims, organisations seeking to promote human-rights outcomes through the use of aid have a very easy place from which to start: themselves. Ensuring that their internal personnel management and decision-making procedures are non-discriminatory, non-exclusionary, transparent, and accountable, for example, especially for field offices, may well be a minor revolution. Adding to this the application of the same criteria to an organisation's dealings with its closest direct partners in the field increases the impact: does it hire its employees, or provide its services, on a non-discriminatory basis? Does it function in a manner that is accountable and transparent? Does it promote these outcomes through all means possible: dialogue, support, principled communication?

In addition, the human-rights approach to development clearly implies an absolute requirement of participation, whose suspension, abrogation, or limitation is only allowable in the most extreme of circumstances. In practice, this means that aid agencies should ensure that they provide all relevant information to those concerned, in local languages if necessary; that they strictly monitor and ensure the security of those who do choose to participate; that they do all that is possible to ensure that under-represented groups are brought into the process as well; that they meet all the costs that participation may cause, both to themselves and to the potential participants. Let's face it: this costs money. Besides money, the strong requirement for participation also entails a strict duty for donor agencies to be transparent, to ensure that their aims, assessments, resources, and constraints are known (or could be known) by all those concerned.

The resulting clarity may benefit not only wide participation and frank discussion among all parties concerned: it may also contribute significantly to an increase in donor credibility. It also calls for a broad commitment by aid agencies to give much greater priority to promoting local dialogues, to stimulate local knowledge-generation and research, to find ways of making people's voices heard by those in power – both out of respect for the dignity of people, and because they are the ones who have to live with the consequences of being wrong.

Acknowledgements

1.   This chapter draws substantially on my earlier piece 'On moral high ground: the incorporation of human rights by the development enterprise', *Praxis: The Fletcher Journal of Human Security* XVII:19–26 (2002), available at http://fletcher.tufts.edu/praxis/xvii/Uvin.pdf/ and also in *Development and Human Rights* (Kumarian Press, 2004). I thank Andrea Cornwall for her excellent editing.

References

DFID (2000) *Realizing Human Rights for Poor People*, Strategy Paper, London: DFID.

Donnelly, Jack (1999) 'Human rights, democracy, and development', *Human Rights Quarterly* 21 (3): 608–32.

Duffield, Mark (2000) *Global Governance and the New Wars: The Merging of Development and Security*, London: Zed Books.

de Feyter, Koen (2001) *World Development Law*, Antwerp: Intersentia.

Frankovits, André and Patrick Earle (eds.) (2000) *Working Together: The Human Rights Based Approach to Development Cooperation*, Report of the NGO Workshop, SIDA, Stockholm 16–19 October.

Human Rights Council of Australia (HRCA) (2001) *Submission to the Joint Standing Committee on Foreign Affairs, Defense and Trade Inquiry into the Link between Aid and Human Rights*, Canberra: HRCA.

Lovelace, James C. (1999) 'Will rights cure malnutrition? Reflections on human rights, nutrition, and development', *SCN News*, 18.

Mukasa, Stella and Florence Butegwa (2001) 'An Overview of Approaches to Economic and Social Rights in Development in Uganda – Draft Report for DANIDA', Kampala: Nordic Consulting Group.

Obiora, L. Amede (1996) 'Beyond the rhetoric of a right to development', *Law and Policy* 18, 3/4 (July- Oct): 355–418.

Rosas, Allan (1995) 'The right to development', in Asbjorn Eide, Catarina Krause and Allan Rosas (eds.) *Economic, Social and Cultural Rights. A Textbook*, Dordrecht: Martinus Nijhoff, pp. 247–256.

Sano, Hans-Otto (2000) 'Development and human rights: the necessary, but partial integration of human rights and development', *Human Rights Quarterly* 22(3): 734–52.

Sen, Amartya K. (1999) *Development as Freedom*, New York, NY: Alfred A. Knopf.

Sengupta, Arjun (2000a) 'Realizing the right to development', *Development and Change* 31(3): 553–78.

Sengupta, Arjun (2000b) 'Right to Development', Note by the Secretary-General for the 55th session, August A/55/306.

Shue, Henry (1980) *Basic Rights. Subsistence, Affluence and US Foreign Policy*, New York, NY: Basic Books.

Slinn, Peter (1999) 'The international law of development: a millennium subject or a relic of the twentieth century?', in Wolfgang Benedek, Hubert Isak, and Renate Kicker (eds.) *Development and Developing International and European Law*, Frankfurt: Peter Lang, pp. 299–318.

Tomasevski, Katarina (1993) *Development Aid and Human Rights Revisited*, New York, NY: Pinter.

United Nations (1994) *An Agenda for Development: Report of the Secretary-General*, New York, NY: UN, A/48/935, 6 May.

UNDP (1998) *'Integrating Human Rights with Sustainable Development'*, UNDP Policy Document 2, New York, NY: UNDP.

UNDP (2000) *Human Development Report 2000: Human Rights and Human Development*, Oxford and New York, NY: Oxford University Press.

Uvin, Peter (1998) *Aiding Violence: The Development Enterprise in Rwanda*, West Hartford, CT: Kumarian Press.

Windfuhr, Michael (2000) *'Economic, social and cultural rights and development cooperation'*, in A. Frankovits and P. Earle (eds.)

World Bank (1992) *Governance and Development*, Washington, DC: World Bank.

World Bank (1999) *Development and Human Rights: The Role of the World Bank*, Washington, DC: World Bank.

About the author

Peter Uvin holds the Henry J. Leir Chair of International Humanitarian Studies at the Fletcher School of Law and Diplomacy at Tufts University in Boston. He has worked for a range of development agencies in Africa, especially in the Great Lakes region. His book, *Aiding Violence: The Development Enterprise in Rwanda,* won the African Studies Association's Herskowits Award for most outstanding book on Africa published in 1998.

CHAPTER 16
Civil society

Neera Chandhoke

The idea of civil society has proved very elusive, escaping conceptual grasps and evading surefooted negotiation of the concept itself. Resurrected in a very definite historical setting, that of authoritarian states, the concept of civil society came to signify a set of social and political practices that sought to engage with state power. The close connection with the re-emergence of the concept and the collapse of dictatorial states made civil society attractive to a variety of political agents pursuing different agendas: expanding the market at the expense of the state, transiting from mass politics to single-issue and localised campaigns, undermining confidence in accepted modes of representation such as political parties, and in general shrinking the domain of the state and that of accepted modes of politics. That the concept of civil society could suit such a variety of different political projects is cause for some alarm, for it might well mean that civil society has come to mean everything to everyone remotely interested in it.

Introduction

The concept of civil society was rediscovered and accorded pre-eminence in political practices in a very definite political context: in Stalinist states in Eastern and Central Europe, which had denied their citizens' basic rights, and in Latin America, where military regimes had managed to survive by employment of the same methods. In the context of autocratic states, the concept quickly acquired a subversive edge. It was in civil society that individuals and groups set out to challenge unresponsive and authoritarian states through peaceful and non-violent methods: strikes, protest marches, demonstrations, dissemination of information through informal networks, and the formation of associational life through the setting up of reading clubs and discussion forums. The net effect of mobilisation in civil society is well known: some very powerful states collapsed, in the face of mass protests, like the proverbial house of cards.[1]

In retrospect, two aspects of the argument on civil society appear tremendously significant. The first aspect was the sustained demand for political rights, and more particularly civil rights: the right to freedom of all kinds, from freedom of expression to freedom to form associations. The second aspect was signified by complete disenchantment with vocabularies that spoke of taking over state power through revolutionary means, smashing the state, or transforming the state. Born into a world disenchanted with overbearing states, with political parties that preferred to follow the impulse to power rather than representing their constituencies, and with trade unions which had become bureaucratic and unrepresentative, the concept of civil society highlighted one basic precondition of democracy: state power has to be monitored, engaged with, and rendered accountable through intentional and engaged citizen action.

It is clear that civil societies have won their most momentous victories against authoritarian states. That is why civil society, as the antonym of authoritarianism, 'is on everyone's lips – government officials, journalists, funding agencies, writers, and academics, not to mention the millions of people across the globe who find it an inspiration in their struggles for a better world. Cited as a solution to social, economic, and political dilemmas by politicians and thinkers from left, right, and all perspectives in between, civil society is claimed by every part of the ideological spectrum as its own. But what exactly is it?' (Edwards 2004:2).

From contested concept to consensual 'hurrah word'

There was a time when civil society was interesting, even riveting, for political theorists, simply because rival and often acrimonious interpretations, formulations, and theorisations jostled with each other to impart meaning to the concept. There was a time, in other words, when civil society was an 'essentially contested' concept. Today it has become a consensual concept, a 'hurrah word', and a matter of tiresomely unanimous acclaim. In the process, civil society has been flattened out.

The reasons for this flattening out are the following. Firstly, the close connection between the 'civil society' argument and the demise of authoritarian regimes came to be perceived by many multilateral and donor agencies as a sure recipe for democracy. Secondly, the generalised discontent that political parties and trade unions as agents of representation had become bureaucratic, unresponsive, and concerned more with the pursuit of power than with representation of their constituencies led scholars and activists to look to other agents in civil society to deepen democracy. In the process, civil society came to be interpreted as an alternative to the formal sphere of party politics. Thirdly, in the wake of the post-Washington Consensus forged by the World Bank, the state was brought 'back in': it was expected that the state would share its functions with civil-society organisations. In other words, the state came to be pluralised, and a number of NGOs emerged to perform the many tasks heaped upon the shoulders of civil society.

Closely allied as they are to the agendas of the donor agencies, contemporary versions of civil society have drastically emptied the sphere of any other agency, such as social movements or political struggles. Civil society consists only of voluntary agencies, and what is euphemistically termed the 'third sector'. Witness the tragedy that has befallen the proponents of the concept: people struggling against authoritarian regimes had demanded civil society; what they got instead was NGOs! In the process of being presented as an alternative to the formal sphere of politics, the state driven by the logic of power, and also the market driven by the logic of profit, the concept has been abstracted from all debates and contestations over its meaning, stripped of its ambiguities, its dark areas, and its oppressions, and presented to us as an area of solidarity, self-help, and goodwill.

The idea that civil society can provide an alternative to the state and to the market helps funding organisations to bypass the 'Third World' state and disburse aid directly to organisations in civil society. The sovereignty of the 'Third World state' has been compromised by this fact alone. However, the very idea that civil society can be protected from the reach of the state is astounding, when the essential conditions of civil society – for instance, the rule of law, which regulates the public sphere and guarantees the rights of its inhabitants – are institutionalised by the state. The belief that civil society can give us an alternative both to the state and to the market is utopian at best and dangerous at worst, for it simply messes up our comprehension of what the sphere is about.

Nowhere in the history of civil society has it been conceptualised as an alternative to or as independent of the state. For de Tocqueville (1835, 1840), civil society limits the state; for Hegel (1821), civil society is a necessary stage in the formation of the state; for Marx, civil society is the source of the power of the state; and for Gramsci (1929–1935), civil society is the space where the state constructs its hegemony in alliance with the dominant classes. Not only are the state and civil society a precondition each for the other, but the logic of one actually constitutes the other. Today, however, the two have been un-coupled. Whatever the reason for this uncoupling, the moment that we think of civil society as a welcome alternative to the state, we conveniently forget that the concept has always been problematic for political theory. Anxious questions about the sphere have almost always outstripped the answers to these questions. Today, however, civil society is readily and smoothly presented as an answer to the malaise of the contemporary world.

If civil society is hailed by almost everyone, from trade unions, social movements, the United Nations, the International Monetary Fund, the World Bank, NGOs, lending agencies, and borrowing agencies to states – both chauvinistic and democratic – as the ideal elixir to counter the ills of the contemporary world, there must be something wrong. To put it bluntly, if the concept of civil society can be used by groups of every ideological stripe and hue with equal dexterity and presumably much profit, civil society must surely prove advantageous for all. Why? Because it has ceased to mean anything? Because it has been reduced to a project that Western funding agencies seek for their own reasons to promote in other parts of the world? Because it has been watered down? Or because this understanding of the concept excludes much more than it includes? The emergence on our theoretical horizon of a truncated, flattened out, jaded avatar of civil society, stripped of all contradictions and tensions, may justifiably give us cause for thought.

The ubiquity of a concept, we can conclude somewhat regretfully, may prove ultimately to be its undoing. For if it comes on to everyone's lips with a fair amount of readiness, it must have lost both shape and content. Amid all this acclaim, ritual invocations of civil society as a panacea for the ills of the modern world simply sound insipid and dreary. Where in all of this are the grey areas of civil society that Hegel spoke of? Where are the exploitations and the oppressions of civil society that Marx passionately castigated? Where is the state-inspired project of hegemony that Gramsci unearthed so brilliantly and perceptively? What we are left with is a one-dimensional, watered-down concept that has ceased to have any meaning, least of all for those who are supposed to benefit from it.

Tracing the emergence of 'civil society'

The concept of civil society swept into prominence in the 1980s for reasons that are by now well known. Intellectuals in Eastern Europe began to realise that the two options that had been historically available to people struggling to emancipate themselves from unbearable political situations were no longer accessible to them. The first option was reform of state power from above. The second was that of revolution from below. Both had been ruled out by the Brezhnev doctrine, namely that the (former) Soviet Union would not hesitate to intervene in the affairs of Eastern European states, wherever and whenever the need arose.

Reeling under obdurate state power and imperious bureaucracies, people found the lack of civil and political liberties, state monopoly over economic and social transactions, and absence of participative citizenship or representativeness both claustrophobic and intolerable. Some remedy had to be found. The only option that presented itself as credible in this context was to carve out a 'free zone' within the existing system. Here people could associate and express their sentiments without fear amid warm networks of solidarity. The Eastern Europeans called this free zone, peopled by social associations, self-help and self-management organisations, and characterised by mutual solidarity, '*civil society*'.

Theorised as a metaphorical space between the household and the state, the call to civil society served to repopulate the public sphere, which had been disastrously emptied out by regimes intent on monopolising the nooks and crannies of social and political life. The slogan of civil society naturally appeared attractive to people who for long had inhabited politically arid, remorseless, and desolate political spaces. It offered the promise that a rather tormenting deficit in the lives of people would be filled up by warm and personalised social interaction, even as these very people turned their back on the state.

Forged as it was in the historical context of Eastern Europe, three features of the civil-society argument stand out as significant. First, it announced the determination of people who had been banished from the political arena to insert themselves into the political discourse on their own terms. The invocation to civil society conveyed a statement of intent: that ordinary people have the capability to fashion their own lives. Second, the argument asserted that the nurturing of self-help and solidarity through thick and overlapping associations – reading clubs, discussion societies, trade unions, self-education groups – was a good thing in itself, for it provided a counterpoint both to the state and to the atomism of individual life.

Civil society emerged in Eastern Europe as the site where people, organised into groups, could make and pursue democratic projects of all kinds in freedom from bureaucratic state power. Third, then, the argument sought to institutionalise state–society relationships, even as it asserted that procedures such as the rule of law, institutionalisation of political and civil rights, and accountability should be codified in order to limit the power of the state over all areas of social life. In the process, the historical pairing of state and civil society was uncoupled.

The end of politics as social transformation

The argument developed rapidly into a polemical slogan that counter-posed the sphere of voluntary and purposive collective action to dictatorial state power. Matters did not rest here, for an activity that had initially concentrated on carving out a free zone within existing state power was to develop into a powerful political movement, albeit one that was haphazard, spontaneous, and unorganised. In 1989, we were to witness the awesome spectacle of so many powerful states in Eastern Europe literally collapsing before agitating and agitated crowds assembled in the streets.

Even as a purportedly self-limiting social revolution transformed itself into a highly charged political revolution, a fourth dimension was added to the civil-society argument. The civil public, which had initially turned its back on the state, had dramatically transformed itself into the political public, concerned with the form and content of power. The 'civil' in 'civil society' no longer signified non-political; it meant that people inhabiting the sphere outside the state had the right to debate about the nature of the state and the politics that it pursued.

In retrospect, two aspects of the civil-society argument in Eastern Europe give us cause for thought. Firstly, if we look closely at the details of the argument – the demand for civil liberties, especially the right to freedom of expression and the right to associate, rule of law, limited state power, political accountability and the freeing of the market – it is clear that the Eastern Europeans were practically re-enacting the bourgeois revolution that had taken place in England in the seventeenth century against absolutist state power. John Locke, the quintessential liberal thinker, may well have authored the civil-society script for and in Eastern Europe in the 1980s.

Secondly, the message conveyed by the experience of Eastern Europe was to validate precisely what Antonio Gramsci had conceptualised in the 1930s: that wherever and whenever states – whether absolutist or socialist – deny their people political and civil rights, we can expect the eruption of discontent against exclusions from structures of citizenship and representation. Gramsci's dictum that states that do not possess civil societies are more vulnerable than those that do possess them was to prove more than prescient in this case. The tragedy here was that because people in Eastern Europe were deprived of civil rights, and because the civil-society argument concentrated on resuscitating those rights, the Eastern Europeans, through and by the civil-society argument, proclaimed a final end to the revolutionary imagination. The argument effectively killed off the idea of politics as social transformation. From the 1980s onwards, civil society replaced revolution as the prime locus of passions and imaginations. It is not surprising that scholars and political commentators wedded to bourgeois liberalism hastened in the aftermath of the velvet revolutions to proclaim an end to ideology and an end to history.

The rise of the civil-society argument in development

The civil-society argument, fashioned in the historical context of Eastern Europe, was to have a powerful influence on the way that scholars and activists conceptualised the human condition in other parts of the world. It was to prove extraordinarily influential. The reasons had partly to do with the bourgeois liberal acclaim of the end of ideology, its insistence on the bankruptcy of the socialist tradition, and its emphasis on the viability of liberal democracy as the sole option for politics. The attraction of civil society in such instances had less to do with the intrinsic value of the concept and more to do with its ideological association with the end of socialist societies. It was this sentiment that was hijacked by donor agencies, which sought to posit the construction or expansion of civil society as the answer to all kinds of historically specific problems.

The civil-society argument was also enthusiastically embraced by activists and scholars, for reasons that were relatively independent of the 'end of ideology' thesis. These had largely to do with the failure of the state, especially in developing countries, to deliver a minimum standard of life to its people. Powerful bureaucracies and political elites, consolidating their power in the interstices of post-independence states, had simply turned their backs on the very same masses who had put them there in the first place. Scholars in India were to speak of corrupt bureaucracies and of even more amoral and power-hungry political leaders, who were completely impervious to the fact that state-led development had failed miserably. These scholars were to castigate the bankruptcy of the political vision; they were to bemoan the loss of hope, and express a lack of confidence in the capacity, or indeed the willingness, of the state to be responsive to the needs of the people.

It is not as if authoritarian state policies had not been resisted earlier. Since the late 1960s, militant struggles against state power had been launched by the Naxalite movement. The early 1970s saw the formation and consolidation of a number of social movements challenging the agenda of the state, such as the anti-caste movement, the farmers' movement, and the women's movement. After the lifting of the Emergency in 1977, two of the most important movements in contemporary India in the 1980s – the civil liberties movement and the environmental movement – appeared as dominant actors on the political scene. The public sphere of India's civil society became noisy, untidy, vibrant, and creative.

Still, what was needed was a concept, a vocabulary, and an agenda that would (a) locate these struggles; (b) emphasise the legitimate rights of a people in a democracy to make demands on the state; (c) insist on state accountability; and (d) stress the importance of an autonomous site where people could engage in democratic projects for their own sake. This vocabulary and this concept were found in civil society. Oddly enough, the language of civil society, which, as the product of specific historical processes in England and France, is arguably an alien import, proved peculiarly apt for societies that were struggling to consolidate fledgling democracies.

It was in the midst of disenchantment with the overreach of the state – in Africa as well as Asia – that the concept of civil society took hold of the imaginations of both the left and the right. It promised an exit from bureaucratic inefficiency and political indifference. The state could no longer be relief upon; it had failed miserably, despite having exercised untrammelled power for decades. People looked for an alternative to state-led projects and state-inspired developments. The wave of protest movements that overtook Africa in the early 1990s, movements that were popularly hailed as the second liberation of the continent, were accordingly conceptualised as civil society *versus* the state.

The inhabitants of Western European societies were to make roughly the same complaint: that of the unresponsiveness of the state and the indifference of the bureaucracy. If socialism had failed in the eastern part of Europe, liberal democracy was not doing too well in the western part of the continent. Civil societies had been rendered passive and quiescent, even as state-dominated strategies had colonised what Habermas (1987) felicitously termed the 'life world'. In the USA, theorists complained about the disappearance of civic virtue among the inhabitants of civil society. Robert Putnam (1994, 2000) remonstrated about the lack of associational life, and Francis Fukuyama (1995) complained about the absence of what he called 'trust'. A vibrant and politicised civil society, as the Eastern European case had shown, promised the rebuilding of both political activism and civic virtue.

Civil society as a project

The moment we perceive civil society from the vantage point of marginalised groups, we may be forced to accept that there is a deep and perhaps irresolvable tension between the acknowledged virtues of the sphere and its actual functioning. Yet social movements can, through struggle, expand and even transform the sphere of civil society. They can do this by demanding that civil society deliver what it promises in theory: freedom from domination, freedom to achieve self-realisation, freedom to assert selfhood. Far from being a given, civil society is a project whereby individuals can realise their self through engagement, contestation, and affirmation.

Civil society is a project in another sense. Theorists as eminent as Adam Smith (1776) and Georg Hegel (1821), who were to conceptualise civil society in the first instance, saw it as a deeply troublesome sphere. They were perfectly aware of the many incivilities that civil society was capable of; and for neither could the sphere reproduce itself without deliberate intervention to tame it. We only need to look at post-'velvet revolution' Eastern Europe in order to insert a word of caution into the celebratory notes on civil society: for, once civil society had been resurrected in this context, people found that they really did not want it.

The dismantling of state institutions and the opening out of markets has inevitably led to uncompromising austerity, massive unemployment, discrimination against ethnic minorities, and resultant ethnic explosions. The rolling back of the state from any kind of responsibility for the people has left those who cannot fend for themselves at the mercy of those who are in a position to profit from new arrangements. People in this part of the world, it is obvious, have been as quickly disenchanted with civil society as they had been enchanted by the invocation of the concept.

Yet for all the hubris associated with civil society, it remains a valuable term. This is not because it is a precondition for democracy, or 'democratisation' as political conditionalities would have it, but because it is a site where various groups can engage with each other in projects of all kinds. Its absence would mean the absence of democracy, and of the freedom that is necessary for democratic engagement. By asserting civil society, people demand that regimes recognise the competence of the political public to chart out a discourse on the content and the limits of what is politically desirable and democratically permissible. In the heady days when theorists brought 'Civil Society Back In', the domain came to be increasingly conceptualised without reference to the state. Now any self-respecting scholar knows that civil society can be conceptualised only in relation to the state, and *vice versa*.

The de-linking of the state and civil society has greatly impoverished our understanding of both concepts. Those theorists who waxed eloquent on the need for people to connect were to stray away from the shadowy peripheries of actually existing civil societies and underplay the ambiguous relationship of this sphere with democracy. Such formulations obfuscate the conflict within, and the general incivility of much of civil society, because they are completely indifferent to the notion of power.

Taking a long hard look within civil society itself focuses our attention on power equations of all kinds: on material deprivation, unevenly shared conceptual understanding, dominant and marginal languages, and the many oppressions, the many incivilities, the many banishments of civil society. Some groups possess overlapping political, material, symbolic, and social power; others possess nothing, not even access to the means of life. The former find a space in civil society, and civil society finds a place for them; the latter are banished to the dark periphery of the sphere. The irony is that even though most countries of the developing world are primarily rural, it is the urban middle-class agenda that is best secured by the invocation of civil society. The agenda of oppressed and marginal peasants, or of the tribals who are struggling for freedom, remain unrepresented either in the theory or in the practice of civil society. Therefore, in order to find a voice, marginal groups may well have to storm the ramparts of civil society, to break down the gates, and make a forcible entry into the sphere.

Beyond normativity

Like other domains of collective interaction, civil society too is a contested site. That is why dreams of a democratic civil society are also a project of civil society. But for this, we have to accept that it is not enough that there be a civil society, or even a civil society that is independent of the state. It is not something that, once constructed, can be left to fend for itself; nor is it an institution. Civil societies are what their inhabitants make of them. They can easily become hostages to formal democracy at best, and undemocratic trends at worst. There is nothing in civil society that automatically ensures the victory of democratic projects. All that civil society does is to provide actors with the values, the space, and the inspiration to battle for democracy.

It is critical to go beyond the buzzword that 'civil society' has become if it is to regain the vitality that it once had as an essentially contested concept. In this chapter, I suggest that it is vital to disentangle normative expectations from the analysis of actually existing civil societies, and to see what civil society actually does or does not do for different people who inhabit the sphere. If we want to see what kind of civil society is feasible and possible for our historical agendas, then we cannot allow our political passions and normative concerns to obfuscate our understanding of this sphere.

Note

1.   This chapter draws substantially on Chandhoke (2003).

References

Chandhoke, Neera (2003) *The Conceits of Civil Society*, New Delhi: Oxford University Press.

Fukuyama, Francis (1995) *Trust: The Social Virtues and Creation of Prosperity*, New York, NY: Free Press.

Gramsci, Antonio (1971) [1929–1935] *Selections from Prison Notebooks of A. Gramsci* (Q. Hoare and G.N. Smith eds.), New York, NY: International Publishers.

Habermas, Jürgen (1987) *Theory of Communicative Action*, Vol. 2. Lifeworld and System: A Critique of Functionalist Reason, Boston, MA: Beacon Press.

Hegel, Georg Wilhelm Fredrik (1942) [1821] *The Philosophy of Right* (trans. T.M Knox), Oxford: Oxford University Press.

Putnam, Robert D. (2000) *Bowling Alone: The Collapse and Revival of American Community*, New York, NY: Simon & Schuster.

Putnam, Robert with Robert Leonardi and Raffaelle Y. Nanetti (1994) *Making Democracy Work: Civic Traditions in Modern Italy*, Princeton, NJ: Princeton University Press.

Smith, Adam (1952) [1776] *An Inquiry into the Nature and Causes of the Wealth of Nations*, in Robert Maynard Hutchin (ed.) *Great Books of the Western World*, Chicago, IL: William Benton.

Tocqueville, Alexis de (1955) [1835 and 1840] *The Old Regime and the French Revolution* (trans. Stuart Gilbert), Garden City, NY, Doubleday Press.

About the author

Neera Chandhoke is Professor of Political Science and Director of the Developing Countries Research Centre at the University of Delhi. Her most recent works include *The Conceits of Civil Society* (2003) and *Beyond Secularism: The Rights of Religious Minorities* (1999).

CHAPTER 17

Public advocacy and people-centred advocacy: mobilising for social change

John Samuel

Public and people-centred advocacy are shaped by the political culture, social systems, and constitutional framework of the country in which they are practised. It is the practice of advocacy that determines the theory, and not vice versa. If advocacy is not rooted in grassroots realities and is practised only at the macro level, the voice of the marginalised is increasingly likely to be appropriated by professional elites. However, the very credibility of advocacy practitioners depends on their relationship with mass-based movements and grassroots perceptions of what constitutes desirable social change.

Introduction

'Public advocacy' has become a bandwagon that everyone is clambering on to. But hardly anyone seems to know what it really is. The bandwagon is certainly very appealing. The 'fast-food' toolkits on the streets of the development market find a ready-made clientele. But they turn the ideas and action required for long-term social change into trivial, quick-fix tools for 'scaling up impacts'. In the process, public advocacy becomes a victim of the bandwagon syndrome. Many people claim that they are promoting or doing advocacy without really thinking about what they mean by this. How many of its proponents know that it is about actions that are rooted in the history of socio-political and cultural reform? Few seem to go beyond the bandwagon syndrome to redefine the concept and practice of advocacy in promoting social change.

As a form of social action, the nature and character of both public and people-centred advocacy are very much shaped by the political culture, social systems, and constitutional framework of the country in which they are practised. And they are influenced by the ways in which decision making and public policies are influenced by public-interest or social-action groups in different contexts. It is the practice of advocacy that determines the theory, and not vice versa. The trouble is that 'public advocacy' is used to signify a broad sweep of practices, ranging from public relations, market research, and report-writing to lobbying, public-interest litigation, and civil disobedience.

Public advocacy can be considered from three perspectives: political, managerial, or technical. While effective public advocacy integrates all three, the emphasis will depend on the beliefs and background of the proponent. For instance, a social or political activist will perceive public advocacy basically as a political process, which may involve some professional skills or technical understanding of the appropriate methods. But someone with a managerial background may see it as the effective use of technical devices, skills, and professional practices, with or without much of a political component. Hence the need for a long-term political and historical perspective on the concept and practice of public advocacy and people-centred advocacy, and their relevance for advancing a more humane, just, and equal world.

Understanding advocacy: a political perspective

Public advocacy is a set of deliberate actions designed to influence public policies or public attitudes in order to empower the marginalised. The main difference between it and people-centred advocacy is that such actions are undertaken in ways that empower people, particularly the marginalised. In a liberal democratic culture, public advocacy uses the instruments of democracy and adopts non-violent and constitutional means. It is perceived as a value-driven political process, because it seeks to question and change existing unequal power relations in favour of those who are socially, politically, and economically marginalised. In the Indian context, grassroots organisation and mobilisation are used to generate an awareness of and assert one's rights as a citizen, and lend credibility, legitimacy, and crucial bargaining power to public advocacy.

Advocacy therefore involves the following:

- Resisting unequal power relations (such as patriarchy) at every level, from the personal to public, from family to governance.
- Engaging institutions of governance to empower the marginalised.
- Creating and using 'spaces' within the system, in order to change it.
- Strategising the use of knowledge, skills, and opportunities to influence public policies.
- Bridging micro-level activism and macro-level policy initiatives.

In India, one of the major thrusts of public advocacy is the implementation of existing social-justice legislation and social-security programmes. Progressive legislation such as the Equal Remuneration Act, the Dowry Prohibition Act, the Bonded Labour Prohibition Act, and the Prevention of Atrocities against Scheduled Caste and Scheduled Tribe Act is often honoured more in the breach than in the observance. This is principally because we lack the political will and administrative efficiency to put the legislation into practice, but also because of the incompatibility between libertarian or liberal constitutional values and traditional socio-cultural practices (like caste) and religious values (like fatalism).

Since, in a liberal democratic framework, public policies play a vital role in determining the directions of social justice, political and civil liberties, and the long-term interests of the environment and the general public, the primary focus of advocacy is to influence policy formulation, change, and implementation. But public policies are a function of the dominant political equation at a given time. Hence, in order to influence public policies, it is necessary to influence the prevailing power relations in favour of the marginalised.

Influencing power relations is a complex process involving confrontation and negotiation among different interest. To do this effectively depends on having other sources of power. In the context of public advocacy, there are six major sources of power:

- the power of people, or citizens' mobilisation
- the power of information and knowledge
- the power of constitutional guarantees
- the power of direct grassroots experience and linkages
- the power of networking alliances and solidarity
- the power of moral convictions.

Advocacy does not depend only on having information, but on being able to transform such information into knowledge by interpreting it with reference to specific values.

Advocacy in India

India has seen public advocacy on issues such as environmental degradation, the rights of *dalits* and tribal peoples, women's rights, civil rights, and many others. While voluntary organisations and activist groups have focused on social, developmental, and political interventions at the micro level, their efforts to influence the formulation or implementation of public policies have tended to be fragmented, with little national impact. Even so, successful advocacy campaigns like the Silent Valley Movement in Kerala (described below) and the amniocentesis campaign in Maharashtra illustrate the potential of organised advocacy in exerting pressure to enact progressive legislation.

As the lives of ordinary Indians are increasingly affected by economic liberalisation, so there is a growing realisation among social-action groups of the need to empower the people to influence public policies. The isolated 'murmurs of dissent' can be amplified and channelled through advocacy efforts. Clearly the methods and approaches that are adopted must be grounded in the Indian context. It is also necessary to understand the limitations of public advocacy, as well as its potential for achieving social change in India. In many of the more effective advocacy campaigns, mass mobilisation, improvised forms of non-violent protest and persuasion, public-interest litigation, pressure for legislative change, lobbying of public officials, and media work were strategically and simultaneously used to build up an effective public argument.

Advocacy without mobilisation is unlikely to achieve much. The credibility and socio-political legitimacy of advocacy efforts largely depend on the means and the ends being consistent and compatible. In the Indian context, grassroots support rather than professional background is what most determines a lobbyist's credibility. A major challenge is therefore to safeguard and extend the political space in which to advocate for the cause of the marginalised, resisting the agendas set by others, whether the multinational corporations or various kinds of fundamentalism.

For practical as well as ethical reasons, then, public advocacy needs to go beyond public policy to the larger arena of influencing societal attitudes and practices so as to transform an oppressive value system into a more just and humane one. Public advocacy cannot be undertaken in a vacuum. Issues of deprivation, injustice, and rights violation are its impetus. Without an issue, what would one advocate for? The second part of this chapter therefore considers the question of communication in creating the momentum for people-centred advocacy for social change.

People-centred advocacy

People-centred advocacy seeks to challenge and change unjust power relations at all levels: people are the alpha and omega. Though focused on public policies, the larger purpose of people-centred advocacy is social transformation such that all people realise their human rights, including civil, political, economic, and social rights. It seeks to promote social and economic justice, equitable social change, and sustainable development. Public-policy change is one means of achieving these goals.

Social-change communication is central to people-centred advocacy, seeking to inform and educate a large number of people in such a way that they are enabled to change or redefine their attitudes and values and become more socially responsible and empowered citizens. In the past 20 years, there have been concerted efforts to build effective communication strategies on issues such as human rights, women's rights, development, and ecology. While these strategies helped to increase the outreach and efficiency of information dissemination, a big question mark hangs over their effectiveness in terms of bringing about attitudinal change.

Communication is ideally a sort of communion or sharing or exchanging the same set of thoughts, feelings, and attitudes. Creativity, communication, and community are what distinguish human beings from other living species. Language and symbols make for an organic and dynamic interplay between human creativity, a primordial urge to communicate, and the need for community living. One of the crises of the post-modern condition is that these organic linkages have broken down. Language and symbols have become subservient to highly mechanised tools for disseminating information. Hence MTV, Star New, Zee TV, BBC, Doordarshan, the Internet, etc. all have their own language and symbols. When the content is determined by the medium, the act of communication becomes increasingly alienated from real communities. Even if such media do give rise to imagined or virtual communities who feel connected through them, these individuals are not organically connected to each other.

When communication ceases to be grounded in communities, it is reduced to a dehumanised form of conveying information or entertainment. The absence of dynamic symbols and language that connect communities and communication has a negative effect on human creativity, particularly aesthetic creativity. The bewildering perplexity and anarchy of many of the 'music albums' disseminated through MTV or V channels illustrate the phenomenon. Fragmented and frozen images stare and laugh at you in the cacophony of sound and fury. Where does this leave us? How do social-change communicators locate themselves in this jangle? Why is it that we can inform people but somehow fail to change their attitudes and beliefs?

A recent example of this 'mal-communication' is the AIDS-awareness campaigns intended to educate people and to change their attitudes and behaviour. The international aid agencies imported sophisticated communication frameworks and mandarins to develop communication strategies and implementation channels. Millions of dollars were spent on five-star workshops and five-star consultants. But at the end of the day, the exercise had created more 'buzz' about AIDS than actual changes in people's attitudes about the socio-political implications of being HIV-positive, or more informed attitudes towards sexual choices. Even among the better-run campaigns on environmental protection or women's rights, information was transmitted and received, but without producing much change in attitudes. Partly, this is due to the inability of dehumanised forms of communication to touch people's hearts. In the proliferation of methods to disseminate information, values, feelings, and cultural ethos get marginalised or completely lost.

Furthermore, even the best of modern communication strategies generally fail to get beyond a middle-class audience; even if the information does reach relatively marginalised people in urban slums or rural areas, the message is often received without being digested. In the case of India, this means that the vast majority of people are either alienated from or simply not reached by post-modern communication tools and strategies. The lack of ethical clarity or political positions tends to produce ambiguous messages. So on the question of people who are HIV-positive, WHO has one stand and UNDP has a different one, though both of them are in the business of popular communication about the issue. The result is that ambiguous messages get lost in the labyrinth of tools and strategies.

Medium in search of a message

Many social-change organisations are like a medium in search of a message. This is further complicated when the communication process is guided by institutional interests or by project priorities, rather than by conviction in the message. In the enthusiasm to create new methods, the conviction in and clarity of the message for social change somehow get lost. One of the major obstacles to changing people's attitudes is the gap between communication that is mediated through media such as television or the Internet, and socially mediated communication. The former tends to treat people as 'targets' and 'objects' that can be influenced or acted upon.

By contrast, in socially mediated or community-oriented communication, people participate in the process. Hence, they themselves become the medium and own the process. This makes it impossible to remain indifferent to what is being communicated. In the formal or technically driven media, the message is treated like a 'product' to be delivered to a 'target' audience. Indeed, focused information dissemination is almost like shooting at a target, so its communication strategies tend to emphasise 'packaging' the 'product' to make it more saleable. In socially mediated and community-oriented communication, it is the interaction that matters, and involves either the entire community or its 'opinion formers'.

Interactive communication not only helps to ensure that a message is delivered, but enables the recipients to analyse and interpret it in the language and cultural ethos that define their collective identity. In other words, it leads to an interpretative process that is capable of changing attitudes. Modern communication tools are highly efficient for broadcasting or for mass dissemination, but remain relatively dehumanised. Hence, they are unlikely to change people's attitudes. The socially mediated communication methods are rather slower and best suited for narrow-cast or community-based communication. The advantage of folk communication is that it is a creative and humanising community-based process.

The medium is the message

I myself experienced the effectiveness of community-oriented communication in the social-change campaigns initiated by Kerala Sasthra Sahitya Parishat (KSSP) in the early 1980s. Through a series of low-cost, community-oriented communications, involving thousands of young people, KSSP was able to change people's attitudes in a very significant way. The best example is that of the Campaign against the Hydroelectric Project in the Silent Valley, popularly known as the Silent Valley Campaign. In the late 1970s when the campaign began, almost all the political parties, trade unions, and newspapers were either against it or indifferent to the cause. People were by and large indifferent to environment issues. But the situation dramatically changed over a period of two years, as large numbers of ordinary people began to support the campaign. There were processions and popular participation in almost all parts of Kerala. The campaign triggered off a debate on the effectiveness of the development models and paradigms. It emerged as one of the most effective people-centred advocacy campaigns for environmental protection and sustainable development.

There was no imported framework, no communication mandarins, no swadeshi (local) or videshi (foreign) funding, no big institution. What made the difference was people's participation in a communicative process and communicative action: the community-oriented folk methods clicked; they drew people into debates and discussions. This did not give people much space for indifference. Communication took the form of grounded debates at the grassroots. The issue was discussed and debated in the local teashops with the morning cup of tea and newspaper. The press could not afford to ignore an issue that had become the focus of such interest. As student activists, we made posters, wrote songs, and performed street plays to build up a public debate and discourse. No one told us what the strategy was, but we knew what the message was. We were emotionally and intellectually involved. We had a language and a song on our tongues. We had grown up with the symbols of folklore. We were from the people. Many of us were at our creative best. We were the grassroots. Without learning any theory of communication, I instantly realised the organic linkages between creativity, community, and communication.

Fifteen years later, when I studied the Silent Valley Campaign from the perspective of public advocacy, I was keen to know what exactly had changed public perceptions. Then I realised it was the active involvement of four poets and five poems that played a major role in drawing young people to the campaign. Poetry, *Sanmskarika Jathas* (cultural processions), street plays, indigenous and spontaneous poster campaigns, village-level debates, and pamphlets were all extensively used. But the major factor was the conviction in and clarity of the main message. The message preceded the medium, tools, and strategies. There were no institutional interests or communication framework to mediate between the people and the message. People became the medium, and the message travelled across drawing rooms to back yards, to tea shops, to schools and colleges, to the countryside and city streets. There was no television or newspaper advertising. But there was a lot of poetry and lots of people. It played a major role in my own and many others' formative years of convictions and activism.

I have also experienced the power of socially mediated communication in the villages of Mizoram. Mizoram has a unique press culture, hosting scores of newspapers of different shapes and sizes. There is a culture of discussion and debate on issues of social importance. The Young Mizo Association (YMA) makes use of songs and community-level discussions. When communication gives rise to action, it creates a social momentum with the power to influence people's attitudes. The key is in the organic linkages between the process of communication with popular collective action. Communication without potential action is a passive exercise. The best examples of such linkages can be seen in the ways that religious leaders such as Buddha or Christ and reformers like Thukkaram and Kabir communicated. Parables were powerful ways for communicating with the people. The messages were clear, simple, and straightforward. Messages were for action. That linkage changed people's attitudes, and it changed history. The songs of Kabir do not need any 'extra' music; they go straight to the heart.

Reclaiming 'public advocacy'

There is a time for everything: a time to make words and tools, a time to market them, a time to consume them, and a time to discard them in the development garbage bin. Those who would promote and defend the use of 'public advocacy' to bring about social change need to go back to the people to (re-)learn their language, symbols, and ethos. We need to be clear about the message before we define the strategies or reach for the tools. We need to become equal participants in social communication, rather than playing the role of highly paid experts travelling around with our ready-made toolkits and frameworks for prescribing the best communication medicine. A real danger of professional advocacy is that the real issues become diluted or marginalised in the labyrinth of strategies, tactics, and skills.

If public advocacy is not rooted in grassroots realities and is practised only at the macro level, the voice of the marginalised is increasingly likely to be appropriated by urban (or international) elites who have the necessary information and skills. Conversely, the credibility of advocacy practitioners is on the line if they become alienated from mass-based movements, seduced by their own influence and co-opted by the power structure, lost in a maze of vested interest politics. We need therefore to reclaim the organic linkages between creativity, communication, and communities, bridging the vast gap between technical *communications* and social *communication*. We need to be more clear and convinced about the message of social change. If we ourselves don't believe in what we say, people are not going to listen, even if we use the very latest strategies and tools. Let us create the message, and let us become a medium for inspiring and rejuvenating the barren lands of imagination and social action.

About the author

John Samuel is International Director of ActionAid International Asia as well as a human-rights activist and co-editor of *Infochange News and Features*.

CHAPTER 18

NGOs: between buzzwords and social movements

Islah Jad

*The associations that the term 'NGO' has acquired in development discourse
need to be critically analysed in relation to practice on the ground. Drawing on
an analysis of the rise of NGOs in Palestine, the author suggests that the development of the NGO movement served to demobilise Palestinian civil society
in a phase of national struggle. Through professionalisation and projectisation
brought about by donor-funded attempts to promote 'civil society', a process of
NGOisation has taken place. The progressive de-politicisation of the women's
movement that NGOisation has brought about has created a vacuum that has
been increasingly filled by the militancy of the Islamic Movement (Hamas). As
this case shows, 'NGOs' may be a development buzzword, but they are no magic
bullet. Rather than taking for granted the positive, democratising effects of the
growth and spread of NGOs as if they represented 'civil society' itself, this chapter
contends, a more critical approach is needed, one that takes greater account of the
politics of specific contexts and of the dynamics of institutionalisation.*

Introduction

The growth of NGOs is a worldwide phenomenon. It is commonly seen as
evidence of the weakening of ideological political parties and the retreat
of the state from providing social entitlements and services, in response to
structural adjustment policies imposed on most Third World countries by
the World Bank and the IMF, and under the pressure of neo-liberal reforms
(Hann 1996; Edwards and Hume 1995; Omvedt 1994). Some see NGOs as
the product of neo-liberal policies, as financially dependent on neo-liberal
sources, and as directly involved in competing with socio-political movements for the allegiance of local leaders and activist communities (Petras
1997). Others see them as mechanisms deployed for the 'creation of civil
society by external intervention' (Sampson 1996:121–42), noting the problematic conflation of 'NGOs' with 'civil society' itself. A number of studies
emphasise the negative impact of NGOs on social movements (Petras 1997;
Hann 1996) and explore the impact of what Sonia Alvarez (1998) has termed
'NGOisation' on mobilisation and social action.

Many scholars view the proliferation of NGOs in the Middle East as evidence of a vibrant civil society (Ibrahim 1995; Norton 1995; Moghadam 1997). NGOs are conflated not only with the 'democratising' features of civil society but with social mobilisation itself: an association which this chapter seeks to bring into question. Little has been done to evaluate the impact of the proliferation of NGOs on the empowerment of the various social groups that NGOs claim to represent in the Middle East. Nor has their claim to success in mobilising such groups to assert their rights been verified. Equally, few studies on the Middle East focus on how NGOs affect and interlink with other forms of social organisation, whether in the form of unions, political parties, or social movements involving students, women, or workers.

In this chapter, I draw on research in Palestine to explore the consequences of the mushrooming of NGOs, and, in particular, the NGOisation of Palestinian social movements. I suggest that empowering consequences have not been brought about by NGOisation – as the process through which issues of collective concern are transformed into projects in isolation from the general context in which they are applied and without due consideration of the economic, social, and political factors affecting these projects. On balance, my research has found that the rights-based agenda of women's NGOs has had a negative impact on the mobilising potential of mass-based women's organisations; and that this impact, in turn, created a space that has helped Islamist groups to establish themselves as a powerful and hegemonic force in Palestinian civil society.

Palestinian NGOs: a brief history

The role played by Palestinian NGOs before the 1993 Oslo Agreement differs significantly from their role in the post-Oslo phase. Before the formation of the Palestinian Authority (PA), Palestinian society was organised in and around political parties and mass grassroots organisations. NGOs were linked to these parties under the umbrella of the Palestine Liberation Organization (PLO), which encouraged and financially supported the parties and their satellite organisations. While the PLO and its political parties were banned by Israel, their satellite organisations were to some extent allowed to work, since they were seen as service-providing organisations. Between the end of the 1987 *intifada* and the signing of the Oslo Agreement, the NGO sector was the main channel of foreign aid aimed at providing services at the grassroots level. This included clinics, schools, kindergartens, and income-generating projects. The result was that these NGO actors became important and acquired even more power than their parent parties.

The role of NGOs in the West Bank and Gaza shifted under the influence of the state-building process initiated by the 1991 Madrid Conference. The dynamics of state building and their impact on different forms of organisation in civil society are important in understanding the process through which the Palestinian women's movement was demobilised. The dual dynamics of state building and NGOisation led to more fragmentation and demobilisation of all social movements. The limited life-cycle of 'projects' induced fragmentation, rather than bringing about what Tarrow (1994) called 'sustainable networking', whereby ties made with members and organisations are maintained on a regular basis.

Women's NGOs in the Arab world are considered by some to be important agents for development and democratisation and consequently modernisation (Kandil 1995). Yet, along with being regarded as 'donor driven', reflecting a Western agenda and representing elite women (Shalabi 2001; Hammami 1995; Hanafi and Tabar 2002), in terms of culture (and social change), these NGOs are seen as reproducing rather than seeking to transform patriarchal and kin-based social structures (Joseph 1997). Not only may NGOs serve to reinforce the less 'participatory' elements of existing social and political culture, but NGOisation itself has cultural dimensions, spreading values that favour dependency, lack of self-reliance, and new modes of consumption. In Palestinian newspaper advertisements, it is common to read about collective community actions organised by groups of youth, such as cleaning the streets, planting trees, painting walls, and so on, followed by a little icon indicating the name of the donor who funded these projects. It is also noticeable that many NGO activities are held in fancy hotels, serving fancy food, distributing glossy materials, hiring 'presentable' young people to help to organise the event or the activity. This phenomenon has led to the gradual disappearance of the traditional image of the casual activist with a peasant accent and appearance.

It is, however, with the political dimensions of NGOisation that this chapter is more concerned: as a process that also introduces changes in the composition of the women's movement elites (Goetz 1997). In the case of Palestine, the rise of NGOs and the process of NGOisation can be seen to have resulted in a shift in power relations: from 'power to' women at the grassroots to 'power over' them by the new elite (Jad 2004). While 'NGO' may be a synonym for 'progressive' and 'participatory' among the well-meaning supporters of well-known international NGOs, such associations are wishful thinking at best and illusory at worst.

The creation of a new Palestinian 'civil society'

The new NGOs that mushroomed in the post-Oslo period distinguish themselves from the older forms that are categorised as either charitable societies or popular mass organisations (*uttor jamaheryya*), which had an entirely different structure, discourse, leaders, projects, and networks (Taraki 1989; Shalabi 2001). The older mass organisations were open-access structures with public agendas, aiming to mobilise the largest number of students, workers, women, and youth into organisations serving each of these sectors. The newer ones, in contrast, are active in cities, run by an urban middle-class elite, and are smaller entities, dependent upon foreign funding.

The decline of popular grassroots organisations started in the early 1990s and was related to the decline of what Vivian (1994) calls 'institutional politics': politics practised through institutions such as unions and parties. The peace process triggered a process of state building in which the gender agenda became a pawn, claimed by those seeking a new basis for legitimacy after the split of their party, those who wanted to build a new constituency, and those who wanted to forge a new public space by claiming the state for citizens' and women's rights. By the mid-1990s, Hamas was yet to formulate a coherent gender vision. However, by concentrating on discrediting any group or organisation that might claim to change the *shari'a*, they managed to mount an orchestrated campaign to discredit and de-legitimise the women's organisations that followed a rights-based approach, and with them all other women's organisations. Meanwhile the new NGOs triggered conflicts with the earlier forms of mass-based organisation over legitimacy, resources, and space in public arenas.

The move from the gender agenda to a renewed interest in the national agenda was not based on continuing linkages with Palestinian constituencies or any involvement in national activism. Rather, it was brought about by international NGOs and other international players with a key role in choosing their Palestinian counterparts, whom they handpicked to speak on behalf of the Palestinian national interest. The national agenda, after the second *intifada*, was effectively hijacked by international NGOs and foreign states and donors, and concentrated on a particular set of issues concerning peace building, conflict resolution, and related issues. This created a constituency of entire groups that became the interlocutors of international agencies.

The need for professionals – or, in local parlance, *motakhassissin* (specialists) – came alongside the growing activities of women's organisations. Women's activists were in need of people with specialist skills to 'push our work forward'. The inclusion of professionals, on boards or in administration, introduced different interests and an alternative vision. The period from 1988 to 1994 witnessed a proliferation of feminist women's organisations. These new organisations propagated a new discourse on women and women's status, but within the context of a steady decline in women's mobilisation. The dichotomy between 'professional' and 'political' was one of the factors that undermined the kinds of initiative found previously among women's organisations in Palestine. Professionalisation produces upward rather than downward accountability, exclusion rather than inclusion; and 'scaling up' brings with it bureaucratisation. As Friedman notes, the result is that 'power tends to drift upward, professionalisation (which is almost always dis-empowering) takes over' (1992: 142).

There was, at this period, an increased demand by the international women's and human rights organisations to include a Palestinian voice in their activities. This led to what Palestinians call the 'militant with a suitcase – *monadel bel hakiba*' or 'jet-setting militants'. If the first *intifada* witnessed the de-linking of many women's leaders from the mass-based organisations in favour of their linkages to the international community (through participation in many activities and conferences), the second *intifada* witnessed a shift to NGO leaders representing the voice of Palestinian 'civil society'. Analysing this shift, Tabar and Hanafi refer to what they call the emergence of a Palestinian 'globalised elite', tied more closely to the global actors – in other words international NGOs and donors – than to local constituencies. They were characterised by being informed by a global agenda, supporting the peace process, and being urban and professional (Hanafi and Tabar 2002). It was noted that the 'globalised elite' had overturned the old elite (charitable societies and women's grassroots groups), through a process of competition and through vying for organisational continuity.

The NGOisation of the national agenda

Women's activists were heavily involved in the Palestinian national movement from the outset. They sought to mobilise public opinion, whether in the Arab world or in the world at large, in supporting their national rights to independence and self-determination. That role was recuperated later on by the General Union of Palestinian Women (GUPW), mainly outside the Occupied Territories. In the course of the first Palestinian uprising and the move of the centre of the struggle to the Occupied Territories, that role was largely taken over by the Palestinian women's movements in the Occupied Territories, who were better equipped to express their suffering and their daily realities under the policies practised by the Israeli Occupation Forces.

From the 1990s onwards, however, the effects of NGOisation started to be felt within the formulation of the national agenda. This position is credible, since some of the main donors for Palestinian NGOs insisted upon 'correct political conditions' in an attempt to separate these organisations from politics. But, again, it would be an oversimplification to perceive NGOs as passive recipients, and donors as simply following or executing their government policies. It was argued that local NGOs, as well as international actors, have a space to negotiate their mutual relationships. Cohen and Comaroff, for example, state that NGOs 'do not respond to a need, but negotiate relationships by convincing the other parties of the meaning of organisations, events and processes [...] they act as brokers of meanings' (Cohen and Comaroff 1976: 88, cited in Hilhorst 2003: 191).

In order to carve out a new basis for legitimacy, distinct from that gained by the participation of grassroots women's leaders in the national struggle, the new activists (NGO leaders) made excessive use of the language of 'expertise' and emphasised their links with international donors. It was common, in these meetings, to hear how many important state representatives and news agencies had met with these new women's leaders, and how many international prizes they had been granted for their efforts in the 'peace process' and women's advancement. However, this language failed to convince the old leaders and was sometimes even met with derision, as one of the 'old' leaders put it:

When we organise demonstrations, they stop their cars in front of the demonstrations, get their banners out and stand in the first row to be photographed. They can sell this to the outside, but nobody buys this internally.

The transformation of a cause for social change into a project with a plan, timetable, and fixed budget needs to be 'owned' for reporting and to secure further funding. This is exacerbated by the 'magic bullet syndrome' (Vivian 1994): the view among NGO staff members responsible for designing, implementing, and reporting on projects that they must demonstrate success if they are to maintain their funding. A corollary of the syndrome is a tendency to gloss over mistakes and to present the project as an unqualified success story. An explanation that relies exclusively on donor pressure is insufficient, however, since NGOs can also be seen to be complicit in the donors' success stories. If donors are driven by the logic of efficacy of their funds, then NGOs are driven by the imperatives of professionalism and delivery. It is therefore the 'project logic', the NGOisation of issues related to social change and popular participation, that should be better scrutinised. Nowhere is this more true than in relation to activities associated with 'peace' in this region.

Projectising peace

The visual display of the 'peace process' (the handshake between Rabin and Arafat in the lounge of the White House in 1993) was accompanied by an abundance of internationally funded projects on conflict resolution, peace-building measures, building trust, 'engendering the peace process', and 'parallel negotiations'. These projects, written in highly technical English, usually involved women's activists in conferences in Europe or in the USA where they could meet with their Israeli counterparts, in order to dismantle psychological barriers, push women into decision making, and enhance gendered parallel negotiations. In most cases, it was the international actors who chose their local interlocutors.

Many political positions concerning vital issues related to refugees, Jerusalem, forms of resistance, and the formation of the future state are adopted by the participants of international conferences without consulting anyone back home. One might argue that there is no single interlocutor to consult with. This may be true, and indeed many male actors in the international arena do not consult 'back home'. The difference for Palestinian NGO activists is that they lack the backing of any legitimate political actors in the PA or civil society, since they have no constituency or political party or organisations to belong to. Claiming feminist credentials and professionalism are the main criteria to qualify as participants in these forums. In this context, professionally written reports and easy and efficacious channels of communications are important. However, their lack of political training as activist leaders weighs heavily on the legitimacy back home of some of these NGO elites.

The prevalence of particular kinds of project is usually linked to the power of the donor community to dictate or influence local NGO agendas (Kunibert and Singer 1996; Pinto-Duschinsky 1991). Some claim that this flow of projects does not necessarily reflect a well-orchestrated policy by international NGOs and donors. The international donor community is not monolithic, but is driven by different interests, visions, and politics. Chabbott (1999), for example, suggests that there are some international development professionals who have used their concerns, which are distinct from those of their own donors, to carve out a larger role for international NGOs in the world polity over time. She suggests that these international actors have developed 'a discourse of development, which placed increasing emphasis on the role of external factors in national development, simultaneously constraining nation-state autonomy and creating space for non-state actors in development' (1999: 238).

I would argue that, besides their ability to convince international donors of the vitality of their work, 'peace activists' are driven in this process by their own interests. The involvement in 'peace process' activities by many NGOs, aside from getting funding, supports their claim to acquire more power and legitimacy. 'Peace process' activism might after all come to constitute a power base for the NGO elite to reach decision-making positions, whether in the PA or in the leadership of the Palestinian women's movements and other social movements.

The new professionals

A combination of schooling and work experience has produced a specialised cadre of international development professionals who spend the bulk of their working lives on a series of assignments in global metropolises and the capitals of low-income countries. Carapico suggests that these professionals become somewhat detached from their countries of origin; their perspectives and concerns may be quite different from those of legislators and ordinary citizens who fund international development organisations. Given their distance from the funders, they face significant opportunities and temptations to exercise personal and professional prerogatives. It is these professionals, rather than national politicians or diplomats, who have generated the international development discourse, written the UN reports, drafted conference statements, designed conference follow-up strategies, and helped new nation-states to draft national development policies (Carapico 2000). An industry of funding and projects has developed around issues related to democracy, peace building, and women's rights; democracy-brokers in Europe, North America, and Australia are kept busy writing proposals and bids to public bureaucracies for their projects in the Arab world (Carapico 2002).

Given the power of the international NGOs, one might imagine that some of this power might trickle down and give more leverage to local professionals in 'doing the professional job', i.e. the implementation of the project plan, and reporting and evaluation, on the ground. The better the quality of the professional work, the better and stronger the relations with the donor. The more that local professionals can meet expectations, the better their chance of being part of the 'virtual community' (Castells 1996), which creates a common career path set out by those humanitarian-oriented organisations that shape their common culture and belief system. This system includes a belief in the centrality of development to human progress, in the responsibility of governments to promote it, in the imperative for international development assistance to support it, in the definition of development in 'human' rather than strictly economic (or political) terms (Chabbott 1999). Thus, the link with international donors is not a one-way relationship, but donors and local actors interlink in a web of relations that is far more complicated than one party imposing its will on the other. This is not to say that both parties have equal power, but simply to problematise the links between them to include the personal interests of both donors and recipients that give them the power to decide what to take and what to leave.

Concluding remarks

In the above analysis, I argue that professionalisation, as part of an NGO-isation process, might not lead to more participation for the 'target groups' or the grassroots. 'Project logic' pushes towards upward vertical participation and not downward horizontal participation, and can lead to further concentration of power in the hands of administrators or technocrats. NGOisation leads to the transformation of a cause for social change into a project with a plan, a time-table, and a limited budget, which is 'owned' for reporting and used for the purposes of accountability *vis-à-vis* the funders. This concentration of power might impede the spread of a social movement in continuous need of networking, deliberation, and mobilisation, based on daily contact and personal connections. This process of dissemination is time-consuming and hard to frame in timetables, especially in the constantly changing situation in Palestine. In this context, professionalism and the project logic also provided a new power base for NGO elites to determine which women's issues should be brought to public attention. Lack of awareness by NGO professionals of the forces active in civil society and the public sphere risks weakening calls for more equitable gender relations and empowering more conservative actors in civil society.

NGOs are often presented as passive recipients of external influence, at the mercy of the whims of donors: yet analysis of the 'Do[nor]-NGOs' in Palestine shows the extent to which NGO representatives also have the power to manipulate, re-negotiate, and legitimise donor agendas, using funds earmarked for peace to further their own agendas. They are part of a 'globalised elite', in that they are tied to international players and informed by global agendas. These links proved instrumental to the 'NGOisation' of the national agenda in Palestine, transforming it from a struggle to realise self-determination and sovereign statehood into 'projects' for donor funding, in which donors play a vital role in choosing their local interlocutors.

What we see as a result of the rise of 'NGO' as a development buzzword is the mistaken tendency to assume that any and all of the organisations who adopt this term are thereby describing themselves as progressive and democratic. In the case of Palestine, the discourse of NGOs was used to forge a space in the public arena at the expense of old mass-based organisations. It recast the 'old' basis for legitimacy founded on resistance and sacrifice as a basis for women's subordination and isolation. And it spoke less to the overall social, economic, and political context than to the desires of the donors and elites who were to propel the rapid growth of these organisations in this setting. Against this background, I believe that women's NGOs and the new discourses that they brought to the public sphere might – however inadvertently – have acted to disempower, de-legitimise, and fragment civil-society secular actors and their movements in Palestine.

For all the assumptions that circulate in international development circles about NGOs being closer to 'the people', able to speak for 'the grassroots', and a motor of democratisation and development, the Palestinian case is a vivid reminder of the need to get beyond the buzzword itself and take a long, hard look at what is actually going on. That, as I suggest here, the NGOisation of Palestinian women's movements and the use by women's NGOs of the currency of rights talk promoted by international NGOs has contributed to the growing power and legitimacy of the Islamists is consequence enough for such circumspection to be necessary.

References

Alvarez, Sonia (1998) 'Women's movements and gender politics in the Brazilian transition', in J. Jaquette (ed.), *The Women's Movement in Latin America: Feminism and the Transition to Democracy*, London: Unwin Hyman.

Carapico, Sheila (2000) 'NGOs, INGOs, Go-NGOs and Do-NGOs: making sense of non-governmental organizations', *Middle East Report* 214: 12–15.

Carapico, Sheila (2002) 'Foreign aid and democratisation', *Middle East Journal*, 56(3): 379–95.

Castells, Manuel (1996) *The Information Age: Economy, Society and Culture Vol. I: The Rise of the Network Society*, Oxford: Blackwell.

Chabbott, Colette (1999) 'Development INGOs', in John Boli and George Thomas (eds.), *Constructing World Culture: International Nongovernmental Organisations Since 1875*, Stanford, CA: Stanford University Press.

Edwards, Michael and D. Hulme (eds.) (1995) *Non-Governmental Organisations: Performance and Accountability: Beyond the Magic Bullet*, London: Earthscan and Save the Children.

Friedman, John (1992) *Empowerment: The Politics of Alternative Development*, Oxford: Blackwell.

Goetz, Anne Marie (ed.) (1997) *Getting Institutions Right for Women in Development*, London: Zed Books.

Hammami, Rema (1995) 'NGOs: the professionalization of politics', *Race and Class* [Special Issue on Palestine: Diplomacies of Defeat] 37(2): 51–64.

Hanafi, Sari and Linda Tabar (2002) 'NGOs, elite formation and the Second Intifada', *Between the Lines* 2(18): 31–37.

Hann, Chris (1996) 'Introduction: political society and civil anthropology', in Chris Hann and Elizabeth Dunn (eds.), *Civil Society: Challenging Western Models*, London and New York: Routledge.

Hilhorst, Dorothea (2003) *The Real World of NGOs: Discourses, Diversity and Development*, London: Zed Books.

Ibrahim, S.E. (1995) 'Civil society and prospects of democratisation in the Arab world' in Augustus R. Norton (ed.), *Civil Society in the Middle East*, Vol. I. Leiden: E.J. Brill.

Jad, Islah (2004) 'The "NGOisation" of the Arab women's movement', *IDS Bulletin*, 35(4): 34–42.

Joseph, Suad (1997) 'The reproduction of political process among women activists in Lebanon: "shopkeepers" and "feminists"', in Dawn Chatty and Annika Rabo (eds.), *Organizing Women: Formal and Informal Women's Groups in the Middle East*, Oxford: Berg.

Kandil, Amani (1995) *Civil Society in the Arab World*, Washington, DC: Civicus.

Kunibert, Raffer and H.W. Singer (1996) *The Foreign Aid Business: Economic Assistance and Development Co-Operation*. Cheltenham and Brookfield: Edward Elgar.

Moghadam, Valentine (1997) *Women, Work and Economic Reform in the Middle East and North Africa*, Boulder, CO: Lynne Rienner.

Norton, Augustus Richard (ed.) (1995) *Civil Society in the Middle East*, Vols. I and II, Leiden: E.J. Brill.

Omvedt, Gail (1994) 'Peasants, dalits and women: democracy and India's new social movements', *Journal of Contemporary Asia* 24.1: 35–48.

Petras, James (1997) 'Imperialism and NGOs in Latin America', *Monthly Review* 49(7), available at www.monthlyreview.org/1297petr.htm (retrieved 15 April 2007).

Pinto-Duschinsky, Michael (1991) 'Foreign political aid: the German political foundations and their US counterparts', *International Affairs* 67(1): 33–66.

Sampson, Steven (1996) 'The social life of projects: improving civil society in Albania', in Chris Hann and Elizabeth Dunn (eds.), *Civil Society: Challenging Western Models*, London: Routledge.

Shalabi, Yasser (2001) *'al-ta'thirat al-dawleya 'ala tahdid ro'aa al-monathmat ghayr al-hokomeyya alfelastineyya wa-adwareha'* [International and Local Impacts on the Visions and Roles of Palestinian NGOs], unpublished MA thesis, Palestine: Bir Zeit University.

Taraki, Lisa (1989) 'Mass organizations in the West Bank', in N. Aruri (ed.), *Occupation: Israel Over Palestine*, Massachusetts, MA: Belmont.

Tarrow, Sidney (1994) *Power in Movement: Social Movements, Collective Action and Politics*, Cambridge and New York: Cambridge University Press.

Vivian, Jessica (1994) 'NGOs and sustainable development in Zimbabwe: no magic bullets', *Development and Change* 25(1): 167–93.

About the author

Islah Jad is Assistant Professor of Gender and Development at Bir Zeit University in Palestine, where she co-founded the Institute of Women's Studies. She has published widely on Palestinian and Arab women's political participation and is co-author of the 2005 *Arab Human Development Report*.

CHAPTER 19

Capacity building: who builds whose capacity?

Deborah Eade

This chapter focuses on the role that development NGOs play in capacity build-ing, arguing that many conventional NGO practices are ultimately about retain-ing power, rather than empowering their partners. This leads to tunnel vision and to upward rather than downward or horizontal accountability, based on the assumption that the transfer of resources is a one-way process. At worst, this un-dermines rather than strengthens the capacities of the organisations that NGOs are attempting to assist. Sharing responsibilities and risks, mutual accountability, and committing to the long term rather than to short-term projects are more likely to create partnerships that can withstand vicissitudes and contribute to lasting change.

Building or undermining capacities?

The danger of working in any kind of aid agency is that one begins to see the world through its eyes; and, as identities gradually merge, it is increasingly difficult to look at the world afresh, or to see ourselves as others see us.

This is particularly so in the case of international aid agencies, where the reality-checks of working up-close and personal are muted in unfamiliar cul-tural settings, as well as being distorted by asymmetries of power, and by com-plex insider–outsider dynamics (Eyben 2006). Too easily, 'development' and 'aid' are used synonymously; and both are assumed to be good. Too readily, aid agencies assume that *their* priorities (which are necessarily shaped by their upward accountability, and fed by their own public-relations priorities) will naturally coincide with those of the people on the receiving end, or can be bolted on without too much problem. When they become fashion accessories, or mere buzzwords invoked in order to negotiate bureaucratic mazes, the use of concepts such as 'gender', or 'empowerment', or 'capacity building' is not only drained of any remaining political content, but may actually end up crushing local capacities rather than releasing their potential.[1]

But if capacity building means anything, it is surely about enabling those out on the margins to represent and defend their interests more effectively, not only within their own immediate contexts but also globally. Unless one believes that the Development Industry in all its expressions is inherently self-serving, the 'good cop' of international aid *vis à vis* the 'bad cop' of international capitalism, then it follows that hindering social transformation is not the intended outcome. So what is it that goes so wrong?

There are no easy answers, as every context presents its own specific challenges: the sustained political violence that wracks Colombia is not the same as the gang violence throughout much of Central America, though doubtless they share some of the same roots in drug trafficking. And regions that seem quite calm, at least to an outsider, can erupt apparently overnight. Witness the Zapatista uprising in Chiapas, which burst into life on 1 January 1994, the very day that the North American Free Trade Agreement (NAFTA) came into effect.

My focus here is on the role that development NGOs might play in the areas of capacity building. This is partly because I have worked mainly in the development NGO sector for almost 30 years, but more importantly because it is often *assumed* that NGOs have some unique ability or role to play in this arena.[2]

In time-honoured feminist tradition, I shall start with a thumbnail sketch of where I am coming from in order to locate myself in this analysis. For most of my professional career I have worked in the international NGO sector. For ten years I was on the spending side, based in a regional office for Mexico and Central America. Though at pains to establish relationships that were *not* predicated only on money, we and our 'partners' were under no illusions about the fact that it was our job to decide who should be funded to do what, for how long, and on what conditions; and to defend these decisions within our own regional team and to our managers and oversight committees in the UK. We saw our role as twofold: on the one hand to provide critical accompaniment to our counterparts, and on the other to marry these to the NGO's values and criteria in a way that allowed everyone to feel comfortable in the relationship.

Then followed a wretched time spent working as a bureaucrat in the UK. Now my job was not to relate to our counterparts, but to police the money. Counting beans offers no food for the soul, so it was a relief to take on the editorship of *Development in Practice*. But as a result, I found my job security depending initially on a trickle of one-year grants (with the plug likely to be pulled at short notice), being 'evaluated' by managers with no particular expertise in journals publishing, chasing funding applications that had languished in someone's in-tray for months, having to meet reporting requirements that bore no relation to the needs and rhythms of the project, and so on. In short, this experience was the same as that of hundreds of thousands of organisations worldwide that depend on Northern NGO 'partners'. (The contribution to this volume by my former colleague in Mexico, Miguel Pickard, addresses this problem in greater depth.)

Having been on both sides of the partnership fence has given me some insight into what constitutes 'good capacity-building practice', and into how many NGO practices are ultimately about holding on to their own power, rather than empowering others. This leads me to pose three questions:

- What do we understand by capacity building in the context of development, and specifically of development aid?
- How central are NGOs in taking forward a capacity-building agenda? What is their track record in this? Do they really make a difference?
- How can the South engage with the North in capacity building?

A background to capacity building

A glance through the development literature – from scholarly articles to agency PR – confirms the 'buzzword' status of *capacity building*. Some dismiss it for this reason as a sloppy piece of aid jargon. For others, it is a synonym for institutional or organisational development. Often it is no more than a serious-sounding alternative to 'training'. After all, no NGO could admit to funding one-off training workshops whose impact may be short-lived, or that risk serving mainly as social events for the same old bunch of tired aid junkies. But simply changing the name does not change the practice, and adopting a narrow view of capacity building as in-service or vocational training is just as unhelpful as using it as a catch-all to mean everything and nothing.

The intellectual and political roots of capacity building lie partly in the rights-centred *capacitación* of Liberation Theology and the *conscientização* work of Paulo Freire. Southern feminists and 'gender and development' policy makers and activists have also deepened the understanding of 'empowerment' and social exclusion (see, for instance, Srilatha Batliwala's contribution to this volume). Amartya K. Sen's work on entitlements and capabilities provides insights into the dynamic nature of the exclusion that capacity building seeks to address. This has influenced the pivotal work of UNDP on human development in articulating an alternative to the economic view of 'human capital' associated with the international financial institutions (see also Ben Fine's contribution to this volume on the subject of social capital). However, these institutions – most notably the World Bank (now re-cast as the Global Knowledge Bank) – have also adopted the language of capacity building and participation, relating this to the neo-liberal agenda of rolling back the state, privatising public services (the 'marketisation' of social welfare), good governance, and democratisation. (Evelina Dagnino's contribution to this volume develops this theme in relation to the co-option of the popular democratisation project in Brazil.) In the post-Washington Consensus era, the role of civil society (another woolly and contested term) is crucial. And, within the international development context, NGOs are considered – and often consider themselves – to occupy pride of place as 'civil society'. The list of NGOs with consultative status at the United Nations runs to 60 pages, each with about 40 entries – that's one NGO a day for six and a half years or, if you don't have that much time, roughly one per minute for an entire 24-hour day. And they are only the ones at the tip of the iceberg.

My point here is that capacity building originally drew on a generally left-leaning range of intellectual and political traditions, but is today commonly used to further a neo-liberal 'pull-yourself-up-by-your-bootstraps' kind of economic and political agenda. If NGOs are not aware of these competing agendas, their role in capacity building will be at best insignificant, at worst damaging.

Engaging with the wider context

Capacity building is not a 'thing' or a commodity that can be reduced to a set of ingredients for a universal recipe on 'how to do it'. Recognising that there are many diverse and competing actors in development, we can nevertheless state that its early origins lay in the belief that the role of an engaged outsider is to support the capacity of local people to determine their own values and priorities, to organise themselves to act upon and sustain these for the common good, and to shape the moral and physical universe that we all share.

Because aid agencies exist to channel resources from one part of the world to another, and because the currency of aid remains the Project, despite the growing Northern NGO focus on advocacy and 'one-programme frameworks', it is tempting to take short cuts in order to get things done. This leads to NGOs taking too little time to understand the local political and cultural environment as well as the international policy context within which people, their organisations, and their governments are functioning. Aid agencies, particularly but not exclusively NGOs, characteristically see the aspect of people's lives that relates to their project-defined 'target groups', but often fail to see the cat's cradle of shifting inter-relationships in which these same people are embedded (Eade and Williams 1995: 17–19). If NGOs live in a kind of Project World theme park, they will fail to see the less visible processes that will undermine the impact of their projects. A case in point is the belated discovery that providing micro-credit to women in Bangladesh, notwithstanding the remarkable achievements of Mohammad Yunus and the Grameen Bank, does not always benefit them. Why? Because men use women as a means to get credit for themselves (Rahman Khan 1995), or because their fathers, brothers, and husbands feel threatened by women's greater financial independence, and so literally beat them back into submission (Schuler et al. 1998). Taking more time to understand the non-project realities and underlying gender-power dynamics may pre-empt these unintended impacts.

And what are the capacities that NGOs seek to build? They may be intellectual, organisational, social, political, cultural, representational, material, technical, practical, or financial – and most likely a shifting combination of all of these. The ability to articulate and mobilise around specific interests or demands is intimately linked to the development of a civil society in which divergent interests can be represented, and which has appropriate mechanisms for adjudicating among these. Civil society flourishes best when the state is capable of balancing competing claims in the interests of the common good. Good governance is not served if a state is encouraged to abandon its responsibilities to its citizens, or when it transfers these piece-meal to institutions (including NGOs) that see this as a great capacity-building opportunity, but are not themselves accountable to those who use their services – a point to which I shall return.

A capacity-building approach therefore means getting out of Project World, focusing less on supporting scores of projects and more on seeing any intervention within the wider context of social and other kinds of change – local, national, regional, and global. Training may be successful in its own terms, but contribute very little to enabling participants to change their realities. International NGOs may claim spectacular campaigning achievements, but translating these successes into sustainable changes in people's lives means a long-term commitment and listening to what they themselves say. Rather than viewing support for this or that organisation or activity in a fragmented or insular fashion, it is necessary to look intelligently at the whole web of social relations within which these organisations and their activities are embedded. A change in one bit of the system may have many repercussions on another part, not necessarily positive. For instance, if public services are put out to tender, NGOs that previously co-operated with each other may start to compete for a lucrative contract. An opportunity for one quickly becomes a threat to others.

Development NGOs

How relevant are development NGOs to capacity building? Reading some of the literature, one could be forgiven for thinking both that capacity building is an exclusively Southern 'need', and that international NGOs are among those best placed to meet it.

The sad reality is that most development aid has precious little to do with building the capacities of 'The Poor' to transform their societies. Not even the best-intentioned NGOs are exempt from the tendency of the Development Industry to ignore, misinterpret, displace, supplant, or undermine the capacities that people already have. Recognition of this danger is precisely what lies behind NGO initiatives to establish standards of behaviour and accountability in the humanitarian field: initiatives such as the Sphere Project, ALNAP (Active Learning Network for Accountability in Humanitarian Action), or HAP (Humanitarian Accountability Partnership). Even so, how often do 'end-users' or 'clients' get to shop around to choose their service provider? The Salvadoran refugees who withdrew their co-operation with the European NGO charged with providing medical assistance remain an exception that proves the rule.[3]

There are two points to be made here. The first is that while NGOs may be no worse than other development actors, they do not have any inherent capacity to build the capacities of 'The Poor'. Some are of course better equipped than others to do so: the local faith-based NGO that replaced the ousted European agency in the Salvadoran case was committed to training the refugee community alongside its provision of health-care services, although this came hand in hand with what many regarded as a conservative and authoritarian theology.

Conventional wisdom holds that operational NGOs tend to replace rather than build local capacities, but even here it is difficult to generalise. One British co-operant-sending organisation, for example, has moved away from exporting 'experts' to work overseas for a couple of years towards employing local experts who can commit to a longer period, building up new social relationships in the process. Similarly, it is often thought that material inputs and capacity building are at opposite ends of the aid spectrum. Capacity building is *about people* and therefore not about *things*, so training and education are all right, while bricks and mortar are not. The reality is seldom so stark. I well recall spending a Sunday morning helping a network of health workers in the outskirts of San Salvador to build a small clinic, while the afternoon heat was spent under the mango trees in more conventional health education activities. For them, both were essential: they needed a place to meet and to attend to patients, particularly in the rainy season, and building a joint community clinic was critical to establishing mutual trust; they also, of course, needed to acquire new skills and knowledge. They saw both activities as being on the same capacity-building spectrum. I learned a lot about building techniques that day. And I learned a lot more about building a shared vision based on trust and co-operation.

To take a slightly different example, a Northern NGO that advocates energetically on behalf of its 'partners' in the South may be experienced by them as diminishing their own voices and knowledge, rather than helping them to acquire the skills needed to undertake their own lobbying, in their own time and in their own way – arguments reminiscent of the 'nothing about us without us' slogan that originated in the South African disability-rights movement.[4] What this means is that we cannot look at an input in isolation and say *a priori* that X represents capacity building while Y doesn't. It is much more a question of understanding the subtleties of the context and direction; an approach, rather than a thing.

The second point is that a capacity-building approach hinges on the capacity for self-criticism. We have heard a thousand times that if you give a man a fish, you feed him for a day, and if you teach him to fish, you feed him for a lifetime. But, as a friend in El Salvador once asked: What if that fisher is not a man but a woman? And what if she doesn't own the water in which she is fishing? Or her customary fishing rights have been taken away from her? An NGO in South Africa takes the question a step further: what if the NGO does not even know how to fish? For NGOs to make a lasting difference means that they must reflect hard on their own role(s) and be alert to changes in the environment in which they operate. It also means a commitment to learning as *intrinsic* to their interventions to build the capacities of others.

Simply invoking concepts like partnership is not enough to steer NGOs through these issues. The re-defined role of the state is a case in point. An NGO may have been doing commendable education with village health workers for many years, complementing government services. However, if the government privatises its health services, or charges user-fees that place health care out of the reach of those most in need, then that same NGO may find itself performing a *de facto* 'gap-filling' role within a quite different political agenda, one that is bent on reducing the role of the state and privatising public services. My point here is not whether neo-liberalism is good or bad, but how easily NGOs with a narrow project focus can become unwitting pawns in others' chess games.

What does the North have to learn?

This brings me to my third question. What are the kinds of skill that Northern NGOs need if they are to adopt a capacity-building approach to their work?

Some have been identified already: self-awareness, self-criticism, and a degree of modesty. Then the ability to distinguish between different agendas and fads, rather than spinning around like a weathervane in a windstorm. It also calls for a wide repertoire of engagement. By and large, Northern NGOs engage with the South via the transfer of financial and technical resources: in other words, through money-driven partnerships. Although this donor–recipient relationship has been extended in recent years, notably in the area of advocacy, it essentially remains what it always was. 'Hard' resources are transferred from North to South in return for 'soft' resources in the form of information, 'stories', and *New Internationalist*-cum-Benetton photos that in turn feed into the Northern NGO's capacity to raise funds or recruit campaign supporters. 'Soft' resources may also be used in policy- or issue-focused lobbying and campaigning. But again, the agendas and timetables are almost invariably set by Northern NGOs and not by their Southern 'partners' – even though the principal policy targets may be *global* institutions, *global* processes, and respect for *universal* rights.

But, you might say, if this division of labour works, what does it matter? If you espouse a capacity-building approach, it matters quite a lot. First, because if a relationship is only as sustainable as its money supply, then power games and dependency lie at its heart. All power corrupts, but absolute dependency undermines absolutely. The Northern NGO depends on getting money from its domestic public, or (increasingly) from governments (and this has its own implications in relation to the 'too close for comfort' arguments presented by Hulme and Edwards 1996); the Southern 'partner' can function only by virtue of a dripfeed administered by philanthropic outsiders. If the dosage changes, or runs out, the life of the Southern partner is threatened.

Second, a partnership that is based on a one-way transfer of resources (whether these are financial or intellectual) is profoundly asymmetrical, a fact which will tend to distort the functioning and dignity of the weaker partner, as well as fostering the hubris of the stronger one. Organisations that have priorities projected on to them, however subtly, are almost bound to shift their agendas to match those of their donors. Few Southern organisations have the capacity to generate 'no strings' funds from the general public. In-country fundraising is beginning to happen in nations with large and wealthy middle-classes such as Brazil, India, Mexico, or South Africa – while remittances from migrant workers may be more important in weaker economies or in particular regions of stronger ones (Jennings and Clarke 2005). Southern organisations that depend on Northern funding are thereby compromised in their role as civil-society organisations. Obviously, it makes no sense for Southern organisations to do less local advocacy and mobilising because of the constraints imposed by financial dependency. But it is also dangerous for any NGO to assume functions for which it is not equipped or not accountable, simply because it has the financial muscle to do so. Jenny Pearce (1993) has shown how, by taking on more political roles in public life – roles for which they were not *politically* accountable – Chilean NGOs effectively *depoliticised* the social movements that they set out to serve, and which had given them their legitimacy in the first place: something that Sonia Alvarez (1998) has called the 'NGOization of social movements', a phenomenon that she attributes to their 'professionalization' and recasting as 'gender experts rather than as citizens' groups' (Alvarez 1999). And all thanks to Northern NGO support.

Because administrative accountability has been fashioned around money, the systems have tended to move upwards from recipient to donor, not the other way around. Yet, as we have seen, the intended beneficiaries seldom get to choose which NGO is going to provide services or advocate on their behalf. The victims of floods and mudslides in Manila or Tegucigalpa – or, come to that, New Orleans – may not much care whether they are helped to safety by Catholic Relief Services, by any or all of the Oxfams, by a local Red Cross volunteer, or (most likely) by their next-door neighbour. But when it comes to the longer-term reconstruction effort, it may make a great difference whether the work is designed and financed by the World Bank as opposed to, say, World Neighbors. The Bank is likely to promote small-enterprise development, the fostering of the spirit and capacity to compete in the marketplace (Moxham 2005); the NGO on organisational skills and on healing social divisions. The intended beneficiaries of international development assistance may be consulted about this or that, but they rarely have the opportunity to tell an aid agency to just leave them alone (although there are countless examples of ways in which people express their displeasure by deliberately subverting aid projects). NGOs, on the other hand, insist on *their* right to choose whom to help and how, and what they want in return.

Don't get me wrong here. The relative autonomy of NGOs can be vital. In the 1980s, for instance, it is what permitted Northern (mainly European and Canadian) NGOs in Central America to work with local organisations and informal structures that enjoyed the trust of people working for social change, and not to be sucked into the brutal counter-insurgency effort. It is what made it possible to claim the right to 'humanitarian space' to assist civilians living in the conflict zones in El Salvador and Guatemala. The same held true of NGOs that supported clandestine opposition to Apartheid in South Africa, or to the Marcos regime in the Philippines.

But there is another side to the autonomy coin. NGOs can, and do, pick up and then abandon their Southern 'partners' without being called to account. NGOs that are concerned to help to build capacity, in full recognition of the social, political, and ethical responsibilities that this entails, should first scrutinise their downward and horizontal accountability. They need to look at the impacts of their support on the webs of relationships in which their chosen 'partners' function. They need to look at how they learn from their 'partners', not just gathering 'stories and pictures', but in terms of their values, their perceptions, their analyses, concerns, and aspirations. They need to check their feedback and communication mechanisms, because without these there is no mutual accountability. Consultation is not just a question of asking, but of accounting back for decisions taken. The list could go on. But the basic message is that if NGOs want to take capacity building seriously, then they must be prepared to change their own structures and practices in order to reflect this commitment to partnership, reciprocity, shared risk-taking, and inter-dependence.

Finally, all this takes time. Aid agencies are always in a hurry. They feel the need to spend in order to justify their existence to their constituencies and to their donors. But there are no prizes for coming first, and a lot of collateral damage can be done by taking things too fast – or indeed by packing up as soon as the funded activity is over. The workshops have been held, the participants gave positive feedback on their evaluation forms, and so capacity has been built. A year later, there is nothing to show for it. A more sustained relationship may not yield spectacular results, but these results may well be more lasting. An example from Honduras illustrates this. In the mid-1980s we began funding an incipient social-education programme run by a *campesina* whose goal was to create a peasant women's movement. However, the self-esteem of most of the women who came along to the meetings was so low that they would simply wait for her to tell them what to do. She did not want to reproduce the static top–down structure found in all the other popular organisations and local NGOs, whatever their professed radicalism. I put her in touch with a feminist social worker and former nun in Mexico who had worked for many years with non-literate women. She visited the programme and, with them, developed a self-help manual that would help them, and women like them, to tackle the deep sources of their oppression. Given their Christian faith, she drew on positive images of women in the Bible to help get the message across. Imagine my delight *nearly 10 years later* when I was sent a copy of the manual, by then a best-selling publication; and a video showing women who had been too shy even to say their names addressing mass rallies calling for women's right to own land. And when, *more than 20 years later*, I was invited to the inaugural meeting of the peasant women's movement that had grown out of such humble beginnings. If we had expected concrete results after the three-year grant came to an end, we would have been sorely disappointed. But how genuinely interested are NGOs in what happens after 'their' project has finished? While they might adopt a more programme- based approach to grant making, with the aim of 'scaling up' or at least ensuring that the whole is more than the sum of the parts, seldom does this extend beyond the final report on how the funds were used. More often than not, the grant is disbursed, the 'project' does what is expected, accountability for the use of funds is assured, and the final report ends up gathering dust deep in the organisational archives.[5]

Conclusion

Capacity building is an approach to solidarity-based partnerships with an in-finite variety of expressions. While some of the ingredients can be identified, there is no global recipe, no quick fix. Partnership entails mutual accountabili-ty, and you cannot have one without the other. This includes accounting back honestly for decisions that affect others. This approach is demanding, and it calls for time, flexibility, shared risk taking, open dialogue, and a willingness *on both sides* to respond to feedback. Co-development is also far more reward-ing than trying to be a catalyst, which exerts 'an impact or change on another component within a system without itself changing' (Eyben 2006: 48).

NGOs can foster the capacities of those Southern organisations whose aspi-rations they support. Partnership is not about accepting anything and every-thing that each other does, but for Northern NGOs it almost certainly means getting out of the driving seat and learning to trust their chosen partners' navigational skills. Just because they paid to fill up the tank does not give NGOs the right to determine the route. What is abundantly clear is that you can't build capacities in others that you don't have yourself. And if you can't learn, you can't teach either.

That said, disengagement is not an option. The gulf between rich and poor diminishes our humanity. Another world is possible, but only by building on the capacity of the most oppressed to repudiate injustice, and work for mutual respect and solidarity.

Notes

1. This essay draws on my earlier work, in particular Eade 1997; Eade and Williams 1995.
2. The focus on development NGOs is certainly not limited to international or Northern NGOs; nor are the issues peculiar to the NGO sector. The NGO world does not divide into neat North–South, good–bad, powerful–powerless categories. Nor should one deny the real contests and diver-gences that exist between and often within them. Rather, my concern is

with NGOs as holders and brokers of power *vis-à-vis* those who have more or less power than they do.

3. The reasons for this 'vote of no confidence' have of course been variously interpreted, but they revolve essentially around political agency. The refugees argued that the NGO imposed a 'doctor knows best' philosophy, while they wanted to develop skills as community health workers in preparation for their return to El Salvador. The NGO claimed that it was vital to keep medical supplies under firm control, in order to prevent them leaking out to the FMLN fighters, and that the refugees were either FMLN sympathisers, or were the victims of political manipulation and threats (Terry 2002).

4. Space does not permit discussion on the vexed issue of advocacy by Northern NGOs; suffice it to say that Southern activists and academics alike complain that all too often the role assigned to them is that of providing local evidence to fuel Northern advocacy on their behalf, or 'case studies' to illustrate Northern analyses of the problems facing the Global South. See Eade 2002, in particular the chapters by Maria Teresa Diokno-Pascual, Dot Keet, Paul Nelson, and Warren Nyamugasira; and Olukoshi, cited in Utting 2006:121.

5. Staff turnover seriously impedes long-term Northern NGO engagement with Southern organisations beyond the grant period. The director of a small agency that receives funds from various Northern NGOs once commented to me that he usually knew far more about each NGO's history in Chiapas than did the successive 'new brooms' sent down to sweep through his agency's funding requests. A curious reversal of roles indeed when Southern 'partners' end up safeguarding the histories of their Northern NGO benefactors! Central Americans interviewed in 1997 made similar points: 'The international aid agencies, particularly the NGOs, "lived through the process with us" and often identified deeply with it. Suddenly it was all change. The new emphasis was on technical issues, efficiency, efficacy, and so on – but without recognising and taking into account the more subjective elements' (Ardón 1999:63); 'Many of the international aid workers are new. They did not live through the war years, and do not have a detailed knowledge of the context. This has made working with them far harder, since it is like having to start all over again – which takes up a lot of time' (*ibid.*: 66).

References

Alvarez, Sonia (1998) 'The NGOization of Latin American feminisms' in S. Alvarez, E, Dagnino, and A. Escobar (eds.) *Cultures of Politics, Politics of Culture: Re-visioning Latin American Social Movements*, Boulder, CO: Westview Press.

Alvarez, Sonia (1999) 'Advocating feminism: the Latin American Feminist NGO "boom"', *International Feminist Journal of Politics* 1(2): 181–209.

Ardón, Patricia (1999) *Post-war Reconstruction in Central America: Lessons from El Salvador, Guatemala, and Nicaragua*, Oxfam Working Papers, Oxford: Oxfam GB.

Eade, Deborah (1997) *Capacity-Building: An Approach to People-Centred Development*, Oxford: Oxfam (UK and Ireland).

Eade, Deborah (ed.) (2002) *Development and Advocacy,* A Development in Practice Reader, Oxford: Oxfam GB.

Eade, Deborah and Suzanne Williams (1995) *The Oxfam Handbook of Development and Relief (3 vols.)*, Oxford: Oxfam (UK and Ireland).

Eyben, Rosalind (2006) *Relationships for Aid*, London: Earthscan.

Hulme, David and Michael Edwards (eds.) (1996) *NGOs, States and Donors: Too Close for Comfort?*, Basingstoke: Palgrave Macmillan.

Jennings, Allen and Matthew Clarke (2005) 'The development impact of remittances to Nicaragua', *Development in Practice* 15(5): 685–91.

Moxham, Ben (2005) 'The World Bank's land of kiosks: community driven development in Timor-Leste', *Development in Practice* 15(3&4): 522–8.

Pearce, Jenny (1993) 'NGOs and social change: agents or facilitators?', *Development in Practice* 3(3): 222–7.

Rahman Khan, Mahmuda (1995) 'Women entrepreneurs in the Bangladeshi restaurant business', *Development in Practice* 5(2): 240–4.

Schuler, Sidney Ruth, Syed M Hashemi, Shamsul Huda Badal (1998) 'Men's violence against women in rural Bangladesh: undermined or exacerbated by microcredit programmes?', *Development in Practice* 8(2): 148–57.

Terry, Fiona (2002) *Condemned to Repeat? The Paradox of Humanitarian Action*, Ithaca, NY: Cornell University Press.

Utting, Peter (ed.) (2006) *Reclaiming Development Agendas: Knowledge, Power and International Policy Making*, Basingstoke: Palgrave Macmillan and UNRISD.

About the author

Deborah Eade was Editor of *Development in Practice* from 1991 to 2010, and had previously worked for 10 years for a number of national and international agencies in Mexico and Central America. She has published extensively on international development and humanitarian issues. She is now an independent writer and editor based in the Geneva area.

CHAPTER 20

Harmonisation: how is the orchestra conducted?

Rosalind Eyben

Harmonisation of donor efforts is one of the current buzzwords in the world of official aid. However, while it is an attractive idea in theory, as long as donors do not recognise and address the operations of power in the aid relationship, harmonisation is likely to be counterproductive in promoting locally initiated responses to development challenges.

In response to the Government's well-orchestrated preparation process for a high quality Poverty Reduction Strategy Paper (PRSP) for Bangladesh – DFID, the World Bank, the Asian Development Bank (ADB), and the Government of Japan, Bangladesh's major development partners (accounting for over 80% of development assistance) joined the orchestra to harmonise their support for the PRSP. (DFID 2006)

'Harmonisation' in the language of Aidland means donors trying to have common programmes and procedures, so that the recipient need communicate with only one single set of financing agencies. Harmonisation is judged to be especially important in highly aid-dependent countries such as Mozambique, where 50 per cent of the public capital-expenditure budget is donor-financed, and there are 49 official donors.[1]

Aid co-ordination failures have become legendary. According to a Government of Cameroon representative, in 2004 his government received 400 project missions, and there were 60 co-ordination/management units among the 14 donors.[2] Such stories support the case for empowering recipient governments through better donor co-ordination.

The OECD Development Assistance Committee (DAC) was established in 1960 to co-ordinate the policies and practices of governments' aid programmes. Ever since, donors have been trying to be part of the same orchestra, if not necessarily playing from the same score. Harmonisation, co-ordination, and alignment are major pillars in today's aid-effectiveness agenda. Identified as important at the 2002 Monterrey Conference on Financing for Development, in 2003 they became the subject of a High-Level Forum in Rome; two years later in Paris, along with 'country ownership' and 'managing for results', they became elements in the 2005 Paris Declaration on Aid Effectiveness.[3] The signatories to the Rome Declaration make clear their understanding of how disharmony impedes aid effectiveness: it is through efficiency losses:

> The totality and wide variety of donor requirements and processes for preparing, delivering, and monitoring development assistance are generating unproductive transaction costs for, and drawing down the limited capacity of, partner countries. (Rome Declaration paragraph 2)[4]

In what follows, I consider how harmonisation, co-ordination, and alignment – sometimes known as HAC, but which henceforth I shall refer to simply as *harmonisation* – are a good idea in principle and sometimes in practice, yet become an additional distraction from the really serious issues donors should be tackling.

The virtues of harmonisation

The case for harmonisation is that it reduces transaction costs for the recipient organisation because it has to deal with only a single interlocutor. Instead of having to report separately to many different donors, the recipient need send only one report against an agreed plan and performance indicators that it has developed previously.

I have always been a supporter of harmonisation – or at least co-ordination – when it means empowering the recipient, reducing donor rivalry, and ensuring that resources are used optimally. I took a lead in the DAC Women in Development (WID) working group's initiative to co-ordinate donor support of participation by civil-society organisations (CSOs) at the 1995 Fourth World Conference on Women held in Beijing. This was largely successful, despite the enormous challenges posed by each donor's different funding and accountability procedures. It may have worked because it was run by a group of feminists, conscious of issues of power and competition, and more committed to Beijing's objectives than to the requirements of their respective employers. It was 'us against them'. We bent and sometimes broke the rules. I carried this experience with me when moving to Bolivia in 2000 as head of the country office of DFID (the UK government's Department for International Development), but I failed to reflect sufficiently that what matters is the way in which harmonisation is implemented.

Bolivia was a pilot in the World Bank's Comprehensive Development Framework (CDF) initiative, which included a harmonisation agenda. The eventual aim was to put all donor money directly into the government's budget in support of a national poverty-reduction strategy.

As an interim step, the donors learned to work together by constructing 'basket funds' at sector or programme level. A 'basket fund' is when several donors put their money into a single fund that is managed by the recipient, without each donor's contribution being 'projectised' or earmarked for specific activities. An easy pilot initiative was carried out with the Office of the Ombudsperson (*Defensoría del Pueblo*), because of the strong leadership of the person in charge and the belief that corruption in the Office was minimal. About eight bilateral donors had been supporting the Office previously, with each cherry-picking aspects of its work that resonated with its own interests – or even offering the Office money for doing something that otherwise it would not have done. Getting rid of all these separately funded projects was empowering for the recipient.[5]

My recommendation to London that we contribute to this basket fund was well received. Senior management already saw DFID as being in the vanguard of harmonisation efforts. However, those responsible for financial procedures thought otherwise. I was told that it was procedurally not possible. To my humiliation, even 'unlike-minded' donors such as Belgium were finding this easier to do than DFID. Still fired up by the experience from the DAC WID group, I saw harmonisation as a challenge to the *status quo*. I engaged in a six-month battle – with much behind-the-scenes lobbying – to persuade the finance people eventually to change their procedures. This struggle is reflected in an OECD-commissioned report that studied donor practices in relation to harmonisation and alignment in four countries, including Bolivia:

> Donors have their own procedures and policy directions, which are often adapted from their domestic procedures. For example, donors have a mechanism through which the expenditure of public funds is made accountable to their own taxpayers. This accountability is often the responsibility of an intermediary audit authority or reporting to a democratic assembly. The different traditions, mechanisms and arrangements determine the way donors operate in practice and constitute a key factor in the harmonisation process. This is particularly the case with multi-donor initiatives and budget support. (OECD 2003:113)

The resistance to harmonisation by donors' procedural units led to the OECD commissioning another report into how to change incentives in aid agencies. The study concluded:

> Organisations with management cultures which promote and reward innovation in all fields including harmonisation, and welcome challenges to the status quo and suggestions for improvements, are more likely to engage in harmonisation than organisations which mostly reward compliance with existing rules and procedures. (de Renzio *et al.* 2005: vi)

Yet, meanwhile, harmonisation has become the new orthodoxy in Aidland, where its practice reveals several vices.

Harmonisation: the new orthodoxy and its vices

The **first vice** of harmonisation is that of donors ganging together and thus exerting greater power over the recipient (Edgren 2003). Even when Ministries of Finance *appear* to be conducting the donor orchestra, as was the case when I was in Bolivia, we donors used to meet behind closed doors to agree what we were going to play before going to the official co-ordination meeting. It is noteworthy that recipient countries that are not aid-dependent, such as China and India, are not at all interested in donor harmonisation and successfully object to its practice. Harmonisation as it is currently practised in highly aid-dependent countries becomes a problem. It turns donors into a cartel or monopolistic supplier.

Some find it a strange irony that the economists-turned-managers who govern Aidland advocate *co-operation* among themselves on efficiency grounds, while on exactly the same grounds they impose polices based on principles of *competition* on their recipients (Severino and Charnoz 2003). Easterly (2002) argues that aid agencies have always colluded when it was to their advantage to do so, collectively hiding bad outcomes while advertising good outputs. If a smaller aid agency tried to step out of line, it would be vulnerable to public relations attacks by the others. At a recent meeting at one of the smaller European aid agencies, staff told of harassment by a bigger donor for declining to join a programme of harmonised support for the education sector in a certain African country because of their misgivings about government corruption.

The **second vice** is that harmonisation reflects an underlying view of the world in which poverty reduction is achieved through broad-based consensus, whereby everyone in a recipient country can agree to a national poverty strategy behind which donors can line up. This is a bland, apolitical view of the world and frankly bizarre, given that donors know that back home in their own countries, generally more stable and orderly than those to which they are giving aid, such harmonious political consensus would be rarely achievable. In countries where strategies are owned by the few, donors are co-ordinating to re-inforce the power of a non-democratic ruling elite (see Buiter, in this volume).

The Paris Declaration emphasises the importance of a single diagnosis of the problems of poverty in any aid-recipient country. This tends to mean a diagnosis by the larger donors in consultation with the recipient government's Ministry of Finance. An alternative would be for different donors deliberately to support diagnoses by diverse local actors (in or outside government) who are likely to have varied understandings of the causes and consequences of poverty. This would mean donors playing a role in encouraging rather than suppressing different perspectives, helping to provide space for democratic dialogue, and recognising that optimal solutions often emerge through on-going, often confused, and highly politicised debate and argument (Bond 2006).

The **third vice** relates more specifically to the Paris Declaration's emphasis on providing all aid through the government, to the detriment of supporting the development of autonomous civil society (INTRAC 2006). Anecdotal information from DFID staff confirms a reduction in the number of projects for civil-society organisations (CSOs).

To sum up, harmonisation becomes a vice when it strengthens long-standing donor habits of pretending that poverty is not political. It is a new orthodoxy that reinforces, on the grounds of efficiency, the tendency for donor bureaucracies to talk only with their counterparts in the recipient government. By largely ignoring civil society and parliaments, they put at risk their stated commitment to broad-based country ownership of aid.

What is happening to the harmonisation effort?

As I discovered in Bolivia, negotiating a shared diagnosis, approach, and set of procedures means donors spending a great deal of time talking to each other. One solution is to form an inner cartel of just a few donors who agree what is to be done, and then invite others to join the process. This is what happened in Bangladesh:

> Government was initially worried about the four 'big ones ganging up on conditionality', but is now strongly in favour as the partnership is supportive of its harmonisation action plan. The wider donor community would ideally have liked a more inclusive process but the four partners were initially concerned to keep the venture manageable...With these basic foundations in place for a harmonised support by the four partners for the Government led PRSP, the outcome matrix was shared with the wider donor community on 22 February 2006, inviting them to join the process. (DFID 2006)

Another solution is to establish a division of labour so that just a few donors work in each sector. This is agreed through a 'Joint Assistance Strategy'. Some sectors are more popular than others and are referred to as 'donor darlings'. Others, such as gender, become 'donor orphans'.[6]

Some donors would like to avoid supporting sectors completely and provide general budget support. This means they need speak to only a limited number of staff in the Ministry of Finance and leave it to Finance to talk to the line ministries such as Education or Roads. This is appropriate, because country ownership points to this conversation being *their* job, not the donors'. An evaluation of Burkina Faso's General Framework Agreement for Organizing Budgetary Assistance to Support the PRSP hints, however, that such conversations within the recipient government do not always take place:

> Ownership has taken place and is reflected in the leadership role played by the Government, represented by the Minister of Finance and Budget (MFB). This is evidenced by the fact that the MFB is assuming all its responsibilities and is effectively co-ordinating discussions related to budgetary assistance and public finance. However, there is some uncertainty as to whether the other departmental offices have assumed ownership of the process to the same degree.[7]

Doubts concerning the increasingly predominant role of ministries of finance within recipient governments emerged in the 2005 Joint Review of aid to Mozambique, with line ministries expressing disquiet about the higher proportion of aid going to general budget support (Government of Mozambique 2005).

Along with the World Bank under Wolfensohn, DFID has been the most enthusiastic champion of harmonisation. The ideal for DFID is to co-finance the Bank's Poverty Reduction Support Credit, which is negotiated with the Ministry of Finance. This enthusiasm stems from DFID's wanting to spend more money with fewer people, as the result of a Treasury decision to cut the number of civil servants while increasing the quantity of aid (Gershon 2004). The 2006 DAC peer review of UK aid criticises DFID for pushing too hard its own interpretation of harmonisation as meaning general budget support:

> DFID enthusiasm for certain initiatives is not always shared by other partners and British advocacy can be perceived as promoting DFID's own model rather than leading and encouraging complementary donor action. (OECD 2006)

While these murmurs from the bilateral community concerning DFID are becoming stronger, collectively the donors are undermining the principles of harmonisation and country ownership by increasingly putting much of their money through global programme funds that bilaterals have set up with the World Bank and United Nations agencies. A recent evaluation notes that these programmes are largely donor-driven, with insufficient alignment between global and country objectives and priorities (Lele *et al.* 2005).

Interestingly, the harmonisation agenda recently seemed to be unravelling for another reason. Those bilaterals close to the World Bank were worried that its then President, Paul Wolfowitz, was refusing to approve Bank loans in circumstances where there was evidence of major government corruption. By so doing he was blocking harmonised spending by other donors such as DFID, including its co-financing of a major loan to India. If harmonisation leads to slower disbursement, donors will become disenchanted.

Meanwhile, the harmonisation agenda has resulted in a very large number of papers, management tools, consultancies, training workshops, and international conferences, which surprisingly no one seems to have identified as transaction costs. At the same time, as noted in the DAC Review of UK aid, 'Country office staff should spend more time out of capital cities. Greater effort should be made in getting key staff closer to the development realities they support' (OECD 2006:7). This comment would apply to many other aid agencies. A staff member of a bilateral agency recently told me: 'Joint Assistance Strategies are the thing ... Donor country heads now earn their spurs by being seen to deliver the Paris Declaration. Not quite sure where country ownership appears in all this' (personal communication 2006).

Conclusion

Harmonising donor expenditures to achieve greater efficiency is an attractive idea in theory. In practice, however, as long as donors do not recognise and address the operations of power in the aid relationship, it is likely to be subject to the following problems:

- Harmonisation enables the major donors to exert undue influence on the recipient and on minor donors to accept a development agenda pre-determined by the major donors.
- The agenda determined by the major donors prioritises budget support, which has lower administrative costs, over civil-society projects which are more expensive to administer but likely to achieve greater and longer-term progressive social change.
- Curiously, while the major donors prescribe *competition* to recipient countries as the way to achieve efficiency, they prescribe to themselves *co-operation* (read: *cartelisation*) to achieve this same result.
- Harmonisation tends to suppress trying out different approaches to local problems. The harmonisation agenda is politically naïve in assuming that there is a national development strategy that all can agree to – disregarding the internal (including gender-related) power relations in the recipient country.
- While trumpeting harmonisation, the major donors are undermining country ownership by increasingly spending aid monies through 'global programme funds', whose agenda is largely donor-driven.

Notes

1. I am grateful to Sarah Ladbury for these figures, as well as for her overall feedback on an earlier draft of this chapter.
2. Report of workshop on the Paris Declaration: implications and implementation, Bamako, 27–29 March 2006, page 5. The document was retrieved on 24 June 2006 at www.aidharmonization.org/, but Google provides a clue, revealing that the website's former address was www.worldbank.org/harmonization/
3. The High-Level Forum took place in Paris, 28 February-2 March 2005. The Paris Declaration on Aid Effectiveness is available at www.worldbank.org/harmonization/Paris/FINALPARISDECLARATION.pdf (retrieved 12 October 2006).
4. The High-Level Forum took place in Rome, 24–25 February 2003. The Rome Declaration on Harmonization is available at www.aidharmonization.org/ah-wh/secondary-pages/why-RomeDeclaration (retrieved 12 October 2006).
5. The same applies to funding local NGOs. Harmonised support from international NGOs can give recipients space to become learning organisations when they no longer have to spend so much time learning the various procedures of the organisations funding them (Shutt 2006).
6. From a discussion at the DAC GenderNet meeting in July 2006 on the implications of the Paris Declaration for gender equality.
7. 'Burkina Faso: General Framework Agreement for Organizing Budgetary Assistance to Support the PRSP', independent evaluation mission April 2006, page 3, available at www.aidharmonization.org retrieved 30 June 2006.

References

Bond, P. (2006) 'A review of progression and regression in debt, aid, trade, relations, global governance and the MDGs', *AFRODAD Occasional Papers No. 3*, Harare: AFRODAD.

de Renzio, P., with David Booth, Andrew Rogerson, and Zaza Curran (2005) *Incentives for Harmonisation and Alignment in Aid Agencies*, ODI Working Paper No. 248 London: Overseas Development Institute.

Department for International Development (DFID) (2006) 'Aid Effectiveness Network News', www.dfid.gov.uk/mdg/aid-effectiveness/newsletters/joint-strategy-bangladesh.asp (retrieved 30 June 2006).

Easterly, W. (2002) 'The cartel of good intentions: the problem of bureaucracy in foreign aid', *The Journal of Policy Reform* 5(4): 223–50.

Edgren, G. (2003) 'Donorship, ownership and partnership: issues arising from four Sida studies of donor– recipient relationships', *Sida Studies in Evaluation No. 3*, Stockholm: Sida.

Gershon, P. (2004) *Releasing Funds to the Front Line*, Independent Review of Public Sector Efficiency, London: HMSO.

Government of Mozambique (2005) 'Joint Review – 2005 Aide-Me´moire (Final version)', 12 May 2005, www.dfid.gov.uk/pubs/files/mozambique-aide-memoire.pdf (retrieved 12 October 2006).

INTRAC (2006) 'Aid harmonisation: challenges for civil society' *Ontrac 33*, May.

Lele, U., N. Sadik, and L. Simmons (2005) 'The changing aid architecture: can global initiatives eradicate poverty?', *DAC News*, www.oecd.org/dataoecd/48/6/37046754.htm.

OECD (2003) 'Harmonising Donor Practices for Effective Aid Delivery', Development Assistance Committee, Paris: OECD.

OECD (2006) 'Summary of DAC Peer Review of UK Aid', Paris: OECD, www.oecd.org

Severino, J.-M. and O. Charnoz (2003) 'A paradox of development', *Revue d'Économie du Développement* 17(4): 77–97.

Shutt, C. (2006) 'Money matters in aid relationships', in R. Eyben (ed.) *Relationships for Aid*, London: Earthscan.

About the author

Rosalind Eyben is a Fellow at the Institute of Development Studies at the University of Sussex, following a long career in the world of aid policy and practice. Her recent publications include the edited volume *Relationships for Aid* (2006).

CHAPTER 21

'Country ownership': a term whose time has gone

Willem H. Buiter

The term 'country ownership' refers to a property of the conditionality attached to programmes, processes, plans, or strategies involving both a 'domestic' party (generally a nation state) and a foreign party (generally the IMF, the World Bank, the Regional Development Banks, and other multilateral and bilateral institutions). Under what circumstances and how can the concept of country ownership be relevant to a country with a myriad heterogeneous and often conflicting views and interests? Or to a country whose government's representational legitimacy or democratic credentials are in question? The author argues that the term has been abused to such an extent that it is at best unhelpful and at worst pernicious: a term whose time has gone.

Words matter. They can enlighten or obscure. Jargon is an example of the destructive use of words. It creates artificial barriers to understanding and participation and thus generates obscurity rents that the insiders can appropriate. Scientific disciplines, professions, and institutions all have their own jargon. So do the international financial institutions (IFIs) and multilateral development banks (MDBs). The term 'country ownership' and the associated adjective 'country-owned' have become particularly pernicious examples of politically correct IFI-speak. 'Country ownership' may have been a useful term at some point. Regrettably, it has been used and abused in so many ways to gloss over realities deemed uncomfortable, and to create a pleasant buzz to distract the uninformed and unwary, that it now needs to be put out of its misery.

Country ownership is a property of programmes, processes, plans, or strategies involving both a 'domestic' party (generally a nation state) and a foreign party. More specifically, it is a property of the conditionality attached to these programmes. The foreign parties I have in mind are the international financial institutions (IFIs): the IMF, the World Bank, the Regional Development Banks, and other multilateral institutions. However, most of what I have to say applies equally to bilateral relations between a developing country and a donor country and to the relationship between the EU and developing countries and emerging markets. The programmes/processes in question include the Poverty Reduction Strategy Papers (PRSPs) and Interim Poverty Reduction Strategy Papers (I-PRSPs) and the consultative processes associated with them, co-managed by the World Bank and the IMF, the IMF's Poverty Reduction and Growth Facility (PRGF), the World Bank's and IMF's Highly Indebted Poor Country Initiative (HIPC), The World Bank's Country Assistance Strategies (CAS), the World Bank's Low Income Countries Under Stress Initiative (LICUS), IMF Standby Arrangements, World Bank Structural Adjustment Facilities (SAFs), Structural Adjustment Loans and Sector Adjustment Loans (SALs), and a range of similar stabilisation, structural adjustment, and reform programmes.

'Country ownership' can refer to a number of dimensions of the multidimensional relationship of the domestic party to the programme/process and its conditionality. Specifically, it can mean one or more of the following:

- *'The country* has designed and drafted the programme'; or its weaker siblings, ranging from *'The country* has had a significant involvement in the drafting and design of the programme' to *'The authorities of the country* were informed of the programme after it had been drawn up by other parties, typically the World Bank and the IMF'.
- *'The country* agrees with the objectives of the programme.'
- *'The country* believes that the implementation of the programme as envisaged will achieve the programme's objectives.'
- *'The country* implements the programme', or its weaker siblings, ranging from *'The country* plays a significant role in the implementation of the programme' to *'The authorities of the country* are kept informed of how and when the programme has been implemented'.

Until this point I have gone along with the sloppy usage of the word 'country' as referring to a single purposefully acting agent. This anthropomorphic approach obscures reality and confuses the argument. Who or what is or are 'the country' that owns the programme, in any of the four senses just referred to?

A country is made up of populations ranging from the tens of thousands to the billion plus. All countries, even the smallest and most homogeneous – racially, ethnically, culturally, religiously etc. – contain many individuals and groups with diverse, often divergent and conflicting views, interests, policy objectives, and programmes. Under what circumstances and how can the concept of *country ownership* be relevant to a country with a myriad heterogeneous and often conflicting views and interests?

If the country has institutions for political and economic governance that are representative and legitimate, there may be a limited number of national representative voices that can claim with some validity to 'speak for the country' or to 'represent the interests of the country'. The range of views and interests in the country may be so wide, however, that not even the representatives of the legitimate government and of the worlds of work and business can claim to speak for 'the country' whose ownership is being sought for a programme. In the case of the PRSPs, recognition of this reality has led to the development of *ad hoc* consultative processes of ever-increasing complexity and duration. Not only representatives of the government (central, state, and municipal) and of parliament are now involved, but also representatives of many other groups, associations, agencies, institutions, and organisations. Increasingly, the PRSP process tries to involve a wide range of special interests and lobby groups, including political, environmental, cultural, and religious NGOs (both local and international) and other representatives of civil society.

Quite how the views and voices of such a range of sectional and special interests are aggregated into an operative concept of country ownership remains a mystery. Also, despite the large number of NGOs and civil-society groups, organisations, and factions involved in some of the PRSP consultative processes, the representativeness of the consultations remains an open issue. For instance, the spectacular under-representation of the enterprise sector, and especially the private-enterprise sector, in most PRSP consultative processes represents a serious dent in its claim to be representative of all the parties whose efforts are essential to a successful attack on poverty or who are affected by it.

Moreover, it is only in a limited number of cases that there is a realistic prospect for putting together a consultative process (let alone a process that actually drafts the programme and designs the conditionality) that can make any claim to being representative of the interests, wishes, and views of the majority of the country's population. Unrepresentative and often repressive governments frequently preclude representative PRSP processes. This should come as no surprise.

Why do countries become candidates for stabilisation, structural adjustment, or reform programmes? Why do countries take part in the HIPC initiative or the PRSP process? It is because they need and seek external assistance of three kinds:

- They need external financial resources and cannot access these through the markets, because they are not creditworthy.
- They need external expertise and do not have the resources to pay for this on market terms.
- They need an external commitment device because of weak domestic political institutions.

Countries that need one or more of these external desiderata – finance, expertise, commitment – are countries that are in trouble, countries that cannot help themselves, countries that are in a mess.

It is possible for a country with good institutions, good political leadership, and good policies nevertheless to be in a mess. The cause(s) could be 'exogenous bad luck': bad neighbours preventing trade and transit and restricting the country's ability to participate effectively in the regional and global economy; armed conflict inflicted on a peaceful nation; natural disasters and public-health disasters such as tsunamis, earthquakes, or the AIDS pandemic; bad initial conditions, such as those encountered by many of the new CIS countries following the collapse of the Soviet Union. History can be a curse.

Most of the time, however, bad luck does not explain why a country is confronted with the programmes and conditionality associated with external assistance. The most frequent reasons are bad institutions, bad political leadership, and bad policies. Countries subject to IFI programmes and the associated conditionality often have political systems that are unrepresentative and repressive, ranging from mildly authoritarian to brutally totalitarian. The political leadership and the elites supporting it are often corrupt and economically illiterate. Rent-seeking and cronyism offer higher returns to effort than socially productive labour and entrepreneurship. Public administration is weak, corrupt, and has very limited implementation capacity. Moreover, the countries with the most unrepresentative and repressive governments do not permit a representative cross-section of civil society to participate. Indeed, civil society tends to be weakest precisely in those countries where it is most needed.

What would country ownership mean in Zimbabwe, in the Democratic Republic of the Congo (a HIPC-initiative country), and in Sudan? These are extreme examples, and neither Zimbabwe nor Sudan currently has a World Bank or IMF programme, but there are many others. What does country ownership mean in Algeria, in Egypt, or in the People's Republic of China? In Iraq after the fall of Saddam Hussain, and in Afghanistan? Closer to my operational home, we have the CIS-7 poor countries: Moldova, Georgia, Armenia, Azerbaijan, Tajikistan, the Kyrgyz Republic, and Uzbekistan. All but Uzbekistan have produced PRSPs. In Uzbekistan the World Bank Group has a modest programme of lending, technical assistance, and analytical and policy advice. There is no IMF programme, although an Article 4 Consultation was completed in June 2004. What would country ownership mean in Uzbekistan? That the agreement of President Karimov has been obtained?

The term 'country ownership' is used to describe both positive and normative features of IFI programmes. These alternative uses are exemplified by the following two statements, both of which are commonly heard. First, *'Unless an IMF programme and the conditionality it embodies are country-owned, the programme will fail'*. Second, *'Unless an IMF programme and the conditionality it embodies are country-owned, the program deserves to fail'*. I take the first statement to mean that for an IMF programme to be successful certain actions are required of 'local' agents. Unless these agents are willing and able to implement these actions, the programme will fail. This statement is true, but not very enlightening. A programme and the plan of action that it involves have to be incentive-compatible to be credible and to succeed.

The local agents whose actions are necessary for the programme to succeed are, however, not necessarily those who speak for the country in the meetings or consultative processes where these programmes are drafted and the conditionality is designed. And those on whom the success of the programme depends may not include all those affected by it. Often the majority of those affected by a programme have had no voice in the design of the conditionality, and the programme may not serve their interests, regardless of whether their efforts are essential to its success, and regardless of whether they can be cajoled or induced to implement it and make it 'successful'. If this is the reality in a country that is a candidate for a programme, it is beyond the ability of the IMF, World Bank, and other IFIs to remedy it. The effective choice for the IFIs is then between not having a programme and having one that is not 'country owned' in the sense of not in the interest of and supported by the majority of the population. There can be little doubt that at times programmes have been designed and implemented that served the interests of an unrepresentative few at the expense of the unrepresented many. Such illegitimate programmes do not deserve to be implemented. In many other cases, however, the case is less clear-cut.

Even legitimate programmes (that is programmes that are widely viewed as fair and desirable) are constrained by the requirement that their implementation must be incentive-compatible. If they depend for their success on the adoption of rules or on actions that are not incentive-compatible, they are not credible. Conditionality (sticks or carrots conditional on outcomes, processes, performance, or actions) is a means of enhancing the incentive compatibility and thus the credibility of programmes. In practice, ensuring post-implementation irreversibility of reforms, policies, and actions is the hardest part of programme design. Most incentives (for example, the disbursement of a tranche of a loan or grant) have a natural expiry date. Good conditionality creates effective and lasting or irreversible incentives to take certain actions.

Conditionality can apply to actions, outcomes, or processes. Ideally, incentives should be designed to increase the likelihood of actions that contribute to desirable outcomes. In practice, key outcomes may lag far behind actions, and the contribution of the action to the eventual outcome may be hard to identify, measure, and verify. The effect of privatisation on economic performance is an obvious example. Process conditionality does not directly target specific actions, policies, or outcomes. Instead it focuses on promoting good governance, in the hope that more accountable, transparent, responsive, representative, and democratic government institutions will produce better actions, policies, and outcomes. Process conditionality focuses on capacity building broadly defined, and requires that a process (like the consultative PRSP process) be implemented, or that certain institutions be in place to enhance the transparency and representativeness of governance at different levels. Making aid available to countries whose governments and institutions for political and economic governance are most effective (or at least meet certain minimum thresholds, defined, say, by international standards and codes) is an example of process or institutional conditionality. The US Millennium Challenge Account embodies this process approach to conditionality.

If process conditionality and country ownership are to be taken seriously, we would need international standards and codes to benchmark acceptable practice. Failure to meet these benchmarks would mean that the country would not have access to the external funds, expertise, and credibility brought by an IFI-mediated programme. Sources of benchmarks could be initiatives or reports like the *Extractive Industries Transparency Initiative*; the *Publish What You Pay, Publish What You Receive* initiative; the *FATF* for anti-money-laundering benchmarks; the *Corruption Perceptions Index* of Transparency International; and the reports of the Organization for Security and Co-operation in Europe (OSCE) and of the Council of Europe on electoral and political performance. Standards for other key aspects of the accountability of the government to the domestic population could be set by defining benchmarks or minimum standards for freedom of the media, independence of the courts, freedom to organise and register independent political parties and labour unions, the right of peaceful assembly and protest, and the right to strike.

Process conditionality *is* political or governance conditionality. The European Bank for Reconstruction and Development (EBRD) has long practised this form of conditionality because of the political nature of its mandate, which in that regard is unlike that of the other IFIs.[1] The requirement that we operate only in '...*countries committed to and applying the principles of multiparty democracy, pluralism and market economics*' has meant that the Bank no longer engages in new public-sector projects in Turkmenistan and in Belarus, and that similar constraints have been imposed on the Bank's ability to work with the sovereign in Uzbekistan.

While process conditionality and political benchmarks may give one a warm glow inside, an unavoidable implication of their adoption is that a number of potential countries of operation will fail to qualify. The EBRD still operates, albeit at a low level of activity, in Turkmenistan, Belarus, and Uzbekistan, because the primary mandate of the Bank is in the private sector. The World Bank and IMF would be out of business altogether if they could no longer operate in and with the public sector. More generally, if the IFIs were to get serious about country ownership, there would be many fewer programmes.

In conclusion, the concept of 'country ownership' has been used and abused in so many ways that it now is at best unhelpful and at worst misleading and obfuscating. When the statement 'this programme is country-owned' means no more than 'this programme is supported by the people who own the country', it is time to purge it from our vocabulary.

Acknowledgements

This chapter is based on remarks prepared for the Development Policy Forum 'Conditionality Revisited', organised by the World Bank at the World Bank Conference Center in Paris on 5 July 2004. The views expressed are those of the author, who was then Chief Economist at the European Bank for Reconstruction and Development (EBRD). They do not represent the views of the EBRD. The paper is reproduced here with the kind permission of the author, who holds copyright.

Note

1. The preamble to the Agreement Establishing the European Bank for Reconstruction and Development states:

   The contracting parties, Committed to the fundamental principles of multiparty democracy, the rule of law, respect for human rights and market economics; Recalling the Final Act of the Helsinki Conference on Security and Co-operation in Europe, and in particular its Declaration on Principles; Welcoming the intent of central and eastern European countries to further the practical implementation of multiparty democracy, strengthening democratic institutions, the rule of law and respect for human rights and their willingness to implement reforms in order to evolve towards market-oriented economies; ...

   Article 1 of the Agreement states:

   Purpose In contributing to economic progress and reconstruction, the purpose of the Bank shall be to foster the transition towards open market-oriented economies and to promote private and entrepreneurial initiative in the central and eastern European countries committed to and applying the principles of multiparty democracy, pluralism and market economics.

About the author

Willem H. Buiter is Professor of European Political Economy at the London School of Economics and Professor of Economics at the University of Amsterdam. He has held professorships at the Universities of Bristol, Cambridge, and Yale, and advisory roles to government ministries in several countries in Latin America and the Caribbean.

CHAPTER 22

Best of practices?

Warren Feek

In this brief critique of the idea of 'best practice', the author argues that good practice is not replicable or uniform; it cannot be reduced to its component parts for replication elsewhere. Furthermore, the criteria for what constitutes 'best practice' are at best unscientific and tend to discourage diversity and local experimentation.

OK, let's start with a little quiz. Picture yourself in a meeting or just chatting with a colleague. Is there a particular word or phrase which when used by participants in the meeting or by this colleague in an informal chat gets you just a little agitated? Maybe very agitated? I am sure you know the feeling. The blood moves a little quicker. You feel a little more edgy and itchy. You wish you could ban that word or phrase being used – or at least restrict it to, let's say, five times a meeting or conversation. Ironically, though internally agitated, externally you may show contradictory signs. You slump a little in your chair. Shoulders droop a little. A 'here we go again' feeling gently inhabits you. And it is even worse when you find yourself uttering that very word or phrase that agitates you!

The word or phrase will be different for different people. Some have mentioned 'empowerment', 'capacity building', 'developing countries', or any word that has the root 'particip' – 'participation', 'participatory', 'participative' – among their 'I get agitated' prompts. It can have a theme: for example, any phrase related to American sports (which are a mystery to most of us!), such as 'who will quarterback this programme?', 'we are in a full-count situation', 'that came out of left field', 'this needs a full-court press', and many others. The word can be an everyday one: 'culture', 'context', and 'community' have been cited. It might be one of our own little inventions: 'results-based management' gets a number of votes. I witnessed a whole meeting actually demonstrate open agitation when someone tried to use Mr Potato Head as a metaphor. Sorry, no time to explain to the uninitiated what is Mr Potato Head![1]

I have avoided telling you – but can delay no longer. The phrase that really gets me going is 'best practice'. And this makes my life difficult, as 'best practice' seems to be everywhere. Most organisations I know have a person or a team of people trying to identify and/or describe 'best practice' related to their field, and there are all manner of 'best practice' publications in existence and being produced regularly.

Can someone please tell me what is best practice, and why do we spend so much time trying to identify it? I understand 'good practice', 'innovative practice', 'excellent practice', and 'creative practice'. But how do you decide what is 'best' when all practice – all development action, including communication interventions, addressing priority development issues – takes place in different contexts, with different purposes, different population groups, and significantly different opportunities, involving challenges within widely varying cultural, political, and resource environments. Compounding this problem is the implication of judging something the 'best': that we all need to think about also doing what that practice is doing because it is the best. The 'best practice' highlighted after an exhaustive international search may work in the poor *barrio* on the outskirts of Cali, Colombia, but may be completely inappropriate – perhaps even 'bad practice' – if replicated in Blantyre, Malawi; Puna, India; Kuala Trenggannu, Malaysia; and even the town in which I was raised: New Plymouth, New Zealand. Probably even Barranquilla, Colombia would not do what they do in Cali, because it just would not work in Barranquilla. Things are different in Barranquilla! And, if the point of labelling something the 'best' is not that others replicate it, then why label it the 'best'?

As can be seen from the above paragraph, I got a little agitated – although I must say, it does feel good to get it out there (I am sure therapy has a word for this). As a result, the calming-down process has now kicked in!

Why are 'best practice' and its natural extensions of 'replication' and 'going to scale' bad for progress on development issues? I would suggest the following reasons.

- They imply uniformity, when we need greater diversity: diversity matching the number of contexts – an almost infinite number.
- They have the strong possibility of disempowering people and organisations: those who are doing great stuff in their contexts see something rated as the best which they know will not work in their situations, and they wonder why they do not get the recognition they feel they deserve.
- They bias the suggested required action towards the large agencies, international agencies, and away from the small, local organisations.
- They send the wrong message, namely that what really matters is the detailed programme itself, rather than the principles to which that programme works or the lessons learned from their experience – not as the best lessons learned, but as an overall contribution to building a body of knowledge for the work.
- Finally, they are not exactly the result of a 'scientific' decision-making process. How is one piece of practice 'best' and not another? Who decides, and on what basis?

Now before anyone says 'Aha! But the whole of The Communication Initiative process is based on sharing best practice', let me try to clarify! We are not. We try to share everything. There are now over 35,000 pages of summarised practice, thinking, and initiatives (so that you can quickly review if information and ideas on a page are useful to you and your work). The experiences, ideas, and information on those pages come from you within the network. We put them up without favour or qualification. Why? Because you will all have different interests and demands. So, we try to put the power in your hands. You can decide – in your setting – what is the 'best practice' for you to learn from. And, by using the review forms at the bottom of each page, you can provide your view of the idea, experience, and information on any page – a peer-review process – providing a practitioner's and network view on practice.

So if you are in a meeting with me and someone says 'best practice', please do not all look my way. I will not know what to do. Probably just shrink a little in my chair!

Thanks for considering this.

Acknowledgement

This piece was originally placed on The Communication Initiative website on 3 March 2005, and is reprinted here with kind permission of The Communication Initiative.

Note

1. According to the Wikipedia entry of 14 November 2006, Mr Potato Head is a popular children's doll, consisting of a plastic model of a potato. Originally, the potato is blank; however, it can be decorated with numerous attachable plastic parts to make a face, including a moustache, hat, nose, and other features.

About the author

Warren Feek is Executive Director of The Communication Initiative (www.comminit.com) and is based in Canada.

CHAPTER 23
Peacebuilding does not build peace

Tobias Denskus

The concept of peacebuilding is a buzzword of the development policy and practice mainstream. The recent introduction of managerial tools and the focus on measuring the 'effectiveness' of peacebuilding have marginalised and depoliticised critical questions about the causes of violent conflict, and have replaced them with comforting notions for donors that peace can be built and measured without challenging Western understanding of economy, governance, and social aspirations of people.

Everything becomes stories and it is not important when or where something happened, how it happened or whether it happened at all ... Everything can be influenced in the telling and so nothing is how it is, nothing stays how it was once the telling begins, and everything can be told and you tell yourself as a story with every word, with every lie. (Jäkle 2006)

The question of whether 'peacebuilding' builds peace remains highly relevant almost a decade after Charles-Philippe David's article of the same title (David 1999). 'Peacebuilding' first appeared as a word in a UN document (Boutros Ghali 1992), but it has turned into a 'non-place', like the airports or supermarkets invoked in Marc Augé's anthropological–philosophical account of 'supermodern' places. Incorporated into the new aid discourse of results-based management, and the subject of innumerable manuals and frameworks, 'peacebuilding' has lost any sense of context, and of the people in that context. The sites of peacebuilding have become 'non-places'. This chapter reflects on what has happened to a word that has lost the ability to tell us stories, to make us angry or happy, and to connect people affected by war and violence and those who are offering external advice through the international aid system for a more peaceful world. I take a critical look at the 'non-place' that peacebuilding describes and I consider what it would take to populate it with those whose stories might have something to offer in transforming contemporary approaches to development, and to war and peace.

What *is* peacebuilding?

> The inclusion of so many activities, levels and actors under the umbrella term peacebuilding has rendered its definition so broad that it is in danger of becoming meaningless. (Llamazares 2005: 2–3)

The 'Agenda for Peace' is one of the cornerstones for the international debates on how to build peace after violent conflicts. When the Cold War ended and new – mainly intra-state – wars were on the rise, the international community needed new forms of engagement to continue the delivery of 'development'. Right from the beginning, 'peacebuilding' was not regarded as a concept that would seek to *transform* societies in or emerging from conflict, but to maintain stability. Beth Fetherston argues:

> If conflict is caused, enabled, reproduced by particular social structures and institutions which favour a dominant group, we cannot hope to remove or alleviate those causes, without altering those structures. Then, peacekeeping becomes another aspect of a system which only seeks stability within the confines of that system, a system which already made the war possible. (Fetherston 2000a: 196).

Ever more institutional arrangements and operational guidelines were adopted by international aid organisations to operationalise 'peacebuilding'. An entire industry of 'peacebuilding' consultants, experts, and practitioners sprang up to service these arrangements. After its failed engagement in Rwanda, the international community became more interested in the approach encapsulated by the 'do no harm' position (Anderson 1999). But the heavy weight of five decades of 'development' made it difficult to escape explaining 'contemporary processes and phenomena through a dominant conceptual framework marked by Northern economic and social philosophy' (Gosovic 2000: 447) and 'Western intellectual traditions – expectations, values and rationality' (Duffey 2001: 143).

The framing of 'peace' and ways of 'building' it led to a preferred set of methods and methodologies. As elsewhere in development, quantitative research – such as that of Paul Collier for the World Bank (Collier *et al.* 2003) – gained prominence, offering a powerful instrument to legitimise interventions by aid organisations. However, the deployment of such approaches to research not only served to erase the particularity of places and experiences through its inevitable generalisations, but it also had further costs. Fetherston comments: 'The trend towards increasingly complex statistical analyses tends to leave people out altogether. After all how can social space, cultures of violence and militarization, and discourses be statistically analysed?' (2000a: 194).

The 'peacebuilding' 'discourse coalition' (Hajer and Wagenaar 2003) that has emerged over the past decade or so relies on a web of academics/academic institutions, researchers and practitioners, and different units in different aid organisations. In the field of 'peacebuilding', new conceptual and organisational arrangements have been implemented to legitimise it for various constituencies in 'Northern' countries and 'Southern' capital cities. One example of a virtual (and therefore global) meeting place is the *Berghof Handbook* that features a range of contributions to engage with 'peacebuilding' but puts an emphasis on 'PCIA' (Peace and Conflict Impact Assessment) and related methodologies to merge 'peacebuilding' with the 'results-based management' needs of aid organisations (for example, Anderson 2004; Hoffman 2004).

Paffenholz and Reychler's 'aid for peace' approach is another such example, peppered with phrases from the world of international aid:

> In presenting our approach we have shown that a *unified framework* is not only possible but also a useful starting point for all actors as it links the analysis of the conflict and peacebuilding environment with the implementation of interventions in conflict zones in a *systematic step-by-step* process. It also links the core of peace research (a theory of social change) with *operational requirements* and provides *methods and tools* to assess or anticipate conflict-related risks as well as effects (*outcomes and impact*) by introducing peace-and-conflict *results chains and indicators* as well as other tools. (Paffenholz and Reychler 2005: 16, my emphasis)

By introducing managerial tools – such as the current focus on measuring the 'effectiveness' of peacebuilding (Paffenholz and Reychler 2007; Anderson 2004; Hoffman 2004) – critical questions about the causes of violent conflict and the future outlook of societies emerging from conflict are depoliticised (cf. Ferguson 1994). These tools have become part of the daily life-worlds of people working on 'peacebuilding', as shown by the following small excerpts from a conversation between the author and a desk officer from the 'conflict unit' of a large bilateral donor agency in its European headquarters:

> Part of my culture shock [when returning from a field assignment in Kosovo] was about the importance of manuals and check-lists that are perceived very differently in the field (...) The introduction of the new conflict matrix has created needs for [in-house] consultancy. If people from the field approach us, we provide them with manuals and check-lists or examples of TORs for external consultants (...) If you talk to some of the people in the field offices about the new conflict matrix, you get hit by the collected frustrations about development co-operation. This is a sort of 'anti-mainstreaming': People work with the conflict matrix to be left in peace [sic!], but they do not engage with the actual meaning and contents; this is similar to what I have observed with the 'gender' topic.

In addition to the 'conflict matrix', the government of the country has recently approved a 'cross-sectoral policy concept' on peacebuilding and runs a special network of different implementing organisations that collect and disseminate 'best practices' on peacebuilding – among many other initiatives to 'professionalise' and 'institutionalise' peacebuilding. Such institutional and practical arrangements are tailored to the (perceived) need to present 'success' (Mosse 2005). But they never actively include those whose experience might help to turn them from the artefacts of a 'non-place' into something that could respond to the particular issues that matter in particular places – neither the field staff and development and peace workers of aid organisations, nor the people in (post-) conflict situations that should 'benefit' from the projects and programmes.

The limits of 'peacebuilding'

Critical literature on the limitations on 'peacebuilding' is available for all the countries where external engagement took place from the mid-1990s until today (Paris 2004). In the case of Latin America, for example, Colombia, El Salvador, and Guatemala are three countries where 'peacebuilding' has failed after decades of war and violence (comprising all aspects of 'gendered' violence against children and women as well as gang and criminal violence mainly involving men), and poverty is widespread (Preti 2002; Pearce 1999). This should come as no surprise, because although the 'root causes' of the conflict are known (including land distribution, income inequality, and a small powerful elite running the country), the engagement of the international community, especially of the international financial institutions (IFIs), showed that imposing short-sighted liberal governance frameworks helped to stabilise existing elite structures. Large sections of the elite had accepted the need for economic liberalisation, but had not accepted 'the need for redistribution or even responsibility to invest domestic resources in the reconstruction of the country' (Boyce 1999: 57). They let the international community take care of the '87 per cent majority' in Guatemala, because fundamental changes, for example through land reforms, were dismissed as 'left-wing, communist' experiments by US policy makers and IFI staff.

One could argue that these were early examples of 'peacebuilding', and that the special US history in this region makes it difficult to regard them as 'representative' cases; but the more general point here is that 'peacebuilding' as defined by the international community could never carry transformative potential. Instead, it often became a cover for familiar development interventions. And, as elsewhere in development, there was little critical attention paid to systemic shortcomings, and to 'worst practices' from around the 'peacebuilding' globe (East Timor, Kosovo, Mozambique, Sri Lanka, or Rwanda, for example).

Augé remarks that 'certain places exist only through the words that evoke them, and in this sense they are non-places, or rather, imaginary places' (1995: 95). In the non-place of 'Aidland' (Apthorpe 2005), peacebuilding has become such a word; and 'building peace in [country name]' has certainly become an imaginary place. Discursive interactions, governed by accepted methodologies, terms, and frameworks, have established rules of engagement that are similar to the rules of the road and 'instructions for use' that Augé describes in his travels through 'non-places':

This establishes the traffic conditions of spaces in which individuals are supposed to interact only with texts, whose proponents are not individuals, but "more entities" or institutions (airports, airlines, Ministry of Transport; commercial companies, traffic police, municipal councils [or aid organisations, NGOs, think tanks,...]). (1995: 96)

Kathmandu in 2006: donor amnesia in 'Aidland'

In Nepal, after five decades of 'development' and ten years of violent conflict between the army and Maoist insurgents/rebels/terrorists, Kathmandu remained in a 'bubble of innocence', as one donor representative described the state of mind in the city that seems remarkably far away from 'underdevelopment' or 'war'. When the people formed a democracy movement in April 2006 and demonstrated on the streets of the capital, few conflict advisers and inhabitants of the bubble were able to predict the fundamental political changes that were about to happen. But they quickly shared their relief that the promising signs of the Maoist party joining 'mainstream politics', a forthcoming constituent assembly, and parliamentary elections will put Nepal back on the 'road to development'.

Some donors were relieved that they could now continue with work they had planned before the violent conflict, and that the small Nepali elite in Kathmandu seems to be willing to address the challenges, 'root causes' that have kept Nepal in 'poverty' for the past 55 years. In this fast-moving environment, people in Kathmandu did not or could not spend time to reflect on the conflict that has cost around 13,000 lives so far, but started to look forward to the bright 'post-conflict' future of the country.

INGOs, individuals, and aid specialists from other post-war 'non-places' quickly arrived in Kathmandu to share their approaches, always stressing that they needed to be tailored to Nepal, of course. 'Arms management', 'security sector reforms', 'transitional justice' – the Fall 2006 collection arrived in Kathmandu straight from the peacebuilding catwalks in Europe without looking outside the 'bubble', or searching for stories in the remote villages of Nepal, asking local people about the future direction of their country. A former 'conflict adviser' of a European donor observes:

> When I first attended the meetings of the conflict advisors' group I was surprised to find them talking over simple and conservative conflict analyses and I immediately started to wonder whether these guys [all but one were men at that time] should know these things by now and before coming to Kathmandu.

Harmonisation may be all the rage in today's Aidland, but, as this donor went on to comment, donor co-ordination in the peacebuilding industry seems somewhat over-enthusiastic: *'We had 400 meetings after the February 1 coup of the King in 2005. I knew more about what the Japanese and Americans were doing than about our projects in the field.'*

The professional life-world in Kathmandu was also matched by the sheltered private lifestyle of most international inhabitants of 'Aidland', because the Maoist violence never reached the Kathmandu Valley. As another donor representative remarked half-jokingly:

> Travelling to the field was declared as 'too dangerous' from a very early stage of the conflict. So how did the international community experience 'the conflict'? During one of the longest *bandhs* [general strikes and blockades announced by the Maoists] people had to switch from fresh groceries to the canned Dole-stuff in the supermarkets and then had something to talk about for days!

'Peacebuilding' is almost always linked to issues of 'governmentality' – making 'chaotic' and 'unsafe' places fit for (neo)liberal democracy. Nepal is doomed to be a success-story of how a violent conflict can be transformed through peaceful, democratic means and adoption of the latest fashion in 'peacebuilding'. Neither critical voices nor lessons learned from the failed development of Nepal, nor indeed the history of failed 'peacebuilding' interventions elsewhere, will enter the narrative of 'success'.

The end of history?

'Peacebuilding' has become a lifestyle for a small community of global 'cosmopolitans' who travel from aid city to aid city. As the current situation in Kathmandu shows, post-war engagement always seems to start from zero, without history or critical baggage. The simple word 'peacebuilding' has become a 'non-space', part of the supermodern aid industry. But even if it sounds paradoxical after such a devastating overview, we still know very little about the inner workings of this 'non-place'. Beth Fetherston points out that the 'irrationality of warzones' is not understood by those who promote 'peacebuilding':

> Understandings of war implied in the definitions, researches and methodologies of conflict settlement and CR [Conflict Resolution] lack connection to the everydayness of the warzone. These kinds of descriptions of war and its aftermath fail to catch its complexity and deep effects on social space and meaning. (Fetherston 2000b: 9)

Anthropological micro-studies have recently begun to emerge that raise uncomfortable questions about agency, participation, and inner workings of wars (Hoffman and Lubkemann 2005; Richards 2005; Utas 2005; Nordstrom 2004). Such accounts highlight alternative forms of 'governance' and order that 'peacebuilding' finds difficult to address, because they lie outside the normative framework of the liberal democratic model. They show that a great many people benefit from war, and some are even 'empowered' by it; and they challenge taken-for-granted understandings about the gender dynamics of war and peace. What such studies make apparent is that it is only by better understanding how social interactions change during war, and how relationships and power are maintained after its 'end', that the 'non-place' of peacebuilding can be peopled with the diversity of experiences of war and peace of those who live in situations of conflict.

To make sense of the disconnect between the virtual world created by the peacebuilding narrative and lived experience, further study is also needed of the outside actors who engage in 'peacebuilding', those who send dedicated and motivated people into 'post-war' situations or sit at the geographical or thematic desks in ministries, aid organisations, and research institutions. 'Aidnography' has emerged as a term to describe ethnographic research in the realities of aid projects to uncover relationships, negotiation processes, and the 'being' of development projects. This is also needed for the organisations and projects that aim at 'building peace'.

These two avenues of further inquiry are not separate, because they are both looking into complexity, the everyday reality of war and 'peacebuilding', and different forms of sensemaking of the realities that constitute the 'non-place' of peacebuilding. The development workers in the headquarters in Europe, in the aid cities, and in the projects in 'the field' will be a key factor in pricking the 'bubble'. Listening to people living in war and in peace, acknowledging their stories and those of the people who inhabit Aidland, and naming the uncertainties and failures that are part of these worlds, can help to bring a transformative element into a debate that is currently buried under the high pressure of supermodern aid management.

Without these stories, and without more reflection on our own engagement and more qualitative insights into the social dynamics of war and peace, 'peacebuilding' will not even remain a buzzword. It will become another 'airport' on the global development travel routes – 'This is the final call for the *Aidlines* flight from "gender" to "peacebuilding", with a quick stop-over in "participation" '. Gillie Bolton's example from medical professionals could be an entry point for the development and peace profession as well:

> Bringing our everyday stories into question is an adventure. No one adventures securely in their backyard. Professionals need to face the uncertainty of not knowing what's round the corner, where they're going, how they'll travel, when they'll meet dragons or angels, and who the comrades are. They even have to trust why they're going. A student commented: 'What a relief it is to know that this uncertainty is essential; knowing that makes me feel less uncertain of being uncertain. Now uncertainty is my mantra'. (Bolton 2006: 210)[1]

Acknowledgements

I would like to thank Andrea Cornwall and Deborah Eade for their helpful comments and editorial support.

Note

1. I have to thank Gael Robertson for sharing this reference with me.

References

Anderson, Mary B. (2004) 'Experiences with impact assessment: can we know what good we do?', in David Bloomfield, Martina Fischer and Beatrix Schmelzle (eds.) *Berghof Handbook for Conflict Transformation*, Berlin: Berghof Research Center for Constructive Conflict Management, available online at www.berghof-handbook.net.

Apthorpe, Raymond (2005) 'Postcards from Aidland', paper presented at the Institute of Development Studies (IDS), Brighton, 10 June.

Augé, Marc (1995) *Non-places: Introduction to an Anthropology of Supermodernity*, London: Verso.

Bolton, Gillie (2006) 'Narrative writing: reflective enquiry into professional practice', *Educational Action Research* 14(2): 203–18.

Boutros-Ghali, Boutros (1992) *An Agenda for Peace*, www.un.org/Docs/SG/agpeace.html.

Boyce, James K. (1996) *Economic Policy for Building Peace. The Lessons of El Salvador*, Boulder, CO: Lynne Rienner.

Collier, Paul, V.L. Elliott, Håvard Hegre, Anke Hoeffler, Marta Reynal-Querol, and Nicholas Sambanis (2003) *Breaking the Conflict Trap: Civil War and Development Policy*, New York, NY: Oxford University Press.

David, Charles-Philippe (1999) 'Does peacebuilding build peace? Liberal (mis) steps in the peace process', *Security Dialogue* 30(1): 25–41.

Denskus, Tobias (2002) 'The System Seems Always to be Less than the Sum of its Parts: International Post-War Reconstruction and the Role of Peacebuilding', unpublished MA Dissertation, Bradford: University of Bradford, Department of Peace Studies.

Duffey, Tammy (2001) 'Cultural issues in contemporary peacekeeping', in Tom Woodhouse, Oliver Ramsbotham: *Peacekeeping and Conflict Resolution*, London: Frank Cass.

Ferguson, James (1994) *The Anti-Politics Machine: 'Development', Depoliticization, and Bureaucratic Power in Lesotho*, Minneapolis, MN: University of Minnesota Press.

Fetherston, Beth (2000a) *From Conflict Resolution to Transformative Peacebuilding: Reflections from Croatia*, Working Paper 4, Bradford: Centre for Conflict Resolution.

Fetherston, Beth (2000b) 'Peacekeeping, conflict resolution and peacebuilding: a reconsideration of theoretical frameworks', in Tom Woodhouse and Oliver Ramsbotham (eds.) *Peacekeeping and Conflict Resolution*, London: Frank Cass, pp. 190–218.

Gosovic, Branislav (2000) 'Global intellectual hegemony and the international development agenda', *International Social Science Journal* 52(4): 447–56.

Hajer, Marten A., and Hendrik Wagenaar (2003) *Deliberative Policy Analysis. Understanding Governance in the Network Society*, Cambridge: Cambridge University Press.

Hoffman, Daniel and Stephen Lubkemann (2005) 'Warscape ethnography in West Africa and the anthropology of "events"', *Anthropological Quarterly* 78(2): 315–27.

Hoffman, Mark (2004) 'Peace and conflict impact assessment methodology', in David Bloomfield, Martina Fischer, and Beatrix Schmelzle (eds.) *Berghof Handbook for Conflict Transformation*. Berlin: Berghof Research Center for Constructive Conflict Management, available online at www.berghof-handbook.net.

Jäkle, Nina (2006) Type case 5, *Mercedes Benz Texttracks Volume 1*, www.mercedes-benz.com/texttracks.

Llamazares, Monica (2005) *Post-War Peacebuilding Reviewed: A Critical Exploration Of Generic Approaches To Post-War Reconstruction*, Working Paper 14, Bradford: Centre for Conflict Resolution.

Mosse, David (2005) *Cultivating Development. An Ethnography of Aid Policy and Practice*, London: Pluto Press.

Nordstrom, Carolyn (2004) *Shadows of War: Violence, Power, and International Profiteering in the Twenty-First Century*, Berkeley, CA: University of California Press.

Paffenholz, Thania and Luc Reychler (2005) 'Towards better policy and programme work in conflict zones: introducing the "Aid for Peace" approach', *Journal of Peacebuilding and Development* 2(2): 1–18.

Paffenholz, Thania and Luc Reychler (eds.) (2007) *Aid for Peace: A guide to planning and assessment for conflict zones*, Baden-Baden: Nomos Verlag.

Paris, Roland (2004) *At War's End: Building Peace After Civil Conflict*, Cambridge: Cambridge University Press.

Pearce, Jenny (1999) 'Peace-building in the periphery: lessons from Central America', *Third World Quarterly* 20(1): 51–68.

Preti, Alessandro (2002) 'Guatemala: violence in peacetime: a critical analysis of the armed conflict and the peace process', *Disasters* 26(2): 99–119.

Richards, Paul (2005) *No Peace, No War: An Anthropology of Contemporary Armed Conflict*, Athens, OH and Oxford: Ohio University Press and James Currey.

Utas, Mats (2005) 'Victimcy, girlfriending, soldiering: tacit agency in a young woman's social navigation of the Liberian war zone', *Anthropological Quarterly* 78(2): 403–30.

About the author

Tobias Denskus has worked in Afghanistan and Nepal and undertaken research on German peacebuilding projects in Macedonia. He is studying at the Institute of Development Studies at the University of Sussex, and describes himself as having dual citizenship of both 'Aidland' and 'Reflectionland'.

CHAPTER 24

The uncertain relationship between transparency and accountability

Jonathan Fox

The concepts of transparency and accountability are closely linked: transparency is supposed to generate accountability. This chapter questions this widely held assumption. Transparency mobilises the power of shame, yet the shameless may not be vulnerable to public exposure. Truth often fails to lead to justice. After exploring different definitions and dimensions of the two ideas, the more relevant question turns out to be: what kinds of transparency lead to what kinds of accountability, and under what conditions? The chapter concludes by proposing that the concept can be unpacked in terms of two distinct variants. Transparency can be either 'clear' or 'opaque', while accountability can be either 'soft' or 'hard'.

The right to information is increasingly recognised as a fundamental democratic right, although it was clearly stated in Article 19 of the United Nations Universal Declaration of Human Rights a half-century ago.[1] More than 60 countries around the world have now launched 'right-to-know' reforms, starting with Sweden in 1766, and now including dozens of developing countries (Banisar 2006). Their content varies widely, however: one can only imagine how effective the 2002 reforms in Zimbabwe and Tajikistan have been. Yet in the same year, Mexico passed what became the most far-reaching law on public access to information in the developing world (Sobel *et al.* 2006; Fox *et al.* 2007). Mexico's breakthrough was then surpassed by India's remarkable 2005 reform, which followed years of state-level reforms and grassroots campaigns.

Civil-society campaigners around the world have incorporated the right to know into both their strategies and their tactics, with the hope that transparency will empower efforts to change the behaviour of powerful institutions by holding them accountable in the glare of the public eye. More broadly, the twin principles of transparency and accountability have become adopted by an extraordinarily broad array of political and policy actors in a remarkably brief period of time. This appeal is testimony to their trans-ideological character – and to the convergence of forces from above and below that have appropriated them. This underscores the need to specify what exactly the terms mean, to whom, and in what context. One person's transparency is another's surveillance. One person's accountability is another's persecution.

Where one stands on these issues depends on where one sits. Both concepts are inherently relational: who is to be transparent to whom, and who is to be accountable to whom? Yet what they share is the fact that such a wide range of actors agree that transparency and accountability are key to all manner of 'good governance', from anti-poverty programmes to corporate responsibility, participatory budgeting, and NGO management.

Not coincidentally, the terms *transparency* and *accountability* are both quite malleable and therefore – conveniently – can mean all things to all people. For example, while the transparency banner has been held high by the environmental movement for decades, calling for public hearings to assess environmental impacts and for the obligatory reporting of toxic emissions, corporate investors also took up the charge in the wake of the Enron collapse, calling for managements to open their books. While accountability has long been the watchword of human-rights movements around the world, calling for truth with justice, technocratic managers and anti-union politicians also use it to impose their goals on ostensibly unresponsive public bureaucracies (using the reporting tools of tests and other quantifiable indicators). Campaigners have long challenged the World Bank on the grounds of lack of transparency and advocate holding it accountable for development disasters, yet World Bank managers now call for borrowing governments to be more transparent, and claim that they are holding corrupt governments and contractors accountable for misusing development funds. Bank managers even now converge with the World Social Forum in support for participatory budgeting, a local-government reform strategy that brings transparency and accountability together.

The views of various 'stakeholders' on these issues – to use another development buzzword – depend heavily on how exactly transparency and accountability are defined, and such definitional decisions are path-dependent. In other words, the question of 'what counts' as transparency and accountability depends on how their conceptual boundaries are drawn. Moreover, in many national and international debates over how and whether to enforce social and environmental standards, the following trend appears to be quite pronounced: while critics call for accountability, powerful elites respond by offering some measure of transparency instead. The implication is that monitoring and reporting measures (sometimes by interested parties) are the cure for all ills. They offer a 'market-friendly' substitute for the threat of authoritative sanctions (now stigmatised as 'command and control' measures). One notable example was in the US debate over the North American Free Trade Agreement, when labour and environmental side-agreements that could only promise public hearings and modest investigations were sold as the solution to the poor enforcement of minimum standards (in the USA as well as in Mexico). In brief, better and more information is supposed to make both markets and public authorities work better. But does it? What does the evidence show?

The conventional wisdom about the power of transparency is straightforward: transparency generates accountability. Several related phases come to mind, such as 'information is power', 'the truth shall set you free', and 'speak truth to power'. Or, as one of the founders of public-interest law and later US Supreme Court Justice Louis Brandeis put it 90 years ago: '[p]ublicity is justly commended as a remedy for social and industrial diseases, sunshine is said to be the best disinfectant, electric light the best policeman' (1913).[2]

This proposition makes a great deal of sense, yet a review of the research literature on this issue revealed two major puzzles. First, the actual evidence on transparency's impacts on accountability is not as strong as one might expect. Second, the explanations of transparency's impacts are not nearly as straightforward as the widely held, implicitly self-evident answer to the 'why' question would lead one to expect.

To evoke the power of sunshine is both intuitive and convincing. Indeed, these principles have guided my past 15 years' work.[3] Nevertheless, recently, a review of the empirical evidence for the assumed link between transparency and accountability shows that one does not necessarily lead to the other. Those who make this assumption are confusing the normative (that which our democratic values lead us to believe in) with the analytical (that which the social sciences allow us to claim). If the power of transparency is fuelled by the 'power of shame', then its influence over the really shameless could be quite limited.[4] It turns out that transparency is necessary but far from sufficient to produce accountability.

In this context, it is important to reframe the question in the following terms, more analytical than normative: *under what conditions* can transparency lead to accountability? To be explored in practice, such a question requires still more precision. Both the concepts of transparency and accountability refer to a broad range of processes, actors, and power relations. To reframe the question: what *types* of transparency manage to generate what *types* of accountability?

Both transparency and accountability share a conceptual problem: they are rarely defined with precision. For both, you know it when you see it. At least until recently, transparency has received more practical than conceptual attention.[5] In contrast, the concept of accountability has been reviewed and deepened from diverse perspectives.[6] Yet if one is interested in understanding whether and how transparency *generates* accountability, it is crucial to disentangle rather than conflate the two ideas. To preview the discussion, one must take into account the distinction between two dimensions of accountability: on the one hand, the capacity or the right to demand answers (what Schedler calls 'answerability') and, on the other hand, the capacity to sanction (1999).

Transparency pathways

Instruments for public access to information generally fall into one of two categories: proactive and demand-driven. *Proactive dissemination* refers to information that the government makes public about its activities and performance. Practical expressions can range from toxic-release inventories to organic certification, third-party policy evaluations, and post-authoritarian truth commissions. *Demand-driven access* refers to an institutional commitment to respond to citizens' requests for specific kinds of information or documents which otherwise would not be accessible. Institutions can range from classic freedom-of-information laws to ombudsman offices, 'social accountability' agencies, and investigative bodies such as the World Bank's Inspection Panel.

The idea of transparency can also be unpacked in terms of its directionality. Disclosure cuts both ways, channelling information upwards as well as downwards. 'Right to know' reforms refer to measures that promote 'downwards transparency', from the state to society. In contrast, state imperatives to monitor citizens can be understood as a form of 'upwards transparency'. Consider the examples of conditional cash-transfer social programmes, in which states closely monitor family behaviour, or the lack of guaranteed ballot secrecy, which leads voters to suspect that authorities will learn how they voted. In other words, transparency can be another word for surveillance, which in turn allows state actors to hold citizens accountable for perceived transgressions.

From transparency to accountability

It remains unclear why some transparency initiatives manage to influence the behaviour of powerful institutions, while others do not. Public oversight institutions that seek to bolster checks and balances emphasise the production of transparency. Through inspections, reports, audits and investigations, legislative hearings, ombudsmen, truth commissions, complaint offices, and human-rights commissions, these agencies of 'horizontal accountability' shed light on abuses.[7] Civil-society organisations and independent media also invest heavily in encouraging these official watchdogs to do their job. Yet these oversight bodies rarely have sufficient institutional clout to be able to *act* on their findings, whether by proposing mandatory sanctions, policy changes, protection from violations, or compensation for past abuses. As a result, the power of transparency, defined in terms of the tangible impacts of the public spotlight, depends in practice on how *other* actors respond. These reactive responses can be indirect, when the mass media, opposition political parties, or voters make an issue of newly revealed abuses; or they can be direct, as when the judicial or elected authorities make binding decisions in response.

This observation raises a few dilemmas. The first involves the difference between accountability targets: institutions or individuals? The second involves the problem of quality control for official information. The third involves a conceptual distinction between two different kinds of transparency: clear and opaque. The fourth point brings this distinction together with two kinds of accountability: soft and hard, which will allow us to return to the initial question by defining transparency and accountability with greater precision.

Transparency's different goals: individual vs institutional accountability

Beyond the general assumption that transparency reforms can limit abuses of power, they can have different goals. While some are intended to tackle corruption, and therefore focus on crime, others attempt to encourage improved institutional performance more generally. These different goals imply distinct strategies. The first would be more legalistic, tending to focus on individual failures, while the second would address more systemic flaws. Within the field of budget transparency, for example, the first approach would focus more on revealing the details of public-sector contracts, for instance, and assuring that funds were spent as intended. The second strategy, in contrast, would focus more on the impacts of public spending: how agencies actually used the funds, and to what effect. This strategy requires both highly disaggregated public-spending data and reliable, publicly accessible, third-party policy evaluations.[8] From a civil-society perspective, policy impact is also likely to depend on 'vertical integration' between national public-interest groups that monitor the big picture and grassroots organisations that can 'ground-truth' the claims of official data (Fox 2001).

The goals of individual vs institutional accountability may be not only different: they may sometimes conflict. Any institutional action is the result of decisions by many individuals, which complicates efforts to establish responsibility with precision. Thompson characterised this as 'the problem of many hands' (1987). If the goal is to reveal which individuals were responsible for a specific transgression, then the spotlight often falls on those immediately responsible, usually at lower or middle levels of an agency, which lets higher-level officials off the hook.[9]

Data or information?

A second dilemma involves the difference between official data and relevant, reliable information. Here there is a big difference between disclosure that is voluntary, nominally mandatory vs. really obligatory. Voluntary disclosure would seem to be inherently limited, given the incentive to conceal damaging information – but with a notable exception. Firms that choose to submit to certification of their compliance with social and environmental standards presumably lose some control over the transparency process.[10] This has led to major debates over which certifiers are truly 'arms-length', as in the case of manufacturers that hire commercial accounting firms to certify their subcontractors, which fail to use the key instrument of *unannounced* factory inspections.[11]

When considering obligatory disclosure of performance data, the challenge of assuring quality control becomes clear when examining the 'paradigm case' for impact of transparency reforms: the toxic-release inventory system. Since 1986, in the USA and now many other countries, private firms that emit certain chemicals are required to report the quantities of their emissions to a government agency, which in turn makes the data public. The assumption is that this dissemination provides tools to the public to inform and motivate civic and media campaigns to encourage compliance with environmental laws.[12] Many analysts have argued that the USA's toxic-release inventory was responsible for the reported 46 per cent reduction in emissions between 1988 and 1999 (for example, Fung and O'Rourke 2000; Graham 2002; Konar and Cohen 1997; Stephan 2002). Nevertheless, evaluations by the federal government's accountability office found that the Environmental Protection Agency did not assure reliable and consistent reporting by private firms (GAO 1993, 2001). As a result, polluters did not have to fear sanctions for under-reporting. When public-interest groups did their own assessment in the city of Houston, they found that independently estimated actual levels of emissions were four times greater than had been officially reported (Environmental Integrity Project 2004). These findings do not mean that the reform had no impact, but they do raise serious questions about the claims made for this widely recognised public alternative to so-called 'command-and-control' approaches (for example, Dietz and Stern 2002). Disclosure that was mandatory in theory turned out to be less than mandatory in practice.

The two faces of transparency

This leads us to a third dilemma: how do we explain why some forms of transparency are better able to leverage accountability than others? Here it is relevant to distinguish between two different kinds of transparency: clear and opaque. This distinction is relevant, because insofar as transparency discourse becomes increasingly fashionable, the forces opposed to it will tend to go underground. They will express their opposition indirectly, by providing less than clear transparency.

Opaque or 'fuzzy' transparency involves the dissemination of information that does not reveal how institutions actually behave in practice, whether in terms of how they make decisions, or the results of their actions. The term also refers to information that is divulged only nominally, or which is revealed but turns out to be unreliable. For example, in principle, in the USA, data on who gets farm subsidies, and how much, are considered to be in the public domain. But for the information to be publicly accessible in practice, a public-interest watchdog organisation, the Environmental Working Group, had to invest US$ 12 million in six years of difficult technical work (Becker 2002). Now one simply needs to access www.ewg.org to see exactly who gets how much. This case reminds us that an enormous civil-society investment may be required to translate nominally public data into clearly transparent information.

Clear transparency refers both to information-access policies and to programmes that reveal reliable information about institutional performance, specifying officials' responsibilities as well as where public funds go. Clear transparency sheds light on institutional behaviour, which permits interested parties (such as policy makers, opinion makers, and programme participants) to pursue strategies of constructive change. Examples of clear transparency would include civil-society data about human-rights violations, reliable certification of private-sector compliance with environmental standards, independent ombudsman reports, publicly accessible third-party policy evaluations, and even the World Bank's Inspection Panel reports.[13]

This distinction between clear and opaque is grounded on the premise that if transparency policies are going to meet their goals of transforming institutional behaviour, then they must be explicit in terms of who does what, and who gets what. Nevertheless, clear transparency by itself does not guarantee hard accountability, which would require the intervention of other public-sector actors. Returning to the example of farm subsidies, even though public-interest groups generated an impressive impact in the media, afterwards US government payments to large agribusiness corporations not only were not reduced, they increased enormously (because of their electoral logic).

From the two faces of transparency to the two faces of accountability

In conclusion, the distinction between opaque and clear transparency provokes reflection about their relationships with accountability. Space does not permit a full review of the multiple variants of public accountability, but they share an emphasis on the fundamental right to call those in authority to justify their decisions – the idea of 'answerability'. For many, however, answerability without consequences falls short of accountability.

This discussion will be limited to distinguishing between two basic dimensions of accountability. One could call answerability the 'soft face', while the 'hard face' includes answerability plus the possibility of sanctions. Tables 1 and 2 are organised around this distinction. They show how the presence or absence of certain institutional capacities is associated with either opaque or clear transparency on the one hand, and either hard or soft accountability on the other. Three kinds of institutional capacity are depicted in terms of varying shades of grey: dissemination of and access to information, answerability, and the power to sanction/compensate. The relationship between transparency and accountability is illustrated by these differences in institutional capacity.

Table 1 suggests that when only information access is present, at one extreme, an institution is transparent, but not accountable. On the right-hand side, accountability includes the capacity to sanction or compensate. The intermediate category refers to the capacity to demand explanations, which is posed here as an area of *overlap* between transparency and accountability. The most meaningful kind of answerability is produced by those public and civil-society agencies that have the power not only to reveal existing data, but also to investigate and *produce* information about actual institutional behaviour. This *capacity to produce answers* permits the construction of the *right* to accountability.

Table 2 takes this distinction a step further by unpacking both transparency and accountability in terms of their two respective dimensions: the opaque

Table 1. A first approximation of the relationship between transparency and accountability

Transparency	Accountability
Dissemination and access the information	
Institutional answerability	
	Sanctions, compensation and/or remediation

Table 2. Unpacking the relationship between transparency and accountability

Transparency		Accountability	
Opaque	Clear	Soft	Hard
Dissemination and access the information			
	Institutional answerability		
		Sanctions, compensation and/or remediation	

and the clear, as well as the hard and the soft. By recognising these distinctions, one can identify the area of overlap with greater precision: institutional 'answerability'.

In conclusion, the point of departure for this exploration of the relationship between transparency and accountability was that we are obliged to distinguish between the two concepts because one does not necessarily generate the other. To circle back to the question of how transparency relates to accountability, Table 2 suggests that the two concepts do indeed overlap. *Clear transparency* can be understood as a form of *soft accountability*. This distinction allows us to identify both the limits and the possibilities of transparency, which at minimum should help to calibrate realistic expectations. One should not expect answerability from opaque transparency, and one should not expect hard accountability from answerability. To take the next step and address hard accountability would involve going beyond the limits of transparency and dealing with both the nature of the governing regime and civil society's capacity to encourage the institutions of public accountability to do their job.

Notes

1. This chapter is a revised and abridged translation of Fox (2008a).
2. It is worth noting that this same thinker and activist, defender of transparency as a tool to fight the abuse of concentrated power, also invented and defended the concept of the right to privacy (Warren and Brandeis 1890). The transparency of the state and citizens' privacy are two sides of the same coin.

3. See, among others, Fox and Brown (1998) and Clark *et al.* (2003). On recent campaigns, see www. bicusa.org/.
4. Regarding the 'mobilisation of shame', above all by human-rights defenders, see Drinan (2001), among others.
5. For exceptionally comprehensive works, see Florini (2003), Graham (2002), Hood and Heald (2006), Monsiváis (2005), Roberts (2006), and Oliver (2004). For analyses of the Mexican experience by civil society, see Fox (2008b).
6. See, for example, Ackerman (2008), Behn (2001), Bovens (1998), Fox *et al.* (2007), Isunza Vera and Olvera (2006), Mainwaring and Welna (2003), O'Donnell (1999), and Schedler (1999).
7. On horizontal accountability, see O'Donnell (1999, 2003). On truth commissions, see Rotberg and Thompson (2000) and Gibson (2005), among others.
8. Recall, for example, the distinction between *policy inputs* (such as budget appropriations and contracts for building schools), *results* (whether or not the schools were actually built and staffed, student attendance rates), and *impacts* (to what degree did the students learn). Though third-party evaluations are now very much in vogue, and their focus on measuring impacts is welcome, they run the risk of assuming the reliability of official data regarding the inputs that are then correlated with outputs.
9. Long before low-ranking soldiers took all of the official blame for torture at Abu Ghraib in Iraq, classic cases would include the 1968 My Lai massacre in Vietnam, in which a low-ranking officer was found guilty of ordering the mass murder of 500 civilians. In a rare conviction, he was first sentenced to life imprisonment and ended up serving three and a half years of 'house arrest' on a military base. He claimed that he was 'following orders', and indeed he was carrying out a counter-insurgency strategy that was the result of decisions made at the highest levels of the US government.
10. For an overview of fair trade, see Nichols and Opal (2004). On voluntary certification in the timber case, see Cashore *et al.* (2004).
11. See, among others, Esbenshade (2004), Richter (2001), and Rodríguez-Garavito (2005).
12. See, for example, the tools at www.scorecard.org/.
13. On the latter experience, see Clark *et al.* (2003) and World Bank (2003).

References

Ackerman, John Mill (ed.) (2008) *Más allá del Acceso a la Información: Transparencia, Rendición de Cuentas y Estado de Derecho*, Mexico, DF: Instituto de Acceso a la Información Pública (IFAI)-Instituto de Investigaciones Jurídicas UNAM.

Banisar, David, (2006) *Freedom of Information Around the World 2006: A Global Survey of Access to Government Information Laws*, London: Privacy International.

Becker, Elizabeth (2002) 'Web site helped change farm policy', *New York Times*, 24 February.

Behn, Robert D. (2001) *Rethinking Democratic Accountability*, Washington, DC: Brookings Institution.

Bovens, Mark (1998) *The Quest for Responsibility: Accountability and Citizenship in Complex Organizations*, Cambridge: Cambridge University Press.

Brandeis, Louis (1995) [1913] *Other People's Money and How the Bankers Use It*, Boston, MA: Bedford Books of St. Martin's Press.

Cashore, Benjamin, Graeme Auld, and Deanna Newsom (2004) *Governing Through Markets: Forest Certification and the Emergence on Non-State Authority*, New Haven, CT: Yale University Press.

Clark, Dana, Jonathan Fox, and Kay Treakle (eds.) (2003) *Demanding Accountability: Civil Society Claims and the World Bank Inspection Panel*, Lanham, MD: Rowman & Littlefield.

Dietz, Thomas and Paul C. Stern (eds.) (2002) *New Tools for Environmental Protection: Education, Information and Voluntary Measures*, Washington, DC: National Academy Press, National Research Council.

Drinan, Robert (2001) *The Mobilization of Shame: A World View of Human Rights*, New Haven, CT: Yale University Press.

Environmental Integrity Project (2004) 'Review of 10 toxic air emissions finds "startlingly" bad data reaching public; key flaw: EPA's failure to act and new steps to undermine accuracy of reporting', 22 June, available at www.commondreams.org/news2004/0622-14.htm (retrieved 8 March 2007).

Esbenshade, Jill (2004) *Monitoring Sweatshops: Workers, Consumers and the Global Apparel Industry*, Philadelphia, PA: Temple University Press.

Florini, Ann (2003) *The Coming Democracy: New Rules for Running a New World*, Washington, DC: Island Press.

Fox, Jonathan (2001) 'Vertically integrated policy monitoring: a tool for civil society policy advocacy', *Nonprofit and Voluntary Sector Quarterly* 30(3): 616–27.

Fox, Jonathan (2008a) 'Transparencia y rendición de cuentas: dos conceptos distintos y una relació′n incierta', in John Mill Ackerman (ed.) op. cit.

Fox, Jonathan (2008b) *Accountability Politics: Power and Voice in Rural Mexico*, Oxford: Oxford University Press.

Fox, Jonathan and L. David Brown (eds.) (1998) *The Struggle for Accountability: The World Bank, NGOs and Grassroots Movements*, Cambridge, MA: MIT Press.

Fox, Jonathan, Libby Haight, Helena Hofbauer, and Tania Sánchez (eds.) (2007) *Mexico's Right to Know Reforms: Civil Society Perspectives*, Mexico, DF: FUNDAR/Woodrow Wilson Center.

Fung, Archon and Dara O'Rourke (2000) 'Reinventing environmental regulation from the grassroots up: explaining and expanding the success of the toxic release inventory', *Environmental Management*, 25(2): 115–27.

General Accounting Office (GAO) (1993) 'Environmental Enforcement: EPA Cannot Ensure the Accuracy of Self-Reported Compliance Monitoring Data', Washington, D.C.: GAO, Report to the Chairman, Committee on Governmental Affairs, US Senate, GAO/RCED-93-21, March.

General Accounting Office (GAO) (2001) 'Environmental Protection: EPA Should Strengthen Its Efforts to Measure and Encourage Pollution Prevention', Washington, DC: GAO, Report to Congressional Requestors, GAO-O1-283, February.

Gibson, James L. (2005) 'The truth about truth and reconciliation in South Africa', *International Political Science Review*, 26(4): 341–61.

Graham, Mary (2002) *Democracy by Disclosure: The Rise of Technopopulism*, Washington, DC: Brookings Institution.

Hood, Christopher and David Heald (eds.) (2006) *Transparency: The Key to Better Governance?* Oxford: British Academy/Oxford University Press.

Isunza Vera, Ernesto and Alberto Olvera (eds.) (2006) *Democratización, Rendición de Cuentas y Sociedad Civil: Participación Ciudadana y Control Social*, Mexico DF: CIESAS, Universidad Veracruzana/ Ed. Miguel Angel Porrua.

Konar, Shameek and Mark A. Cohen (1997) 'Information as regulation: the effect of community right to know laws on toxic emissions', *Journal of Environmental Economics and Management* 32(1): 109–24.

Mainwaring, Scott and Christopher Welna (eds.) (2003) *Democratic Accountability in Latin America*, Oxford: Oxford University Press.

Monsiváis, Alejandro (ed.) (2005) *Políticas de transparencia: Ciudadanía y rendición de cuentas*, Mexico, DF: Instituto Federal de Acceso a la Información Publica/ Centro Mexicano para la Filantropía, pp. 17–30.

Nicholls, Alex and Charlotte Opal (2004) *Fair Trade: Market-Driven Ethical Consumption*, London: Sage.

O'Donnell, Guillermo (1999) 'Horizontal accountability in new democracies', in Andreas Schedler, Larry Diamond, and Marc F. Plattner (eds.) *The Self-Restraining State: Power and Accountability in New Democracies*, Boulder, CO: Lynne Reinner, pp. 29–51.

O'Donnell, Guillermo (2003) 'Horizontal accountability: the legal institutionalization of mistrust,' in Mainwaring and Welna (eds.), pp. 34–54.

Oliver, Richard (2004) *What is Transparency?*, New York, NY: McGraw Hill.

Richter, Judith (2001) *Holding Corporations Accountable: Corporate Conduct, International Codes and Citizen Action*, London: Zed Books.

Roberts, Alasdair (2006) *Blacked Out: Government Secrecy in the Information Age*, Cambridge: Cambridge University Press.

Rodríguez-Garavito, César (2005) 'Global governance and labor rights: Codes of Conduct and anti-sweatshop struggles in global apparel factories in Mexico and Guatemala', *Politics and Society* 33(2): 203–33.

Rotberg, Robert and Dennis Thompson (eds.) (2000) *Truth v. Justice: The Morality of Truth Commissions*, Princeton, NJ: Princeton University Press.

Schedler, Andreas (1999) 'Conceptualizing accountability', in Andreas Schedler, Larry Diamond and Marc F. Plattner (eds.) *The Self-Restraining State: Power and Accountability in New Democracies*, Boulder, CO: Lynne Reinner, pp. 13–28

Sobel, David, Bethany A. Davis Noll, Benjamin Fernández Bogado, TCC Group, Monroe Price (2006) *The Federal Institute for Access to Public Information in Mexico and a Culture of Transparency*, Philadelphia, PA: University of Pennsylvania, Annenberg School for Communication, Project for Global Communication Studies.

Stephan, Mark (2002) 'Environmental information disclosure programs: they work, but why?' *Social Science Quarterly* 83(1): 190–205.

Thompson, Dennis (1987) *Political Ethics and Public Office*, Cambridge, MA: Harvard University Press.

Warren, Samuel and Louis D. Brandeis (1980) 'The right to privacy', *Harvard Law Review* 4(5), 15 December.

World Bank (2003) *Accountability at the World Bank: The Inspection Panel 10 Years On*, Washington, DC: World Bank.

About the author

Jonathan Fox is Professor of Latin American and Latino Studies at the University of California, Santa Cruz and has published widely on the issues of democratisation and the strengthening of civil society, particularly in Mexico.

CHAPTER 25
Corruption

Elizabeth Harrison

This chapter engages with the ways in which corruption has taken centre stage in much development policy making and rhetoric. It argues that there is a need to destabilise 'taken for granted' assumptions about what corruption is and how it operates. This means generating an understanding of how meanings of corruption vary, and how this variation is determined by the social characteristics of those engaged in corruption talk. It also means examination of how discourses of corruption and anti-corruption are translated from international to national and local stages – from the anti-corruption 'establishment' to the realities of bureaucratic encounters in diverse contexts.

What is the value in dissecting the use of the word 'corruption' in development rhetoric? Like most of the expressions examined in this volume, 'corruption' is frequently used sloppily, and its use may disguise political agendas, or further the interests of the powerful. 'Corruption' is unlike some of the more bland development 'buzzwords' (*social protection, harmonisation, country ownership*), in that they primarily describe fashionable ways of getting development done. There is more to it than this, perhaps because 'corruption' describes not so much how to get things done, but something that is perceived to be hampering those efforts. 'Corruption' is also similar to 'poverty', in that it attempts to describe something, however inadequately, which exists 'in the real world' and can make people's lives miserable.

When it comes to 'corruption', destabilising its 'taken for granted' quality might help us to better identify where corruption hurts, and whom. This means understanding what corruption means for different people, who is able to define an act as corrupt or not, and who is included in or excluded from discourses of corruption. This is not to present a relativistic position where, for example, corruption is re-labelled as 'gift giving' and thus excused as culturally acceptable. Rather it is about understanding the social characteristics which influence corruption talk: gender, age, religion, ethnicity, and so on may all play a role, as will differential engagement with international anti-corruption discourses themselves.

Corruption takes centre stage

The profile of 'corruption' in development talk has grown hugely in recent years. On the international stage, anti-corruption work takes a prominent place in the work of both bilateral and multilateral donors. From the time of James Wolfensohn's speech in 1996, when he famously, and for some, shockingly, referred to the 'cancer of corruption' in Africa, the World Bank has taken a leading role in the anti-corruption 'crusade' (Sampson 2005). Others, such as the UK government's Department for International Development (DFID), have dedicated teams focused on the control of corruption. In the 2005 Report of the Commission for Africa, corruption control takes a prominent place as a vital part of the solution to the continent's ills. The NGO Transparency International (TI) has chapters in 85 countries, all devoted to campaigning against and exposing corruption. It is funded both by the major donors and by businesses keen to be associated with more transparent and virtuous business practices. The world of anti-corruption produces significant research, its findings largely disseminated through a range of anti-corruption portals, such as CORIS and ANCORR.[1] In fact, the Internet has provided a medium in which the volume of anti-corruption information and analysis is so large as to be almost unmanageable.

Concern with corruption is not just a phenomenon of donor development discourse. In both Northern and Southern countries, there is a mounting focus on transparency, accountability, and the rule of law. The Right to Information Movement in India has had significant success in bringing corrupt bureaucrats to account. Anti-corruption campaigners such as John Githongo in Kenya have a high profile and are, rightly, celebrated for speaking out, often putting themselves at personal risk. When the UK High Commissioner to Kenya, Edward Clay, condemned that country's corruption in rather colourful terms, he was fêted in the British media.[2]

And who could argue with the need for more freedom of speech, and the exposure of corrupt and money-grabbing politician or bureaucrats? But when we look closer, the targets of anti-corruption talk become more slippery, less easy to identify. To be sure, a Minister salting donor funds away in a foreign bank is a problem. But what about an agricultural extension worker favouring his brother in the delivery of farm inputs – or, indeed, the brother who receives those inputs? Are they as morally culpable, and how are we to decide? To what extent should we take into account the constraints under which they operate, or the other moral considerations that may be coming into play? As Pardo argues,

> ...in any given society corruption is a changing phenomenon, some of its aspects and received morality are culturally specific and its conceptualization is affected by personal interest, cultural values and socio-economic status. In this key sense, corruption needs to be treated contextually and diachronically. (Pardo 2004: 2)

On rhetoric and meaning

There is a well-developed literature on the definition and meaning of corruption, much of it arising from social anthropology. This explores the nuances between *bribery, nepotism, graft, extortion* and so on, and reflects on the relationships between people and bureaucracies (for example, Leys 1965; Olivier de Sardan 1999; Gupta 1995; Miller *et al.* 2001; Parry 2000). However, when it comes to the control of corruption in development policy making and public statements, such nuance tends to disappear. More complicated views or definitions become reduced to short phrases with a strong rhetorical quality, which become accepted as truths and articles of faith. Thus, for many years, the generally accepted definition of corruption was '*the abuse of public office for private gain*'. This implies a firm dichotomy between the public/impersonal and the private/personal spheres, and the importance of keeping the two separate. It is derived from a Weberian notion of rational–legal bureaucratic organisation. However, unlike for Weber, who was clear that this was an ideal type which 'cannot be found empirically anywhere in reality' (Weber 1949: 90), such a bureaucratic ideal is sometimes presented as a basic model from which to develop policy. For example, in 2004, the World Bank funded a study which examined the 'Weberianess' of individual governments (Evans and Rauch 2004).

A series of scandals involving private-sector firms such as Enron and Worldcom in the USA has prompted some rethinking of the 'abuse of public office' definition. Transparency International and others now refer to '*the abuse of trusted authority for private gain*'. Nonetheless, this still relies on a fairly simplified distinction between the public and private spheres, and glosses over whether, for example, those involved in particular acts see them as corrupt or not. Once the definition has been accepted and repeated, the problems with understanding its application do not trouble its users. Thus, the widespread acceptance that Africa is riddled with corruption like a diseased body is not scrutinised.

Such a view is compounded by the popularity of measures such as the Corruption Perceptions Index (CPI). The CPI, developed by TI, is a composite measure which brings together the views of 'chief financial officers', 'executives in top and middle management', and 'US-resident country experts', as well as a number of other categories of 'business experts' (TI 2005). It reports on perceptions of levels of corruption in more than 150 countries and publishes results in a form of league table in which we can see which countries are perceived to be more, and which less, corrupt. Not surprisingly, Scandinavian countries top the league, while at the bottom Southern, particularly African, countries predominate. In the 2005 CPI, Bangladesh and Chad had the dubious distinction of coming last, while Iceland was at the top. The CPI has obvious attractions, particularly for donors seeking to justify anti-corruption efforts. The fact that it is a measure only of 'perceptions', not of corrupt practices, is seldom treated as important. Nor is the fact that those on whose opinion it relies are likely to be educated, articulate, and share a particular worldview and set of values about the negative effects of corruption.

To be fair, the CPI has been criticised recently, most strongly by one of its originators, Fredrik Galtung, who has left TI to be part of a new anti-corruption network, Tiri (www.tiri.org). Galtung (2005) has argued that the CPI has a number of significant failings. These include the fact that it relies on an imprecise, yet narrow, definition of corruption, focuses only on the takers and not the givers, and draws its information from often ignorant sources. To respond to criticism, TI now also produces a Bribe-Payers Index (BPI) and the Global Corruption Barometer (GCB). The GCB polled 55,000 people in 69 countries in 2005 to hear their perceptions about corruption. According to TI, it 'takes the temperature of the people whose lives and views are touched by corruption' (TI 2005). Significantly, however, this is still only a measure of 'perceptions'.

Research from anthropology suggests that perceptions of corruption may in fact bear little relationship to its incidence. For example, Parry's (2000) ethnography of a government-run steel plant in Madhya Pradesh, India, indicates that, while there was a strong perception that it was virtually impossible to get a job without recourse to an intermediary, in practice very few people actually paid bribes for employment. Parry argues that this illustrates the internalisation, rather than the rejection, of particular values of bureaucratic practice. 'Corruption has seemed to get worse and worse not (only) because it has, but also because it subverts a set of values to which people are increasingly committed' (Parry 2000: 53). Arguably, the very success of anti-corruption rhetoric may result in more and more people believing that corruption is a problem. The more there is talk about the problem of corruption, the more widely it is perceived to be a national blight.

The Global Corruption Barometer is seen as a tool to combat 'corruption', but behind its impressive and emotive language, the slipperiness about what corruption is persists. For the GCB, the focus is 'bribery', and the argument is made that 'corruption's impact on personal and family life is most dramatic on poor households' (TI 2005). But petty bribery, the kind that makes a young mother lose hope for the future because she believes that securing her child's health requires a 'hand under the table', is not the same as the kind of grand corruption that much anti-corruption rhetoric focuses upon. Some might say it is worse, or that it is what really matters. Others might stress how single acts of grand corruption do much more harm. The differences between different practices which are all lumped together as 'corruption' lie in the different conceptions of what kind of moral boundary line has been crossed in particular instances. This is something that is not part of the moral certainty that drives anti-corruption rhetoric. But, in classifying corruption as a simple phenomenon, the diverse ways in which people engage with morality are overlooked. Comprehension of how opportunities are shaped, both to engage in and to escape from corruption, is important. It seldom occurs.

Why corruption has come to matter – and why now?

So why has anti-corruption become so pre-eminent in donor discourse, with such under-specification of what corruption itself is? Two opposed explanations are possible. On the one hand, there are those who strongly associate themselves with anti-corruption and for whom academic speculation about contested moralities is at best a waste of time and at worst a dangerous diversion. For these, the pre-eminence of corruption in international discourse is merely and self-evidently a reflection of the importance of the phenomenon. It may also be something of a moral victory for those who have 'right' on their side. On the other hand is a growing body of scholars who see the growth of anti-corruption as part of a project of 'normalisation' (Hindess 2004). Among these are those such as Szeftel, who has argued (1998) that the anti-corruption agenda fundamentally misunderstands the nature of the state in Africa; and Brown and Cloke (2004), who see it as the manifestation of a neo-liberal policy agenda. For several, anti-corruption is closely associated with the governance agenda in development, itself a manifestation of greater intrusion of neo-liberalism in the architecture of aid. Szeftel also suggests that anti-corruption may reflect a desire to both explain and divert attention from the failure of structural-adjustment policies. These criticisms together become even more pertinent when the accountability and moral purity of international development institutions themselves are called into question. Has insufficient attention been paid to the internal anti-corruption mechanisms of such institutions? And does the focus on anti-corruption, with its attendant increase in privatisation, concessions, and contracting-out, in turn open the door for greater corruption among multinational corporations (Hall 1999; Hawley 2000)?

Of course, the answer lies somewhere in between. Corruption does exist, *and* its pre-eminence in international discourse is not innocent of neo-liberal values. To develop this point, reflection on the working of the anti-corruption 'establishment' itself is valuable. Like all discourses, that of anti-corruption does not exist in an institutional vacuum: it is used and developed by particular actors and demonstrates particular sets of practices. In examining this world, a picture emerges which may imply less intentionality than a neo-liberal conspiracy, but which goes some way towards explaining the nature of anti-corruption talk.

In this, the role of academic discipline emerges as significant. The World Bank is now a (perhaps *the*) major player in anti-corruption activity (Marquette 2003; Polzer 2001). Despite its nominal independence, TI has strong links with the Bank, and was indeed founded by former Bank employees, whose connections have been important in its rapid growth. From being an organisation whose Articles of Confederation forbade its involvement in 'politics', the Bank has now come to accept the intimate connection between politics and economic outcomes. The Bank is also, despite some shifts, still dominated by economists. Arguably, the way that the Bank has defined and used the concept of corruption is influenced by this.

Corruption becomes something that it is legitimate for the Bank to pronounce upon, precisely because it becomes defined as an economic concept. For example, the formula developed by Klitgaard – *'Corruption may be represented as following a simple formula: $C = M + D - A$. Corruption equals Monopoly plus Discretion minus Accountability'* (Klitgaard 1998: 4) – is widely quoted.

There are parallels with the arguments that Ben Fine (2001; see also his contribution to this volume) has made with regard to the concept of social capital: that economics has succeeded in 'colonising' the other social sciences, by applying its methods to non-market and non-economic relations and treating them as if they were all economic. In this way, the world is characterised as more predictable and controllable than it actually is.

The world of anti-corruption

Beyond the dominance of economics, there are other processes at work. Recent research by Steven Sampson into anti-corruption activity in the Balkans, including that of TI, has revealed that the world of anti-corruption is a complex one, involving a confluence of money and power with strongly held moral and ethical beliefs (Sampson 2005). It is significant that the field of anti-corruption has become increasingly well funded. This is effectively illustrated by the professionalism and high fees charged at a series of prestigious anti-corruption conferences. TI itself administers more than €6 million of donated funds. Accordingly, those with undoubtedly strong moral imperatives have also become caught up in a struggle for resources which Sampson labels 'projectisation'. In this, simple formulas and descriptions of corruption become important for attracting grants and 'technical assistance'. The idea of the 'Corruption Fighters' Toolkit' (a product from TI) is attractive in its simplicity; it is also eminently fundable. This is not to imply that all anti-corruption activity is a cynical attempt to obtain funding. However, it does account somewhat for the processes of simplification.

The world of anti-corruption described by Sampson is an important part of the picture. Equally important are the ways in which its messages are translated and adapted into different settings, from the Kenyan national anti-corruption discourse, with its 'gluttonous politicians', to the 'crisis of corruption' in an Indian steel plant, or the 'young woman seeking health care' for her child. Corruption is a word with distinctly Western origins. The ways in which it is used in different, especially non-Western, contexts will reflect a complicated mixture of interpretation, moral judgement, and opportunism. Reflecting on this picture requires keeping in mind that corruption is *both* a normative concept *and* a set of practices with effects that can hurt people.

Conclusion

'Corruption', but more particularly the anti-corruption lobby that has expanded so dramatically in recent years, needs closer examination. Riding on a wave of righteous virtue, anti-corruption talk comes from diverse quarters and, for many, is unquestionable. Indeed, to do so is slightly heretical; corruption is so obviously harmful that querying this is equivalent to excusing immorality. As I have discussed, there are good reasons to have some sympathy with this position. However, in lumping together all 'corruption' under the same heading, the anti-corruption lobby underplays the very different meanings that are attached to diverse transactions. More significantly, it also provides a neat explanation for the ills of both countries and continents that leaves moral culpability entirely with the supposedly corrupt. Ethnographic engagement with practices that are seen as corrupt may be valuable. Equally, though, such engagement needs to extend to questions of how, and why, anti-corruption has risen to its current prominence.

Notes

1. CORIS is Transparency International's anti-corruption information service; ANCORR is the OECD's anti-corruption website.
2. The text of his speech includes the following: 'We never expected corruption to be vanquished overnight. We all implicitly recognised that some would be carried over to the new era. We hoped that it would not be rammed in our faces. But it has: evidently the practitioners now in government have the arrogance, greed and perhaps a desperate sense of panic to lead them to eat like gluttons. They may expect we shall not see, or notice, or will forgive them a bit of gluttony because they profess to like Oxfam lunches. But they can hardly expect us not to care when their gluttony causes them to vomit all over our shoes'; available at http://bbc.co.uk, (retrieved 3 August 2004).

References

Brown, E. and J. Cloke (2004) 'Neoliberal reform, governance and corruption in the South: assessing the international anti-corruption crusade', *Antipode* 36(2): 272–94.

Evans, P. and J. Rauch (2004) 'Bureaucracy and Growth: A Cross National Analysis of the Effects of 'Weberian' State Structures on Economic Growth', http://sociology.berkeley.edu/faculty/evans/burperf.html (retrieved 6 December 2006).

Fine, B., C. Lapavitas, and J. Pincus (eds.) (2001) *Development Policy in the 21st Century*, London: Routledge.

Galtung, F. (2005) 'Measuring the immeasurable: boundaries and functions of (macro) corruption indices' in F. Galtung and C. Sampford (eds.) *Measuring Corruption*, London: Ashgate.

Gupta, A. (1995) 'Blurred boundaries: the discourse of corruption, the culture of politics and the imagined state', *American Ethnologist* 22(2): 375–402.

Hall, D. (1999) 'Privatisation, multinationals, and corruption', *Development in Practice* 9(5): 539–56.

Hawley, S. (2000) *Exporting Corruption: Privatisation, Multinationals and Bribery*, The Corner House, Briefing No. 19, Dorset: The Corner House, available at www.thecornerhouse.org.uk/item.shtml?x=51975 (retrieved 6 December 2006)

Hindess, B. (2004) *'International Anti-corruption as a Program of Normalization'*, paper presented at the ISA Conference, Montreal, 17–20 March.

Klitgaard, R. (1998) 'International cooperation against corruption', *Finance and Development*, March, pp. 3–6, available at www.worldbank.org/fandd/english/pdfs/0398/080398.pdf (retrieved 5 December 2006).

Leys, C. (1965) 'What is the problem about corruption?', *Journal of Modern African Studies* 3(2): 215–24.

Marquette, H. (2003) *Corruption, Politics and Development: The Role of the World Bank*, Basingstoke: Palgrave Macmillan.

Miller, W. L., A. B. Grodeland, and T. Y. Koshechkina (2001) *A Culture of Corruption? Coping With Government in Post-Communist Europe*, Bucharest: Central European University Press.

Olivier de Sardan, J.-P. (1999) 'African corruption in the context of globalisation', in R. Fardon, W. van Binsbergen, and R. van Dijk (eds.) *Modernity on a Shoestring: Dimensions of Globalisation, Consumption and Development in Africa and Beyond*, Leiden and London: EIDOS.

Pardo, I. (ed.) (2004) *Between Morality and the Law: Corruption, Anthropology and Comparative Society*, Aldershot: Ashgate.

Parry, J. (2000) 'The crisis of corruption and the idea of India – a worm's eye view', in I. Pardo (ed.) *Morals of Legitimacy: Between Agency and System*, Oxford: Berghahn Books.

Polzer, T. (2001) 'Corruption: deconstructing the World Bank discourse', *Working Papers Number 01–18*, London: Development Studies Institute, LSE.

Sampson, S. (2005) 'Integrity warriors: global morality and the anticorruption movement in the Balkans', in C. Shore and D. Haller (eds.) *Corruption: Anthropological Perspectives*, London: Pluto Press.

Szeftel, M. (1998) 'Misunderstanding African politics: corruption and the governance agenda', *Review of African Political Economy* 76: 221–40.

Transparency International (2005) 'Global Corruption Barometer', www.transparency.org/news_room/latest_news/press_releases/2005/09_12_2005_barometer_2005 (retrieved 6 December 2006).

Weber, M. (1952) 'The essentials of bureaucratic organization: an ideal type construction' in R. K. Merton, A. P. Gray, B. Hockey, and H. C. Selvin (eds.) *Reader in Bureaucracy*, New York, NY: The Free Press.

About the author

Elizabeth Harrison is a Senior Lecturer in Anthropology at the University of Sussex. Her research has been broadly within the 'anthropology of development', and has included work on the generation and use of key concepts within development thinking, with a focus on gender and participation.

CHAPTER 26

'Good governance': the itinerary of an idea

Thandika Mkandawire

The concept of good governance originated among African scholars in relation to state–society relations in Africa, expressing the concern that these be developmental, democratic, and socially inclusive. The term has since been taken up by the international development business – in particular the World Bank – and used by them as a new label for aid conditionality, in particular structural adjustment in all its various manifestations.

The belief that lack of 'good governance' might be the main hindrance to economic growth in Africa was firmly set in the minds of the international community following a World Bank report published in 1989 which categorically declared: 'Underlying the litany of Africa's development problems is a crisis of governance'. By 'governance' is meant the exercise of power to manage a nation's affairs. Since then, the expression has attained the status of a mantra in the development business. It is presented as the discovery of new truths that must be hammered into the benighted minds of African policy makers. The Africans themselves often consider it as one more item on the list of aid conditionalities.

Rarely recognised, even by Africans, is that the inspiration came from African scholars and that the current use of the concept diverges significantly from their own original understanding. In the preparation of the 1989 report, the World Bank did the then unusual thing of consulting African scholars and commissioning them to prepare background papers, apparently at the insistence of Africans within the Bank. Among the scholars were Claude Ake, Nakhtar Diouf, and Ali Mazrui. Their papers focused on state–society relations in Africa as the main problem. In the introduction to a volume of background papers to its Long-Term Perspective Study (LTPS), the World Bank acknowledged the contributions of the Africans:

> Consideration of these aspects was very much a result of the collaborative approach adopted early in the preparation of this report. In the process, it became clear that any assessment of the region's performance in the past and directions for the future would have to be informed by issues that cut across various disciplines to include history, culture, politics, and the very ethos of Africa. By listening to the report's African and other collaborators, it was evident that a report with a scope such as

that of the LTPS could no longer evade these issues. These collaborators greatly strengthened that ability of the LTPS to address, if not authoritatively, at least in a well-informed manner, the deep-seated concerns that ultimately shape and direct the course of economic growth and development. The ten papers presented in this third volume of the LTPS Background Papers contain some of those invaluable contributions.

The general understanding within African intellectual circles then was that the main challenge of development was the establishment of state–society relations that are (a) developmental, in the sense that they allow the management of the economy in a manner that maximises economic growth, induces structural change, and uses all available resources in a responsible and sustainable manner in highly competitive global conditions; (b) democratic and respectful of citizens' rights; and (c) socially inclusive, providing all citizens with a decent living and full participation in national affairs. Good governance should therefore be judged by how well it sustains this triad. The urgency of the democratic aspect of good governance was highlighted by the clamour for democracy by social groups that had opposed misgovernment and the imposition of policies by unelected institutions – national or foreign.

Downsized states and instability

This widespread view in African intellectual circles followed the concern with the failure of authoritarian regimes in Africa to ensure both human rights and development. It was informed by the belief that the downsizing of the state insisted upon by donors addressed only the short-term issues of stabilisation, while undermining long-term developmental capacities. And, given the potential for ethnic conflicts and the growing social blindness of economic policy, there was also the view that poor state–society relations only exacerbated political instability. Good governance would therefore have to pay special attention to issues of equity and inclusion.

The initial response to the 1989 report from staff of the International Monetary Fund (IMF) and the World Bank, especially the economists, was at best lukewarm for a number of reasons. First, it was felt that the focus on politics was distracting attention from the task of 'getting the macroeconomic fundamentals right'. Indeed, a report on Africa produced five years later (World Bank 2000) stridently argued that orthodox adjustment policies work, and that the poor performance of African economies was due to their failure to implement agreed-upon adjustment policies. There was hardly any mention of governance. Second, the new focus did not leave much room for the World Bank. Its insistence on the importance of local initiatives, political accountability to the citizens, and the need to reconcile African traditions and institutions with 'modern' ones were not exactly the types of thing the World Bank could relate to in a quantifiable and operational manner.

A few years later, however, with African economies showing signs of recovery, there was an orchestrated campaign by the Washington-based financial institutions to highlight the 'turnaround' in policy adoption in Africa. These institutions attributed the turnaround to their own persistence with their own policies, and to the emergence of African leaders with a new awareness of the demands of globalisation. A major World Bank report on Africa, published in 2000, stated that 'many countries have made major gains in macroeconomic stabilization, particularly since 1994'; and that there had been a turnaround because of 'on-going structural adjustment throughout the region which has opened markets and has had a major impact on productivity, exports, and investment'. There had indeed been a sea-change in the African policy landscape and, as a result, arguments that African countries had refused or been slow to adjust, or that enough time had not passed, became less credible.

However, as had happened many times before, these reforms did not lead to the expected outcomes, and celebration of 'recovery' proved premature. Considerable evidence – including some from within the Bank itself – suggested that adoption of the prescribed policies had not worked. Much of the 'recovery' could be explained by so-called exogenous factors – weather, terms of trade, plain good luck, and end of conflicts – rather than adjustment.

Thus came the question: 'Why is it that even when the recommended policies were implemented (often under the aegis of and conditionalities from the International Monetary Fund and the World Bank), the results hoped for did not materialise?' The answer was 'institutional weakness' or 'bad governance'. The new proponents of good governance argued that the policies themselves were sound, and that good governance must also mean implementing orthodox economic policy. Good governance thus simply became one more instrument for ensuring the implementation of adjustment programmes. Because macroeconomic policies were sacrosanct, it was important that the democratic institutions that might come with good governance were not used to undermine economic policy. This was ensured by introducing institutional reforms that effectively compromised the authority of elected bodies through the insulation of policy technocrats and the creation of 'autonomous' authorities.

As a consequence, the current use of 'governance' is still very much business as usual. Thus although the IMF took on good governance, it also insisted that the many reforms (fiscal, financial, etc.) in which it had been involved were indeed core components of good governance. Many other donors have followed suit, simply re-labelling various divisions from one thing to 'governance'.

The approach to good governance and economic policy that finally became dominant differed radically from that of the African contributors who were strongly opposed to adjustment policies because not only were they deflationary and thus not developmental, but also because they were externally imposed, weakened the state, and undermined many of the post-colonial 'social contracts'. For the African contributors, good governance related to the larger issues of state–society relations and not just to the technocratic transparency-accountability mode that it eventually assumed in the international financial institutions. The actual use of the concept of good governance sidestepped the central concerns of the Africans and rendered the notion purely administrative. And all too often, it looked like a fallback position for failed policies.

References

World Bank (1989) *Sub-Saharan Africa: From Crisis to Sustainable Growth: A Long-Term Perspective Study*, Washington, DC: World Bank.
World Bank (1994) *Adjustment in Africa: Reforms, Results and the Road Ahead*, Washington, DC: World Bank.
World Bank (2000) *Can Africa Claim the 21st Century?*, Washington, DC: World Bank.

About the author

Thandika Mkandawire is Professor of African Politics at the LSE and was previously Director of UNRISD and Executive Director of CODESRIA.

CHAPTER 27
The discordant voices of security

Robin Luckham

This chapter examines the links between development and 'security', situating these concepts within their philosophical and political contexts, particularly in relation to contemporary wars, including the 'war on terror', and the so-called 'securitisation' of development. The security of states does not necessarily ensure the security of their citizens, and the very concept of security is both complex and contested. The author provides a succinct summary of various interpretations of security – of states, collectivities, and individuals – showing how each is double-edged or ambivalent.

In today's world, we understand that security is a global need and that countries must work together to achieve it. Security and development are linked.
(DFID: Fighting Poverty to Build a Safer World. A Strategy for Security and Development 2005)

[T]he indivisibility of security, economic development and human freedom.
(United Nations: A More Secure World, 2004)

There's only one issue here. It's security. People are sick of invasions and rebels and war.
(Deputy Mayor of Goma, Democratic Republic of Congo, during the country's presidential election, October 2006)

While the link between security and development is routinely made in official reports and academic papers – and by ordinary people – it is a recent and controversial addition to development discourse. The 1980 Brandt Report on International Development (Independent Commission on International Development Issues 1980) and the 1982 Palme Report on Disarmament and Security (Independent Commission on Disarmament and Security Issues 1982) connected the two issues in the early 1980s. Yet development agencies still refused to engage with security questions, which were seen as too political or beyond their mandate. They only took an interest when the violence already disfiguring much of the developing world during the Cold War was re-presented as a development problem after the latter ended.

The global shifts which brought security into development discourse are complex, and will not be discussed in detail here. They have given birth to the perception that development is being 'securitised' and subordinated to the security priorities of the major global players, including the 'war on terror'.

Even more than development, security is a contested concept, with multiple layers of history and meaning, containing dark corners in which demons hide. Yet most people who talk security do so as if they know what security is, and for the most part they treat it as unproblematic. 'Security' is used as an abstract noun, describing a desirable existential state. But what security? Whose security? How achieved? And from what? There are no easy answers to any of these questions.

Insecurity is seemingly easier to define. Fear and violence are all around us. They are tangible realities for enormous numbers of people, and (to an extent) can be measured. Commonsense notions of security indeed characterise it in terms of personal safety, or 'freedom from fear' in the words of the 2004 UN Report cited above. The links between 'freedom from fear' and other existential risks, like 'freedom from want' are at the core of the concept of 'human security'. They resonate within a wider family of meanings, such as 'social security', 'food security', and, in the context of capitalist property relations, 'security of tenure'.

However, even in these relatively benign senses security cannot be used without a safety warning. From the time of Thomas Hobbes, security has been embedded in the theory and practice of modern statehood. It has been a discourse of the powerful, even more than of the insecure and weak. Writing in 1651 soon after the English Civil War, Hobbes argued that the people's safety was the business of the 'great Leviathan called a Commonwealth or State'. For 'without a common power to keep them all in awe', they 'are in that condition which is called war; and such a war as is of every man against every man'.

There was an implied social contract, by which the state delivered peace and security, and citizens consented to its sovereign authority. This contract was backed the state's right to use force, for 'covenants without the sword, are but words and of no strength to secure a man at all'. State sovereignty was absolute, and loyalty unconditional, for 'to resist the sword of the Commonwealth ... no man hath liberty; because such liberty takes away from the sovereign the means of protecting us, and is therefore destructive of the very essence of government'. Even so, there was an important proviso, namely that 'the obligation of subjects to the sovereign is understood to last as long, and no longer than, the power lasteth by which he is able to protect them'. Weak rulers, according to Hobbes, were invariably deprived of the right to govern by external conquest or internal rebellion.

While Hobbes himself was primarily concerned with the nature of political obligation, and used the word 'security' sparingly, his thinking still permeates security analysis in the twenty-first century. Security discourse continues to frame politics and governance in the language of threat, risk, insecurity, and violence – Hobbes' war of All Against All. In contrast to development, whose language is firmly rooted in the grand narrative of the Enlightenment, the discourse of security arises from the double-edged and ambivalent nature of development, including its roots in a destructive capitalism which demolishes livelihoods, communities, and even states – indirectly through the structural violence of poverty, and directly through war and political violence.

On the one hand there are benign, ameliorative discourses of entitlement, associated with the state's 'responsibility to protect': 'social security', 'human security', etc. On the other, there are more conservative threat-based discourses, mistrustful of change, fearful of others, and protective of established interests: 'national security', 'regime security', 'security from terror', etc. Matters are complicated by the fact that such threat-based discourses are often dressed up in the language of global enlightenment. 'International security' and 'collective security' are widely (and rightly) seen as desirable in a conflict-torn and insecure world. But at the same time, they tend to be structured around the interests of the powerful, who are able to define who and what are seen as 'threats' to the global order.

For all the talk about the corrosive impacts of globalisation, that global order still to a considerable extent revolves around the world of Westphalian nation states that began to be constructed from around the time Hobbes wrote *Leviathan*. States are as much ideological constructions as they are configurations of power and resources. Security discourses have been central to how the idea of the modern state was constructed.

First, by endorsing force as the state's distinctive prerogative its 'monopoly of legitimate violence', as Max Weber was later to phrase it in the early twentieth century.

Second, through the claim that the principal responsibility for protecting citizens and ensuring their security resides with states and the rulers of states, security is seen as a public good and is thus bound up with the distinction between public and private, state and market, which has been a distinctive feature of modern, especially capitalist, states.

Third, by elevating *raison d'état* as the defining principle of governance, meaning that rulers who deploy the coercive powers of the state for the common good cannot be held accountable by the same moral standards as their citizens (an idea increasingly challenged in democratic political systems, but still adhered to in practice by political elites).

Fourth, through the contrast drawn between peace and security within well-ordered states and the endemic international insecurity which remains the hallmark of realist accounts of international relations. This is the foundation of the distinction between 'internal' security, ensured through policing and justice systems, and the 'external' security provided by the military and intelligence apparatuses of the modern state. As Hobbes graphically described it:

> But though there had never been any time wherein particular men were in a condition of war one against another, yet in all times kings and persons of sovereign authority, because of their independency, are in

continual jealousies, and in the state and posture of gladiators, having their weapons pointing, and their eyes fixed on one another; that is, their forts, garrisons, and guns upon the frontiers of their kingdoms, and continual spies upon their neighbours, which is a posture of war.

It is, however, precisely such a view of national and international security which is now being challenged. States and indeed the entire state-system are called in question by globalisation and by new security challenges, which render realist paradigms of state security ever more incoherent. States also face unprecedented challenges to their legitimacy and capacity to govern – above all, but not only, in 'failing' or 'collapsed' states. Even major powers are not immune, despite a 'Revolution in Military Affairs', which supposedly endowed them with flexible, precise, and deadly instruments of coercion, optimising use of new information technologies. Their capacity to resolve global security issues by overwhelming displays of military force has been mercilessly exposed in Iraq, Afghanistan, and other imperial wars. At the same time, new visions of human security, human development, and a rights-based international order have sprung up to dispute the entire moral basis of state sovereignty, security, and international relations.

Linked to this is the increasing privatisation of security and security provision at a number of levels: the growth of global markets in military and security goods and services; the subcontracting of core security functions, even by global military powers like the USA; global firms which subcontract the protection of their installations to state security bodies as well as private military companies; the growth of private security firms and gated communities offering protection to the middle classes; 'conflict' resources driving civil wars; the emergence of military/security entrepreneurs for whom insecurity has become a source of employment and profit; and the erosion of weak states and their national boundaries by flows of weapons, combatants, and 'conflict resources' across national boundaries. The factors driving these changes are complex and multi-layered. What is crucial is how they create new articulations between states and markets, and weaken the traditional distinctions between the public and the private spheres, and between 'internal' and 'external' security, on which state practice and security discourse in modern states has been based.

Even so, it would be premature to celebrate the decline of the state, or the irrelevance of military force, or the demise of realist paradigms of international security. While contested as never before, all three remain entrenched in global politics, in the security practices of powerful states, and in international law. Even those who hold that states have a 'sovereign responsibility to protect' citizens of their own and other states from violence, rights abuses, and acute insecurity, presuppose the continuing relevance of a world of sovereign states.

Indeed critics of this view argue, to the contrary, that the discourse and practice of security have increasingly tended to 'securitise' development, forging new 'regimes of truth' around the security–development nexus. Having been banished by neo-liberal development paradigms from the development realm, the state is being smuggled back in under the 'security and development' rubric.

Security's discursive energy still partly derives from its association with state and military power, and it is reinforced by the logic of *raison d'état,* which has been enjoying a resurgence, for instance in the current erosion of civil liberties in Western states. When development problems, like extreme poverty, population displacement, or bad governance, are labelled as security threats, they are assigned crisis status, seeming to require emergency action – which may extend to the 'humanitarian' use of force by the international community, or by powerful states claiming to act on its behalf.

The concept of 'securitisation' has been popularised to describe this process of labelling (see, for instance, Duffield 2001). It implies first that 'hard' military and state security concerns tend to prevail over the 'soft' concerns of human and collective security. And second that security discourse tends to colonise and appropriate other discourses, including those of development, governance, democracy, and humanitarian and human rights, which are considered to be defining attributes of 'global liberal governance'.

There is much in the present international context that might seem to justify such an analysis. Yet it is somewhat one-dimensional. Security not only has multiple definitions, but these have become the epicentre of protracted contests over meaning, in turn rooted in global, regional, and national struggles for power, wealth, and resources. These discursive struggles are by no means always settled in favour of the dominant realist security paradigms. Indeed they have become more intense, precisely because of the crisis of confidence in existing global, regional, and national security arrangements. This crisis of confidence has in turn inspired a number of alternative conceptualisations of security, challenging state-centred paradigms, and beginning to re-centre security around the safety and welfare of citizens and human beings.

These struggles over the meaning of security are reflected in the multiplicity of interlinked yet discordant security discourses, sketched out below. Each of the conceptualisations has two faces, the reverse side of which is spelt out in italics.

International security: the outer gaze of the modern state

- States exist in an international system of states; hence national security and international security are mutually dependent.
- The architecture of the international system, including the UN, is still largely built on the building block of the sovereign state.
- Clubs are trumps: we still inhabit a Hobbesian world of force and threats to use force.
- Insecurity and unregulated violence are endemic in inter-state relations.

- Security discourse remains dominated by the language of fear and threats.
- Realist and neo-realist theories of security remain the dominant way of thinking about international relations.

- *Attempts to ensure international security are constantly undercut by 'security dilemmas' – i.e. the pursuit of security by accumulating military power. This encourages military competition and is a source of insecurity in its own right.*
- *The international state system in practice prioritises the security of the most powerful states.*
- *Purely state-centred security is increasingly inadequate in a globalised world of complex interdependence.*
- *It is also weakened by the privatisation of security provision and the emergence of global markets in security goods and services.*
- *'New' threats and insecurities, such as terrorism or resource insecurities, traverse national boundaries, and are increasingly difficult to manage within a state-centred paradigm.*
- *States are increasingly constrained by international law, as well as by international and regional institutions.*

National security: the inner gaze of the modern state

- National security remains rooted in Weberian conceptions of the state: territorial control; politics as 'power backed up by violence'; the state's 'monopoly of the legitimate use of physical force'.
- States (even democratic ones) are in many respects national security states, with their authority buttressed by coercion and surveillance.
- State and nation building remain priorities, especially in the developing world.
- Political order and stability tend to take precedence over social transformation, rights, and justice.
- Neo-mercantilism and national security go hand in hand: national security and national development are in synergy.
- National security tends to be structured around changing economic models, including (latterly) neo-liberalism.

- *Military power by itself is an insecure foundation for state power: 'despotic' power is less sustainable than 'infrastructural' power (i.e. state capacity to provide public goods and manage development).*
- *States themselves may be called into question by violent conflict or state fragility.*
- *State security institutions can themselves become agents of insecurity.*
- *State building is insufficient when not founded upon legitimate public authority and an active political and civil society.*
- *State security and development priorities may conflict.*

- *States may be undermined by economic vulnerabilities (including dependence on donors) as well as military insecurity.*
- *Both national security and development policy tend to be subverted by market forces and networks of power beyond the state, e.g. flows of weapons and conflict resources.*

Security as hegemonic project

- Hegemonic security is characteristic of a world of unequal states, and is also linked to unequal concentrations of corporate wealth and power.
- Hegemony reflects global shifts, such as the transition from Cold War bipolarity to unipolar or multipolar order.
- Military power by itself is not enough to ensure dominance, hence it tends to be reinforced by other hegemonic practices, including 'soft' (ideological, media, economic etc.) power.
- 'Soft power' tends to deploy international security, humanitarianism, human rights, and democratic governance as legitimising discourses.

- *Hard and soft power are not necessarily mutually reinforcing: they may also conflict (e.g. the role of Western media in criticising the US-led intervention in Iraq).*
- *Collisions tend to emerge between new forms of global hegemony and new forms of resistance, as in the 'war on terror'.*
- *Weapons of the weak, including terrorism and other forms of asymmetric conflict, create new security challenges. These are not easily contained by the conventional instruments of military power.*
- *The spread of democracy, human rights, and international humanitarianism – sometimes deployed as instruments of 'soft power' – also open spaces in which to challenge security-dominated conceptions of the state and of international relations.*

'Common' or 'collective' security: a global public good

- Ideas of common security are linked to global development and to North–South collaboration (as in the recent UN Reports, *A More Secure World* and *In Larger Freedom*).
- They imply collective action based on shared goals, rather than zero-sum competition.
- They also link the instruments of security policy to those of economic policy (trade, development co-operation, etc.).
- Common security is associated with other global public goods: international development, environmental sustainability, tackling health pandemics like HIV and AIDS, etc.
- It is also reinforced by the growth of international law and institutions (UN, EU, regional bodies).

- The media have fostered conceptions of a global village in which human suffering and insecurity are of concern to all.
- Common security is framed in a discourse of universal human rights and entitlements, as are the discourses of democracy and international humanitarianism.
- It gives legitimacy to new forms of international co-operation, including conflict prevention, peace building, and post-conflict reconstruction.

- *Insecurity and violent conflict are also being globalised, being sustained by markets in conflict goods and resources and by new actors (e.g. terrorists).*
- *Common security remains problematic in a world where states lack sustained commitment to it.*
- *Unilateralism has tended to undermine multilateralism in a global order shaped by the security concerns of a single superpower.*
- *Collective-action problems are inherent and very difficult to overcome: it is hard in practice to guarantee international commitment to common goals, still more to implement them.*
- *Common security is undermined by powerful economic and political forces sustaining violent conflicts and insecurity.*
- *Global institutions and collective action are constrained by huge global inequalities in wealth, power, and military capabilities.*
- *In such a global context, it may be argued that common security and 'global liberal governance' reinforce new forms of global hegemony.*

Security as the state's 'sovereign responsibility to protect': a national public good

- Security cannot be provided by citizens acting on their own, or purchasing it on the market.
- It is grounded in the Hobbesian social contract between state and citizen, which implies the state's 'sovereign responsibility to protect'.
- Legitimate public authority is of the essence, thus implicitly connecting security and democracy.
- Security is embedded in public order, the rule of law, and a 'well-policed state'.
- Security is thus also an aspect of governance: in principle the same principles of public accountability apply to security institutions as to other state institutions.
- If states fail to exercise their 'sovereign responsibility to protect', the international community can and should step in as provider of security to the poor, marginalised, and oppressed.

- *In practice, security tends to be a very imperfect public good: it is top–down, unequally distributed, and harnessed to the interests of elites.*

- *It is also undermined by the privatisation of violence, including new networks of power and profit working around the state, together with the spread of conflicts across national boundaries.*
- *The failure of weak or repressive states to exercise their 'sovereign responsibility to protect' opens the door to potentially problematic humanitarian military interventions.*

Security as risk-management: new topologies of threat and risk

- Security is increasingly redefined in terms of widened conceptions of risk: economic, resource, environmental, health-related, etc., and the actual or assumed inter-connections among them.
- Such risks tend to be perceived as existential threats to human survival, calling for collective action by the international community.
- These expanded conceptions of security link to conceptions of human security (see below).

- *'Securitisation' – the discursive interpretation of such risks as security threats, rather than shared global problems requiring collective action – tends to be problematic.*
- *This entails the risk that anti-terrorism agendas may distort development goals.*
- *Neo-Malthusianism rides again: security is re-framed in terms of competition for resources, and is seen as source of new anarchy.*
- *Blowback: insecurities in the developing South are reframed as threats to the developed North – through resource scarcities, refugees, disease pandemics, and terrorism.*

'Human security': as an entitlement of citizens; and of human beings

- Human security posits a fundamental challenge to state-centric views of security, as well as those prioritising the threat or use of force.
- It prioritises protection of individuals from crime and violence, including state violence.
- It is conceptually rooted in ideas of democratic citizenship and human rights.
- It implies the state's 'sovereign responsibility to protect' citizens from insecurity, violence, and poverty.
- Security from day-to-day violence interconnects with security from famine, disease, displacement, and the other risks suffered by individuals and communities.
- Human security implies action to redress insecurities associated with gender and other marginalised identities.
- It implies collective action by citizens, whether to put pressure on the state, or to organise to provide their own security.

- *There are potential conflicts between citizen and human security (e.g. of refugees and other non-citizens).*
- *Collective action to improve human security tends to be constrained and distorted by social, political, and economic inequalities.*
- *Ideas about universal and citizens' entitlements often become problematic in identity conflicts, where citizens may be pitted against each other, interpreting group differences as threats.*
- *It is enormously difficult to ensure accountability for failure to provide human security when states fail or are absent, and individuals suffer exploitation and violence at the hands of non-state armed and criminal groups.*

'Security and development' as a new donor discourse

- 'Security and development' has emerged as a new orthodoxy among donors and international NGOs, linked to increasingly interventionist promotion of economic and political liberalisation and of 'good governance'.
- New donor-policy instrumentalities like 'security sector reform' and (in post-conflict states) 'disarmament, demobilisation, and reintegration' (DDR) are used to reconstruct military and security institutions in order to deliver security not insecurity.
- Democratic oversight and rule of law become benchmarks for the governance of security.
- Security for the poor is prioritised and linked to public safety, policing, and access to justice.
- The international 'responsibility to protect' citizens of failing and repressive states is used to legitimise humanitarian intervention, including the use of force.
- 'Peace building' and 'post-conflict reconstruction' have entered the vocabulary of aid agencies and NGOs, and have become new sites of donor intervention.

- *However, deep problems of collective action arise where donors and local stakeholders lack shared goals, interests, and procedures.*
- *Donor leverage is often much less than it appears in the complex political and economic landscape of post-conflict states.*
- *Potentially perverse consequences arise from humanitarian aid and intervention, sometimes including the perpetuation of conflicts.*
- *Security-sector reform, DDR, etc. tend to challenge elite control of the state – and hence tend to be resisted, or implemented half-heartedly, or co-opted by elites.*
- *Post-conflict reconstruction takes place in a highly contested political arena in which donor goals may be mutually inconsistent, as well as conflicting with local interests.*

- *The presence of powerful market and political forces (e.g. natural-resource exploitation, global and regional markets in conflict-related goods, privatised violence) often subverts peace building.*
- *There is an ever-present risk that humanitarian and development agendas may be co-opted to serve the security goals and economic interests of powerful states and global corporations.*
- *Development, human rights, humanitarianism, democracy, etc. tend to be discursively represented as ideological building blocks for a hegemonic conception of global liberal governance.*

Conclusion

This brief summary of the multiple meanings of security prompts three central observations. First, 'security' by itself is too general a word to have much meaning. It is usually linked to qualifying terms locating it in particular discursive practices: 'international' security, 'national' security, 'human' security, and so on. Second, although it contains an implicit claim that security is a value and thus normatively desirable, one should always ask *whose* security and *from whom or what?* This tends to be answered in different ways in varying security discourses. Security is not and cannot be neutral. It is both public good and private asset. It follows, third, that it is always contested, always disputed, and shot through with contradictions.

References

DFID (2005) *Fighting Poverty to Build a Safer World: A Strategy for Security and Development*, London: Department for International Development.

Duffield, Mark (2001) *Global Governance and the New Wars: The Merging of Development and Security*, London: Zed Books.

Independent Commission on International Development Issues (1980) *North–South: A Programme for Survival* (The Brandt Report), London: Pan Books.

Independent Commission on Disarmament and Security Issues (1982) *Common Security: A Blueprint for Survival* (The Palme Report), New York, NY: Simon & Schuster.

United Nations (2004) *A More Secure World: Our Shared Responsibility*, Report of the Secretary-General's High-Level Panel on Threats, Challenges and Change (A59/565), presented at the UN General Assembly, New York, 2 December.

About the author

Robin Luckham is a Research Associate of the Institute of Development Studies (IDS) at the University of Sussex. A political sociologist, he has written extensively on militarism and democracy in sub-Saharan Africa.

CHAPTER 28
Fragile states

Eghosa E. Osaghae

Since the 1990s, states that lack the capacity to discharge their normal functions and drive forward development have been referred to as 'fragile states'. This chapter focuses on Africa, which not only has the largest concentration of prototypical fragile states, but has been the focus of attention for scholars, international development agencies, and practitioners. The author reviews competing analyses of the post-colonial African state and concludes that its characteristics of weak institutions, poverty, social inequalities, corruption, civil strife, armed conflicts, and civil war are not original conditions, but are rooted in specific historical contexts. It is essential to understand both the external and internal factors of fragility if such states are to get the assistance and empowerment that they need – not only for the benefit of their impoverished citizens, but also for the sake of global peace, prosperity, and security. Ultimately, it is the citizens of the countries concerned who are responsible for determining when states are no longer fragile – not 'benevolent' donors and the international community, whose prime motivation for interventions supposedly to strengthen the state is to ensure that fragile states find their 'rightful' places in the hegemonic global order.

The development process and state fragility

The image of the state as a powerful and overarching entity that effectively controls a geo-political domain has influenced the key agency roles assigned to it in development discourse (Evans *et al.* 1985). This is true whether the state is conceived as a centralised organisational structure, a sovereign whose decisions are binding, an instrument of coercion and domination, or an engine of growth and development. When one thinks of the state as the mainstay of political order (with economic and social order in tow), the agency roles are justifiable. The problem is that the state has not always been able to play the roles expected of it. It is precisely for this reason that the Third World state has attracted a great deal of attention in development discourses.

This chapter discusses the meaning and historicity of the 'fragile state', a concept that has gained currency in development discourses since the 1990s, characterised as distressed states that generally lack the capacity to discharge the functions traditionally associated with them and to drive forward development. While the image of fragility is historically associated with the Third World in general, the focus here is mainly on Africa. The continent not only has the largest concentration of prototypical fragile states but has also received the greatest attention of scholars, international development agencies, and practitioners. This is partly because, as Laasko and Olukoshi (1997:8) put it, 'it is perhaps in Africa, more than in other parts of the world, that the crisis of the nation-state project has been most obvious and overwhelming' (see also Davidson 1992; Zartman 1995).

The concept of fragile states

The search for how to characterise and possibly remedy problematic and troublesome states has provided the context for the evolution of the concept of fragile states, which has been popularised by the World Bank and the international development community since the early 1990s.[1] The dominance of World Bank and donor perspectives of state fragility have not always tallied with local perspectives, making it necessary to adopt a more discerning and critical (some would add balanced) approach to the interrogation of fragile states. In general, the concept of fragile states may be regarded as an all-encompassing summation of the pathologies of problematic states that have over the years been variously described as *weak, soft, overdeveloped, illegitimate, poor, irrelevant, de-rooted, rogue, collapsed,* and *failed,* each description attempting to capture one or a few problematic elements. As with other development concepts, fragility and its associated descriptive terms are relative. In this case, they suggest deviance and aberration from the dominant and supposedly universal (but Western) paradigm of the state, which played a key role in the development of capitalism.

The relativity of state fragility makes it an empirical rather than normative construct (Jackson and Rosberg 1982). Conventional wisdom defines the state in terms of four core attributes: defined territory, population, government, and recognition by other states. The first three constitute the empirical referents, and the fourth constitutes the juridical. A state is expected to be effective on all counts: establish strong and effective institutions; control and defend its territory; have a stable, loyal, and cohesive population; exercise sovereign and legitimate power within its territory and possess the resources to ensure the well-being of its citizens; and, finally, enjoy the recognition and respect of other states as a credible member of the global community. The changing realities and paradigm shifts of the post-Cold War period have seen further elaboration and extension of these attributes to include good governance variables (strong and effective political institutions and civil society, democracy, rule of law, accountability, transparency, conflict management) and the material correlates of just and equitable resource management, poverty alleviation, and economic growth and development.

A fragile state, in contrast, may be defined as a distressed state that lacks the elements necessary to function effectively. Specifically, fragile states are characterised by one or more of the following:

- Weak, ineffective, and unstable political institutions and bad governance, conducive to loss of state autonomy, informalisation, privatisation of state, personal and exclusionary rule, neo-patrimonialism, and prebendal politics.
- Inability to exercise effective jurisdiction over its territory, leading to the recent concept of 'ungoverned territories'.
- Legitimacy crisis, occasioned by problematic national cohesion, contested citizenship, violent contestation for state power, perennial challenges to the validity and viability of the state, and massive loss and exit of citizens through internal displacement, refugee flows, separatist agitation, civil war and the like.
- Unstable and divided population, suffering from a torn social fabric, minimum social control, and pervasive strife that encourage exit from rather than loyalty to the state. Underdeveloped institutions of conflict management and resolution, including credible judicial structures, which pave the way for recourse to conflict-ridden, violent, non-systemic and extra-constitutional ways in which to articulate grievances and seek redress.
- Pervasive corruption, poverty, and low levels of economic growth and development, leading to lack of fiscal capacity to discharge basic functions of statehood, including, most importantly, obligations to citizens such as protection from diseases like AIDS and guarantees of overall human security.[2]

With these characteristics, especially the stress of mal-governance and poverty as well as violent contestations of citizenship and statehood – which typically produce civil war, armed conflict, population displacement, and refugee and humanitarian problems – fragile states 'muddle through' at best, and constantly face the threat of collapse, break-up, or disintegration. As Jackson and Rosberg (1982) found from their study, extremely fragile states – like Somalia or Sierra Leone – collapsed at different points in time, but remained states only in name and because of their extant recognition by international law. Chabal and Daloz (1999) suggest that political disorder may be less a consequence of state fragility than a political instrument employed by the power-holding elite. So, rather than a pathology or aberration, disorder (in the form of weak institutions, informalisation of political processes, legitimacy crisis, civil strife, armed conflict) may very well be a deliberate strategy of politics in fragile states. (See also Bayart *et al.* 1999.)

The instability of fragile states and the stress that they impose on neighbouring states and the international community through refugee flows and proliferation of small arms make them a threat to global peace, security, and prosperity (Stiglitz 2003; Chua 2004). Two further factors reinforce the threat posed by fragile states. The first is that with the heightening of global economic inequalities, the number of states judged by the World Bank to be 'fragile' has almost doubled: from 14 to 26 between 2000 and 2006 (World

Bank 2006), of which 14 are in sub-Saharan Africa. The other factor is neglect of the plight of poor states by the international community. The failure of the United Nations and other key global actors to respond promptly to civil wars in Rwanda, Liberia, Chad, Côte d'Ivoire, Somalia, and Sudan (Darfur) contributed in large measure to state collapse and fragility-inducing stress inflicted on neighbouring countries. Direct foreign investment and flows to distressed states, especially in Africa, have remained very low, ostensibly because of the high risk of doing business there. While these reasons can be rationalised in terms of the competitiveness of the global economy, the point remains that global peace and security calls for greater will and commitment on the part of the international development community.

The historicity of fragile states

Although the concept of fragile states gained currency in the 1990s, it represents some kind of old wine in a new bottle. The phenomenon that it describes has a history that is almost as old as the contemporary – or post-colonial – state in the Third World (Osagahae 1999a; 2005). Two periods of engagement can be distinguished. The first began at independence and spanned the period of the Cold War. In this period, state structural disabilities (weak and fragile institutions, authoritarian tendencies, weak economies, contested nationhood, armed conflicts, separatist agitations, over-dependence on foreign aid, susceptibility to external shocks) were recognised, but the circumstances of the Cold War assured such states a great deal of understanding and support, even if they left debilitating foreign debt in their wake. The second period of engagement covers the years from the end of the Cold War at the end of the 1980s to the present. Its hallmark was a deterioration of the material conditions of most developing countries and the capacities of their states to promote and consolidate development, leaving states more vulnerable to external shocks and interventions. This was accompanied by the increased tendency to treat the state as an independent or autonomous system and deny the externalities of its problems (Herbst 1996/1997). The triumph of (neo-)liberalism saw the emergence of a new more hegemonic and interventionist global order, whose major pastime became whipping deviant states into line.

Gone are the indulgences of the Cold War era. Here instead is a regime that seeks to reproduce the liberal state through political, economic, and social reforms imposed as conditionalities and benchmarks by the World Bank, IMF, and the international development community, and at times through military intervention. This hegemonic character of global politics, which has elicited counter-revolutionary mobilisation on a global scale, including terrorism, also makes global peace and security a key objective of interventions. These elements have led to a rethinking of the state that is not shy of considering dissolution of 'troublesome' states. Kothari (1988) captures this new thinking in a thesis of 'dispensability', which he believes informs the new agenda for a world order in which the fruits of progress can be held secure for certain privileged regions of the world. The thesis is as follows:

> Certain states, communities and regions...have become an unacceptable burden on the world economy. These segments are incapable and unwilling to mend their ways. They subsist as parasites on the rest of the world. To allow their continued existence as parasites...would gravely endanger the health and future of the world economy. They must be dispensed with, and left to fend for themselves. (Kothari 1988: 4–5)

Kothari may have stated the thesis in rather strong terms, but it does reflect the realities of engagement with fragile states in the post-Cold War era. The pressure is on states to salvage themselves, discharge their obligations to donors and benefactors, and meet set targets such as the Millennium Development Goals (MDGs) under the guidance of the World Bank, IMF, and other champions of neo-liberalism or be left out of the active and competitive global system. Notions of self-inflicted marginalisation, Afro-pessimism, and 'basket cases', which African states have worked hard to dispel, tell part of the story – as do the closures of entry to affluent societies to economic migrants from poor and conflict-torn countries, which make it incumbent on the states to get their acts together. Unlike the Cold War period, scholars, development practitioners, and donors no longer seem willing to help fragile states to survive at all costs. This raises the stakes.

Let us now turn to examine the hows and whys of fragility. For this purpose we must move beyond the mere empirical characterisations and typologies that have dominated World Bank/IMF perspectives to analyse the bases of fragility. While it is true that fragile states are low-income and poorly governed, with a high prevalence of corruption, poverty, food insecurity, malnutrition, and disease, and prone to violent conflict and war, these attributes do not in and of themselves explain why they are fragile. In other words, state fragility is a dependent variable and not an independent or original condition. Migdal et al. (1994: 2) identify society and the socio-economic determinants of politics as key in this regard, because 'societies affect states as much as, or perhaps more than, states affect societies'. To these we shall add external forces that have historically shaped state and social formations in the Third World.

Exploring the bases of fragility

The deviant, non-conventional, and unique characters of state formations in the Third World have long been recognised. Major signposts include the initial 'discovery' of non-Western state systems, which necessitated the formulation of new tools and concepts of analysis. It has been argued that, because of its epochal effects, colonialism is the most important explanatory factor for the unique trajectory of state growth in the Third World and the subsequent problems, the bottom line being that the state model was imported wholesale and imposed on erstwhile colonies (Ekeh 1975, 1983; Alavi

1979; Young 1994). The failure to properly graft or adapt the 'migrated' state structures to the circumstances of the colony and post-colony is said to have created a disjunctive duality between state and society that left the state suspended above society like a balloon (Hyden 1980).

This was the context within which fragile states evolved. The first set of problems concerned the nature of the colonial state itself. It remained aloof from indigenous or native society and enforced its will through violence and repression, placing emphasis on the rudiments of law and order that were sufficient to ensure economic exploitation and uphold the standards of European settlers (Young 1994). A second set of problems arose from the nature of relations between the state and (native) society, as well as the anomalies of the migration of state structures from Europe. As many scholars have argued, it became impossible for the 'natives' to appropriate the state, which they perceived as alien and serving the interests of the coloniser and not those of the colonised (Ake 1985; Davidson 1992; Osaghae 1989, 1999a). This gave rise to the endemic legitimacy crisis that marooned the colonial state and its post-colonial successor.

The overall relevance of the state for the citizens was always a contested issue (Ihonvbere 1994). This encouraged exit and opposition by alienated, marginalised, and excluded segments, and the development of shadow state structures, mainly communal self-help organisations which emerged to fill the void left by state failure (Osaghae 1999b). For Alavi (1979), the fact that the social formations of the colony upon which migrated state structures were imposed were at a lower level of development than in Metropolitan Europe meant that the state was 'overdeveloped'. Overdevelopment gave the state the appearance of powerfulness, but its 'omnipresence' did not translate into 'omnipotence' (Chazan 1988). Young (1994) attributes the crisis of national cohesion, one of the defining elements of state fragility, to the fact that the imported state lacked the nationhood that had defined and underpinned its growth in Europe. This was why nationalism, the avowed ideology of cohesion, overarching loyalty to the central state, and self-determination were unable to salvage the state as had been expected.

Opinions are divided on the significance of colonialism for subsequent state fragility in Africa. Ake (1985) suggests that what happened at independence was a changing of the guard, rather than a change in the character of the state which, by the nature of its peripheral formation and integration into the global system, was an appendage of the dominant centres. Ekeh (1983) questions the validity of episodic perspectives, which consider the period of colonialism too limited in Africa's long history to have the kinds of epochal effect claimed for it. Post-colonial states have, it has been argued, shown a great deal of diversity and unevenness in their abilities to cope with the challenges of development, which suggests that factors other than colonialism have to be examined in order to explain state fragility. Why, for instance, have the Asian tigers succeeded and the African states failed? Why has Botswana done well, and Nigeria and Ghana have not?

Yet others argue that the focus on colonialism distracts attention from autochthonous factors. The argument that then follows is that the pathologies of the state in the Third World, especially the African species, are partly – and in some cases largely – endemic to indigenous formations. Contrary to the suggestion that the colonial and post-colonial states were artificial, Bayart (1991: 53) argues that they 'were built upon their own social foundations'. Similarly, Chabal and Daloz (1999:4) have pointed out that 'the state in Africa was never properly institutionalised because it was never significantly emancipated from [indigenous] society'. The import of these claims is that corruption, violent politics, bad governance, and other fragile state variables are products of the appropriation of the state by autochthonous forces. The point missed by Bayart and others, however, is that the acts of state creation, including the determination of boundaries, were undertaken by European colonisers and were not negotiated with the colonised. It is in this sense that the states are regarded as artificial. The other point missed by Bayart and others is that the so-called indigenous social structures that survived under colonialism were actually *transformed indigenous structures*, having undergone changes of epochal magnitude during the colonial encounter. What colonialism did was to turn society upside down and inside out (Ekeh 1983). The post-colonial indigenous sector is no different: it is a product of the encounters with powerful forces of globalisation that have created 'states of disarray' (UNRISD 1995; Osaghae 2005).

Colonialism certainly laid the foundations for externalities and disarticulations that have cumulatively since independence tended to disable rather than strengthen the state (Bose 2004). The devastating effects of Cold War interventions linger on. In the post-Cold War period, states in the Third World have fared much worse. Economic and political reforms, especially structural adjustment programmes, have demonstrably weakened their economies and governments, and raised the stakes of what is now popularly known as the National Question, precipitating authoritarianism, anti-state mobilisations, armed conflicts and civil war (Gibbon *et al.* 1992; van de Walle 2001). The distorted structures and practices of the WTO, as well as the double standards and barricades erected by the USA and other leading industrialised countries, have restricted exports, encouraged dumping and smuggling, and slowed down industrial and economic growth in peripheral formations. Huge foreign debts have also limited the options available to fragile states.

None of this absolves fragile states of blame. The fact that many states in the Third World remain afloat and have in fact been effective drivers of the development process in spite of the common historical trajectories means that we must also look inwards at internal cultural, social, economic, and political factors in order to explain the phenomenon of fragile states. Clearly, problems such as poor resources and the 'mono-crop' nature of economies which depend on only one agricultural or mineral commodity, weak and fragile institutions, bad governance variables, corruption, 'politics of the belly', high unemployment, food insecurity, patrimonialism and tendencies toward personal authoritarian rule, poor management of the public domain, capital flight, brain drain, social inequalities occasioned by unequal and discriminatory citizenship, high incidence of violent crimes, and underdevelopment of structures of conflict management and resolution are internally located and, notwithstanding the externalities that may attend them, have to be resolved from within.

There is an even more important reason why there should be a closer focus on the internal dynamics of fragile states than on externalities. This is the fact that the states have been the sites of popular struggles by coalitions of citizens and civil society, which seek to redeem and salvage the state through appropriation and ownership to make it an effective manager of development. In Africa, these struggles have been analysed in terms of the first (anti-colonial) and second (anti-authoritarian state) liberation or independence movements (Ekeh 1997; Osaghae 2005). The objective of these movements 'is to transform the state in such a way that it becomes an ally rather than an obstacle in the democratisation [and development] process' (Nzongola-Ntalaja and Lee 1997:8). The implication of the local struggles 'from below' is that the definition and turnaround of fragile states is not all about what the World Bank/IMF, donors, and the international development community think or do, which is substantially the case at present. As has happened in one or two cases (Ghana and Uganda readily come to mind), the danger in such one-sidedness is the possible disconnection between the evaluation of the World Bank/IMF and donors and that of the citizens and local coalitions. Thus Ghana and Uganda were judged by the Bank to be reform success cases in the 1990s, but the citizens of both countries thought otherwise because their material conditions did not show any remarkable improvement and, as a consequence, the anti-state struggles persisted. The need for synergy between the dominant and hegemonic global actors and local constituents in the engagement with fragile states cannot be overemphasised.

Conclusion

The concept of fragile states is appropriate for characterising problematic and troublesome states that have potential not only to self-destruct but also to endanger global peace, prosperity, and security. As an empirical construct, it is valid and is therefore likely to remain a development buzzword for some time to come. It does not have the ideological image and baggage of *rogue state*, for example, or the finality of the *failed or collapsed state*, and offers a 'window of opportunity' for redemption and strengthening if the right diagnosis is made and appropriate medicines are administered, which is the framework within which the World Bank/IMF and international development partners ought to be engaging fragile states. However, this conceptual logic has not been followed through for at least two reasons.

First, 'fragile states' remains a characterisation or typological construct, and the assumption is that the pathologies of such states are inherent to deviant statehood. But certainly, weak institutions, poverty, social inequalities, corruption, civil strife, armed conflicts, and civil war cannot be and are not original conditions. Second, the failure to historicise state fragility and to assign the full weight of externalities and externally induced disarticulations has so far prepared the ground for wrong therapies. The tendency to ignore the local/internal conceptions of state fragility and the struggles to redeem them, and the preference for curtailment or possible elimination of the threat potential of fragile states (through isolation or military intervention or outright neglect and indifference, for instance), which is the essence of the dispensability thesis advanced by Kothari and discussed earlier, misses the point about superpower complicity that can only be remedied through composite global–local action. The argument in this chapter is that the external and internal factors of fragility have to be fully interrogated if these countries are to get the kind of assistance and empowerment that they so clearly deserve – at least for the sake of global peace, prosperity, and security, if not for that of the impoverished citizens of fragile states. But, ultimately, the responsibility for determining when states are no longer fragile is that of the citizens of the countries concerned and not that of 'benevolent' donors and the international development community, whose prime motivation for supposed state-strengthening interventions is to ensure that fragile states take their 'rightful' places in the hegemonic global order.

Notes

1. Some of the major publications which marked the 'entry' of fragile states from a substantially African perspective include the World Bank's *World Development Reports* (from 1988), *Sub-Saharan Africa: From Crisis to Sustainable Growth* (1989) and *Governance and Development* (1992); Migdal (1988), Wunsch and Olowu (1990), Joseph (1990), Hyden and Bratton (1992) and Zartman (1995).
2. Among others, Myrdal (1968) analysed the *soft* state, which he defined as a state that is unable to enforce its will, especially in areas which demand moral rectitude (see also Rothchild 1987); Ekeh (1975) interrogated the evolution and interactions of the *two publics* in Africa; Alavi (1979) examined the *overdeveloped* state. Others have analysed the *weak state* (Migdal 1988), *weak leviathan* (Callaghy 1987), *neopatrimonial* statehood (Bratton and van de Walle 1994), centralisation and powerlessness (Kohli 1994), governance and politics (Hyden and Bratton 1992), prebendal politics (Joseph 1987), and *politics of the belly* (Bayart 1993).

References

Ake, C. (1985) *Political Economy of Nigeria*, Lagos: Longman.
Alavi, H. (1979) 'The state in post-colonial societies: Pakistan and Bangladesh', in H. Goulbourne (ed.), *Politics and State in the Third World*, London: Macmillan.

Bayart, J.-F. (1991) 'Finishing with the idea of the Third World: the concept of the political trajectory', in J. Manor (ed.) *Rethinking Third World Politics*, London: Longman.

Bayart, J.-F. (1993) *The State in Africa: The Politics of the Belly*, London: Longman.

Bayart, J.-F., S. Ellis, S. and B. Hibou (1999) *Criminalization of the State in Africa*, Oxford: James Currey.

Bose, S. (2004) 'De-colonization and state building in South Asia', *Journal of International Affairs* 58(1): 95–113.

Bratton, M. and N. van de Walle (1994) 'Neopatrimonial regimes and political transitions in Africa', *World Politics* 46: 453–89.

Callaghy, T. (1987) 'The state as a lame leviathan: the patrimonial-administrative state in Africa', in Z. Ergas (ed.) *African State in Transition*, London: Macmillan.

Chabal, P. and J. Daloz (1999) *Africa Works: Disorder as Political Instrument*, Oxford: James Currey.

Chazan, N. (1988) 'State and society in Africa: images and challenges', in D. Rothchild and N. Chazan (eds.) *The Precarious Balance: The State and Society in Africa*, Boulder, CO: Westview.

Chua, A. (2004) *World on Fire: How Exporting Free Market Democracy Breeds Ethnic Hatred and Global Instability*, New York, NY: Anchor Books.

Davidson, B. (1992) *The Black Man's Burden: Africa and the Curse of the Nation-State*, London: James Currey.

Ekeh, P.P. (1975) 'Colonialism and the two publics in Africa: a theoretical statement', *Comparative Studies in Society and History* 17(1): 91–112.

Ekeh, P.P. (1983) *Colonialism and Social Structure in Africa: An Inaugural Lecture*, Ibadan: Ibadan University Press.

Ekeh, P.P. (1997) 'The concept of second liberation and the prospects of democracy in Africa: a Nigerian context', in P. Beckett and C. Young (eds.) *Dilemmas of Democratization in Nigeria*, Rochester, NY: University of Rochester Press.

Evans, P., D. Reuschmeyer, and T. Skocpol (eds.) (1985) *Bringing the State Back In*, Cambridge: Cambridge University Press.

Gibbon, P., Y. Bangura, and A. Ofstad (eds.) (1992) *Authoritarianism, Democracy and Adjustment: The Politics of Economic Reform in Africa*, Uppsala: Nordiska Afrkainstitutet.

Herbst, J. (1996/1997) 'Responding to state failure in Africa', *International Security* 21(4): 120–144.

Hyden, G. (1980) *Beyond Ujamaa in Tanzania*, London: Heinemann.

Hyden, G. and M. Bratton (eds.) (1992) *Governance and Politics in Africa*, Boulder, CO: Lynne Rienner.

Ihonvbere, J.O. (1994) 'The "irrelevant" state, ethnicity and the quest for nationhood in Africa', *Ethnic and Racial Studies*, 17(1): 42–60.

Jackson, R.H. and C. G. Rosberg (1982) 'Why Africa's weak states persist: the empirical and the juridical in statehood', *World Politics* 35(1): 1–24.

Joseph, R.A. (1987) *Democracy and Prebendal Politics in Nigeria: The Rise and Fall of the Second Republic*, Cambridge: Cambridge University Press.

Joseph. R.A. (1990) *African Governance in the 1990s*, Atlanta, GA: Carter Center.

Kohli, A. (1994) 'Centralization and powerlessness: India's democracy in a comparative perspective', in J.S.Midgal, A. Kohli, and V. Shue (eds.).

Kothari, R. (1988) *State Against Democracy: In Search of Humane Governance*, New Delhi: Ajanta Publications.

Laasko, L. and A. O. Olukoshi (1997) 'The crisis of the post-colonial nation-state project in Africa', in A.O. Olukoshi and L. Laasko (eds.) *Challenges to the Nation-State in Africa*, Uppsala: Nordiska Afrikainstitutet.

Migdal, J.S. (1988) *Strong Societies and Weak States: State–Society Relations and State Capabilities in the Third World*, Princeton, NJ: Princeton University Press.

Migdal, J.S., A. Kohli, A. and V. Shue (eds.) (1994) *State Power and Social Forces: Domination and Transformation in the Third World*, Cambridge: Cambridge University Press.

Myrdal, G. (1968) *Asian Drama: An Inquiry into the Poverty of Nations*, Harmondsworth: Penguin.

Nzongola-Ntalaja, G. and M. Lee (1997) 'Introduction', in G. Nzongola-Ntalaja and M. Lee (eds.) *The State and Democracy in Africa*, Harare: AAPS Books.

Osaghae, E. E. (1989) 'The character of the state, legitimacy crisis, and social mobilization in Africa: an explanation of form and character', *Africa Development*, 14(2): 27–47.

Osaghae, E. E. (1999a) 'The post-colonial African state and its problems', in P. McGowan and P. Nel (eds.) *Power, Wealth and Global Order*, Cape Town: University of Cape Town Press.

Osaghae, E. E. (1999b) 'Exiting from the state in Nigeria', *Journal of African Political Science* 4(1): 83–98.

Osaghae, E. E. (2005) 'The state of Africa's second liberation', *Interventions: International Journal of Postcolonial Studies* 7(1): 1–20.

Rothchild, D. (1987) 'Hegemony and state softness: some variations in elite responses' in Z. Ergas (ed.) *African State in Transition*, London: Macmillan.

Stiglitz, J.E. (2003) *Globalization and its Discontents*, New York, NY: WW Norton.

UNRISD (1995) *States of Disarray: The Social Effects of Globalization*, Geneva: UNRISD.

van de Walle, N. (2001) *African Economies and the Politics of Permanent Crisis, 1979–1999*, Cambridge: Cambridge University Press.

World Bank (1988–2000) *World Development Reports*, New York, NY: Oxford University Press.

World Bank (1992) *Governance and Development*, Washington, DC: World Bank.

World Bank (2006) *Engaging with Fragile States: An IEG Report of World Bank Support to Low Income Countries under Stress*, Washington, DC: World Bank.

Wunsch, J.S. and D. Olowu (1990) *The Failure of the Centralized State: Institutions and Self-Governance in Africa*, Boulder, CO: Westview.

Young, C. (1994) *The African Colonial State in Comparative Perspective*, New Haven, CT: Yale University Press.

Zartman, I.W. (1995) *Collapsed States: The Disintegration and Restoration of Legitimate Authority*, Boulder, CO: Lynne Rienner.

About the author

Eghosa E. Osaghae is Professor of Comparative Politics and Vice Chancellor of Igbinedion University in Nigeria. He has published extensively on the post-colonial state in Africa, and won the 'Best Article Award for 2004' at the 2005 African Studies Association for his article 'Political Transitions and Ethnic Conflict in Africa', published in the *Journal of Third World Studies*.

CHAPTER 29

'Knowledge management': a case study of the World Bank's research department

Robin Broad

This chapter looks at 'knowledge management', using a case study of the World Bank's research department, located in the Bank's Development Economics Vice-Presidency (DEC). Despite the Bank's presentation of its research arm as conducting 'rigorous and objective' work, the author finds that the Bank's 'knowledge management' involves research that has tended to reinforce the dominant neo-liberal globalisation policy agenda. The chapter examines some of the mechanisms by which the Bank's research department comes to play a central role in what Robert Wade has termed 'paradigm maintenance', including incentives in hiring, promotion, and publishing, as well as selective enforcement of rules, discouragement of dissonant views, and manipulation of data. The author's analysis is based both on in-depth interviews with current and former World Bank professionals and on examination of the relevant literature.

Knowledge and its management

Let me start with a confession: when I began the research project that would lead to this chapter (among others), I did not even know that the term 'knowledge management' existed. I was then and am still a professor of international development at a university in the USA. I had done a significant amount of research and writing on the international financial institutions and 'development' (buzzword alert) since I first lived in the rural Philippines in the 1970s.

It turns out that, while I was teaching and writing about such things, 'knowledge management' had become a pretty big deal in the private sector. Not only is there a growing literature on knowledge management – generically defined as 'how organizations create, retain, and share knowledge' (Cummings 2003:1) – but also there are whole publications devoted to the subject. Witness *The Journal of Knowledge Management Practice* (formerly the *Journal of Systemic Knowledge Management*) or *Inside Knowledge: The Original Knowledge-Management Publication*. The point, as the latter explains on its website, is that:

> The knowledge that exists within your organisation is your only sustainable source of competitive advantage. We believe this makes knowledge management a strategic imperative for you. But how do you ensure that

your KM initiative is effective, that it delivers on its promises and that your organisation sees a return on its KM investment?[1]

And it also turns out that the 'development industry' (buzzword? contradiction in terms?) was leaping into the 'knowledge management' arena. This, I must quickly assure you lest you stop reading, I did know. Indeed, by the late 1990s, key public institutions that 'do' development were in need of a new meta-word and meta-fix. This was especially the case at the World Bank, where then-president James Wolfensohn was presiding over an institution that needed a clearer mission to keep it centre-stage. Yes, the World Bank still had its project-lending function. And yes, the Bank still had its focus on making sure that recipient countries structurally adjusted to the 'correct' set of neo-liberal macro-economic policies.[2] But the problem was that its central role as a lender was waning. The heyday of the debt crisis was over (so countries, especially middle-income countries, were no longer as desperate for loans), and commercial banks were once again lending to 'Third World' countries (so there were other potential sources for loans). So too was China on the horizon as a lender. Being a provider of 'aid' or 'development assistance' via project loans or even policy-based lending was not going to be enough to ensure that the World Bank would remain the powerful player that it had become.

So, in 1996, then-Bank president James Wolfensohn launched an initiative to magnify the research and dissemination role of the World Bank by transforming the institution from what was called a 'lending bank' into *the* 'Knowledge Bank':

> Development knowledge is part of the 'global commons': it belongs to everyone, and everyone should benefit from it. But a global partnership is required to cultivate and disseminate it. The [World] Bank Group's relationships with governments and institutions all over the world, and our unique reservoir of development experience across sectors and countries, position us to play a leading role in this new global knowledge partnership.

> We have been in the business of researching and disseminating the lessons of development for a long time. But the revolution in information technology increases the potential value of these efforts by vastly extending their reach....We need to become, in effect, the Knowledge Bank. (Wolfensohn 1996)[3]

The implication was that the World Bank was a place where all views, all ideas, all empirical data on development would be available to the world. Given this mission to increase the World Bank's role in creating, aggrandising, distributing, and brokering 'knowledge' – that is, in 'knowledge management' – it makes sense to look more carefully at how World Bank research is conducted and distributed to see if this is, in fact, the case.

The Knowledge Bank or the Paradigm-Maintenance Bank?

The World Bank is not only the main lender for 'development'. It is also the world's largest development research body, a role that is centred in the World Bank's Development Economics Vice-Presidency (DEC).

DEC is important also because it serves as a research department for other bilateral aid agencies and other multilateral development banks, which often follow the course laid out by the Bank. So too with the World Trade Organisation, which, according to an internal Bank document, 'looks to the Bank to provide analysis on trade integration policies'.[4] And Bank research is consulted by policy makers across the globe. In academia, as well, relevant courses often rely heavily on Bank research papers. In short, DEC is the research powerhouse of the development world.

And DEC is important to this chapter because it demonstrates how badly the Bank fails in this regard – or, depending on one's view, how well it succeeds at controlling the definition of development 'knowledge' and at managing its distribution and projection to suit the Bank's purposes.

The Bank likes to claim that DEC conducts the *crème-de-la-crème* of development research – with 'research projects' that are and 'must be rigorous and objective'.[5] After a careful look inside DEC (including a couple of dozen interviews with former and current Bank staff), I have reached a different conclusion: through its research, the World Bank has played a critical role in the legitimisation of the neo-liberal 'free-trade' paradigm over the past 25 years, and its research department has been vital to this role.

The work of perhaps the best-known World Bank researcher, David Dollar, exemplifies the 'paradigm-maintenance' role.[6] For many in the media, academia, and policy-making circles, Dollar's work on trade and economic growth has been transformed into a widely cited, empirically proven fact (read 'knowledge') that 'globalisers' – Dollar's term for countries wedded to the Washington Consensus, especially to liberalised trade – experience higher economic growth rates than 'non-globalisers'. Indeed, Dollar's and his co-author's work is the one source cited by Thomas Friedman in his best-selling book *The World Is Flat* as proof that 'economic growth and trade remain the best antipoverty program in the world' (Friedman 2005: 315). As Dollar phrased it in a co-authored 2002 article in *Foreign Affairs*: '...openness to foreign trade and investment, coupled with complementary reforms, typically leads to faster growth'.

How did Dollar's work become so prominent? Why does the work of DEC researchers who support the dominant knowledge framework – the neo-liberal policy agenda – get widespread attention? I discovered a set of six inter-related processes and mechanisms through which DEC, at times collaborating with other parts of the World Bank, performs its paradigm-maintenance role by privileging knowledge producers and knowledge that 'resonate' with the neo-liberal globalisation ideology. These mutually reinforcing structures include a series of incentives – increasing an individual's chances to be hired, to advance one's career, to be published, to be promoted by the Bank's External Affairs department, and, in general, to be assessed positively. And they also include selective enforcement of rules, discouragement of dissonant discourse, and even the manipulation of data to fit the paradigm. This incentive or reward system is typically unstated, may even negate the formal or stated procedures and, as such, functions as soft law. This is done in a way that undermines debate and nuanced research conclusions, instead encouraging the confirmation of *a priori* neo-liberal hypotheses as *de facto* knowledge.[7]

There follows a brief overview of the six sets of mechanisms.

Hiring

The structures through which these incentives play out are multiple, and they begin with hiring biases. While countries of birth and nationality may lead to a superficial assessment that the staff are international and diverse, the Bank is far from diverse. Bank staff are overwhelmingly PhD economists. Boundaries of disciplines in and of themselves set intellectual boundaries, defining acceptable questions and methods. DEC houses fewer than a handful of non-economist social scientists.

Further concentrating thought, the USA and the UK (and primarily the former) university economics departments supply most of the PhD economists doing research and writing within DEC (and within the Bank in general). The Bank's generous pay scale and benefits are also part of this incentive structure. This is what a former Bank economist terms 'the golden handcuffs'. (Unless buzzwords or otherwise stated, quotes are from my interviews.) While the Bank claims these are necessary to attract the best and the brightest, what they actually do is limit dissent by increasing the 'opportunity cost' of any dissidence.

Promotion

There are a number of ways in which promotion incentives help to shape the work towards paradigm maintenance.

The overarching goal of any researcher who wants to make a career of the Bank is to achieve, after five years, 'regularisation', the Bank equivalent of academic tenure. Along the way, there are annual reviews. It is important to note that '...most Bank employees are on short-term contracts. There is substantial anecdotal evidence that this is distorting incentives away from creative thinking and towards career-path management' (Gilbert *et al.* 2000: 81).

To get good reviews, DEC professionals need to publish, ideally in both internal Bank publications and externally, especially in academic journals. Reviews also look at a DEC researcher's influence on Bank operations and policy. The Bank has set up formal structures to try to ensure the transfer of research 'knowledge' to operations. Most notable is that one-third of a researcher's time must be spent doing what is called operational 'cross-support'. In devising a work programme, the researcher is aware that he/she will 'need marketability for 1/3 time' when she/he is a *de facto* 'free agent'. In terms of the characteristics of a 'marketable' DEC researcher, as one Senior Economist in DEC explains, 'Operations looks for high-profile folks with "resonance"'. To paraphrase, if you are in Operations and you are looking to buy the time of a researcher, you look to add someone who is likely to improve the chances of your project getting through. 'You want a Dollar', one interviewee states bluntly without provocation. Conversely, asks one non-neo-liberal-economist researcher rhetorically: 'Why would Operations want me?'

Selective enforcement of rules

DEC's paradigmatic bias is also reflected in the process of reviewing on-going research for publication. The Bank likes to claim that there is uniform, objective, external review, but that is not the perception of individual researchers themselves. While there may be written rules with specific requirements (which this author has yet to see, despite repeated attempts), evidence suggests and interviews confirm that reviews of proposed research, manuscripts, and individuals are done 'selectively'.

Most of those interviewed for this chapter commented that research critical of the neo-liberal model or opening the door to alternatives (i.e. without that necessary 'resonance') is likely to undergo stricter external review and/or be rejected. The review process, says a former Bank professional, 'depends on what the paper is [about] and who the author is. If you are a respected neoclassical economist, then [approval] only needs one sign-off, that of your boss. If it's critical, then you go through endless reviews, until the author gives up...'

Discouraging dissonant discourse

Rather than revealing the Bank to be an honest agent of different views or even an institution willing to broker debate, my research exposes a number of ways in which dissonant discourse, while allowed at the 'fringe' of the research department, is generally discouraged. Dissent is allowed on more marginal issues, but seldom on the core tenets of the neo-liberal model. How does this discouragement of dissent occur?

Discourse is part of the answer. On numerous occasions when the author asked Bank staff about someone whose work has raised dissent, the response was invariably that the person was 'idiosyncratic' or 'iconoclastic', or 'disaffected'. In other words, people who do not project the Bank's paradigm are diminished or ostracised or deemed 'misfits'. Former DEC official David Ellerman has described the Bank as 'an organization where open debate is not a big part of the culture' (Ellerman 2005: xix).

This lack of openness to dissent is all the more troubling in the context of the rapidly evolving post-Seattle and post-Asian-crisis debate on development. Since the late 1990s, with the rise of a global backlash against the neo-liberal model, there has been – outside the Bank – a vibrant theoretical and policy debate about neo-liberal economic globalisation, as evidence grows of its negative impacts on economic, environmental, and social development. During this period, Bank projects and policy-based lending have come under heavy attack for contributing to these negative impacts. Yet, the Bank has been able to continue to operate relatively unchecked in its research work.

Take David Dollar's work.[8] There has been widespread external criticism of Dollar's methodology by non-doctrinaire economists outside the Bank – from Harvard economist Dani Rodrik, Center for Economic and Policy Research director/economist Mark Weisbrot, London School of Economics Robert Wade, to Cornell professor (and former Bank professional) Ravi Kanbur, and others (including the present author). Rodrik, for example, reaches a conclusion opposite to Dollar's: 'The evidence from the 1990s indicated a positive (but statistically insignificant) relationship between tariffs and economic growth' (Rodrik 2001:22).

Yet, the Bank continues to project Dollar's work as if it is undisputed fact. This suggests a certain presumption within the Bank about what the right answers should be, and a willingness to ignore or discard evidence that complicates the answer. Ignoring the complications or caveats allows for the presentation of subjective and conditional conclusions as objective and scientific discourse – as knowledge. 'The point,' explains a DEC economist, 'is that one type of research is encouraged, people know what type it is and they produce it, while another type is given short-shrift.'

Selective presentation of data

What does the Bank do if data/research do not support a neo-liberal hypothesis? There is disturbing evidence that the Bank crafts, and even manipulates, the executive summaries and press releases of reports so that they reinforce the neo-liberal paradigm. A case in point of an executive summary that is so well crafted that it no longer meshes with the text of the report is a 350-plus-page 2003 Bank document on 'Lessons from NAFTA for Latin American and Caribbean Countries' (World Bank 2003). The summary (p. viii) states that 'real wages [in Mexico] have recovered rapidly from the 1995 collapse ...'. However, the text itself does not support this conclusion, as researcher Sarah Anderson noticed as she read it carefully: 'Table 1 of the summary shows that real wages in both local currency and in dollars have dropped since 1994.... Figure 4 in the main body of the report shows that real Mexican wages relative to those in the US are also below their 1994 levels.'[9]

Anderson wrote to the report's co-author Daniel Lederman to ask how a table showing a drop in real wages in the 1994–2001 period could have been summarised as a return to a level 'roughly equal' to 1994. Lederman responded that the wage trends were complicated and therefore the summary was meant to 'be vague'. As Anderson replied: '... to say that wages have returned to their 1994 levels when they have not is not merely "vague" but is inaccurate'.

Yet, Anderson seems to have been one of the few to read the report carefully enough to note this key discrepancy (or 'falsehood', as she more accurately phrases it). Indeed, on 9 January 2004, the *Washington Post* ran a long, lead editorial on the success of NAFTA, based in part on the World Bank report. Incredibly enough, the *Post* editorial chastised NAFTA critics who say that wage growth has 'been negligible', and instead noted that 'wage levels that match those existing before the peso crisis represent an achievement'. In other words, the Bank seems to understand and play to the fact that most people, including most journalists, will read only the press release and summary. In this case, in a significant arena for potential policy debate and reform, the Bank fooled a major newspaper whose editorials are read and used by key policy makers.

External projection

My research also concluded that the Bank's External Affairs department functions as a projector of DEC's paradigm-maintenance role. Dollar, for instance, did not only have the backing of DEC. The Bank's External Affairs department stepped in to publicise his work; it is External Affairs that has the 'money, media contacts, and incredible clout' to fly an author around the world.

External Affairs' rise in stature dates from the early Wolfensohn years under the leadership of Mark Malloch Brown (1994–1999). (Malloch Brown was later rewarded, becoming Administrator of UNDP and, in 2005, Chief of Staff to UN Secretary General Kofi Annan.) In Wolfensohn's second term, External Affairs' budget soared to become, by 2004–2005, comparable to the full annual budget of the Heritage Foundation. External Affairs has grown, the present author would hypothesise, at least in part in response to the increasing external questioning of the Bank and its model. External Affairs has become vital in the polarised public debate over the Bank's role.

Conclusion

These six sets of incentives raise significant questions about the World Bank's own argument that it produces and disseminates work of the utmost quality and integrity. My research should certainly raise alarm about further concentrating and aggrandising this role of knowledge production and marketing in the World Bank – indeed, alarm about any institution that seeks to monopolise and manage knowledge.

We also get a further, illuminating insight into World Bank 'knowledge management' by its reactions to my research. After reading a draft of my original article, a former consultant to the World Bank mused: 'I wonder what the reaction will be from the people in the Bank. A deafening silence? An invitation to participate in a task force to see how to improve things? A witch hunt to find your informants?'[10] True to form, the knowledge managers burst into action. After the original, longer academic article on DEC appeared in a peer-reviewed academic journal, two gentlemen from the Bank contacted the journal's editors. Although I was not privy to the communication, I gather that the gentlemen found my scholarship to be 'poor' and the journal's review process wanting if such an article could be published.[11] The editors (who had, in fact, overseen a rigorous review process) offered journal space for the two to rebut my article, with the understanding that I would then be given the customary academic opportunity to reply. But such open academic debate appears not to have been to the liking of the complainants – who feared, I infer, that it would give my article further prominence.[12]

Clearly, there was something about my 'knowledge' that needed to be 'managed'. I will let my case – that of one mere academic writing in one mere academic journal – stand as a concluding coda, as further evidence of the need to break up the monopolisation of 'knowledge' and its 'management'. As Susan George, a member of the journal's International Editorial Board, wrote: 'Could it be that the letter of complaint [from the World Bank] helps to prove rather than to disprove Broad's case – it struck me as a classic example of manning the barricades in the interests of paradigm defense.'[13]

My research suggests that there is an urgent need to question 'paradigm maintenance' and to fundamentally re-think research – and knowledge production and dissemination – at the World Bank. Does the Bank really need a biased research department? Does the Bank really need an External Affairs department to tout research that reinforces the highly discredited neo-liberal model? Would not knowledge – and development – be better served by supporting multiple and diverse independent research institutions, especially in the South? Should not the goal be to stimulate a more diverse development debate?

Development knowledge should not be managed. It should, indeed, be debated – not only by academics such as myself, but more importantly by those who are supposed to be its 'beneficiaries'.

Acknowledgement

This chapter includes sections adapted and condensed, with permission, from Robin Broad (2006) 'Research, knowledge, and the art of "paradigm maintenance": the World Bank's Development Economics Vice-Presidency (DEC)', *Review of International Political Economy* 13(3): 387–419, available at the journal's homepage, www.tandf.co.uk/journals/titles/09692290.asp.

Notes

1. 'About *Inside Knowledge* magazine', at www.ikmagazine.com/about.asp, retrieved 27 March 2007.
2. For those readers who are buzzword connoisseurs, structural adjustment loans became known as 'antipoverty loans' and then 'development policy support'.

3. James D. Wolfensohn, Annual Meetings Address, World Bank, Washington, DC, 1 October 1996, retrieved 29 September 2004. See also World Bank 1999. Another term now used is 'knowledge sharing', which the Bank seems to have come to believe has a better buzz than 'knowledge management'. For more on Wolfensohn's Knowledge Bank initiative, see the work of Diane Stone 2000, 2003 as well as the work of Jeff Powell and Alex Wilks at the UK-based Bretton Woods Project. See also King (2002), Ellerman (2002, 2005), Gilbert and Vines (2000), Standing (2000), and Kapur (2006).

4. See 'Leveraging Trade for Development: World Bank Role', paraphrased in Bretton Woods Project, 'World Bank to "Intensify" Work on Trade', 4 April 2001. See also Dethier (2005). The then Chief Economist Stern emphasised this in a 2001 meeting with the *Financial Times*, which reported: '...the chief economist of the World Bank... promised that the bank would provide intellectual firepower to the World Trade Organization... "The World Trade Organization doesn't have the research capacity the World Bank does and looks to us to push the trade research agenda", he said. "... The World Bank is the only organization with the depth of knowledge at the country level you need to discuss trade issues seriously"'(Beattie 2001:14).

5. World Bank, Research Advisory Staff (n.d.) 'Evaluations of World Bank Research: Research Support Budget Projects', available at www.worldbank. org/html/rad/evaluation/home.htm, retrieved 22 October 2004.

6. The term 'paradigm maintenance' is taken, with gratitude, from the perceptive article by Robert Wade (1996).

7. My original article (Broad 2006) from which this present chapter is adapted expands upon these six mechanisms, and provides more detail on DEC's structure, role, and impact; and how DEC came to embrace the neo-liberal globalisation paradigm.

8. A list of Dollar's writings is available at http://ideas.repec.org/e/pdo54.html#works.

9. The sources for this paragraph and the next two are World Bank (2003), along with the relevant press release dated 17 December 2003; Sarah Anderson (2003) letter to 'Fellow NAFTA-watchers', and Sarah Anderson (2003) email exchange with World Bank economist Daniel Lederman, 18–19 December; Daniel Lederman (2003) email exchange with Institute for Policy Studies researcher Sarah Anderson, 18–19 December; and 'NAFTA at 10' (2004) *Washington Post*, editorial, 9 January, A16. See also the response to the Bank report by Bakvis (2003) of the ICFTU.

10. Professor Robert Wade, London School of Economics, email to author, 4 April 2006.

11. The letter is quoted in Susan George, '"Paradigm Maintenance", or why we can't trust the World Bank's research', available atwww.tni/org/archives/george/paradigm.htm (retrieved 3 February 2007). George received the letter of complaint as a member of the journal's International Editorial Board. The website cited here includes George's letter of response to the Editorial Board of 22 November 2006, as well as an introduction (dated 24 January 2007) contextualising her letter. See also

Bretton Woods Project, 'Bank Attempts to Silence Critics', Update #54, 31 January 2007, at www.brettonwoodsproject.org.
12. Soon thereafter, the *Financial Times* (Callan 2006) reported on an extensive external review of DEC headed by (among others) Princeton economist Angus Deaton and former head of research at the IMF Ken Rogoff (Bannerjee *et al.* 2006). The 'audit' review reached conclusions that were shockingly similar to mine.
13. Susan George, letter 22 November 2006 to Editorial Board of *Review of International Political Economy.*

References

Bakvis, Peter (2003), 'Distorted World Bank Report on NAFTA and Labor', available at www.50years.org/cms/ejn/story/ (retrieved 8 April 2007).

Bannerjee, Abijihit, Angus Deaton (Chair), Nora Lustig, and Ken Rogoff (2006) 'An Evaluation of World Bank Research, 1998–2005', available at siteresources.worldbank.org/DEC/Resources/84797-1109362238001/726454-1164121166494/RESEARCH-EVALUATION-2006-Main-Report.pdf

Beattie, A. (2001) 'Bright prospects seen for new trade round: the World Economic Forum Chief Economist pledges World Bank's intellectual firepower ...', *Financial Times*, 30 January.

Broad, Robin (2006) 'Research, knowledge, and the art of "paradigm maintenance": the World Bank's Development Economics Vice-Presidency (DEC)', *Review of International Political Economy* 13(3): 387–419.

Callan, Eoin (2006) 'World Bank "uses doubtful evidence to push policies"', *Financial Times*, 22 December, available at www.ft.com/cms/s/a3433812-9160-11db-b71a-0000779e2340.html

Cummings, Jeffrey (2003) 'Knowledge Sharing: A Review of the Literature', Washington, DC: World Bank Operations Evaluation Department.

Dethier, J. (2005) 'An Overview of Research at the World Bank,' presentation at the Conference 'Research Bank on the World Bank', organised by the Center for Policy Studies, Central European University, Centre for the Study of Globalisation and Regionalisation, University of Warwick, and the World Bank European Office, Budapest, 1–2 April 2005.

Ellerman, David (2002) 'Should development agencies have Official Views?', *Development in Practice* 12(3&4): 285–97.

Ellerman, David (2005) *Helping People Help Themselves: From the World Bank to an Alternative Philosophy of Development Assistance*, Ann Arbor, MI: University of Michigan Press.

Friedman, Thomas L. (2005) *The World Is Flat: A Brief History of the Twenty-First Century*, New York, NY: Farrar, Straus and Giroux.

Gilbert, C. and D. Vines (eds.) (2000) *The World Bank: Structures and Policies*, Cambridge: Cambridge University Press.

Gilbert, Christopher, Andrew Powell and David Vines (2000) 'Positioning the World Bank', in C. Gilbert and D. Vines (eds.).

Kapur, Devesh (2006) 'The 'Knowledge' Bank', in Nancy Birdsall (ed.) *Rescuing the World Bank*, Washington, DC: Center for Global Development, pp. 159–70.

King, K. (2002) 'Banking on knowledge: the new knowledge projects of the World Bank', *Compare* 32(3): 311–26.

Rodrik, Dani (2001) *The Global Governance of Trade as if Development Really Mattered*, New York, NY: UNDP.

Standing, Guy (2000) 'Brave new words? A critique of Stiglitz's World Bank rethink', *Development and Change* 31: 737–63.

Stone, Diane (ed.) (2000) *Banking on Knowledge: The Genesis of the Global Development Gateway*, London: Beacon Press.

Stone, Diane (2003) 'The "Knowledge Bank" and the Global Development Network', *Global Governance* 9(1): 43–61.

Wade, Robert (1996) 'Japan, the World Bank, and the art of paradigm maintenance: the East Asian Miracle in perspective', *New Left Review* I (217) (May/June), available at http://newleftreview.org/?page=article&view=1851 (retrieved 8 April 2007).

World Bank (1999) *World Development Report 1998/99: Knowledge for Development*, New York, NY: Oxford University Press.

World Bank (2003) *Lessons from NAFTA for Latin American and Caribbean Countries*, Washington, DC: World Bank.

About the author

Robin Broad is Professor of International Development at American University and on the board of the Bank Information Center. She has published extensively on issues of economic justice, with a particular focus on the Philippines.

Coda

Thirty-eight thousand development programmes[1]

Paradoxically, much of the instrumental value of the conventional vocabulary of development planning rests in its *im*precision of meaning and its authoritative, technical gloss. Advertising executives and businessmen are very familiar with these 'Buzzwords' – words which make a pleasant noise but have little explicit meaning. One property of these words is that they may be combined into almost infinite permutations and still 'mean' something. To illustrate this we list below 56 words which occur frequently in the planner's lexicon. These will generate 38,316 development programmes: since the publisher is unaccountably reluctant to print the necessary 950 additional pages, we must prey on the reader's patience to elaborate it for him or herself. Select one word from each column at random to compose a four-word phrase: for example, A3, B6, C9, D12 = Systematically balanced cooperative action. Or A12, B9, C6, D3 = Comprehensively mobilised rural participation. These may be immediately recognisable, but what do they *mean*?[2] If two or three people were each to write a paragraph explaining one of these phrases to the masses, on behalf of the government of Ruritania, their *different* interpretations should bear further witness to the malleability of such language.

	A	B	C	D	
1	Centrally	Motivated	Grassroots	Involvement	1
2	Rationally	Positive	Sectoral	Incentive	2
3	Systematically	Structured	Institutional	Participation	3
4	Formally	Controlled	Urban	Attack	4
5	Totally	Integrated	Organisational	Process	5
6	Strategically	Balanced	Rural	Package	6
7	Dynamically	Functional	Growth	Dialogue	7
8	Democratically	Programmed	Development	Initiative	8
9	Situationally	Mobilised	Cooperative	Scheme	9
10	Moderately	Limited	On-going	Approach	10
11	Intensively	Phased	Technical	Project	11
12	Comprehensively	Delegated	Leadership	Action	12
13	Radically	Maximised	Agrarian	Collaboration	13
14	Optimally	Consistent	Planning	Objective	14

Notes

1. 'Thirty-eight thousand development programmes' emerged in the late 1970s. We have tried without success to trace the original source; if its authors or copyright holders come forward, we will be only too happy to credit them.

2. The interesting thing about this game is about how much and how little has changed in the last 30 years. Clearly, it pre-dates the international debt crisis, structural adjustment, the 'lost decade', the 'end of communism', neo-liberalism, and the (now post-) Washington Consensus; it therefore also pre-dates the series of UN conferences of the 1980s and 1990s: Children, Environment, Women, Population, Human Rights, and Social Development, which together provided such fertile ground for new buzzwords. The now ubiquitous language of New Public Management, had yet to permeate the Development Industry: in the 1970s, aid recipients were referred to as 'beneficiaries', or possibly 'partners', but never 'clients', 'stakeholders', or, worse still, 'end-users'. But the essence remains the same, give or take a few missing or *passé* items. Readers may therefore enjoy creating more up-to-date versions of the 56 essential buzzwords, drawing perhaps on some of those critiqued in this volume.

Index

Oxfam GB is a development, relief, and campaigning organisation that works with others to find lasting solutions to poverty and suffering around the world. Oxfam GB is a member of Oxfam International.

As part of its programme work, Oxfam GB undertakes research and documents its programme and humanitarian experience. This is disseminated through books, journals, policy papers, research reports, and campaign reports which are available for free download at: www.oxfam.org.uk/publications

www.oxfam.org.uk
Email: publish@oxfam.org.uk
Tel: +44 (0) 1865 473727

Oxfam House
John Smith Drive
Cowley
Oxford, OX4 2JY

The chapters in this book are available for download from the Oxfam GB website: www.oxfam.org.uk/publications